A CUSTOM EDITION, SECOND EDITION

Microeconomics

Jeffrey M. Perloff

Taken from:
Microeconomics, Fourth Edition
by Jeffrey M. Perloff

PEARSON
Custom
Publishing

PEARSON
Addison
Wesley

Cover Art: *Untitled,* by Armstrong

Taken from:

Microeconomics, Fourth Edition
by Jeffrey M. Perloff
Copyright © 2007 by Pearson Education, Inc.
Published by Addison Wesley, Inc.
Boston, Massachusetts 02116

This special edition published in cooperation with Pearson Custom Publishing.

Printed in the United States of America

5 6 7 8 9 10 0BRV 14 13 12 11 10

ISBN 0-536-44417-X

2007160530

MW

Please visit our web site at *www.pearsoncustom.com*

PEARSON CUSTOM PUBLISHING
501 Boylston Street, Suite 900
Boston, MA 02116

Brief Contents

Contents

Chapter Appendixes

Chapter 1

Introduction

I've often wondered what goes into a hot dog. Now I know and I wish I didn't.
—William Zinsser

I f each of us could get all the food, clothing, and toys we want without working, no one would study economics. Unfortunately, most of the good things in life are scarce—we can't all have as much as we want. Thus scarcity is the mother of economics.

Microeconomics is the study of how individuals and firms make themselves as well off as possible in a world of scarcity and the consequences of those individual decisions for markets and the entire economy. In studying microeconomics, we examine how individual consumers and firms make decisions and how the interaction of many individual decisions affects markets.

Microeconomics is often called *price theory* to emphasize the important role that prices play. Microeconomics explains how the actions of all buyers and sellers determine prices and how prices influence the decisions and actions of individual buyers and sellers.

microeconomics the study of how individuals and firms make themselves as well off as possible in a world of scarcity and the consequences of those individual decisions for markets and the entire economy

1. Microeconomics: the allocation of scarce resources: Microeconomics is the study of the allocation of scarce resources.

2. Models: Economists use models to make testable predictions.

3. Uses of microeconomic models: Individuals, governments, and firms use microeconomic models and predictions in decision making.

distribute Portions

In this chapter, we examine three main topics

1.1 Microeconomics: The Allocation of Scarce Resources

Individuals and firms allocate their limited resources to make themselves as well off as possible. Consumers pick the mix of goods and services that makes them as happy as possible given their limited wealth. Firms decide which goods to produce, where to produce them, how much to produce to maximize their profits, and how to produce those levels of output at the lowest cost by using more or less of various inputs such as labor, capital, materials, and energy. The owners of a depletable natural resource such as oil decide when to use it. Government decision makers—to benefit consumers, firms, or government bureaucrats—decide which goods and services the government produces and whether to subsidize, tax, or regulate industries and consumers.

TRADE-OFFS

People make trade-offs because they can't have everything. A society faces three key trade-offs:

- **Which goods and services to produce:** If a society produces more cars, it must produce fewer of other goods and services, because there are only so many *resources*—workers, raw materials, capital, and energy—available to produce goods.
- **How to produce:** To produce a given level of output, a firm must use more of one input if it uses less of another input. Cracker and cookie manufacturers switch between palm oil and coconut oil, depending on which is less expensive.
- **Who gets the goods and services:** The more of society's goods and services you get, the less someone else gets.

WHO MAKES THE DECISIONS

These three allocation decisions may be made explicitly by the government or may reflect the interaction of independent decisions by many individual consumers and firms. In the former Soviet Union, the government told manufacturers how many cars of each type to make and which inputs to use to make them. The government also decided which consumers would get a car.

In most other countries, how many cars of each type are produced and who gets them are determined by how much it costs to make cars of a particular quality in the least expensive way and how much consumers are willing to pay for them. More consumers would own a handmade Rolls-Royce and fewer would buy a mass-produced Ford Taurus if a Rolls were not 21 times more expensive than a Taurus.

APPLICATION

Flu Vaccine: Prices, Exhortation, or Government Intervention

In 2004, the U.S. government expected a record 100 million flu vaccine doses to be available, but one vaccine maker, Chiron, could not ship 46 million doses because of contamination. As a consequence, the government expected a shortage at the traditional price.

In response, the government and public health officials exhorted young, healthy people to forgo getting shots until the sick, elderly, and other high-risk populations were inoculated. When public spirit failed to dissuade enough people, federal, state, and local governments imposed restrictions. They did not try increasing the price to reduce demand for the shot, as would have been done with most non-health-related goods.[1]

PRICES DETERMINE ALLOCATIONS

An Economist's Theory of Reincarnation: If you're good, you come back on a higher level. Cats come back as dogs, dogs come back as horses, and people—if they've been real good like George Washington—come back as money.

Prices link the decisions about *which goods and services to produce, how to produce them,* and *who gets them.* Prices influence the decisions of individual consumers and firms, and the interactions of these decisions by consumers, firms, and the government determine price.

---

[1]Sources for applications appear at the end of the book.

market
an exchange mechanism
that allows buyers to
trade with sellers

Interactions between consumers and firms take place in a **market**, which is an exchange mechanism that allows buyers to trade with sellers. A market may be a town square where people go to trade food and clothing, or it may be an international telecommunications network over which people buy and sell financial securities. Typically, when we talk about a single market, we refer to trade in a single good or group of goods that are closely related, such as soft drinks, movies, novels, or automobiles.

Most of this book concerns how prices are determined within a market. We show that the *number of buyers and sellers* in a market and the amount of *information* they have help determine whether the price equals the cost of production. We also show that if there is no market—and hence no market price—serious problems, such as high levels of pollution, result.

⬤ APPLICATION

TWINKIE TAX

Many U.S., Canadian, U.K., and Australian jurisdictions are proposing a "Twinkie tax" on unhealthful fatty and sweet foods to reduce obesity and cholesterol problems, particularly among children. One survey found that 45% of adults would support a 1¢ tax per pound of soft drinks, chips, and butter, with the revenues used to fund health education programs.

Many proponents and opponents of these proposed laws seem unaware that at least 25 states and 3 cities differentially tax soft drinks, candy, chewing gum, or snack foods such as potato chips (Chouinard et al., 2005). In addition, Australia, Canada, the United Kingdom, and other countries have or are considering such laws.

New taxes will affect *which foods are produced*, as firms offer new low-fat and low-sugar programs, and *how fast-foods are produced*, as manufacturers reformulate their products to lower their tax burden. These taxes will also influence *who gets these goods* as consumers, especially children, substitute to less expensive, untaxed products.

1.2 | Models

Everything should be made as simple as possible, but not simpler. —Albert Einstein

model
a description of the
relationship between
two or more economic
variables

To *explain* how individuals and firms allocate resources and how market prices are determined, economists use a **model**: a description of the relationship between two or more economic variables. Economists also use models to *predict* how a change in one variable will affect another.

⬤ APPLICATION

Income Threshold Model and China

According to an *income threshold model*, no one who has an income level below a threshold buys a particular consumer durable, which is a good that can be used for long periods of time such as a refrigerator or car. The theory also holds that almost everyone whose income is above the threshold does buy the durable.

If this theory is correct, we predict that, as most people's incomes rise above that threshold in less-developed countries, consumer durable purchases will go from near zero to large numbers virtually overnight. This prediction is consistent with evidence from Malaysia, where the income threshold for buying a car is about $4,000.

Given such evidence from other countries, many firms believed that this model's predictions will apply to China. Incomes are rising rapidly in China and are exceeding the threshold levels for many types of durable goods. As a result, these companies predicted that the greatest consumer durable goods sales boom in history will take place there over the next decade. Anticipating this boom, these companies greatly increased their investments in durable goods manufacturing plants in China. Annual foreign investments went from $916 million a year in 1983 to more than $111 billion in 1993 and $13.4 billion in 2004. Anticipating this growth potential, even traditional political opponents of the People's Republic—Taiwan, South Korea, and Russia—invested in China.

SIMPLIFICATIONS BY ASSUMPTION

We stated the income threshold model verbally, but we could have presented it using graphs or mathematics. Regardless of how the model is described, an economic model is a simplification of reality that contains only its most important features. Without simplifications, it is difficult to make predictions because the real world is too complex to analyze fully.

By analogy, if the manual accompanying your new DVD recorder has a diagram showing the relationships between all the parts in the DVD, the diagram will be overwhelming and useless. In contrast, if it shows a photo of the buttons on the front of the machine with labels describing the purpose of each button, the manual is useful and informative.

Economists make many *assumptions* to simplify their models.[2] When using the income threshold model to explain car purchasing behavior in Malaysia, we *assume* that factors other than income, such as the color of cars, are irrelevant to the decision to buy cars. Therefore, we ignore the color of cars that are sold in Malaysia in describing the relationship between average income and the number of cars consumers want. If this assumption is correct, by ignoring color, we make our analysis of the auto market simpler without losing important details. If we're wrong and these ignored issues are important, our predictions may be inaccurate.

Throughout this book, we start with strong assumptions to simplify our models. Later, we add complexities. For example, in most of the book, we assume that consumers know the price each firm charges. In many markets, such as the New York

[2]An economist, an engineer, and a physicist are stranded on a desert island with a can of beans but no can opener. How should they open the can? The engineer proposes hitting the can with a rock. The physicist suggests building a fire under it to build up pressure and burst the can open. The economist thinks for a while and then says, "*Assume* that we have a can opener. . . ."

Stock Exchange, this assumption is realistic. It is not realistic in other markets, such as the market for used automobiles, in which consumers do not know the prices each firm charges.

TESTING THEORIES

Economic *theory* is the development and use of a model to test *hypotheses*, which are predictions about cause and effect. We are interested in models that make clear, testable predictions, such as "If the price rises, the quantity demanded falls." A theory that said "People's behavior depends on their tastes, and their tastes change randomly at random intervals" is not very useful because it does not lead to testable predictions.

Economists test theories by checking whether predictions are correct. If a prediction does not come true, they may reject the theory.[3] Economists use a model until it is refuted by evidence or until a better model is developed.

A good model makes sharp, clear predictions that are consistent with reality. Some very simple models make sharp predictions that are incorrect, and other more complex models make ambiguous predictions—any outcome is possible—which are untestable. The skill in model building is to chart a middle ground.

The purpose of this book is to teach you how to think like an economist in the sense that you can build testable theories using economic models or apply existing models to new situations. Although economists think alike in that they develop and use testable models, they often disagree. One may present a logically consistent argument that prices will go up next quarter. Another, using a different but equally logical theory, may contend that prices will fall. If the economists are reasonable, they agree that pure logic alone cannot resolve their dispute. Indeed, they agree that they'll have to use empirical evidence—facts about the real world—to find out which prediction is correct.

Although one economist's model may differ from another's, a key assumption in most microeconomic models is that individuals allocate their scarce resources so as to make themselves as well off as possible. Of all affordable combinations of goods, consumers pick the bundle of goods that gives them the most possible enjoyment. Firms try to maximize their profits given limited resources and existing technology. That resources are limited plays a crucial role in these models. Were it not for scarcity, people could consume unlimited amounts of goods and services, and sellers could become rich beyond limit.

As we show throughout this book, the maximizing behavior of individuals and firms determines society's three main allocation decisions: which goods are produced, how they are produced, and who gets them. For example, diamond-studded pocket combs will be sold only if firms find it profitable to sell them. The firms will make and sell these combs only if consumers value the combs at least as much as it costs the firm to produce them. Consumers will buy the combs only if they get more pleasure from the combs than they would from the other goods they could buy with the same resources.

---

[3]We can use evidence on whether a theory's predictions are correct to *refute* the theory but not to *prove* it. If a model's prediction is inconsistent with what actually happened, the model must be wrong, so we reject it. Even if the model's prediction is consistent with reality, however, the model's prediction may be correct for the wrong reason. Hence we cannot prove that the model is correct—we can only fail to reject it.

POSITIVE VERSUS NORMATIVE

The use of models of maximizing behavior sometimes leads to predictions that seem harsh or heartless. For instance, a World Bank economist predicted that, if an African government used price controls to keep the price of food low during a drought, food shortages would occur and people would starve. The predicted outcome is awful, but the economist was not heartless. The economist was only making a scientific prediction about the relationship between cause and effect: Price controls (cause) lead to food shortages and starvation (effect).

positive statement
a testable hypothesis about cause and effect

Such a scientific prediction is known as a **positive statement**: a testable hypothesis about cause and effect. "Positive" does not mean that we are certain about the truth of our statement—it only indicates that we can test the truth of the statement.

If the World Bank economist is correct, should the government control prices? If the government believes the economist's predictions, it knows that the low prices help those consumers who are lucky enough to be able to buy as much food as they want while hurting both the firms that sell food and the people who are unable to buy as much food as they want, some of whom may die. As a result, the government's decision whether to use price controls turns on whether the government cares more about the winners or the losers. In other words, to decide on its policy, the government makes a value judgment.

Instead of first making a prediction and testing it and then making a value judgment to decide whether to use price controls, the government could make a value judgment directly. The value judgment could be based on the belief that "because people *should* have prepared for the drought, the government *should* not try to help them by keeping food prices low." Alternatively, the judgment could be based on the view that "people *should* be protected against price gouging during a drought, so the government *should* use price controls."

normative statement
a conclusion as to whether something is good or bad

These two statements are *not* scientific predictions. Each is a value judgment or **normative statement**: a conclusion as to whether something is good or bad. A normative statement cannot be tested because a value judgment cannot be refuted by evidence. It is a prescription rather than a prediction. A normative statement concerns what somebody believes *should* happen; a positive statement concerns what *will* happen.

Although a normative conclusion can be drawn without first conducting a positive analysis, a policy debate will be more informed if positive analyses are conducted first.[4] Suppose your normative belief is that the government should help the poor. Should you vote for a candidate who advocates a higher minimum wage (a law that requires that firms pay wages at or above a specified level), a European-style welfare system (guaranteeing health care, housing, and other basic goods and services), an end to our current welfare system, a negative income tax (in which the less income a person has, the more the government gives that person), or job training programs? Positive economic analysis can be used to predict whether these programs will benefit poor people but not whether they are good or bad. Using these predictions and your value judgment, you can decide for whom to vote.

Economists' emphasis on positive analysis has implications for what we study and even our use of language. For example, many economists stress that they study

---

[4]Some economists draw the normative conclusion that, as social scientists, we economists *should* restrict ourselves to positive analyses. Others argue that we shouldn't give up our right to make value judgments just like the next person (who happens to be biased, prejudiced, and pigheaded, unlike us).

people's *wants* rather than their *needs*. Although people need certain minimum levels of food, shelter, and clothing to survive, most people in developed economies have enough money to buy goods well in excess of the minimum levels necessary to maintain life. Consequently, in wealthy countries, calling something a "need" is often a value judgment. You almost certainly have been told by some elder that "you *need* a college education." That person was probably making a value judgment— "you *should* go to college"—rather than a scientific prediction that you will suffer terrible economic deprivation if you do not go to college. We can't test such value judgments, but we can test a hypothesis such as "One-third of the college-age population *wants* to go to college at current prices."

1.3 Uses of Microeconomic Models

Have you ever imagined a world without hypothetical situations? —Steven Wright

Because microeconomic models *explain* why economic decisions are made and allow us to make *predictions*, they can be very useful for individuals, governments, and firms in making decisions. Throughout this book, we consider examples of how microeconomics aids in actual decision making. Here we briefly look at some uses by individuals and governments and then examine a series of recent decisions by General Motors.

Individuals use microeconomics to make purchasing and other decisions. Another use of microeconomics is helping you decide for whom to vote based on candidates' views on economic issues.

Your government's elected and appointed officials use (or could use) economic models in many ways. Recent administrations have placed increased emphasis on economic analysis. Today, economic and environmental impact studies are required before many projects can commence. The President's Council of Economic Advisers and other federal economists analyze and advise national government agencies on the likely economic effects of all major policies.

Indeed, probably the major use of microeconomic models by governments is to predict the probable impact of a policy before it is adopted. In Chapter 3, we show how to predict the likely impact of a tax on the prices consumers pay and on the tax revenues raised.

● APPLICATION

Putting Saturn in Orbit

Many firms have staffs of economists to make predictions and evaluate policies. Microeconomic analysis was particularly important to GM when it started selling its line of Saturn cars in 1991. The company broke a lot of its old rules. It built Saturns differently from the way it built its other cars and changed its relationship with its dealers so that they would sell and service the cars in a new way. Did GM's gamble work?

Manufacturing Costs. Starting up the Saturn line was a major risk; GM spent an estimated $5 billion to get Saturn going. To keep manufacturing costs down, GM built a new plant that uses modern technology and a team approach and other Japanese-style management methods to assemble cars. One of these, just-in-time inventories, allows GM to keep its inventory costs down by having suppliers ready to deliver parts almost immediately when needed. The Saturn plant produces relatively few models, and its sharing of engines and other major parts reduces production costs.

In building its new plant and designing its new car, GM had to take into account the federal government's emissions standards and other pollution regulations.

Some industry experts believe that GM lost $500 million a year in the first few years because it couldn't make enough cars to cover its investment. Does it make sense to run a plant at a loss for a while? In keeping the plant operating, GM was counting on Saturn managers' and workers' gaining experience in producing cars, which would lower the costs of production in the future.

Pricing. GM does not sell Saturns the way it sells its other cars. Knowing consumers' tastes with respect to the cars' features, service, and purchasing negotiations was an essential part of GM's new strategy.

Saturn's most striking marketing innovation was the "no-dicker sticker." Saturn dealers charge a fixed price for a car—they don't negotiate with customers as do most dealers. Why? One reason is that, according to a J. D. Power survey, 78% of American car buyers dislike negotiating for a new car. At the very least, this negotiation process is time consuming.

Why do traditional firms want to bargain with customers? It allows them to charge customers different prices. Such price discrimination can raise a firm's profits.

In the past, some consumers who did not bargain well or had little information about costs and prices paid substantially more than the dealer's cost for a car. One dealer claims that car dealers often marked up their price over cost by 24% in the 1960s compared to under 7% today. Now, information about dealers' costs is available on the Internet, allowing some consumers to strike better deals than they could previously.

Dealers. GM wanted its Saturn dealers not only to charge a fixed price, but also to provide superior service. With superior service, they could compete more effectively with dealers of high-quality imported cars and attract repeat customers. Because of its pricing method and its emphasis on service, by the end of the millennium, Saturn was one of consumers' top-rated brands for service, along with Cadillac, Jaguar, Volvo, Land Rover, Mercedes-Benz, and Lexus.

GM ensured that its dealers would earn unusually high profits by limiting the number of Saturn dealers. Initially, GM had only 230 Saturn dealers nationally, compared with 5,000 Chevy dealers. As a result, a Saturn dealer's markup of its price above its costs is greater than it would be if the dealer had to compete with many other local Saturn dealers (see Chapter 6). According to one expert, the typical Saturn price markup is 13% over dealer costs, whereas traditional dealer markups average about half that.

Are higher dealer prices and profits good for GM? On the one hand, the higher retail price cuts current sales of Saturns, which hurts GM. On the other hand, the resulting high profits give dealers an incentive to provide superior service. As one dealer said, "If there were more Saturn dealers, with more competition among ourselves, we couldn't afford to give extra service. The trouble with non-Saturn GM dealers is that they cut their own throats by charging too little and taking most profit out of deals." Extra service should increase the demand for Saturns, which helps GM.

Because its sales staff does not have to spend time negotiating with each customer, Saturn dealers need fewer salespeople. Some dealers calculate that traditional dealers need 30% to 40% more sales staff. Thus the ratio of labor to capital in traditional dealers is different from that in fixed-price dealers.

At traditional dealerships, a salesperson gets a commission of about a quarter of the markup on a final sale. Because they make money from each extra sale, these salespeople use cold calls (phone calls to strangers) and personal contacts to attract customers. In contrast, Saturn sales staff are paid a salary. As a result, Saturn salespeople have less incentive to pursue customers aggressively than salespeople who earn a commission. To offset this effect, some Saturn dealers boost advertising to generate showroom traffic.

Strategy. Why did GM change the way it did business? The reason was that its old approach was not working: GM was losing business and profits to other auto manufacturers.

By the very way it designed the Saturn, GM went after a particular type of customer. Only relatively short customers can fit comfortably in a Saturn. Customers who want sporty or other special features are not going to buy a Saturn. Saturn was apparently designed for customers who want to minimize the hassles in their life. A Saturn customer does not have to negotiate over price and is assured a well-built, well-serviced car—with a loaner available if repairs take a long time. (Chapter 6 discusses how firms aim at specific market niches.)

Other dealers and auto manufacturers did not stand still. In picking its strategies, a firm forms beliefs about how its rival will react to its actions. When GM drops its wholesale price, Ford and Honda respond to prevent the loss of sales and profits. When GM started selling Saturns and some of its other cars at fixed prices, Ford began using fixed prices on two of its vehicles. In 2007, the Saturn Aura sedan will use a new gear box that GM jointly developed with Ford. (Chapter 6 examines how large firms compete with each other in setting their prices or quantities.)

Thus GM made many production, marketing, and strategy decisions based on microeconomic models and predictions. The test that GM uses to determine whether its models and predictions are correct is whether Saturn makes a profit.

Summary

1. **Microeconomics: the allocation of scarce resources:** Microeconomics is the study of the allocation of scarce resources. Consumers, firms, and the government must make allocation decisions. The three key trade-offs a society faces are which goods and services to produce, how to produce them, and who gets them. These decisions are interrelated and depend on the prices that consumers and firms face and on government actions. Market prices affect the decisions of individual consumers and firms, and the interaction of the decisions of individual consumers and firms determines market prices. The organization of the market, especially the number of firms in the market and the information consumers and firms have, plays an important role in determining whether the market price is equal to or higher than marginal cost.

2. **Models:** Models based on economic theories are used to predict the future or to answer questions about how some change, such as a tax increase, affects various sectors of the economy. A good theory is simple to use and makes clear, testable predictions that are not refuted by evidence. Most microeconomic models are based on maximizing behavior. Economists use models to construct *positive* hypotheses concerning how a cause leads to an effect. These positive questions can be tested. In contrast, *normative* statements, which are value judgments, cannot be tested.

3. **Uses of microeconomic models:** Individuals, governments, and firms use microeconomic models and predictions to make decisions. For example, to maximize its profits, a firm needs to know consumers' decision-making criteria, the trade-offs between various ways of producing and marketing its product, government regulations, and other factors. For large companies, beliefs about how a firm's rivals will react to its actions play a critical role in how it forms its business strategies.

Supply and Demand

Talk is cheap because supply exceeds demand.

See Question 21.

When asked, "What is the most important thing you know about economics?" many people reply, "Supply equals demand." This statement is a shorthand description of one of the simplest yet most powerful models of economics. The supply-and-demand model describes how consumers and suppliers interact to determine the *quantity* of a good or service sold in a market and the *price* at which it is sold. To use the model, you need to determine three things: buyers' behavior, sellers' behavior, and how they interact. After reading this chapter, you should be adept enough at using the supply-and-demand model to analyze some of the most important policy questions facing your country today, such as those concerning international trade, minimum wages, and price controls on health care.

After reading that grandiose claim, you may ask, "Is that all there is to economics? Can I become an expert economist that fast?" The answer to both these questions is no (of course). In addition, you need to learn the limits of this model and what other models to use when this one does not apply. (You must also learn the economists' secret handshake.)

Even with its limitations, the supply-and-demand model is the most widely used economic model. It provides a good description of how many markets function and works particularly well in markets in which there are many buyers and many sellers, such as in most agriculture and labor markets. Like all good theories, the supply-and-demand model can be tested—and possibly shown to be false. But in markets where it is applicable, it allows us to make accurate predictions easily.

1. Demand: The quantity of a good or service that consumers demand depends on price and other factors such as consumers' incomes and the price of related goods.

2. Supply: The quantity of a good or service that firms supply depends on price and other factors such as the cost of inputs firms use to produce the good or service.

3. Market equilibrium: The interaction between consumers' demand and firms' supply determines the market price and quantity of a good or service that is bought and sold.

4. Shocking the equilibrium: Changes in a factor that affect demand (such as consumers' income), supply (such as a rise in the price of inputs), or a new government policy (such as a new tax) alter the market price and quantity of a good.

5. Effects of government interventions: Government policies may alter the equilibrium and cause the quantity supplied to differ from the quantity demanded.

6. When to use the supply-and-demand model: The supply-and-demand model applies only to competitive markets.

In this chapter, we examine six main topics

2.1 Demand

Potential consumers decide how much of a good or service to buy on the basis of its price and many other factors, including their own tastes, information, prices of other goods, income, and government actions. Before concentrating on the role of price in determining demand, let's look briefly at some of the other factors.

Consumers' *tastes* determine what they buy. Consumers do not purchase foods they dislike, artwork they hate, or clothes they view as unfashionable or uncomfortable. Advertising may influence people's tastes.

Similarly, *information* (or misinformation) about the uses of a good affects consumers' decisions. A few years ago when many consumers were convinced that oatmeal could lower their cholesterol level, they rushed to grocery stores and bought large quantities of oatmeal. (They even ate some of it until they remembered that they couldn't stand how it tastes.)

The *prices of other goods* also affect consumers' purchase decisions. Before deciding to buy Levi's jeans, you might check the prices of other brands. If the price of a close *substitute*—a product that you view as similar or identical to the one you are considering purchasing—is much lower than the price of Levi's jeans, you may buy that brand instead. Similarly, the price of a *complement*—a good that you like to consume at the same time as the product you are considering buying—may affect your decision. If you eat pie only with ice cream, the higher the price of ice cream, the less likely you are to buy pie.

Income plays a major role in determining what and how much to purchase. People who suddenly inherit great wealth may purchase a Rolls-Royce or other luxury items and would probably no longer buy do-it-yourself repair kits.

Government rules and regulations affect purchase decisions. Sales taxes increase the price that a consumer must spend for a good, and government-imposed limits on the use of a good may affect demand. If a city's government bans the use of skateboards on its streets, skateboard sales fall.

Other factors may also affect the demand for specific goods. Consumers are more likely to have telephones if most of their friends have telephones. The demand for small, dead evergreen trees is substantially higher in December than in other months.

Although many factors influence demand, economists usually concentrate on how price affects the quantity demanded. The relationship between price and quantity demanded plays a critical role in determining the market price and quantity in a supply-and-demand analysis. To determine how a change in price affects the quantity demanded, economists must hold constant other factors such as income and tastes that affect demand.

THE DEMAND CURVE

quantity demanded
the amount of a good that consumers are willing to buy at a given price, holding constant the other factors that influence purchases

demand curve
the *quantity demanded* at each possible price, holding constant the other factors that influence purchases

The amount of a good that consumers are *willing* to buy at a given price, holding constant the other factors that influence purchases, is the **quantity demanded**. The quantity demanded of a good or service can exceed the quantity *actually* sold. For example, as a promotion, a local store might sell music CDs for $1 each today only. At that low price, you might want to buy 25 CDs, but because the store ran out of stock, you can buy only 10 CDs. The quantity you demand is 25—it's the amount you *want*, even though the amount you *actually buy* is only 10.

We can show the relationship between price and the quantity demanded graphically. A **demand curve** shows the quantity demanded at each possible price, holding constant the other factors that influence purchases. Figure 2.1 shows the estimated demand curve, D^1, for processed pork in Canada (Moschini and Meilke 1992).

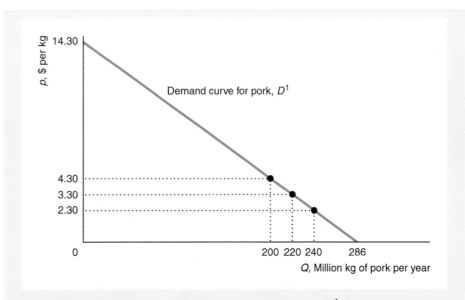

Figure 2.1 **A Demand Curve.** The estimated demand curve, D^1, for processed pork in Canada (Moschini and Meilke, 1992) shows the relationship between the quantity demanded per year and the price per kg. The downward slope of the demand curve shows that, holding other factors that influence demand constant, consumers demand less of a good when its price is high and more when the price is low. A change in price causes a *movement along the demand curve*.

(Although this demand curve is a straight line, demand curves may also be smooth curves or wavy lines.) By convention, the vertical axis of the graph measures the price, p, per unit of the good—here dollars per kilogram (kg). The horizontal axis measures the quantity, Q, of the good, which is usually expressed in some *physical measure* (million kg of dressed cold pork carcass weight) *per time period* (per year).

The demand curve hits the vertical axis at $14.30, indicating that no quantity is demanded when the price is $14.30 (or higher). The demand curve hits the horizontal quantity axis at 286 million kg—the amount of pork that consumers want if the price is zero. To find out what quantity is demanded at a price between these extremes, pick that price on the vertical axis—say, $3.30 per kg—draw a horizontal line across until you hit the demand curve, and then draw a line straight down to the horizontal quantity axis: 220 million kg of pork per year is demanded at that price.

One of the most important things to know about a graph of a demand curve is what is *not* shown. All relevant economic variables that are not explicitly shown on the demand curve graph—tastes, information, prices of other goods (such as beef and chicken), income of consumers, and so on—are held constant. Thus the demand curve shows how quantity varies with price but not how quantity varies with tastes, information, the price of substitute goods, or other variables.[1]

[1]Because prices, quantities, and other factors change simultaneously over time, economists use statistical techniques to hold the effects of factors other than the price of the good constant so that they can determine how price affects the quantity demanded. (See Appendix 2A.) Moschini and Meilke (1992) used such techniques to estimate the pork demand curve. As with any estimate, their estimates are probably more accurate in the observed range of prices ($1 to $6 per kg) than at very high or very low prices.

Law of Demand
consumers demand
more of a good the
lower its price, holding
constant tastes, the
prices of other goods,
and other factors that
influence consumption

Effect of Prices on the Quantity Demanded. Many economists claim that the most important *empirical* finding in economics is the **Law of Demand**: Consumers demand more of a good the lower its price, holding constant tastes, the prices of other goods, and other factors that influence the amount they consume. According to the Law of Demand, *demand curves slope downward*, as in Figure 2.1.[2]

A downward-sloping demand curve illustrates that consumers demand more of this good when its price is lower and less when its price is higher. What happens to the quantity of pork demanded if the price of pork drops and all other variables remain constant? If the price of pork falls by $1 from $3.30 to $2.30 in Figure 2.1, the quantity consumers want to buy increases from 220 to 240.[3] Similarly, if the price increases from $3.30 to $4.30, the quantity consumers demand decreases from 220 to 200. These changes in the quantity demanded in response to changes in price are *movements along the demand curve*. Thus the demand curve is a concise summary of the answers to the question "What happens to the quantity demanded as the price changes, when all other factors are held constant?"

Effects of Other Factors on Demand. If a demand curve measures the effects of price changes when all other factors that affect demand are held constant, how can we use demand curves to show the effects of a change in one of these other factors, such as the price of beef? One solution is to draw the demand curve in a three-dimensional diagram with the price of pork on one axis, the price of beef on a second axis, and the quantity of pork on the third axis. But just thinking about drawing such a diagram probably makes your head hurt.

Economists use a simpler approach to show the effect on demand of a change in a factor that affects demand other than the price of the good. A change in any factor other than price of the good itself causes a *shift of the demand curve* rather than a *movement along the demand curve*.

Many people view beef as a close substitute for pork. Thus at a given price of pork, if the price of beef rises, some people will switch from beef to pork. Figure 2.2 shows how the demand curve for pork shifts to the right from the original demand curve D^1 to a new demand curve D^2 as the price of beef rises from $4.00 to $4.60 per kg. (The quantity axis starts at 176 instead of 0 in the figure to emphasize the relevant portion of the demand curve.) On the new demand curve, D^2, more pork is demanded at any given price than on D^1. At a price of pork of $3.30, the quantity of pork demanded goes from 220 on D^1, before the change in the price of beef, to 232 on D^2, after the price change.

See Problems 22 and 23.

Similarly, a change in information can shift the demand curve. Reinstein and Snyder (2005) find that movie reviews affect the demand for some types of movies. Holding price constant, they determined that if Siskel and Ebert gave a movie a two-thumbs-up review, the opening weekend demand curve shifted to the right by 25% for a drama, but the demand curve did not significantly shift for an action film or a comedy.

---

[2]Theoretically, a demand curve could slope upward however, available empirical evidence strongly supports the Law of Demand.

[3]Economists typically do not state the relevant physical and time period measures unless they are particularly useful. They refer to *quantity* rather than something useful such as "metric tons per year" and *price* rather than "cents per pound." I'll generally follow this convention. From here on, I'll usually refer to the price as $3.30 (with the "per kg" understood) and the quantity as 220 (with the "million kg per year" understood).

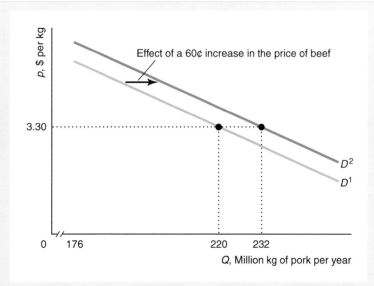

Figure 2.2 **A Shift of the Demand Curve.** The demand curve for processed pork shifts to the right from D^1 to D^2 as the price of beef rises from $4 to $4.60. As a result of the increase in beef prices, more pork is demanded at any given price.

To properly analyze the effects of a change in some variable on the quantity demanded, we must distinguish between a *movement along a demand curve* and a *shift of a demand curve*. A change in the *price of a good* causes a *movement along a demand curve*. A change in *any other factor besides the price of the good* causes a *shift of the demand curve*.

● **APPLICATION**

Sideways Wine

In the Academy Award-winning movie *Sideways*, the lead character, a wine snob, wildly praises pinot noir wine, saying that its flavors are "haunting and brilliant and thrilling and subtle . . ." Bizarrely, the exuberant views of this fictional character apparently caused wine buyers to flock to pinot noir wines, dramatically shifting the U.S. and British demand curves for pinot noir to the right (similar to the shift shown in Figure 2.2).

Between October 2004, when *Sideways* was released in the United States, and January 2005, U.S. sales of pinot noir jumped 16%, to record levels (and 34% in California, where the film takes place), while the price remained relatively constant. In contrast, sales of all U.S. table wines rose only 2% in this period. British consumers seemed similarly affected. In the five weeks after the film opened in the United Kingdom, pinot sales increased 20% at Sainsbury's and 10% at Tesco and Oddbins, which ran a *Sideways* promotion.[4]

---

[4]Sources for the applications appear at the back of the book.

THE DEMAND FUNCTION

In addition to drawing the demand curve, you can write it as a mathematical relationship called the *demand function*. The processed pork demand function is

$$Q = D(p, p_b, p_c, Y), \tag{2.1}$$

where Q is the quantity of pork demanded, p is the price of pork, p_b is the price of beef, p_c is the price of chicken, and Y is the income of consumers. This expression says that the amount of pork demanded varies with the price of pork, the price of substitutes (beef and chicken), and the income of consumers. Any other factors that are not explicitly listed in the demand function are assumed to be irrelevant (the price of llamas in Peru) or held constant (the price of fish).

By writing the demand function in this general way, we are not explaining exactly how the quantity demanded varies as p, p_b, p_c, or Y changes. Instead, we can rewrite Equation 2.1 as a specific function:

$$Q = 171 - 20p + 20p_b + 3p_c + 2Y. \tag{2.2}$$

Equation 2.2 is the estimated demand function that corresponds to the demand curve D^1 in Figures 2.1 and 2.2.[5]

When we drew the demand curve D^1 in Figures 2.1 and 2.2, we held p_b, p_c, and Y at their typical values during the period studied: $p_b = 4$ (dollars per kg), $p_c = 3\frac{1}{3}$ (dollars per kg), and $Y = 12.5$ (thousand dollars). If we substitute these values for p_b, p_c, and Y in Equation 2.2, we can rewrite the quantity demanded as a function of only the price of pork:

$$\begin{aligned}
Q &= 171 - 20p + 20p_b + 3p_c + 2Y \\
&= 171 - 20p + (20 \times 4) + \left(3 \times 3\tfrac{1}{3}\right) + (2 \times 12.5) \\
&= 286 - 20p \tag{2.3}
\end{aligned}$$

The straight-line demand curve D^1 in Figures 2.1 and 2.2—where we hold the price of beef, the price of chicken, and disposable income constant at these typical values —is described by the *linear* demand function in Equation 2.3.

The constant term, 286, in Equation 2.3 is the quantity demanded if the price is zero. Setting the price equal to zero in Equation 2.3, we find that the quantity demanded is $Q = 286 - (20 \times 0) = 286$. Figure 2.1 shows that $Q = 286$ where D^1 hits the quantity axis at a price of zero.

This equation also shows us how quantity demanded changes with a change in price: a movement *along* the demand curve. If the price increases from p_1 to p_2, the change in price, Δp, equals $p_2 - p_1$. (The Δ symbol, the Greek letter delta, means "change in" the following variable, so Δp means "change in price.") As Figure 2.1 illustrates, if the price of pork increases by \$1 from $p_1 = \$3.30$ to $p_2 = \$4.30$, $\Delta p = \$1$ and $\Delta Q = Q_2 - Q_1 = 200 - 220 = -20$ million kg per year.

More generally, the quantity demanded at p_1 is $Q_1 = D(p_1)$, and the quantity demanded at p_2 is $Q_2 = D(p_2)$. The change in the quantity demanded, $\Delta Q = Q_2 - Q_1$, in response to the price change (using Equation 2.3) is

[5]The numbers are rounded slightly from the estimates to simplify the calculation. For example, the estimate of the coefficient on the price of beef is 19.5, not 20, as the equation shows.

$$\Delta Q = Q_2 - Q_1$$
$$= D(p_2) - D(p_1)$$
$$= (286 - 20p_2) - (286 - 20p_1)$$
$$= -20(p_2 - p_1)$$
$$= -20\Delta p.$$

Thus the change in the quantity demanded, ΔQ, is –20 times the change in the price, Δp. If $\Delta p = \$1$, $\Delta Q = -20\Delta p = -20$.

The slope of a demand curve is $\Delta p/\Delta Q$, the "rise" (Δp, the change along the vertical axis) divided by the "run" (ΔQ, the change along the horizontal axis). The slope of demand curve D^1 in Figures 2.1 and 2.2 is

$$\text{Slope} = \frac{\text{rise}}{\text{run}} = \frac{\Delta p}{\Delta Q} = \frac{\$1 \text{ per kg}}{-20 \text{ million kg per year}} = -\$0.05 \text{ per million kg per year.}$$

The negative sign of this slope is consistent with the Law of Demand. The slope says that the price rises by $1 per kg as the quantity demanded falls by 20 million kg per year. Turning that statement around: The quantity demanded falls by 20 million kg per year as the price rises by $1 per kg.

Thus we can use the demand curve to answer questions about how a change in price affects the quantity demanded and how a change in the quantity demanded affects price. We can also answer these questions using demand functions.

SOLVED PROBLEM 2.1

How much would the price have to fall for consumers to be willing to buy 1 million more kg of pork per year?

Answer

1. *Express the price that consumers are willing to pay as a function of quantity:* We use algebra to rewrite the demand function as an *inverse demand function,* where price depends on the quantity demanded. Subtracting Q from both sides of Equation 2.3 and adding $20p$ to both sides, we find that $20p = 286 - Q$. Dividing both sides of the equation by 20, we obtain the inverse demand function:

$$p = 14.30 - 0.05Q \qquad\qquad (2.4)$$

2. *Use the inverse demand curve to determine how much the price must change for consumers to buy 1 million more kg of pork per year:* We take the difference between the inverse demand function, Equation 2.4, at the new quantity, $Q_2 + 1$, and at the original quantity, Q_1, to determine how the price must change:

$$\Delta p = p_2 - p_1$$
$$= (14.30 - 0.05Q_2) - (14.30 - 0.05Q_1)$$
$$= -0.05(Q_2 - Q_1)$$
$$= -0.05\Delta Q.$$

The change in quantity is $\Delta Q = Q_2 - Q_1 = (Q_1 + 1) - Q_1 = 1$, so the change in price is $\Delta p = -0.05$. That is, for consumers to demand 1 million more kg of pork per year, the price must fall by 5¢ a kg, which is a *movement along the demand curve.*

SUMMING DEMAND CURVES

If we know the demand curve for each of two consumers, how do we determine the total demand for the two consumers combined? The total quantity demanded *at a given price* is the sum of the quantity each consumer demands at that price.

We can use the demand functions to determine the total demand of several consumers. Suppose that the demand function for Consumer 1 is

$$Q_1 = D^1(p)$$

and the demand function for Consumer 2 is

$$Q_2 = D^2(p).$$

At price p, Consumer 1 demands Q_1 units, Consumer 2 demands Q_2 units, and the total demand of both consumers is the sum of the quantities each demands separately:

See Problems 29 and 30.
$$Q = Q_1 + Q_2 = D^1(p) + D^2(p).$$

We can generalize this approach to look at the total demand for three or more consumers.

It makes sense to add the quantities demanded only when all consumers face the same price. Adding the quantity Consumer 1 demands at one price to the quantity Consumer 2 demands at another price would be like adding apples and oranges.

⬤ APPLICATION

Aggregating the Demand for Broadband Service

We illustrate how to combine individual demand curves to get a total demand curve graphically using estimated demand curves of broadband (high-speed) Internet service (Duffy-Deno, 2003). The figure shows the demand curve for small firms (1–19 employees), the demand curve for larger firms, and the total demand curve for all firms, which is the horizontal sum of the other two demand curves.

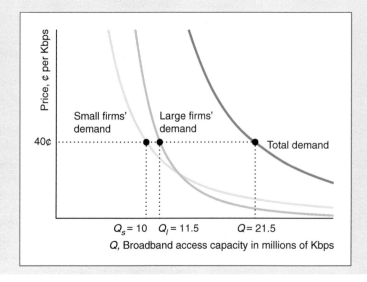

At the current average rate of 40¢ per kilobyte per second (Kbps), the quantity demanded by small firms is $Q_s = 10$ (in millions of Kbps) and the quantity demanded by larger firms is $Q_l = 11.5$. Thus, the total quantity demanded at that price is $Q = Q_s + Q_l = 10 + 11.5 = 21.5$.

2.2 Supply

Knowing how much consumers want is not enough, by itself, to tell us what price and quantity are observed in a market. To determine the market price and quantity, we also need to know how much firms want to supply at any given price.

Firms determine how much of a good to supply on the basis of the price of that good and other factors, including the costs of production and government rules and regulations. Usually, we expect firms to supply more at a higher price. Before concentrating on the role of price in determining supply, we'll briefly describe the role of some of the other factors.

Costs of production affect how much firms want to sell of a good. As a firm's cost falls, it is willing to supply more, all else the same. If the firm's cost exceeds what it can earn from selling the good, the firm sells nothing. Thus, factors that affect costs, also affect supply. A technological advance that allows a firm to produce a good at lower cost leads the firm to supply more of that good, all else the same.

Government rules and regulations affect how much firms want to sell or are allowed to sell. Taxes and many government regulations—such as those covering pollution, sanitation, and health insurance—alter the costs of production. Other regulations affect when and how the product can be sold. In Germany, retailers may not sell most goods and services on Sundays or during evening hours. In the United States, the sale of cigarettes and liquor to children is prohibited. New York, San Francisco, and many other cities restrict the number of taxicabs.

THE SUPPLY CURVE

quantity supplied
the amount of a good that firms *want* to sell at a given price, holding constant other factors that influence firms' supply decisions, such as costs and government actions

supply curve
the *quantity supplied* at each possible price, holding constant the other factors that influence firms' supply decisions

The **quantity supplied** is the amount of a good that firms *want* to sell at a given price, holding constant other factors that influence firms' supply decisions, such as costs and government actions. We can show the relationship between price and the quantity supplied graphically. A **supply curve** shows the quantity supplied at each possible price, holding constant the other factors that influence firms' supply decisions. Figure 2.3 shows the estimated supply curve, S^1, for processed pork (Moschini and Meilke, 1992). As with the demand curve, the price on the vertical axis is measured in dollars per physical unit (dollars per kg), and the quantity on the horizontal axis is measured in physical units per time period (millions of kg per year). Because we hold fixed other variables that may affect the supply, such as costs and government rules, the supply curve concisely answers the question "What happens to the quantity supplied as the price changes, holding all other factors constant?"

Effect of Price on Supply. We illustrate how price affects the quantity supplied using the supply curve for processed pork in Figure 2.3. The supply curve for pork is upward sloping. As the price of pork increases, firms supply more. If the price is

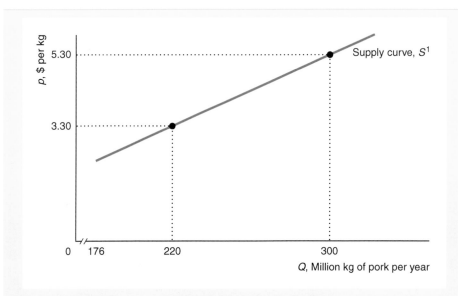

Figure 2.3 **A Supply Curve.** The estimated supply curve, S^1, for processed pork in Canada (Moschini and Meilke, 1992) shows the relationship between the quantity supplied per year and the price per kg, holding cost and other factors that influence supply constant. The upward slope of this supply curve indicates that firms supply more of this good when its price is high and less when the price is low. An increase in the price of pork causes a movement *along the supply curve*, resulting in a larger quantity of pork supplied.

$3.30, the market supplies a quantity of 220 (million kg per year). If the price rises to $5.30, the quantity supplied rises to 300. An increase in the price of pork causes a *movement along the supply curve*, resulting in more pork being supplied.

Although the Law of Demand requires that the demand curve slope downward, there is *no* "Law of Supply" that requires the market supply curve to have a particular slope. The market supply curve can be upward sloping, vertical, horizontal, or downward sloping. Many supply curves slope upward, such as the one for pork. Along such supply curves, the higher the price, the more firms are willing to sell, holding costs and government regulations fixed.

Effects of Other Variables on Supply. A change in a variable other than the price of pork causes the entire *supply curve to shift*. Suppose the price, p_h, of hogs—the main factor used to produce processed pork—increases from $1.50 per kg to $1.75 per kg. Because it is now more expensive to produce pork, the supply curve shifts to the left, from S^1 to S^2 in Figure 2.4.[6] Firms want to supply less pork at any given price than before the price of hogs rose. At a price of processed pork of $3.30, the quantity supplied falls from 220 on S^1, before the increase in the hog price, to 205 on S^2, after the increase in the hog price.

Again, it is important to distinguish between a *movement along a supply curve* and a *shift of the supply curve*. When the price of pork changes, the change in the quantity

---

[6]Alternatively, we may say that the supply curve shifts up because firms' costs of production have increased, so they will supply a given quantity only at a higher price.

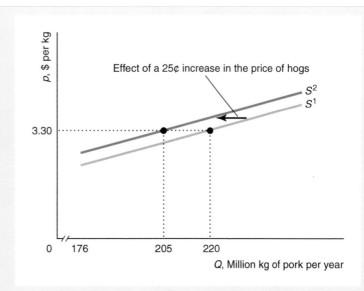

Figure 2.4 **A Shift of a Supply Curve.** An increase in the price of hogs from $1.50 to $1.75 per kg causes the supply curve for processed pork to shift from S^1 to S^2. At the price of processed pork of $3.30, the quantity supplied falls from 220 on S^1 to 205 on S^2.

supplied reflects a *movement along the supply curve*. When costs, government rules, or other variables that affect supply change, the entire *supply curve shifts*.

THE SUPPLY FUNCTION

We can write the relationship between the quantity supplied and price and other factors as a mathematical relationship called the *supply function*. Written generally, the processed pork supply function is

$$Q = S(p, p_h), \tag{2.5}$$

where Q is the quantity of processed pork supplied, p is the price of processed pork, and p_h is the price of a hog. The supply function, Equation 2.5, may also be a function of other factors such as wages, but by leaving them out, we are implicitly holding them constant.

Based on Moschini and Meilke (1992), the linear pork supply function in Canada is

$$Q = 178 + 40p - 60p_h, \tag{2.6}$$

where quantity is in millions of kg per year and the prices are in Canadian dollars per kg. If we hold the price of hogs fixed at its typical value of $1.50 per kg, we can rewrite the supply function in Equation 2.6 as[7]

$$Q = 88 + 40p. \tag{2.7}$$

What happens to the quantity supplied if the price of processed pork increases by $\Delta p = p_2 - p_1$? Using the same approach as before, we learn from Equation 2.7

---

[7]Substituting p_h = $1.50 into Equation 2.6, we find that

$$Q = 178 + 40p - 60p_h = 178 + 40p - (60 \times 1.50) = 88 + 40p.$$

that $\Delta Q = 40 \Delta p$.[8] A \$1 increase in price ($\Delta p = 1$) causes the quantity supplied to increase by $\Delta Q = 40$ million kg per year. This change in the quantity of pork supplied as p increases is a *movement along the supply curve*.

SUMMING SUPPLY CURVES

The total supply curve shows the total quantity produced by all suppliers at each possible price. For example, the total supply of rice in Japan is the sum of the domestic and foreign supply curves of rice.

Suppose that the domestic supply curve (panel a) and foreign supply curve (panel b) of rice in Japan are as Figure 2.5 shows. The total supply curve, S in panel c, is the horizontal sum of the Japanese *domestic* supply curve, S^d, and the *foreign* supply curve, S^f. In the figure, the Japanese and foreign supplies are zero at any price equal to or less than $\underline{p}$, so the total supply is zero. At prices above $\underline{p}$, the Japanese and foreign supplies are positive, so the total supply is positive. For example, when price is p^*, the quantity supplied by Japanese firms is Q_d^* (panel a), the quantity supplied by foreign firms is Q_f^* (panel b), and the total quantity supplied is $Q^* = Q_d^* + Q_f^*$ (panel c). Because the total supply curve is the horizontal sum of the domestic

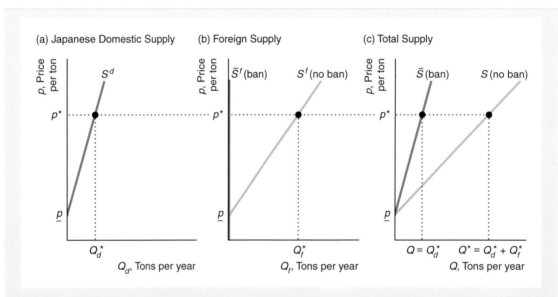

Figure 2.5 **Total Supply: The Sum of Domestic and Foreign Supply.** If foreigners may sell their rice in Japan, the total Japanese supply of rice, S, is the horizontal sum of the domestic Japanese supply, S^d, and the imported foreign supply, S^f. With a ban on foreign imports, the foreign supply curve, $\overline{S}^f$, is zero at every price, so the total supply curve, $\overline{S}$, is the same as the domestic supply curve, S^d.

---

[8]As the price increases from p_1 to p_2, the quantity supplied goes from Q_1 to Q_2, so the change in quantity supplied is

$$\Delta Q = Q_2 - Q_1 = (88 + 40p_2) - (88 + 40p_1) = 40(p_2 - p_1) = 40\Delta p.$$

and foreign supply curves, the total supply curve is flatter than either of the other two supply curves.

EFFECTS OF GOVERNMENT IMPORT POLICIES ON SUPPLY CURVES

We can use this approach for deriving the total supply curve to analyze the effect of government policies on the total supply curve. Traditionally, the Japanese government banned the importation of foreign rice. We want to determine how much less is supplied at any given price to the Japanese market because of this ban.

Without a ban, the foreign supply curve is S^f in panel b of Figure 2.5. A ban on imports eliminates the foreign supply, so the foreign supply curve after the ban is imposed, $\bar{S}^f$, is a vertical line at $Q_f = 0$. The import ban has no effect on the domestic supply curve, S^d, so the supply curve is the same as in panel a.

Because the foreign supply with a ban, $\bar{S}^f$, is zero at every price, the total supply with a ban, $\bar{S}$, in panel c is the same as the Japanese domestic supply, S^d, at any given price. The total supply curve under the ban lies to the left of the total supply curve without a ban, S. Thus the effect of the import ban is to rotate the total supply curve toward the vertical axis.

The limit that a government sets on the quantity of a foreign-produced good that may be imported is called a **quota**. By absolutely banning the importation of rice, the Japanese government sets a quota of zero on rice imports. Sometimes governments set positive quotas, $\bar{Q} > 0$. The foreign firms may supply as much as they want, Q_f, as long as they supply no more than the quota: $Q_f \le \bar{Q}$.

We investigate the effect of such a quota in Solved Problem 2.2. In most of the solved problems in this book, you are asked to determine how a *change* in a variable or policy *affects* one or more variables. In this problem, the policy *changes* from no quota to a quota, which *affects* the total supply curve.

quota
the limit that a government sets on the quantity of a foreign-produced good that may be imported

SOLVED PROBLEM 2.2

How does a quota set by the United States on foreign steel imports of $\bar{Q}$ affect the total American supply curve for steel given the domestic supply, S^d in panel a of the graph, and foreign supply, S^f in panel b?

Answer

1. *Determine the American supply curve without the quota:* The *no-quota* total supply curve, S in panel c, is the horizontal sum of the U.S. domestic supply curve, S^d, and the no-quota foreign supply curve, S^f.

2. *Show the effect of the quota on foreign supply:* At prices less than $\bar{p}$, foreign suppliers want to supply quantities less than the quota, $\bar{Q}$. As a result, the foreign supply curve under the quota, $\bar{S}^f$, is the same as the no-quota foreign supply curve, S^f, for prices less than $\bar{p}$. At prices above $\bar{p}$, foreign suppliers want to supply more but are limited to $\bar{Q}$. Thus the foreign supply curve with a quota, $\bar{S}^f$, is vertical at $\bar{Q}$ for prices above $\bar{p}$.

3. *Determine the American total supply curve with the quota:* The total supply curve with the quota, $\bar{S}$, is the horizontal sum of S^d and $\bar{S}^f$. At any price above $\bar{p}$, the total supply equals the quota plus the domestic supply. For example at p^*, the domestic supply is Q_d^* and the foreign supply is $\bar{Q}_f$, so the total supply is $Q_d^* + \bar{Q}_f$. Above $\bar{p}$, $\bar{S}$ is the domestic supply curve shifted $\bar{Q}$ units to the right. As a result, the portion of $\bar{S}$ above $\bar{p}$ has the same slope as S^d.

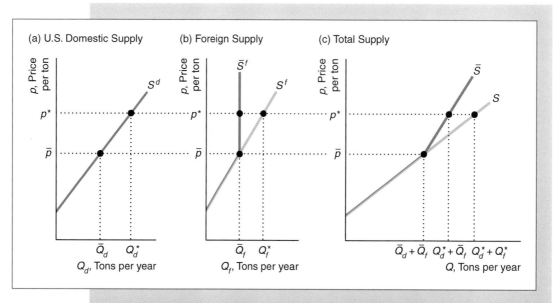

(a) U.S. Domestic Supply (b) Foreign Supply (c) Total Supply

4. *Compare the American total supply curves with and without the quota:* At prices less than or equal to $\bar{p}$, the same quantity is supplied with and without the quota, so $\bar{S}$ is the same as S. At prices above $\bar{p}$, less is supplied with the quota than without one, so $\bar{S}$ is steeper than S, indicating that a given increase in price raises the quantity supplied by less with a quota than without one.

2.3   Market Equilibrium

The supply and demand curves determine the price and quantity at which goods and services are bought and sold. The demand curve shows the quantities consumers want to buy at various prices, and the supply curve shows the quantities firms want to sell at various prices. Unless the price is set so that consumers want to buy exactly the same amount that suppliers want to sell, either some buyers cannot buy as much as they want or some sellers cannot sell as much as they want.

equilibrium
a situation in which no one wants to change his or her behavior

When all traders are able to buy or sell as much as they want, we say that the market is in **equilibrium**: a situation in which no participant wants to change its behavior. A price at which consumers can buy as much as they want and sellers can sell as much as they want is called an *equilibrium price*. The quantity that is bought and sold at the equilibrium price is called the *equilibrium quantity*.

USING A GRAPH TO DETERMINE THE EQUILIBRIUM

This little piggy went to market ...

To illustrate how supply and demand curves determine the equilibrium price and quantity, we use our old friend, the processed pork example. Figure 2.6 shows the supply, *S*, and demand, *D*, curves for pork. The supply and demand curves intersect at point *e*, the market equilibrium, where the equilibrium price is $3.30 and the

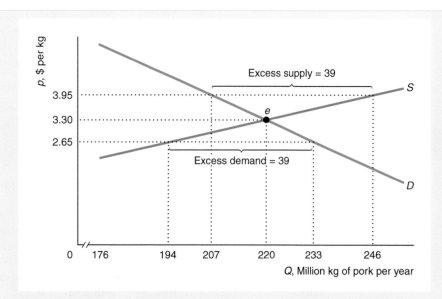

Figure 2.6 **Market Equilibrium.** The intersection of the supply curve, *S*, and the demand curve, *D*, for processed pork determines the market equilibrium point, *e*, where *p* = $3.30 per kg and *Q* = 220 million kg per year. At the lower price of *p* = $2.65, the quantity supplied is only 194, whereas the quantity demanded is 233, so there is excess demand of 39. At *p* = $3.95, a price higher than the equilibrium price, there is excess supply of 39 because the quantity demanded, 207, is less than the quantity supplied, 246. When there is excess demand or supply, market forces drive the price back to the equilibrium price of $3.30.

equilibrium quantity is 220 million kg per year, which is the quantity firms want to sell *and* the quantity consumers want to buy.

USING MATH TO DETERMINE THE EQUILIBRIUM

We can determine the processed pork market equilibrium mathematically, using the supply and demand functions. We use these two functions to solve for the equilibrium price at which the quantity demanded equals the quantity supplied (the equilibrium quantity).

The demand function, Equation 2.3, shows the relationship between the quantity demanded, Q_d, and the price:

$$Q_d = 286 - 20p.$$

The supply function, Equation 2.7, tells us the relationship between the quantity supplied, Q_s, and the price:

$$Q_s = 88 + 40p.$$

We want to find the *p* at which $Q_d = Q_s = Q$, the equilibrium quantity. Because the left-hand sides of the two equations are equal in equilibrium, $Q_s = Q_d$, the right-hand sides of the two equations must be equal:

$$286 - 20p = 88 + 40p.$$

Adding $20p$ to both sides of this expression and subtracting 88 from both sides, we find that $198 = 60p$. Dividing both sides of this last expression by 60, we learn that the equilibrium price is $p = \$3.30$. We can determine the equilibrium quantity by substituting this p into either the supply or the demand equation:

$$Q_d = Q_s$$
$$286 - (20 \times 3.30) = 88 + (40 \times 3.30)$$
$$220 = 220.$$

Thus the equilibrium quantity is 220.

FORCES THAT DRIVE THE MARKET TO EQUILIBRIUM

A market equilibrium is not just an abstract concept or a theoretical possibility. We can observe markets in equilibrium. Indirect evidence that a market is in equilibrium is that you can buy as much as you want of the good at the market price. You can almost always buy as much as you want of such common goods as milk and ballpoint pens.

Amazingly, a market equilibrium occurs without any explicit coordination between consumers and firms. In a competitive market such as that for agricultural goods, millions of consumers and thousands of firms make their buying and selling decisions independently. Yet each firm can sell as much as it wants; each consumer can buy as much as he or she wants. It is as though an unseen market force, like an *invisible hand*, directs people to coordinate their activities to achieve a market equilibrium.

What really causes the market to move to an equilibrium? If the price is not at the equilibrium level, consumers or firms have an incentive to change their behavior in a way that will drive the price to the equilibrium level, as we now illustrate.

If the price were initially lower than the equilibrium price, consumers would want to buy more than suppliers want to sell. If the price of pork is $2.65 in Figure 2.6, firms are willing to supply 194 million kg per year but consumers demand 233 million kg. At this price, the market is in *disequilibrium*, meaning that the quantity demanded is not equal to the quantity supplied. There is **excess demand**—the amount by which the quantity demanded exceeds the quantity supplied at a specified price— of 39 (= 233 – 194) million kg per year at a price of $2.65.

Some consumers are lucky enough to buy the pork at $2.65. Other consumers cannot find anyone who is willing to sell them pork at that price. What can they do? Some frustrated consumers may offer to pay suppliers more than $2.65. Alternatively, suppliers, noticing these disappointed consumers, may raise their prices. Such actions by consumers and producers cause the market price to rise. As the price rises, the quantity that firms want to supply increases and the quantity that consumers want to buy decreases. This upward pressure on price continues until it reaches the equilibrium price, $3.30, where there is no excess demand.

If, instead, price is initially above the equilibrium level, suppliers want to sell more than consumers want to buy. For example, at a price of pork of $3.95, suppliers want to sell 246 million kg per year but consumers want to buy only 207 million, as the figure shows. At $3.95, the market is in disequilibrium. There is an **excess supply**—the amount by which the quantity supplied is greater than the quantity demanded at a specified price—of 39 (= 246 – 207) at a price of $3.95. Not all firms can sell as much as they want. Rather than incur storage costs (and possibly have their unsold pork spoil), firms lower the price to attract additional customers. As long as price remains above the equilibrium price, some firms have unsold pork and want to lower the price further. The price falls until it reaches the equilibrium

excess demand
the amount by which the *quantity demanded* exceeds the *quantity supplied* at a specified price

excess supply
the amount by which the *quantity supplied* is greater than the *quantity demanded* at a specified price

level, \$3.30, where there is no excess supply and hence no more pressure to lower the price further.

In summary, at any price other than the equilibrium price, either consumers or suppliers are unable to trade as much as they want. These disappointed people act to change the price, driving the price to the equilibrium level. The equilibrium price is called the *market clearing price* because it removes from the market all frustrated buyers and sellers: There is no excess demand or excess supply at the equilibrium price.

2.4 Shocking the Equilibrium

Once an equilibrium is achieved, it can persist indefinitely because no one applies pressure to change the price. *The equilibrium changes only if a shock occurs that shifts the demand curve or the supply curve. These curves shift if one of the variables we were holding constant changes.* If tastes, income, government policies, or costs of production change, the demand curve or the supply curve or both shift, and the equilibrium changes.

EFFECTS OF A SHIFT IN THE DEMAND CURVE

Suppose that the price of beef increases by 60¢, and so consumers substitute pork for beef. As a result, the demand curve for pork shifts outward from D^1 to D^2 in panel a of Figure 2.7. At any given price, consumers want more pork than they did before the price of beef rose. In particular, at the original equilibrium price of pork, \$3.30, consumers now want to buy 232 million kg of pork per year. At that price, however, suppliers still want to sell only 220. As a result, there is excess demand of 12. Market pressures drive the price up until it reaches a new equilibrium at \$3.50. At that price, firms want to sell 228 and consumers want to buy 228, the new equilibrium quantity. Thus the pork equilibrium goes from e_1 to e_2 as a result of the increase in the price of beef. Both the equilibrium price and the equilibrium quantity of pork rise as a result of the outward shift of the pork demand curve. Here the increase in the price of beef causes a *shift of the demand curve*, causing a *movement along the supply curve*.

EFFECTS OF A SHIFT IN THE SUPPLY CURVE

Now suppose that the price of beef stays constant at its original level but the price of hogs increases by 25¢. It is now more expensive to produce pork because the price of a major input, hogs, has increased. As a result, the supply curve for pork shifts to the left from S^1 to S^2 in panel b of Figure 2.7. At any given price, firms want to supply less pork than they did before the price of hogs increased. At the original equilibrium price of pork of \$3.30, consumers still want 220, but suppliers are now willing to supply only 205, so there is excess demand of 15. Market pressure forces the price of pork up until it reaches a new equilibrium at e_2, where the equilibrium price is \$3.55 and the equilibrium quantity is 215. The increase in the price of hogs causes the equilibrium price to rise but the equilibrium quantity to fall. Here a *shift of the supply curve* results in a *movement along the demand curve*.

In summary, a change in an underlying factor, such as the price of a substitute or the price of an input, shifts the demand or supply curve. As a result of this shift in the demand or supply curve, the equilibrium changes. To describe the effect of this

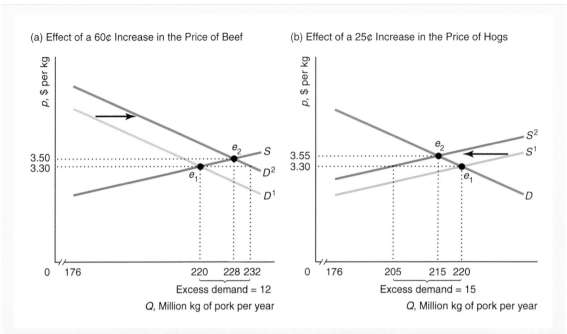

(a) Effect of a 60¢ Increase in the Price of Beef

(b) Effect of a 25¢ Increase in the Price of Hogs

Figure 2.7 Effects of a Shift of a Curve.
(a) An increase in the price of beef by 60¢ causes the demand curve for processed pork to shift outward from D^1 to D^2. At the original equilibrium, e_1, price, $3.30, there is excess demand of 12. Market pres- sures drive the price up until it reaches $3.50 at the new equilibrium, e_2. (b) An increase in the price of hogs by 25¢ causes the supply curve for processed pork to shift to the left from S^1 to S^2, driving the market equilibrium from e_1 to e_2.

change in the underlying factor on the market, we compare the original equilibrium price and quantity to the new equilibrium values.

SOLVED PROBLEM   2.3

Mathematically, how does the equilibrium price of pork vary as the price of hogs changes if the variables that affect demand are held constant at their typical values?

Answer

1. *Solve for the equilibrium price of pork in terms of the price of hogs:* The demand function does not depend on the price of hogs, so we can use Equation 2.3 from before,

$$Q_d = 286 - 20p.$$

To see how the equilibrium depends on the price of hogs, we use supply function Equation 2.6:

$$Q_s = 178 + 40p - 60p_h.$$

The equilibrium is determined by equating the right-hand sides of these demand-and-supply equations:

$$286 - 20p = 178 + 40p - 60p_h.$$

Rearranging terms in this last expression, we find that $60p = 108 + 60p_h$. Dividing both sides by 60, we have an expression for the equilibrium price of processed pork as a function of the price of hogs:

$$p = 1.8 + p_h. \tag{2.8}$$

(As a check, when p_h equals its typical value, \$1.50, Equation 2.8 says that the equilibrium price of pork is $p = \$3.30$, which we know is correct from our earlier calculations.)

We find the equilibrium quantity as a function of the price of hogs by substituting this expression for the equilibrium price, Equation 2.8, into the demand equation (though we could use the supply function instead):

$$Q = 286 - 20p = 286 - 20(1.8 + p_h) = 250 - 20p_h.$$

(Again, as a check, if p_h equals its typical value of \$1.50, $Q = 220$, which we know is the original equilibrium quantity.)

2. *Show how the equilibrium price of pork varies with the price of hogs:* We know from Equation 2.8 that $\Delta p = \Delta p_h$. Any increase in the price of hogs causes an equal increase in the price of processed pork. As panel b of Figure 2.7 illustrates, if the price of hogs increases by $\Delta p_h = \$0.25$ (from \$1.50 to \$1.75), the price of pork, p, increases by $\Delta p = \Delta p_h = \$0.25$ (from \$3.30 to \$3.55).

EFFECTS OF A SHIFT IN THE SUPPLY AND DEMAND CURVES

Some events cause both the supply curve and the demand curve to shift. If both shift, then the qualitative effect on the equilibrium price and quantity may be difficult to predict, even if we know the direction in which each curve shifts. Changes in the equilibrium price and quantity depend on exactly how the curves shift: See the following application and solved problem and the related questions at the end of the chapter.

● APPLICATION

Mad Cow: Shifting Supply and Demand Curves

Government announcements that the fatal disease known as mad cow (bovine spongiform encephalopathy, or BSE) has been found in a country's cattle affect both supply and demand curves. Humans who consume beef products made from diseased animal parts can develop new variant Creutzfeldt-Jakob disease, a deadly affliction that slowly eats holes in sufferers' brains. Mad cow disease can take years to develop in cattle, and symptoms in its human version may not appear for decades. Consequently, identifying the presence of the disease has been difficult.

In 1986, the British government disclosed a case of mad cow disease, but initially asserted that humans were not at risk from eating infected beef. Since then, 180,000 cases of mad cow have been reported in the United Kingdom. Not until 1996 did the British government announce that people were falling victim to a degenerative new brain disease linked to BSE. Following this announcement and similar reports in France, Italy, and Germany, many British and other European consumers stopped buying beef, causing the beef demand curves in European countries to shift to the left. Over time, many cattle were removed from the food chain as European beef producers reduced their herds, so that the supply curves also shifted to the left. Consequently, beef consumption plummeted in Europe in the 1990s.

Japan announced that it had found its first case of mad cow in 2001. Two-thirds of beef sold in Japan in 2001 was imported: 49% of it from Australia and 46% from the United States. Immediately following the domestic mad cow discovery, beef consumption in Japan fell by 60% (including a 30% drop in imports, which were not implicated). A survey of Japanese consumers found that 86% said that they had reduced their consumption since the announcement. To protect and reassure consumers, Japan began conducting BSE tests on all 1.2 million domestic cattle that are slaughtered. By mid-2002, Japan's beef consumption recovered to within 10% to 15% of its pre-announcement levels.

Canada announced its first indigenous case in May 2003 (Canada reported a case in 1993 for a cow imported from Europe). The first U.S. case, in a cow imported from Canada, was reported in December 2003 (and the second in 2005). These announcements affected supply curves and demand curves throughout the world. As soon as the United States revealed the discovery of the single mad cow, more than 40 countries slapped an embargo on U.S. beef, causing beef supply curves to shift to the left in those importing countries. The loss of U.S. producers' largest export market, Japan, cost beef suppliers $1 billion worth of sales; and Canadian exporters lost about $55 million worth of sales to Japan. U.S. exports fell from 1,143 thousand metric tons in 2003 to 209 thousand metric tons in 2004. At least initially, a few people in the United States and Canada stopped consuming beef, causing demand curves in these countries to move slightly to the left. Strangely, the National Cattlemen's Beef Association reported that 89% of U.S. consumers expressed confidence in the safety of U.S. beef after the mad cow announcement, compared to 88% in September 2003. Over a longer period, the U.S. demand curve may have shifted farther to the left as consumers learned more about the disease.

The immediate supply effects in the United States and Canada were larger than the long-run effects. The United States was exporting about 10% of its total production (about $3.8 billion in sales), while the Canadians were exporting 40% of their domestic production. When they were unable to ship the beef abroad, U.S. and Canadian producers had to sell their beef only in their domestic markets, causing domestic supply curves to shift to the right. Thereafter, U.S. and Canadian producers reduced their herds, so that the supply curves shifted to the left in the longer run.

To reopen their export markets, the United States and Canada will have to convince countries that have imposed bans that their testing is adequate to catch future cases. The United States tested only 20,000 cattle out of 23 million slaughtered in 2003. Japan said that it would not allow additional imports unless the United States and Canada started testing all slaughtered animals.

SOLVED PROBLEM   2.4

In the first few weeks after the U.S. ban, the quantity of beef sold in Japan fell substantially, and the price rose. In contrast, three weeks after the first discovery, the U.S. price in January 2004 fell by about 15% and the quantity sold increased by 43% over the last week in October 2003. Use supply and demand diagrams to explain why these events occurred.

Answer

1. *Show how a shift of the Japanese supply curve affects the Japanese equilibrium*: When Japan banned U.S. imports, the supply curve of beef in Japan shifted to the left from S^1 to S^2 in panel a of the figure. (The figure shows a parallel shift, for the sake of simplicity.) Presumably, the Japanese demand curve, D, was unaffected as Japanese consumers had no increased risk of consuming tainted meat. Thus the shift of the supply curve caused the equilibrium to move along the demand curve from e_1 to e_2. The equilibrium price rose from p_1 to p_2 and the equilibrium quantity fell from Q_1 to Q_2.

2. *Show how shifts of both the U.S. supply and U.S. demand curves affect the U.S. equilibrium*: U.S. beef consumers' fear of mad cow disease caused their demand curve in panel b of the figure to shift slightly to the left from D^1 to D^2. In the short run, total U.S. production was essentially unchanged. Because of the ban on exports, beef that would have been sold in Japan and elsewhere was sold in the United States, causing the U.S. supply curve to shift to the right from S^1 to S^2. As a result, the U.S. equilibrium changed from e_1 (where S^1 intersects D^1) to e_2 (where S^2 intersects D^2). The U.S. price fell 15% from p_1 to $p_2 = 0.85p_1$, while the quantity rose 43% from Q_1 to $Q_2 = 1.43Q_1$.

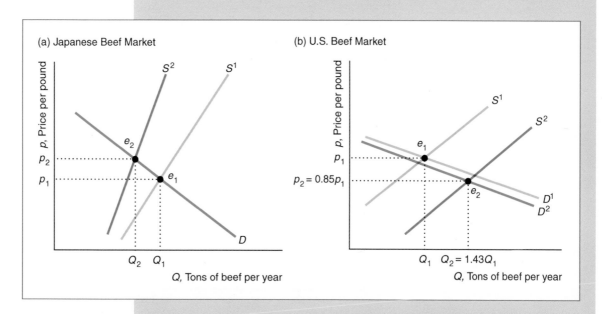

(a) Japanese Beef Market   (b) U.S. Beef Market

See Questions 6 and 9.

Comment: Depending on exactly how the U.S. supply and demand curves had shifted, it would have been possible for the U.S. price and quantity to have both fallen. For example, if D^2 had shifted far enough left, it could have intersected S^2 to the left of Q_1, so that the equilibrium quantity would have fallen.

2.5 ▮ Effects of Government Interventions

A government can affect a market equilibrium in many ways. Sometimes government actions cause a shift in the supply curve, the demand curve, or both curves, which causes the equilibrium to change. Some government interventions, however, cause the quantity demanded to differ from the quantity supplied.

POLICIES THAT SHIFT SUPPLY CURVES

As we saw earlier, quotas on imports affect the supply curve. We illustrate the effect of quotas on market equilibrium.

The Japanese government's ban on rice imports raised the price of rice in Japan substantially. Figure 2.8 shows the Japanese demand curve for rice, D, and the total supply curve without a ban, S. The intersection of S and D determines the equilibrium, e_1, if rice imports are allowed.

What is the effect of a ban on foreign rice on Japanese demand and supply? The ban has no effect on demand if Japanese consumers do not care whether they eat domestic or foreign rice. The ban causes the total supply curve to rotate toward the origin from S (total supply is the horizontal sum of domestic and foreign supply) to $\bar{S}$ (total supply equals the domestic supply).

The intersection of $\bar{S}$ and D determines the new equilibrium, e_2, which lies above and to the left of e_1. The ban causes a shift of the supply curve and a movement along the demand curve. It leads to a fall in the equilibrium quantity from Q_1 to Q_2 and a rise in the equilibrium price from p_1 to p_2. Because of the Japanese ban on imported rice, the price of rice in Japan was 10.5 times higher than the price in the rest of the world in 2001.

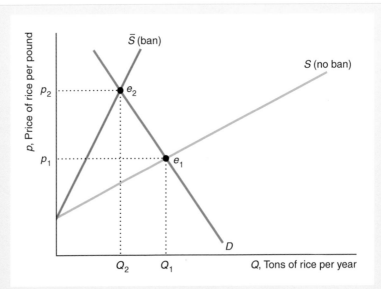

Figure 2.8 **A Ban on Rice Imports Raises the Price in Japan.** A ban on rice imports shifts the total supply of rice in Japan without a ban, S, to $\bar{S}$, which equals the domestic supply alone. As a result, the equilibrium changes from e_1 to e_2. The ban causes the price to rise from p_1 to p_2 and the equilibrium quantity to fall to Q_1 from Q_2.

A quota of $\overline{Q}$ may have a similar effect to an outright ban; however, a quota may have no effect on the equilibrium if the quota is set so high that it does not limit imports. We investigate this possibility in Solved Problem 2.5 and the application that follows it.

SOLVED PROBLEM 2.5

What is the effect of a United States quota on steel of $\overline{Q}$ on the equilibrium in the U.S. steel market? *Hint:* The answer depends on whether the quota binds (is low enough to affect the equilibrium).

Answer

1. *Show how a quota, $\overline{Q}$, affects the total supply of steel in the United States:* The graph reproduces the no-quota total American supply curve of steel, S, and the total supply curve under the quota, $\overline{S}$ (which we derived in Solved Problem 2.2). At a price below $\overline{p}$, the two supply curves are identical because the quota is not binding: It is greater than the quantity foreign firms want to supply. Above $\overline{p}$, $\overline{S}$ lies to the left of S.

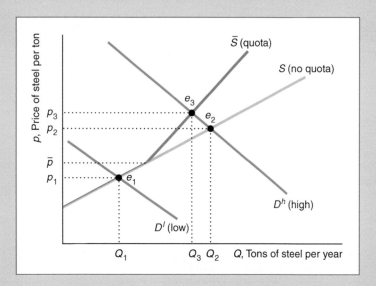

2. *Show the effect of the quota if the original equilibrium quantity is less than the quota so that the quota does not bind:* Suppose that the American demand is relatively *low* at any given price so that the demand curve, D^l, intersects both the supply curves at a price below $\overline{p}$. The equilibria both before and after the quota is imposed are at e_1, where the equilibrium price, p_1, is less than $\overline{p}$. Thus if the demand curve lies near enough to the origin that the quota is not binding, the quota has no effect on the equilibrium.

See Question 16.

3. *Show the effect of the quota if the quota binds:* With a relatively *high* demand curve, D^h, the quota affects the equilibrium. The no-quota equilibrium is e_2, where D^h intersects the no-quota total supply curve, S. After the quota is imposed, the equilibrium is e_3, where D^h intersects the total supply curve with the quota, $\overline{S}$. The quota raises the price of steel in the United States from p_2 to p_3 and reduces the quantity from Q_2 to Q_3.

American Steel Quotas

The U.S. government has repeatedly limited imports of steel into the United States. In some years, the U.S. government negotiated with the governments of Japan and several European countries to limit the amount of steel those countries sold in the United States. Various agreements were in effect from 1969 through 1974. But the quotas were often set so high that they had no effect.

However, in 1971 and 1972, the quotas were binding for most steel products. These quotas raised average U.S. steel prices between 1.2% and 3.5%.

In 1984, President Ronald Reagan negotiated *voluntary* quotas, which covered most steel-exporting countries and limited finished steel imports into the United States to 18.5% of the total U.S. sales for 1985–1989. These limits on imports drove up prices. In 1979–1980, in the absence of quotas, the average U.S. price of steel was approximately the same as the market price in Antwerp, Belgium. In 1984 and 1985, under the Reagan quotas, the average U.S. price was about 25% higher than the corresponding price in Antwerp.

In 1980, pig iron and semifinished steel imports accounted for only 3.5% of domestic steel use, a share that remained virtually unchanged through 1992. Thereafter, in the absence of quotas, imports rose substantially, and the share of imports reached 26.4% by 1998.

In 2002, President George W. Bush imposed a *tariff*, a tax on imported goods, to reduce steel imports. The European Union responded by threatening retaliatory tariffs on U.S. goods. After the World Trade Organization ruled that the tariffs were illegal, President Bush scrapped them at the end of 2003.

POLICIES THAT CAUSE DEMAND TO DIFFER FROM SUPPLY

Some government policies do more than merely shift the supply or demand curve. For example, governments may control prices directly, a policy that leads to either excess supply or excess demand if the price the government sets differs from the equilibrium price. We illustrate this result with two types of price control programs. When the government sets a *price ceiling* at $\overline{p}$, the price at which goods are sold may be no higher than $\overline{p}$. When the government sets a *price floor* at $\underline{p}$, the price at which goods are sold may not fall below $\underline{p}$.

Price Ceilings. Price ceilings have no effect if they are set above the equilibrium price that would be observed in the absence of the price controls. If the government says that firms may charge no more than $\overline{p} = \$5$ per gallon of gas and firms are actually charging $p = \$1$, the government's price control policy is irrelevant. However, if the equilibrium price, p, would be above the price ceiling $\overline{p}$, the price that is actually observed in the market is the price ceiling.

The U.S. experience with gasoline illustrates the effects of price controls. In the 1970s, the Organization of Petroleum Exporting Countries (OPEC) reduced supplies of oil (which is converted into gasoline) to Western countries. As a result, the total supply curve for gasoline in the United States—the horizontal sum of domestic and OPEC supply curves—shifted to the left from S^1 to S^2 in Figure 2.9. Because of this shift, the equilibrium price of gasoline would have risen substantially, from

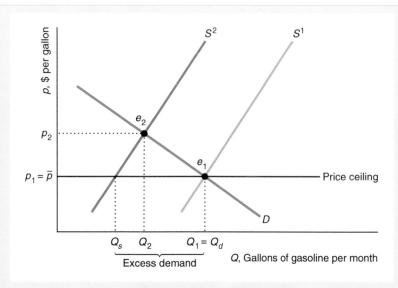

Figure 2.9 **Price Ceiling on Gasoline.** Supply shifts from S^1 to S^2. Under the government's price control program, gasoline stations may not charge a price above the price ceiling $\bar{p} = p_1$. At that price, producers are willing to supply only Q_s, which is less than the amount $Q_1 = Q_d$ that consumers want to buy. The result is excessive demand, or a shortage of $Q_d - Q_s$.

p_1 to p_2. In an attempt to protect consumers by keeping gasoline prices from rising, the U.S. government set price ceilings on gasoline in 1973 and 1979.

The government told gas stations that they could charge no more than $\bar{p} = p_1$. Figure 2.9 shows the price ceiling as a solid horizontal line extending from the price axis at $\bar{p}$. The price control is binding because $p_2 > \bar{p}$. The observed price is the price ceiling. At $\bar{p}$, consumers *want* to buy $Q_d = Q_1$ gallons of gasoline, which is the equilibrium quantity they bought before OPEC acted. However, firms supply only Q_s gallons, which is determined by the intersection of the price control line with S^2. As a result of the binding price control, there is excess demand of $Q_d - Q_s$.

Were it not for the price controls, market forces would drive up the market price to p_2, where the excess demand would be eliminated. The government price ceiling prevents this adjustment from occurring. As a result, an enforced price ceiling causes a **shortage**: a persistent excess demand.

shortage
a persistent excess demand

At the time of the controls, some government officials argued that the shortages were caused by OPEC's cutting off its supply of oil to the United States, but that's not true. Without the price controls, the new equilibrium would be e_2. In this equilibrium, the price, p_2, is much higher than before, p_1; however, there is no shortage. Moreover, without controls, the quantity sold, Q_2, is greater than the quantity sold under the control program, Q_s.

With a binding price ceiling, the supply-and-demand model predicts an *equilibrium with a shortage*. In this equilibrium, the quantity demanded does not equal the quantity supplied. The reason that we call this situation an equilibrium, even though a shortage exists, is that no consumers or firms want to act differently, given the law. Without the price controls, consumers facing a shortage would try to get more output by offering to pay more, or firms would raise prices. With effective government price controls, they know that they can't drive up the price, so they live with the shortage.

What happens? Some lucky consumers get to buy Q_s units at the low price of $\bar{p}$. Other potential customers are disappointed: They would like to buy at that price, but they cannot find anyone willing to sell gas to them.

What determines which consumers are lucky enough to find goods to buy at the low price when there are price controls? With enforced price controls, sellers use criteria other than price to allocate the scarce commodity. Firms may supply their friends, long-term customers, or people of a certain race, gender, age, or religion. They may sell their goods on a first-come, first-served basis. Or they may limit everyone to only a few gallons.

Another possibility is for firms and customers to evade the price controls. A consumer could go to a gas station owner and say, "Let's not tell anyone, but I'll pay you twice the price the government sets if you'll sell me as much gas as I want." If enough customers and gas station owners behaved that way, no shortage would occur. A study of 92 major U.S. cities during the 1972 gasoline price controls found no gasoline lines in 52 of them. However, in cities such as Chicago, Hartford, New York, Portland, and Tucson, potential customers waited in line at the pump for an hour or more.[9] Deacon and Sonstelie (1989) calculated that for every dollar consumers saved during the 1980 gasoline price controls, they lost $1.16 in waiting time and other factors. This experience may be of importance in Hawaii, which imposed gasoline price controls effective in 2005.

● APPLICATION

Zimbabwe Price Controls

In 2001 during a presidential campaign, Zimbabwe's government imposed price controls on many basic commodities, including foods (about a third of citizens' daily consumption), soap, and cement. The controls led to shortages of these goods at retail outlets. Consequently, as the Minister of Finance and Economic Development acknowledged, a thriving *black* or *parallel market*, where controls were ignored, developed. Prices on the black market were two or three times higher than the controlled prices.

Cement manufacturers stopped accepting new orders when the price controls were imposed. Dealers quickly shifted existing supplies to the parallel market. Lack of cement crippled the construction industry. By May 2002, the government had nearly doubled the control price of cement in an effort to induce firms to resume selling cement.

As the price controls made Zimbabwe's sugar significantly cheaper than in the surrounding region, smuggling to other countries increased. Meanwhile, Zimbabwe suffered from a sugar shortage. Similarly, there was a critical maize shortage (which was exacerbated by other shortsighted policies that caused the quantity of maize produced to fall by 30%). Major supermarkets had no maize meal, sugar, and cooking oil on many days. Bakers scaled back operation because

---

[9]See **www.myeconlab.com/perloff**, Chapter 2, "Gas Lines," for a discussion of the effects of the 1973 and 1979 gasoline price controls.

they could obtain only half as much flour as before the controls. These dire shortages pushed many people to the verge of starvation.

In 2005, the government announced new price controls on basic food commodities. Food shortages grew worse. More than a third of the populace is malnourished. Only international food aid has kept millions of these people alive.

Price Floors. Governments also commonly use price floors. One of the most important examples of a price floor is the minimum wage in labor markets.

The minimum wage law forbids employers from paying less than the minimum wage, $\underline{w}$. Minimum wage laws date from 1894 in New Zealand, 1909 in the United Kingdom, and 1912 in Massachusetts. The Fair Labor Standards Act of 1938 set a federal U.S. minimum wage of 25¢. The U.S. federal minimum wage is currently $5.15 an hour. The statutory monthly minimum wage ranges from the equivalent of 19€ in the Russian Federation to 375€ in Portugal, 1,154€ in France, and 1,466€ in Luxembourg. If the minimum wage binds—exceeds the equilibrium wage, w^*—the minimum wage creates *unemployment*, which is a persistent excess supply of labor.[10]

For simplicity, suppose that there is a single labor market in which everyone is paid the same wage. Figure 2.10 shows the supply and demand curves for labor services (hours worked). Firms buy hours of labor service—they hire workers. The

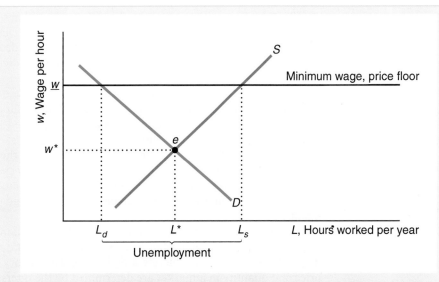

Figure 2.10 **Minimum Wage.** In the absence of a minimum wage, the equilibrium wage is w^* and the equilibrium number of hours worked is L^*. A minimum wage, $\underline{w}$, set above w^*, leads to unemployment—persistent excess supply—because the quantity demanded, L_d, is less than the quantity supplied, L_s.

[10]Where the minimum wage applies to only a few labor markets or where only a single firm hires all the workers in a market, a minimum wage may not cause unemployment (see Card and Krueger, 1995, for empirical evidence). The U.S. Department of Labor maintains at its Web site (**www.dol.gov**) an extensive history of the minimum wage law, labor markets, state minimum wage laws, and other information. For European countries, see **www.fedee.com/minwage.html**.

quantity measure on the horizontal axis is hours worked per year, and the price measure is the wage per hour.

With no government intervention, the market equilibrium is e, where the wage is w^* and the number of hours worked is L^*. The minimum wage creates a price floor, a horizontal line, at $\underline{w}$. At that wage, the quantity demanded falls to L_d and the quantity supplied rises to L_s. As a result, there is an excess supply or unemployment of $L_s - L_d$. The minimum wage prevents market forces from eliminating this excess supply, so it leads to an equilibrium with unemployment. The original 1938 U.S. minimum wage law caused massive unemployment in Puerto Rico.

It is ironic that a law designed to help workers by raising their wages may harm some of them by causing them to become unemployed. A minimum wage law benefits only those who remain employed.[11]

WHY SUPPLY NEED NOT EQUAL DEMAND

The price ceiling and price floor examples show that the quantity supplied does not necessarily equal the quantity demanded in a supply-and-demand model. The quantity supplied need not equal the quantity demanded because of the way we defined these two concepts. We defined the quantity supplied as the amount firms *want to sell* at a given price, holding other factors that affect supply, such as the price of inputs, constant. The quantity demanded is the quantity that consumers *want to buy* at a given price, if other factors that affect demand are held constant. The quantity that firms want to sell and the quantity that consumers want to buy at a given price need not equal the *actual* quantity that is bought and sold.

When the government imposes a binding price ceiling of $\bar{p}$ on gasoline, the quantity demanded is greater than the quantity supplied. Despite the lack of equality between the quantity supplied and the quantity demanded, the supply-and-demand model is useful in analyzing this market because it predicts the excess demand that is actually observed.

We could have defined the quantity supplied and the quantity demanded so that they must be equal. If we were to define the quantity supplied as the amount firms *actually* sell at a given price and the quantity demanded as the amount consumers *actually* buy, supply must equal demand in all markets because the quantity demanded and the quantity supplied are *defined* to be the same quantity.

It is worth pointing out this distinction because many people, including politicians and newspaper reporters, are confused on this point. Someone insisting that "demand *must* equal supply" must be defining demand and supply as the *actual* quantities sold.

Because we define the quantities supplied and demanded in terms of people's *wants* and not *actual* quantities bought and sold, the statement that "supply equals demand" is a theory, not merely a definition. This theory says that the equilibrium price and quantity in a market are determined by the intersection of the supply curve and the demand curve if the government does not intervene. Further, we use the model to predict excess demand or excess supply when a government does control price. The observed gasoline shortages during the period when the U.S. government controlled gasoline prices are consistent with this prediction.

---

[11]The minimum wage could raise the wage enough that total wage payments, wL, rise despite the fall in demand for labor services. If the workers could share the unemployment—everybody works fewer hours than he or she wants—all workers could benefit from the minimum wage.

2.6 When to Use the Supply-and-Demand Model

As we've seen, supply-and-demand theory can help us to understand and predict real-world events in many markets. Briefly, this model is applicable in markets in which:

- **Everyone is a price taker:** Because no consumer or firm is a very large part of the market, no one can affect the market price. Easy entry of firms into the market, which leads to a large number of firms, is usually necessary to ensure that firms are price takers.
- **Firms sell identical products:** Consumers do not prefer one firm's good to another.
- **Everyone has full information about the price and quality of goods:** Consumers know if a firm is charging a price higher than the price others set, and they know if a firm tries to sell them inferior-quality goods.
- **Costs of trading are low:** It is not time consuming, difficult, or expensive for a buyer to find a seller and make a trade or for a seller to find and trade with a buyer.

Markets with these properties are called *perfectly competitive markets*.

Where there are many firms and consumers, no single firm or consumer is a large enough part of the market to affect the price. If you stop buying bread or if one of the many thousands of wheat farmers stops selling the wheat used to make the bread, the price of bread will not change. Consumers and firms are *price takers*: They cannot affect the market price.

In contrast, if there is only one seller of a good or service—a *monopoly* (see Chapter 4)—that seller is a *price setter* and can affect the market price. Because demand curves slope downward, a monopoly can increase the price it receives by reducing the amount of a good it supplies. Firms are also price setters in an *oligopoly*—a market with only a small number of firms—or in markets where they sell differentiated products so that a consumer prefers one product to another. In markets with price setters, the market price is usually higher than that predicted by the supply-and-demand model. That doesn't make the model generally wrong. It means only that the supply-and-demand model does not apply to markets with a small number of sellers or buyers. In such markets, we use other models.

If consumers have less information than a firm, the firm can take advantage of consumers by selling them inferior-quality goods or by charging a much higher price than that charged by other firms. In such a market, the observed price is usually higher than that predicted by the supply-and-demand model, the market may not exist at all (consumers and firms cannot reach agreements), or different firms may charge different prices for the same good.

The supply-and-demand model is also not entirely appropriate in markets in which it is costly to trade with others because the cost of a buyer's finding a seller or of a seller's finding a buyer are high. **Transaction costs** are the expenses of finding a trading partner and making a trade for a good or service other than the price paid for that good or service. These costs include the time and money spent to find someone with whom to trade. For example, you may have to pay to place a newspaper advertisement to sell your gray 1990 Honda with 137,000 miles on it. Or you may have to go to many stores to find one that sells a shirt in exactly the color you want, so your transaction costs includes transportation costs and your time. The cost of a long-distance call to place an order is a transaction cost. Other transaction

transaction costs
the expenses of finding a trading partner and making a trade for a good or service beyond the price paid for that good or service

costs include the costs of writing and enforcing a contract, such as the cost of lawyers' time. Where transaction costs are high, no trades may occur, or if they do occur, individual trades may occur at a variety of prices.

Thus the supply-and-demand model is not appropriate in markets in which there are only one or a few sellers (such as electricity), firms produce differentiated products (music CDs), consumers know less than sellers about quality or price (used cars), or there are high transaction costs (nuclear turbine engines). Markets in which the supply-and-demand model has proved useful include agriculture, finance, labor, construction, services, wholesale, and retail.

Summary

1. **Demand:** The quantity of a good or service demanded by consumers depends on their tastes, the price of a good, the price of goods that are substitutes and complements, their income, information, government regulations, and other factors. The *Law of Demand*—which is based on observation—says that *demand curves slope downward*. The higher the price, the less of the good is demanded, holding constant other factors that affect demand. A change in price causes a *movement along the demand curve*. A change in income, tastes, or another factor that affects demand other than price causes a *shift of the demand curve*. To get a total demand curve, we horizontally sum the demand curves of individuals or types of consumers or countries. That is, we add the quantities demanded by each individual at a given price to get the total demanded.

2. **Supply:** The quantity of a good or service supplied by firms depends on the price, costs, government regulations, and other factors. The market supply curve need not slope upward but usually does. A change in price causes a *movement along the supply curve*. A change in the price of an input or government regulation causes a *shift of the supply curve*. The total supply curve is the horizontal sum of the supply curves for individual firms.

3. **Market equilibrium:** The intersection of the demand curve and the supply curve determines the equilibrium price and quantity in a market. Market forces—

actions of consumers and firms—drive the price and quantity to the equilibrium levels if they are initially too low or too high.

4. **Shocking the equilibrium:** A change in an underlying factor other than price causes a shift of the supply curve or the demand curve, which alters the equilibrium. For example, if the price of beef rises, the demand curve for pork shifts outward, causing a movement along the supply curve and leading to a new equilibrium at a higher price and quantity. If changes in these underlying factors follow one after the other, a market that adjusts slowly may stay out of equilibrium for an extended period.

5. **Effects of government interventions:** Some government policies—such as a ban on imports—cause a shift in the supply or demand curves, thereby altering the equilibrium. Other government policies—such as price controls or a minimum wage—cause the quantity supplied to be greater or less than the quantity demanded, leading to persistent excesses or shortages.

6. **When to use the supply-and-demand model:** The supply-and-demand model is a powerful tool to explain what happens in a market or to make predictions about what will happen if an underlying factor in a market changes. This model, however, is applicable only in markets with many buyers and sellers; identical goods; certainty and full information about price, quantity, quality, incomes, costs, and other market characteristics; and low transaction costs.

Questions

If you ask me anything I don't know, I'm not going to answer.   —Yogi Berra

* = *answer at the back of this book;* **A** = *an application or other real-world material in the text;* **C** = *use of calculus may be necessary.*

1. In December 2000, Japan reported that test shipments of U.S. corn had detected StarLink, a genetically modified corn that is not approved for human

consumption in the United States. As a result, Japan and some other nations banned U.S. imports. Use a graph to illustrate why this ban, which caused U.S. corn exports to fall 4%, resulted in the price of corn falling 11.1% in the United States in 2001–2002.

2. Increasingly, instead of advertising in newspapers, individuals and firms use Web sites that offer free classified ads, such as Realtor.com, Jobs.com, Monster.com, and portals like Yahoo and America Online. Using a supply-and-demand model, explain what will happen to the equilibrium levels of newspaper advertising as the use of the Internet grows. Will the growth of the Internet affect the supply curve, the demand curve, or both? Why?

3. In 2002, the U.S. Fish and Wildlife Service proposed banning imports of beluga caviar to protect the beluga sturgeon in the Caspian and Black seas, whose sturgeon population had fallen 90% in the last two decades. The United States imports 60% of the world's beluga caviar. On the world's legal wholesale market, a kilogram of caviar costs an average of $500, and about $100 million worth is sold per year. What effect would the U.S. ban have on world prices and quantities? Would such a ban help protect the beluga sturgeon? (In 2005, the service decided not to ban imports.)

4. The U.S. supply of frozen orange juice comes from Florida and Brazil. What is the effect of a freeze that damages oranges in Florida on the price of frozen orange juice in the United States and on the quantities of orange juice sold by Floridian and Brazilian firms?

5. The prices received by soybean farmers in Brazil, the world's second-largest soybean producer and exporter, tumbled 30%, in part because of China's decision to cut back on imports and in part because of a bumper soybean crop in the United States, the world's leading exporter (Todd Benson, "A Harvest at Peril," *New York Times,* January 6, 2005, C6). In addition, Asian soy rust, a deadly crop fungus, is destroying large quantities of the Brazilian crops.

   a. Use a supply and demand diagram to illustrate why Brazilian farmers are receiving lower prices.
   b. If you knew only the *direction* of the shifts in both the supply and the demand curves, could you predict that prices would fall? Why or why not? **W**

6. Japan stopped importing animal feed from Britain in 1996, beef imports and processed beef products from 18 countries including EU members starting in 2001, and similar imports from Canada and the United States in 2003. After U.S. beef imports were banned, McDonald's Japan and other Japanese importers replaced much of the banned U.S. beef with Australian beef, causing an export boom for Australia

("China Bans U.S. Beef," **cnn.com**, December 24, 2003; "Beef Producers Are on the Lookout for Extra Demand," **abc.net.au**, June 13, 2005). Use supply and demand curves to show the impact of these events on the domestic Australian beef market. **A**

7. Increased outsourcing to India by firms in the United States and other developed countries has driven up the wage of some skilled workers by 10% to 15% in the last year (Adam Geller, "Offshore Savings Can Be Iffy," *San Francisco Chronicle,* June 21, 2005: D1, D4). Use a demand and supply diagram to explain why, and discuss the effect on employment.

8. On January 1, 2005, a three-decades-old system of global quotas that had limited how much China and other countries could ship to the United States and other wealthy nations ended. Over the next four months, U.S. imports of Chinese-made cotton trousers rose by more than 1,505% and their price fell 21% in the first quarter of the year (Tracie Rozhon, "A Tangle in Textiles," *New York Times,* April 21, 2005, C1). The U.S. textile industry demanded quick action, saying that 18 plants had already been forced to close this year and 16,600 textile and apparel jobs had been lost. The Bush administration reacted to the industry pressure. The United States (and Europe, which faced similar large increases in imports) pressed China to cut back its textile exports, threatening to restore quotas on Chinese exports or to take other actions. Illustrate what happened, and show how the U.S. quota reimposed in May 2005 affected the equilibrium price and quantity in the United States.

9. In Solved Problem 2.4, we illustrated why the mad cow announcement initially caused the U.S. equilibrium price of beef to fall and the quantity to rise. Show that if the supply and demand curves had shifted in the same directions as in the Solved Problem but to greater or lesser degrees, the equilibrium quantity might have fallen. Could the equilibrium price have risen? **A**

10. Due to a slight recession that lowered incomes, the 2002 market prices for last-minute rentals of U.S. beachfront properties were lower than usual (June Fletcher, "Last-Minute Beach Rentals Offer Summer's Best Deals," *Wall Street Journal,* June 21, 2002, D1).

   a. How does a recession affect the demand curve and the supply curve for rental properties? In answering the supply curve question, consider the two options of owners of beach homes: staying in the homes or renting them to others.
   b. Use a supply and demand analysis to show the effect of decreased income on the price of rental homes. **W**

11. The Federation of Vegetable Farmers Association of Malaysia reported that a lack of workers caused a 25% drop in production that drove up vegetable prices by 50% to 100% in 2005 ("Vegetable Price Control Sought," thestar.com.my, June 6, 2005). Consumers called for price controls on vegetables. Show why the price increased, and predict the effects of a binding price control. **W**

12. What is the effect of a quota $\overline{Q} > 0$ on equilibrium price and quantity? (*Hint:* Carefully show how the total supply curve changes.) **A**

*13. Usury laws place a ceiling on interest rates that lenders such as banks can charge borrowers. Low-income households in states with usury laws have significantly lower levels of consumer credit (loans) than comparable households in states without usury laws (Villegas, 1989). Why? (*Hint:* The interest rate is the price of a loan, and the amount of the loan is the quantity measure.)

14. In 1999, after nearly 20 years of rent control in Berkeley, California, the elimination of the law led to an estimated rise in rents of nearly 40%. Using supply-and-demand models, illustrate how the law and then its elimination affected the rental housing market. Discuss the effects on the equilibrium rental price and the quantity of housing rented.

15. After a major earthquake struck Los Angeles in January 1994, several stores raised the price of milk to over $6 a gallon. The local authorities announced that they would investigate and that they would enforce a law prohibiting price increases of more than 10% during an emergency period. What is the likely effect of such a law?

16. Is it possible that an outright ban on foreign imports will have no effect on the equilibrium price? (*Hint:* Suppose that imports occur only at relatively high prices.) **A**

17. If certain jurisdictions ban the use of skateboards on city streets, what is the likely effect on the market for skateboards? How do such laws affect the supply curve, the demand curve, and equilibrium price and quantity?

18. The *New York Times* reported in 1997 that a crackdown on a cocaine-smuggling ring caused cocaine prices in Manhattan to rise from $20,000 to $30,000 a kilogram. Illustrate in a supply-and-demand diagram why this happened, and explain in words.

19. In 1996, a group of American doctors called for a limit on the number of foreign-trained physicians permitted to practice in the United States. What effect would such a limit have on the equilibrium quantity and price of doctor services in the United States? How are American-trained doctors and consumers affected?

20. Suppose that cotton is produced only in the United States and China. The U.S. government says that if an American farmer sells a bale of cotton at the world price, p, the government will give the farmer $(p^* - p)$ per bale, where $p^* > p$. What happens to the quantities sold by American and Chinese growers and the world price of cotton?

*21. Use a supply-and-demand diagram to explain the statement "Talk is cheap because supply exceeds demand." At what price is this comparison being made? **A**

Problems

*22. Using the estimated demand function for processed pork in Canada (Equation 2.2), show how the quantity demanded at a given price changes as per capita income, Y, increases by $100 a year. **A**

23. Suppose that the price of beef, p_b, in Canada increased by 30%, from $4 to $5.20. How does the demand curve for processed pork shift? **A**

24. Use Equations 2.2 and 2.7 and other information in the chapter to show how the equilibrium quantity of pork varies with income.

25. Using the equations for processed pork demand (Equation 2.2) and supply (Equation 2.6), solve for the equilibrium price and quantity in terms of the price of hogs, p_h; the price of beef, p_b; the price of

chicken, p_c; and income, y. If $p_h = 1.5$ (dollars per kg), $p_b = 4$ (dollars per kg), $p_c = 3\frac{1}{3}$ (dollars per kg), and $y = 12.5$ (thousands dollars), what are the equilibrium price and quantity? **A**

26. If the supply of corn by the United States is $Q_a = a + bp$, and the supply by the rest of the world is $Q_r = c + ep$, what is the world supply?

*27. The demand function for a good is $Q = a - bp$, and the supply function is $Q = c + ep$, where a, b, c, and e are positive constants. Solve for the equilibrium price and quantity in terms of these four constants.

28. The demand function for roses is $Q = a - bp$, and the supply function is $Q = c + ep + ft$, where a, b, c, e, and f are positive constants and t is the average

temperature in a month. Show how the equilibrium quantity and price vary with temperature.

*29. Suppose that the inverse demand function for movies is $p = 120 - Q_1$ for college students and $p = 120 - 2Q_2$ for other town residents. What is the town's total demand function ($Q = Q_1 + Q_2$ as a function of p)? Use a diagram to illustrate your answer. **A**

30. The demand function for movies is $Q_1 = 120 - p$ for college students and $Q_2 = 120 - 2p$ for other town residents. What is the total demand function? Use a diagram to illustrate your answer. (*Hint:* By looking at your diagram, you'll see that some care must be used in writing the demand function.) **A**

31. In the application "Aggregating the Demand for Broadband Service" (based on Duffy-Deno, 2003), the demand function is $Q_s = 15.6p^{-0.563}$ for small firms and $Q_l = 16.0p^{-0.296}$ for larger ones, where price is in cents per kilobyte per second and quantity is in millions of kilobytes per second (Kbps). What is the total demand function for all firms? **A**

32. Suppose that the supply curve for broadband service is horizontal at 40¢ Kbps (firms will supply as much service as desired at that price). Using the information in Problem 31, what is the quantity demanded by small firms, large firms, and all firms? **A**

*33. Green et al. (2005) estimate the supply and demand curves for California processed tomatoes. The supply function is $\ln(Q) = 0.2 + 0.55 \ln(p)$, where Q is the quantity of processing tomatoes in millions of tons per year and p is the price in dollars per ton. The demand function is $\ln(Q) = 2.6 - 0.2 \ln(p) + 0.15 \ln(p_t)$, where p_t is the price of tomato paste (which is what processing tomatoes are used to produce) in dollars per ton. In 2002, $p_t = 110$. What is the demand function for processing tomatoes, where the quantity is solely a function of the price of processing tomatoes? Solve for the equilibrium price and quantity of processing tomatoes (explain your calculations, and round to two digits after the decimal point). Draw the supply and demand curves (note that they are not straight lines), and label the equilibrium and axes appropriately.

34. Using the information in Problem 33, determine how the equilibrium price and quantity of processing tomatoes change if the price of tomato paste falls by 10%.

35. Suppose that the government imposes a price support on processing tomatoes at $65 per ton. The government will buy as much as farmers want to sell at that price. Thus processing firms pay $65. Use the information in Problem 33 to determine how many tons firms buy and how many tons the government buys. Illustrate your answer in a supply-and-demand diagram.

36. Use the information in Problem 32 to show how the quantity of processing tomatoes supplied varies with the price (dQ/dp). (*Hint:* It might be easier for you to exponentiate both sides of the equation first.) **C**

Chapter 3

Applying the Supply-and-Demand Model

Few of us ever test our powers of deduction, except when filling out an income tax form.
— Laurence J. Peter

How large a tax would be necessary to reduce the number of teenagers who smoke by half? If the government were to intercept half the cocaine smuggled into New York City, how much would the price of cocaine rise in the short run and in the long run? We can use supply-and-demand analysis to answer such questions.

When an underlying factor that affects the demand or supply curve changes, the equilibrium price and quantity also change. Chapter 2 showed that you can predict the direction of the change—the *qualitative* change—in equilibrium price and quantity even without knowing the exact shape of the demand and supply curves. In most of the examples in Chapter 2, all you needed to know to give a qualitative answer was the direction in which the supply curve or demand curve shifted when an underlying factor changed.

To determine the exact amount the equilibrium quantity and price change—the *quantitative* change—you can use estimated equations for the demand and supply functions, as we demonstrated using the pork example in Chapter 2. This chapter shows how to use a single number to describe how sensitive the quantity demanded or supplied is to a change in price and how to use these summary numbers to obtain quantitative answers to what-if questions.

In this chapter, we examine five main topics

1. How shapes of demand and supply curves matter: The effect of a shock (such as a new tax or an increase in the price of an input) on market equilibrium depends on the shape of demand and supply curves.

2. Sensitivity of quantity demanded to price: The sensitivity of the quantity demanded to price is summarized by a single measure called the price elasticity of demand.

3. Sensitivity of quantity supplied to price: The sensitivity of the quantity supplied to price is summarized by a single measure called the price elasticity of supply.

4. Long run versus short run: The sensitivity of the quantity demanded or supplied to price varies with time.

5. Effects of a sales tax: How a sales tax increase affects the equilibrium price and quantity of a good and whether the tax falls more heavily on consumers or suppliers depend on the shape of the supply and demand curves.

3.1 How Shapes of Demand and Supply Curves Matter

The shapes of the demand and supply curves determine by how much a shock affects the equilibrium price and quantity. We illustrate the importance of the shape of the demand curve using the processed pork example (Moschini and Meilke, 1992) from Chapter 2. The supply of pork depends on the price of pork and the price of hogs, the major input in producing processed pork. A 25¢ increase in the price of hogs causes the supply curve of pork to shift to the left from S^1 to S^2 in panel a of Figure 3.1. The *shift of the supply curve* causes a *movement along the demand curve*, D^1, which is downward sloping. The equilibrium quantity falls from 220 to 215 million kg per year, and the equilibrium price rises from $3.30 to $3.55 per kg. Thus this supply shock—an increase in the price of hogs—hurts consumers by raising the equilibrium price 25¢ per kg. Customers buy less (215 instead of 220).

A supply shock would have different effects if the demand curve had a different shape. Suppose that the quantity demanded were not sensitive to a change in the price, so the same amount is demanded no matter what the price is, as in vertical demand curve D^2 in panel b. A 25¢ increase in the price of hogs again shifts the supply curve from S^1 to S^2. Equilibrium quantity does not change, but the price consumers pay rises by 37.5¢ to $3.675. Thus the amount consumers spend rises by more when the demand curve is vertical instead of downward sloping.

Now suppose that consumers are very sensitive to price, as in the horizontal demand curve, D^3, in panel c. Consumers will buy virtually unlimited quantities of pork at $3.30 per kg (or less), but, if the price rises even slightly, they stop buying pork. Here an increase in the price of hogs has *no* effect on the price consumers pay; however, the equilibrium quantity drops substantially to 205 million kg per year.

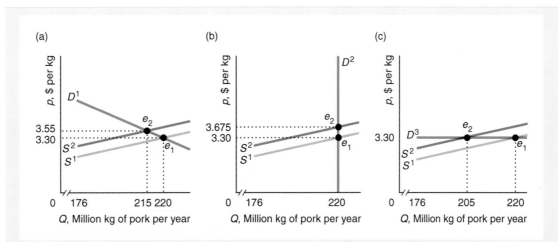

Figure 3.1 **How the Effect of a Supply Shock Depends on the Shape of the Demand Curve.** An increase in the price of hogs shifts the supply of processed pork upward. (a) Given the actual downward-sloping linear demand curve, the equilibrium price rises from $3.30 to $3.55 and the equilibrium quantity falls from 220 to 215. (b) If the demand curve were vertical, the supply shock would cause price to rise to $3.675 while quantity would remain unchanged. (c) If the demand curve were horizontal, the supply shock would not affect price but would cause quantity to fall to 205.

Thus how much the equilibrium quantity falls and how much the equilibrium price of processed pork rises when the price of hogs increases depend on the shape of the demand curve.

3.2 Sensitivity of Quantity Demanded to Price

Knowing how much quantity demanded falls as the price increases, holding all else constant, is therefore important in predicting the effect of a shock in a supply-and-demand model. We can determine how much quantity demanded falls as the price rises using an accurate drawing of the demand curve or the demand function (the equation that describes the demand curve). It is convenient, however, to be able to summarize the relevant information to answer what-if questions without having to write out an equation or draw a graph. Armed with such a summary statistic, the pork firms can predict the effect on the price of pork and their revenues from a shift in the market supply curve.

In this section, we discuss a summary statistic that describes how much the quantity demanded changes in response to an increase in price at a given point. In the next section, we discuss a similar statistic for the supply curve. At the end of the chapter, we show how the government can use these summary measures for demand and supply to predict the effect of a new sales tax on the equilibrium price, firms' revenues, and tax receipts.

PRICE ELASTICITY OF DEMAND

elasticity
the percentage change in a variable in response to a given percentage change in another variable

price elasticity of demand (or *elasticity of demand, ε*)
the percentage change in the *quantity demanded* in response to a given percentage change in the price

The most commonly used measure of the sensitivity of one variable, such as the quantity demanded, to another variable, such as price, is an **elasticity**, which is the percentage change in one variable in response to a given percentage change in another variable. The **price elasticity of demand** (or simply *elasticity of demand*) is the percentage change in the quantity demanded, Q, in response to a given percentage change in the price, p, at a particular point on the demand curve. The price elasticity of demand (represented by ε, the Greek letter epsilon) is

$$\varepsilon = \frac{\text{percentage change in quantity demanded}}{\text{percentage change in price}} = \frac{\Delta Q/Q}{\Delta p/p}, \qquad (3.1)$$

where the symbol Δ (the Greek letter delta) indicates a change, so ΔQ is the change in the quantity demanded; $\Delta Q/Q$ is the percentage change in the quantity demanded; Δp is the change in price; and $\Delta p/p$ is the percentage change in price.[1] For example, if a 1% increase in the price results in a 3% decrease in the quantity demanded, the elasticity of demand is $\varepsilon = -3\%/1\% = -3$.[2] Thus the elasticity of demand is a pure number (it has no units of measure).

See Questions 2 and 3.

---

[1] When we use calculus, we use infinitesimally small changes in price (Δp approaches zero), so we write the elasticity as $(dQ/dp)(p/Q)$. When discussing elasticities, we assume that the change in price is small.

[2] Because demand curves slope downward according to the Law of Demand, the elasticity of demand is a negative number. Realizing that, some economists ignore the negative sign when reporting a demand elasticity. In the example, instead of saying the elasticity is –3, they would say that the elasticity is 3 (with the negative sign understood).

It is often more convenient to calculate the elasticity of demand using an equivalent expression,

$$\varepsilon = \frac{\Delta Q/Q}{\Delta p/p} = \frac{\Delta Q}{\Delta p} \frac{p}{Q}, \qquad (3.2)$$

where $\Delta Q/\Delta p$ is the ratio of the change in quantity to the change in price (the inverse of the slope of the demand curve).

We can use Equation 3.2 to calculate the elasticity of demand for a linear demand curve, which has a demand function (holding fixed other variables that affect demand) of

$$Q = a - bp,$$

where a is the quantity demanded when price is zero, $Q = a - (b \times 0) = a$, and $-b$ is the ratio of the fall in quantity to the rise in price, $\Delta Q/\Delta p$.[3] Thus for a linear demand curve, the elasticity of demand is

$$\varepsilon = \frac{\Delta Q}{\Delta p} \frac{p}{Q} = -b \frac{p}{Q}. \qquad (3.3)$$

As an example, we calculate the elasticity of demand for the linear pork demand curve D in panel a of Figure 3.1. The estimated linear demand function for pork, which holds constant other factors that influence demand besides price (Equation 2.3, based on Moschini and Meilke, 1992), is

$$Q = 286 - 20p,$$

where Q is the quantity of pork demanded in million kg per year and p is the price of pork in dollars per kg. For this demand equation, $a = 286$ and $b = 20$. Using Equation 3.3, we find that the elasticity of demand at the equilibrium e_1 in panel a, where $p = \$3.30$ and $Q = 220$, is

$$\varepsilon = b \frac{p}{Q} = -20 \times \frac{3.30}{220} = -0.3.$$

The negative sign on the elasticity of demand of pork illustrates the Law of Demand: Less quantity is demanded as the price rises. The elasticity of demand concisely answers the question, "How much does quantity demanded fall in response to a 1% increase in price?" A 1% increase in price leads to an $\varepsilon\%$ change in the quantity demanded. At the equilibrium, a 1% increase in the price of pork leads to a -0.3% fall in the quantity of pork demanded: A price increase causes a less than proportionate fall in the quantity of pork demanded.

● APPLICATION

Willingness to Surf

Do you surf the net for hours and download billions of bits of music? Would you cut back if the price of your Internet service increased? At what price would you give up using the Internet?

---

[3]As the price increases from p_1 to p_2, the quantity demanded goes from Q_1 to Q_2, so the change in quantity demanded is $\Delta Q = Q_2 - Q_1 = (a - bp_2) - (a - bp_1) = -b(p_2 - p_1) = -b\Delta p$. Thus $\Delta Q/\Delta p = -b$. (The slope of the demand curve is $\Delta p/\Delta Q = -1/b$.)

Varian (2002) estimated demand curves for connection time by people at a university who paid for access by the minute. He found that the price elasticity of demand was –2.0 for those who used a 128 kilobits per second (Kbps) service and –2.9 for people who connected at 64 Kbps. That is, a 1% increase in the price per minute reduced the connection time used by those with high-speed access by 2% but decreased the connection time by nearly 3% for those with slow, phone-line access. Thus high-speed users are less sensitive to connection prices than slow-speed users.

Some recent studies have found that residential users who pay a flat rate (no per-minute charge) for service have a very inelastic demand for dial-up service: That is, few dial-up users will give up their service if the flat fee rises. Residential customers are more sensitive to the flat-fee price of broadband service, with elasticities ranging from –0.75 to –1.5. That is, if the price of broadband service increases 10%, between 7.5% and 15% fewer households will use a broadband service.

See Question 2.

ELASTICITY ALONG THE DEMAND CURVE

The elasticity of demand varies along most demand curves. The elasticity of demand is different at every point along a downward-sloping linear demand curve; however, the elasticities are constant along horizontal and vertical linear demand curves.

Downward-Sloping Linear Demand Curve. On strictly downward-sloping linear demand curves—those that are neither vertical nor horizontal—the elasticity of demand is a more negative number the higher the price is. Consequently, even though the slope of the linear demand curve is constant, the elasticity varies along the curve. A 1% increase in price causes a larger percentage fall in quantity near the top (left) of the demand curve than near the bottom (right).

The linear pork demand curve in Figure 3.2 illustrates this pattern. Where this demand curve hits the quantity axis ($p = 0$ and $Q = a = 286$ million kg per year), the elasticity of demand is $\varepsilon = -b(0/a) = 0$, according to Equation 3.3. Where the price is zero, a 1% increase in price does not raise the price, so quantity does not change. At a point where the elasticity of demand is zero, the demand curve is said to be *perfectly inelastic*. As a physical analogy, if you try to stretch an inelastic steel rod, the length does not change. The change in the price is the force pulling at demand; if the quantity demanded does not change in response to this pulling, it is perfectly inelastic.

For quantities between the midpoint of the linear demand curve and the lower end where $Q = a$, the demand elasticity lies between 0 and –1: $0 \geq \varepsilon > -1$. A point along the demand curve where the elasticity is between 0 and –1 is *inelastic* (but not perfectly inelastic). Where the demand curve is inelastic, a 1% increase in price leads to a fall in quantity of less than 1%. For example, at the competitive pork equilibrium, $\varepsilon = -0.3$, so a 1% increase in price causes quantity to fall by –0.3%. A physical analogy is a piece of rope that does not stretch much—is inelastic—when you pull on it: Changing price has relatively little effect on quantity.

See Question 1.

At the midpoint of the linear demand curve, $p = a/(2b)$ and $Q = a/2$, so $\varepsilon = -bp/Q = -b(a/[2b])/(a/2) = -1$. Such an elasticity of demand is called a *unitary elasticity*: A 1% increase in price causes a 1% fall in quantity.

At prices higher than at the midpoint of the demand curve, the elasticity of demand is less than negative one, $\varepsilon < -1$. In this range, the demand curve is called

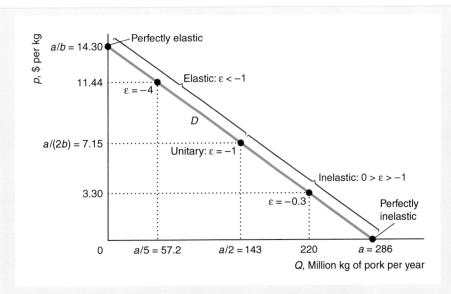

Figure 3.2 **Elasticity Along the Pork Demand Curve.** With a linear demand curve, such as the pork demand curve, the higher the price, the more elastic the demand curve (ε is larger in absolute value—a larger negative number). The demand curve is perfectly inelastic ($\varepsilon = 0$) where the demand curve hits the horizontal axis, is perfectly elastic where the demand curve hits the vertical axis, and has unitary elasticity ($\varepsilon = -1$) at the midpoint of the demand curve.

elastic. A physical analogy is a rubber band that stretches substantially when you pull on it. A 1% increase in price causes a more than 1% fall in quantity. The figure shows that the elasticity is –4 where $Q = a/5$: A 1% increase in price causes a 4% drop in quantity.

As the price rises, the elasticity gets more and more negative, approaching negative infinity. Where the demand curve hits the price axis, it is *perfectly elastic.*[4] At the price a/b where $Q = 0$, a 1% decrease in p causes the quantity demanded to become positive, which is an infinite increase in quantity.

See Question 4.

The elasticity of demand varies along most demand curves, not just downward-sloping linear ones. Along a special type of demand curve, called a *constant-elasticity demand curve,* however, the elasticity is the same at every point along the curve.[5] Two extreme cases of these constant-elasticity demand curves are the strictly vertical and the strictly horizontal linear demand curves.

See Problems 25 and 26.

---

[4]The demand curve hits the price axis at $p = a/b$ and $Q = 0$, so the elasticity is $-bp/0$. As the price approaches a/b, the elasticity approaches negative infinity. An intuition for this convention is provided by looking at a sequence, where –1 divided by 1/10 is –10, –1 divided by 1/100 is –100, and so on. The smaller the number we divide by, the more negative is the result, which goes to $-\infty$ (negative infinity) in the limit.

[5]Constant-elasticity demand curves all have the form $Q = Ap^{\varepsilon}$, where A is a positive constant and ε, a negative constant, is the demand elasticity at every point along these demand curves.

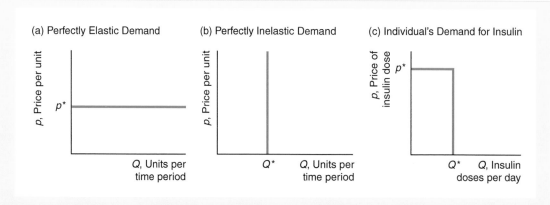

Figure 3.3 **Vertical and Horizontal Demand Curves.** (a) A horizontal demand curve is perfectly elastic at p^*. (b) A vertical demand curve is perfectly inelastic at every price. (c) The demand curve of an individual who is diabetic is perfectly inelastic below p^* and perfectly elastic at p^*, which is the maximum price the individual can afford to pay.

Horizontal Demand Curve. The demand curve that is horizontal at p^* in panel a of Figure 3.3 shows that people are willing to buy as much as firms sell at any price less than or equal to p^*. If the price increases even slightly above p^*, however, demand falls to zero. Thus a small increase in price causes an infinite drop in quantity, so the demand curve is perfectly elastic.

Why would a demand curve be horizontal? One reason is that consumers view this good as identical to another good and do not care which one they buy. Suppose that consumers view Washington apples and Oregon apples as identical. They won't buy Washington apples if these sell for more than apples from Oregon. Similarly, they won't buy Oregon apples if their price is higher than that of Washington apples. If the two prices are equal, consumers do not care which type of apple they buy. Thus the demand curve for Oregon apples is horizontal at the price of Washington apples.

Vertical Demand Curve. A vertical demand curve, panel b in Figure 3.3, is perfectly inelastic everywhere. Such a demand curve is an extreme case of the linear demand curve with an infinite (vertical) slope. If the price goes up, the quantity demanded is unchanged ($\Delta Q/\Delta p = 0$), so the elasticity of demand must be zero: $(\Delta Q/\Delta p)(p/Q) = 0(p/Q) = 0$.

A demand curve is vertical for *essential goods*—goods that people feel they must have and will pay anything to get. Because Jerry is a diabetic, his demand curve for insulin could be vertical at a day's dose, Q^*. More realistically, he may have a demand curve (panel c of Figure 3.3) that is perfectly inelastic only at prices below p^*, the maximum price he can afford to pay. Because he cannot afford to pay more than p^*, he buys nothing at higher prices. As a result, his demand curve is perfectly elastic up to Q^* units at a price of p^*.

OTHER DEMAND ELASTICITIES

We refer to the price elasticity of demand as *the* elasticity of demand. However, there are other demand elasticities that show how the quantity demanded changes in response to changes in variables other than price that affect the quantity demanded.

Two such demand elasticities are the income elasticity of demand and the cross-price elasticity of demand.

Income Elasticity. As income increases, the demand curve shifts. If the demand curve shifts to the right, a larger quantity is demanded at any given price. If instead the demand curve shifts to the left, a smaller quantity is demanded at any given price.

We can measure how sensitive the quantity demanded at a given price is to income by using an elasticity. The **income elasticity of demand** (or *income elasticity*) is the percentage change in the quantity demanded in response to a given percentage change in income, Y. The income elasticity of demand may be calculated as

Income elasticity of demand (or *income elasticity*)
the percentage change in the *quantity demanded* in response to a given percentage change in income

$$\xi = \frac{\text{percentage change in quantity demanded}}{\text{percentage change in income}} = \frac{\Delta Q/Q}{\Delta Y/Y} = \frac{\Delta Q}{\Delta Y} \frac{Y}{Q},$$

where ξ is the Greek letter xi. If quantity demanded increases as income rises, the income elasticity of demand is positive. If the quantity does not change as income rises, the income elasticity is zero. Finally, if the quantity demanded falls as income rises, the income elasticity is negative.

We can calculate the income elasticity for pork using the demand function, Equation 2.2:

$$Q = 171 - 20p + 20p_b + 3p_c + 2Y, \tag{3.4}$$

where p is the price of pork, p_b is the price of beef, p_c is the price of chicken, and Y is the income (in thousands of dollars). Because the change in quantity as income changes is $\Delta Q/\Delta Y = 2$,[6] we can write the income elasticity as

$$\xi = \frac{\Delta Q}{\Delta Y} \frac{Y}{Q} = 2\frac{Y}{Q}.$$

At the equilibrium, quantity $Q = 220$ and income is $Y = 12.5$, so the income elasticity is $2 \times (12.5/220) \approx 0.114$. The positive income elasticity shows that an increase in income causes the pork demand curve to shift to the right. Holding the price of pork constant at $3.30 per kg, a 1% increase in income causes the demand curve for pork to shift to the right by 0.25 (= $\xi \times 220 \times .01$) million kg, which is about one-ninth of 1% of the equilibrium quantity.

See Problem 28.

Income elasticities play an important role in our analysis of consumer behavior. Typically, goods that society views as necessities, such as food, have income elasticities near zero. Goods that society considers to be luxuries generally have income elasticities greater than one.

cross-price elasticity of demand
the percentage change in the *quantity demanded* in response to a given percentage change in the price of another good

Cross-Price Elasticity. The **cross-price elasticity of demand** is the percentage change in the quantity demanded in response to a given percentage change in the price of another good, p_o. The cross-price elasticity may be calculated as

$$\frac{\text{percentage change in quantity demanded}}{\text{percentage change in price of another good}} = \frac{\Delta Q/Q}{\Delta p_o/p_o} = \frac{\Delta Q}{\Delta p_o} \frac{p_o}{Q}.$$

When the cross-price elasticity is negative, the goods are *complements* (Chapter 2). If the cross-price elasticity is negative, people buy less of the good when the price of

---

[6] At income Y_1, the quantity demanded is $Q_1 = 171 - 20p + 20p_b + 3p_c + 2Y_1$. At income Y_2, $Q_2 = 171 - 20p + 20p_b + 3p_c + 2Y_2$. Thus $\Delta Q = Q_2 - Q_1 = 2(Y_2 - Y_1) = 2(\Delta Y)$, so $\Delta Q/\Delta Y = 2$.

the other good increases: The demand curve for this good shifts to the left. For example, if people like cream in their coffee, as the price of cream rises, they consume less coffee, so the cross-price elasticity of the quantity of coffee with respect to the price of cream is negative.

If the cross-price elasticity is positive, the goods are *substitutes* (Chapter 2). As the price of the other good increases, people buy more of this good. For example, the quantity demanded of pork increases when the price of beef, p_b, rises. From Equation 3.4, we know that $\Delta Q/\Delta p_b = 20$. As a result, the cross-price elasticity between the price of beef and the quantity of pork is

$$\frac{\Delta Q}{\Delta p_b} \frac{p_b}{Q} = 20 \frac{p_b}{Q}.$$

See Question 22 and Problem 27.

At the equilibrium where $p = \$3.30$ per kg, $Q = 220$ million kg per year, and $p_b = \$4$ per kg, the cross-price elasticity is $20 \times (4/220) \approx 0.364$. As the price of beef rises by 1%, the quantity of pork demanded rises by a little more than one-third of 1%.

Taking account of cross-price elasticities is important in making business and policy decisions. General Motors wants to know how much a change in the price of a Toyota affects the demand for its Chevy.

● APPLICATION

Substitution May Save Endangered Species

One reason that many species—including tigers, rhinoceroses, pinnipeds, green turtles, geckos, sea horses, pipefish, and sea cucumbers—are endangered, threatened, or vulnerable to extinction is that certain of their body parts are used as aphrodisiacs in traditional Chinese medicine. Is it possible that consumers will switch from such potions to Viagra, a less expensive and almost certainly more effective alternative treatment, and thereby help save these endangered species?

We cannot directly calculate the substitution elasticity between Viagra and these endangered species because their trade is illicit and not reported. However, harp seal and hooded seal genitalia are also used as aphrodisiacs in Asia, and they may be legally traded. Before 1998, Viagra was unavailable (effectively, it had an infinite price). When it became available at about $15 to $20 Canadian per pill, the demand curve for seal sex organs shifted substantially to the left. According to von Hippel and von Hippel (2002, 2004), 30,000 to 50,000 seal organs were sold at between $70 and $100 Canadian in the years just before 1998. In 1998, the price per unit fell to $15 to $20, and only 20,000 organs were sold. By 1999–2000 (and thereafter), virtually none were sold. This evidence suggests a strong willingness to substitute at current prices: a positive cross-price elasticity between seal organs and the price of Viagra. Thus Viagra can perhaps save more than marriages.

See Question 5.

3.3 Sensitivity of Quantity Supplied to Price

To answer many what-if questions, we need information about the sensitivity of the quantity supplied to changes in price. For example, to determine how a sales tax will affect market price, a government needs to know the sensitivity to price of both the quantity supplied and the quantity demanded.

ELASTICITY OF SUPPLY

price elasticity of supply (or *elasticity of supply*, η) the percentage change in the *quantity supplied* in response to a given percentage change in the price

Just as we can use the elasticity of demand to summarize information about the shape of a demand curve, we can use the elasticity of supply to summarize information about the supply curve. The **price elasticity of supply** (or *elasticity of supply*) is the percentage change in the quantity supplied in response to a given percentage change in the price. The price elasticity of supply (η, the Greek letter eta) is

$$\eta = \frac{\text{percentage change in quantity supplied}}{\text{percentage change in price}} = \frac{\Delta Q/Q}{\Delta p/p} = \frac{\Delta Q}{\Delta p}\frac{p}{Q}, \qquad (3.5)$$

where Q is the *quantity supplied*. If $\eta = 2$, a 1% increase in price leads to a 2% increase in the quantity supplied.

The definition of the elasticity of supply, Equation 3.5, is very similar to the definition of the elasticity of demand, Equation 3.1. The key distinction is that the elasticity of supply describes the movement along the *supply* curve as price changes, whereas the elasticity of demand describes the movement along the *demand* curve as price changes. That is, in the numerator, supply elasticity depends on the percentage change in the *quantity supplied*, whereas demand elasticity depends on the percentage change in the *quantity demanded*.

If the supply curve is upward sloping, $\Delta p/\Delta Q > 0$, the supply elasticity is positive: $\eta > 0$. If the supply curve slopes downward, the supply elasticity is negative: $\eta < 0$.

To show how to calculate the elasticity of supply, we use the supply function for pork (based on Moschini and Meilke, 1992), Equation 2.7,

$$Q = 88 + 40p,$$

where Q is the quantity of pork supplied in million kg per year and p is the price of pork in dollars per kg. This supply function is a straight line in Figure 3.4. (The horizontal axis starts at 176 rather than at the origin.) The number multiplied by p in the supply function, 40, shows how much the quantity supplied rises as the price increases: $\Delta Q/\Delta p = 40$. At the equilibrium where $p = \$3.30$ and $Q = 220$, the elasticity of supply of pork is

$$\eta = \frac{\Delta Q}{\Delta p}\frac{p}{Q} = 40 \times \frac{3.30}{220} = 0.6.$$

As the price of pork increases by 1%, the quantity supplied rises by slightly less than two-thirds of a percent.

We use the terms *inelastic* and *elastic* to describe *upward-sloping* supply curves, just as we did for demand curves. If $\eta = 0$, we say that the supply curve is *perfectly inelastic*: The supply does not change as price rises. If $0 < \eta < 1$, the supply curve is *inelastic* (but not perfectly inelastic): A 1% increase in price causes a less than 1% rise in the quantity supplied. If $\eta = 1$, the supply curve has a *unitary elasticity*: A 1% increase in price causes a 1% increase in quantity. If $\eta > 1$, the supply curve is *elastic*. If η is infinite, the supply curve is *perfectly elastic*.

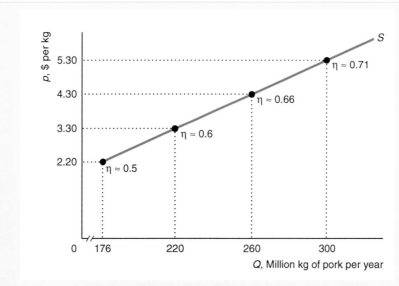

Figure 3.4 **Elasticity Along the Pork Supply Curve.** The elasticity of supply, η, varies along the pork supply curve. The higher the price, the larger is the supply elasticity.

ELASTICITY ALONG THE SUPPLY CURVE

The elasticity of supply may vary along the supply curve. The elasticity of supply varies along most linear supply curves.

The supply function of a linear supply curve is

$$Q = g + hp,$$

where g and h are constants. By the same reasoning as before, $\Delta Q = h\Delta p$, so $h = \Delta Q/\Delta p$ shows the change in the quantity supplied as price changes.

The supply curve for pork is $Q = 88 + 40p$, so $g = 88$ and $h = 40$. Because $h = 40$ is positive, the quantity of pork supplied increases as the price of pork rises.

The elasticity of supply for a linear supply function is $\eta = h(p/Q)$. The elasticity of supply for the pork is $\eta = 40p/Q$. As the ratio p/Q rises, the supply elasticity rises. Along most linear supply curves, the ratio p/Q changes as p rises.

See Problem 29.

The pork supply curve, Figure 3.4, is inelastic at each point shown. The elasticity of supply varies along the pork supply curve: It is 0.5 when $p = \$2.20$, 0.6 when $p = \$3.30$, and about 0.71 when $p = \$5.30$.

Only *constant elasticity of supply curves* have the same elasticity at every point along the curve.[7] Two extreme examples of both constant elasticity of supply curves and linear supply curves are the vertical and the horizontal supply curves.

The supply curve that is vertical at a quantity, Q^*, is perfectly inelastic. No matter what the price is, firms supply Q^*. An example of inelastic supply is a perishable item such as fresh fruit. If the perishable good is not sold, it quickly becomes worthless. Thus the seller accepts any market price for the good.

A supply curve that is horizontal at a price, p^*, is perfectly elastic. Firms supply as much as the market wants—a potentially unlimited amount—if the price is p^* or

---

[7]Constant elasticity of supply curves are of the form $Q = Bp^\eta$, where B is a constant and η is the constant elasticity of supply at every point along the curve.

above. Firms supply nothing at a price below p^*, which does not cover their cost of production.

3.4 Long Run Versus Short Run

The shapes of demand and supply curves depend on the relevant time period. Short-run elasticities may differ substantially from long-run elasticities. The duration of the *short run* depends on how long it takes consumers or firms to adjust for a particular good.

DEMAND ELASTICITIES OVER TIME

Two factors that determine whether short-run demand elasticities are larger or smaller than long-run elasticities are ease of substitution and storage opportunities. Often one can substitute between products in the long run but not in the short run.

When oil prices rose rapidly in the 1970s and 1980s because of actions by OPEC, most Western consumers did not greatly alter the amount of oil they demanded. Someone who drove 27 miles to and from work every day in a 1969 Chevy could not easily reduce the amount of gasoline purchased. In the long run, however, this person could buy a smaller car, get a job closer to home, join a car pool, or in other ways reduce the amount of gasoline purchased.

Gallini (1983) estimated long-run demand elasticities that are more elastic than the short-run elasticity for gasoline in Canada. She found that the short-run elasticity is –0.35; the 5-year intermediate-run elasticity is nearly twice as elastic, –0.7; and the 10-year, long-run elasticity is approximately –0.8, which is slightly more elastic. Thus a 1% increase in price lowers the quantity demanded by only about a 0.35% in the short run but by more than twice as much, 0.8%, in the long run. Similarly, Grossman and Chaloupka (1998) estimate that a rise in the street price of cocaine has a larger long-run than short-run effect on cocaine consumption by young adults (aged 17–29). The long-run demand elasticity is –1.35, whereas the short-run elasticity is –0.96.

For goods that can be stored easily, short-run demand curves may be more elastic than long-run curves. If frozen orange juice goes on sale this week at your local supermarket, you may buy large quantities and store the extra in your freezer. As a result, you may be more sensitive to price changes for frozen orange juice in the short run than in the long run.

SUPPLY ELASTICITIES OVER TIME

Supply curves too may have different elasticities in the short run than in the long run. If a manufacturing firm wants to increase production in the short run, it can do so by hiring workers to use its machines around the clock, but how much it can expand its output is limited by the fixed size of its manufacturing plant and the number of machines it has. In the long run, however, the firm can build another plant and buy or build more equipment. Thus we would expect this firm's long-run supply elasticity to be greater than its short-run elasticity.

Similarly, Adelaja (1991) found that the short-run elasticity of supply of milk is 0.36, whereas the long-run supply elasticity is 0.51. Thus, the long-run quantity response to a 1% increase in price is about 42% (= [0.51 – 0.36]/0.36) more than in the short run.

Oil Drilling in the Arctic National Wildlife Refuge

We can use information about demand and supply elasticities to answer an important public policy question: Would selling oil from the Arctic National Wildlife Refuge (ANWR) substantially affect the price of oil? ANWR, established in 1980, covers 20 million acres, is the largest of Alaska's 16 national wildlife refuges, and is believed to contain massive deposits of petroleum. For decades, a debate has raged over whether the owners of ANWR—the citizens of the United States—should keep it undeveloped or permit oil drilling.[8]

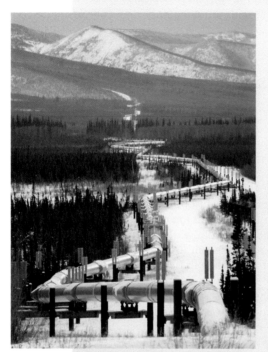

In the simplest form of this complex debate, environmentalists stress that drilling would harm the wildlife refuge and pollute the environment, while President George W. Bush and other drilling proponents argue that extracting this oil would substantially reduce the price of petroleum (as well as decrease U.S. dependence on foreign oil and bring in large royalties). Recent large increases in the price of gasoline and the war in Iraq have heightened this intense debate.

The effect of selling ANWR on the world price of oil is a key element of this debate. We can combine oil production information with supply and demand elasticities to make a "back of the envelope" estimate of the price effects.

A number of studies estimate that the long-run elasticity of demand, ε, for oil is about –0.4 and the long-run supply elasticity, η, is about 0.3. Analysts agree less about how much ANWR oil will be produced. The Department of Energy's Energy Information Service (EIS) predicts that production from ANWR would average about 800,000 barrels per day, or about 1% of the worldwide oil production, which averaged about 82 million barrels per day in 2004. (World output was slightly higher in 2005 and is likely to continue to rise. The EIS estimates that ANWR's oil would increase the volume of production by about 0.7% in 2020.)

A report of the U.S. Department of Energy predicted that ANWR could lower the price of oil by about 50¢ a barrel. Given that the price of a barrel of oil was around $50 (and sometimes much higher) in 2005, that is about a 1% change in the price. Severin Borenstein, an economist who is the director of the U.C. Energy Institute, concluded that ANWR might reduce oil prices by up to a few percentage points so that "drilling in ANWR will never noticeably affect gasoline prices." In the following solved problem, we can make our own calculations of the price effect of drilling in ANWR.

---

[8]I am grateful to Robert Whaples, who wrote an earlier version of this analysis. In the following discussion, we assume for simplicity that the oil market is competitive, and use current values of price and quantities even though drilling in ANWR could not take place for at least a decade.

SOLVED PROBLEM **3.1**

What would be the effect of ANWR production on the world price of oil given that $\varepsilon = -0.4$, $\eta = 0.3$, the pre-ANWR daily world production of oil is $Q_1 = 82$ million barrels per day, the pre-ANWR world price is $p_1 = \$50$ per barrel, and daily ANWR production would be 0.8 million barrels per day? For simplicity, assume that the supply and demand curves are linear and that the introduction of ANWR oil would cause a parallel shift in the world supply curve to the right by 0.8 million barrels per day.

Answer

1. *Determine the long-run linear demand function that is consistent with pre-ANWR world output and price:* At the original equilibrium, e_1, in the figure, $p_1 = \$50$ and $Q_1 = 82$. There the elasticity of demand is $\varepsilon = (\Delta Q/\Delta p)(p_1/Q_1) = (\Delta Q/\Delta p)(50/82) = -0.4$. Using algebra, we find that $\Delta Q/\Delta p$ equals $-0.4(82/50) = -0.656$, which is the inverse of the slope of the demand curve, D, in the figure. Knowing this slope and that demand equals 82 at \$50 per barrel, we can solve for the intercept, because the quantity demanded rises by 0.656 for each dollar by which the price falls. The demand when price is zero is $82 + (0.656 \times 50) = 114.8$. Thus the equation for the demand curve is $Q = 114.8 - 0.656p$.

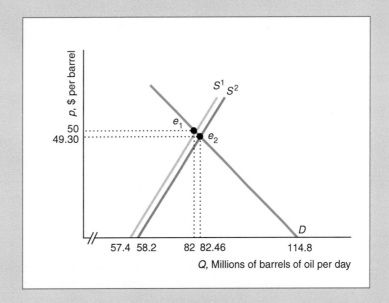

2. *Determine the long-run linear supply function that is consistent with pre-ANWR world output and price:* Where S^1 intercepts D at the original equilibrium, e_1, the elasticity of supply is $\eta = (\Delta Q/\Delta p)(p_1/Q_1) = (\Delta Q/\Delta p)(50/82) = 0.3$. Solving, we find that $\Delta Q/\Delta p = 0.3(82/50) = 0.492$. Because the quantity supplied falls by 0.492 for each dollar by which the price drops, the quantity supplied when price is zero is $82 - (0.492 \times 50) = 57.4$. Thus the equation for the pre-ANWR supply curve, S^1 in the figure, is $Q = 57.4 + 0.492p$.

3. *Determine the post-ANWR long-run linear supply function:* The oil pumped from ANWR would cause a parallel shift in the supply curve, moving S^1 to the right by 0.8 to S^2. That is, the slope remains the same, but the intercept on the quantity axis increases by 0.8. Thus the supply function for S^2 is $Q = 58.2 + 0.492p$.

4. *Use the demand curve and the post-ANWR supply function to calculate the new equilibrium price and quantity:* The new equilibrium, e_2, occurs where S^2 intersects D. Setting the right-hand sides of the demand function and the post-ANWR supply function equal, we obtain an expression in the new price, p_2:

$$58.2 + 0.492p_2 = 114.8 - 0.656p_2.$$

We can solve this expression for the new equilibrium price: $p_2 \approx \$49.30$. That is, the price drops about 70¢, about 1.4%. If we substitute this new price into either the demand curve or the post-ANWR supply curve, we find that the new equilibrium quantity is 82.46 million barrels per day. That is, equilibrium output rises by 0.46 million barrels per day (0.56%), which is only a little more than half of the predicted daily ANWR supply, because other suppliers will decrease their output slightly in response to the lower price.

Comment: Our estimate of a small drop in the world oil price if ANWR oil is sold would not change substantially if our estimates of the elasticities of supply and demand were moderately larger or smaller. The main reason for this result is that the ANWR output would be a very small portion of worldwide supply—the new supply curve is only slightly to the right of the initial supply curve. Thus drilling in ANWR cannot insulate the American market from international events that roil the oil market. A new war in the Persian Gulf could shift the worldwide supply curve to the left by 3 million barrels a day or more (nearly four times the ANWR production). Such a shock would cause the price of oil to soar whether or not we drill in ANWR.

See Problem 30.

3.5   Effects of a Sales Tax

Before voting for a new sales tax, legislators want to predict the effect of the tax on prices, quantities, and tax revenues. If the new tax will produce a large increase in the price, legislators who vote for the tax may lose their jobs in the next election. Voters' ire is likely to be even greater if the tax does not raise significant tax revenues.

In this section, we examine three questions about the effects of a sales tax:

1. What effect does a sales tax have on equilibrium prices and quantity?
2. Is it true, as many people claim, that taxes assessed on producers are *passed along* to consumers? That is, do consumers pay for the entire tax?
3. Do the equilibrium price and quantity depend on whether the tax is assessed on consumers or on producers?

How much a tax affects the equilibrium price and quantity and how much of the tax falls on consumers depend on the shape of the demand and supply curves, which is summarized by the elasticities. Knowing only the elasticities of demand and supply, we can make accurate predictions about the effects of a new tax and determine how much of the tax falls on consumers.

TWO TYPES OF SALES TAXES

Governments use two types of sales taxes. The most common sales tax is called an *ad valorem* tax by economists and *the* sales tax by real people. For every dollar the consumer spends, the government keeps a fraction, α, which is the *ad valorem* tax rate. Since 1997, Japan's national sales tax has been $\alpha = 5\%$. If a Japanese consumer buys a CD player for \$100, the government collects $\alpha \times \$100 = 5\% \times \$100 = \$5$ in taxes, and the seller receives $(1 - \alpha) \times \$100 = \$95$.[9]

The other type of sales tax is a *specific* or *unit* tax, where a specified dollar amount, τ, is collected per unit of output. The federal government collects $\tau = 18.4¢$ on each gallon of gas sold in the United States. Many communities charge a fixed filing fee or tax on every house sold.

EQUILIBRIUM EFFECTS OF A SPECIFIC TAX

To answer our three questions, we must extend the standard supply-and-demand analysis to take taxes into account. Let's start by assuming that the specific tax is assessed on firms at the time of sale. If the consumer pays p for a good, the government takes τ and the seller receives $p - \tau$.

Specific Tax Effects in the Pork Market. Suppose that the government collects a specific tax of $\tau = \$1.05$ per kg of processed pork from pork producers. Because of the tax, suppliers keep only $p - \tau$ of price p that consumers pay. Thus at every possible price paid by consumers, firms are willing to supply less than when they received the full amount consumers paid. Before the tax, firms were willing to supply 206 million kg per year at a price of \$2.95 as the pretax supply curve S^1 in Figure 3.5 shows. After the tax, firms receive only \$1.90 if consumers pay \$2.95, so they are not willing to supply 206. For firms to be willing to supply 206, they must receive \$2.95 after the tax, so consumers must pay \$4. As a result, the after-tax supply curve, S^2, is $\tau = \$1.05$ above the original supply curve S^1 at every quantity, as the figure shows.

We can use this figure to illustrate the answer to our first question concerning the effects of the tax on the equilibrium. *The specific tax causes the equilibrium price consumers pay to rise, the equilibrium quantity to fall, and tax revenue to rise.*

The intersection of the pretax pork supply curve S^1 and the pork demand curve D in Figure 3.5 determines the pretax equilibrium, e_1. The equilibrium price is $p_1 = \$3.30$, and the equilibrium quantity is $Q_1 = 220$. The tax shifts the supply curve to S^2, so the after-tax equilibrium is e_2, where consumers pay $p_2 = \$4$, firms receive $p_2 - \$1.05 = \$2.95$, and $Q_2 = 206$. Thus the tax causes the price that consumers pay to increase ($\Delta p = p_2 - p_1 = \$4 - \$3.30 = 70¢$) and the quantity to fall ($\Delta Q = Q_2 - Q_1 = 206 - 220 = -14$).

See Problem 31.

Although the consumers and producers are worse off because of the tax, the government acquires new tax revenue of $T = \tau Q = \$1.05$ per kg $\times$ 206 million kg per year = \$216.3 million per year. The length of the shaded rectangle in the figure is $Q_2 = 206$ million kg per year, and its height is $\tau = \$1.05$ per kg, so the area of the rectangle equals the tax revenue. (The figure shows only part of the length of the rectangle because the horizontal axis starts at 176.)

How Specific Tax Effects Depend on Elasticities. The effects of the tax on the equilibrium prices and quantity depend on the elasticities of supply and demand. The

[9]For specificity, we assume that the price firms receive is $p = (1 - \alpha)p^*$, where p^* is the price consumers pay and α is the ad valorem tax rate on the price consumers pay. Many governments, however, set the ad valorem sales tax, β, as an amount added to the price sellers charge, so consumers pay $p^* = (1 + \beta)p$. By setting α and β appropriately, the taxes are equivalent. Here $p = p^*/(1 + \beta)$, so $(1 - \alpha) = 1/(1 + \beta)$. For example, if $\beta = \frac{1}{3}$, then $\alpha = \frac{1}{4}$.

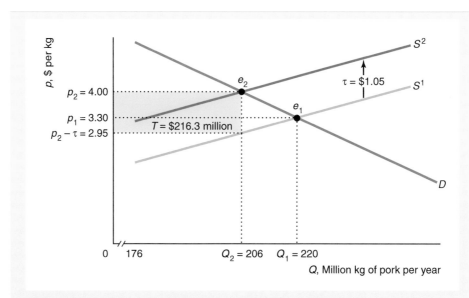

Figure 3.5 **Effect of a $1.05 Specific Tax on the Pork Market Collected from Producers.** The specific tax of $\tau = \$1.05$ per kg collected from producers shifts the pretax pork supply curve from S^1 to the posttax supply curve, S^2. The tax causes the equilibrium to shift from e_1 (determined by the intersection of S^1 and D) to e_2 (intersection of S^2 with D). The equilibrium price increases from $3.30 to $4.00. Two-thirds of the incidence of the tax falls on consumers, who spend 70¢ more per unit. Producers receive 35¢ less per unit after the tax. The government collects tax revenues of $T = \tau Q_2 = \$216.3$ million per year.

government raises the tax from zero to τ, so the change in the tax is $\Delta \tau = \tau - 0 = \tau$. In response to this change in the tax, the price consumers pay increases by

$$\Delta p = \left(\frac{\eta}{\eta - \varepsilon} \right) \Delta \tau, \qquad (3.6)$$

where ε is the demand elasticity and η is the supply elasticity at the equilibrium (this equation is derived in Appendix 3A). The demand elasticity for pork is $\varepsilon = -0.3$, and the supply elasticity is $\eta = 0.6$, so a change in the tax of $\Delta \tau = \$1.05$ causes the price consumers pay to rise by

$$\Delta p = \left(\frac{\eta}{\eta - \varepsilon} \right) \Delta \tau = \frac{0.6}{0.6 - [-0.3]} \times \$1.05 = 70¢,$$

as Figure 3.5 shows.

For a given supply elasticity, the more elastic demand is, the less the equilibrium price rises when a tax is imposed. In the pork equilibrium in which the supply elasticity is $\eta = 0.6$, if the demand elasticity were $\varepsilon = -2.4$ instead of -0.3 (that is, the linear demand curve had a less steep slope through the original equilibrium point), the consumer price would rise only $0.6/(0.6 - [-2.4]) \times \$1.05 = 21¢$ instead of 70¢.

Similarly, for a given demand elasticity, the greater the supply elasticity, the larger the increase in the equilibrium price consumers pay when a tax is imposed. In the pork example, in which the demand elasticity is $\varepsilon = -0.3$, if the supply elasticity were $\eta = 1.2$ instead of 0.6, the consumer price would rise $1.2/(1.2 - [-0.3]) \times \$1.05 = 84¢$ instead of 70¢.

TAX INCIDENCE OF A SPECIFIC TAX

incidence of a tax
on consumers
the share of the tax that
falls on consumers

We can now answer our second question: Who is hurt by the tax? The **incidence of a tax on consumers** is the share of the tax that falls on consumers. The incidence of the tax that falls on consumers is $\Delta p / \Delta \tau$, the amount by which the price to consumers rises as a fraction of the amount the tax increases.

In our pork example in Figure 3.5, a $\Delta \tau = \$1.05$ increase in the specific tax causes consumers to pay $\Delta p = 70$¢ more per kg than they would if no tax were assessed. Thus consumers bear two-thirds of the incidence of the pork tax:

$$\frac{\Delta p}{\Delta \tau} = \frac{\$0.70}{\$1.05} = \frac{2}{3}.$$

Firms receive $(p_2 - \tau) - p_1 = (\$4 - \$1.05) - \$3.30 = \$2.95 - \$3.30 = -35$¢ less per kg than they would in the absence of the tax. The incidence of the tax on firms—the amount by which the price to them falls, divided by the tax—is $\$0.35/\$1.05 = \frac{1}{3}$. The sum of the share of the tax on consumers, $\frac{2}{3}$, and that on firms, $\frac{1}{3}$, adds to the entire tax effect, 1. Equivalently, the increase in price to consumers minus the drop in price to firms equals the tax: 70¢ $- (-35$¢$) = \$1.05 = \tau$.

How Tax Incidence Depends on Elasticities. If the demand curve slopes downward and the supply curve slopes upward, as in Figure 3.5, the incidence of the tax *does not* fall solely on consumers. Firms do not pass along the entire tax in higher prices.

Firms can pass along the full cost of the tax only when the demand or supply elasticities take on certain extreme values. To determine the conditions under which firms can pass along the full tax, we need to know how the incidence of the tax depends on the elasticities of demand and supply at the pretax equilibrium. By dividing both sides of Equation 3.6 by $\Delta \tau$, we can write the incidence of the tax that falls on consumers as

$$\frac{\Delta p}{\Delta \tau} = \frac{\eta}{\eta - \varepsilon}. \tag{3.7}$$

Because the demand elasticity for pork is $\varepsilon = -0.3$ and the supply elasticity is $\eta = 0.6$, the incidence of the pork tax that falls on consumers is

$$\frac{0.6}{0.6 - (-0.3)} = \frac{2}{3}.$$

See Problem 34.

The more elastic the demand at the equilibrium, holding the supply elasticity constant, the lower the burden of the tax on consumers. Similarly, the greater the supply elasticity, holding the demand elasticity constant, the greater the burden on consumers. Thus as the demand curve becomes relatively inelastic (ε approaches zero) or the supply curve becomes relatively elastic (η becomes very large), the incidence of the tax falls mainly on consumers.

SOLVED PROBLEM 3.2

If the supply curve is perfectly elastic and demand is linear and downward sloping, what is the effect of a $1 specific tax collected from producers on equilibrium price and quantity, and what is the incidence on consumers? Why?

Answer

1. *Determine the equilibrium in the absence of a tax:* Before the tax, the perfectly elastic supply curve, S^1 in the graph, is horizontal at p_1. The downward-sloping

linear demand curve, D, intersects S^1 at the pretax equilibrium, e_1, where the price is p_1 and the quantity is Q_1.

2. *Show how the tax shifts the supply curve and determine the new equilibrium:* A specific tax of $1 shifts the pretax supply curve upward by $1 to S^2, which is horizontal at $p_1 + 1$. The intersection of D and S^2 determines the after-tax equilibrium, e_2, where the price consumers pay is $p_2 = p_1 + 1$, the price firms receive is $p_2 - 1 = p_1$, and the quantity is Q_2.

3. *Compare the before- and after-tax equilibria:* The specific tax causes the equilibrium quantity to fall from Q_1 to Q_2, the price firms receive to remain at p_1, and the equilibrium price consumers pay to rise from p_1 to $p_2 = p_1 + 1$. The entire incidence of the tax falls on consumers:

$$\frac{\Delta p}{\Delta \tau} = \frac{p_2 - p_1}{\$1} = \frac{\$1}{\$1} = 1.$$

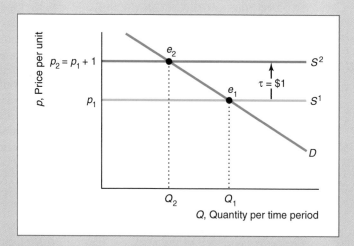

4. *Explain why:* The reason consumers must absorb the entire tax is that firms will not supply the good at a price that is any lower than they received before the tax, p_1. Thus the price must rise enough that the price suppliers receive after tax is unchanged. As consumers do not want to consume as much at a higher price, the equilibrium quantity falls.

Elasticity, Revenue, and Tax Strategy. Governments often use a sales tax to raise tax revenue. However, such a tax harms consumers and producers by reducing the equilibrium quantity.

Some economists and politicians argue that, all else the same, we should tax goods with relatively inelastic demands more heavily. They argue that the less elastic demand is, the less harm a sales tax does in terms of reduced consumption and the more revenue it raises. If the demand curve is vertical at Q_1, the quantity demanded is unchanged by a tax τ, and the revenue is τQ_1. With a downward-sloping demand curve (as in Figure 3.5), the tax reduces the quantity demanded from the original quantity Q_1 to Q_2, and the tax is only τQ_2, which is less than τQ_1.

See Problem 38.

Presumably, most voters would agree with the goal of reducing the harm of taxes. Whether they favor increasing tax revenues is less clear. Moreover, the less elastic the demand, the larger the incidence of the tax that consumers bear.

● **APPLICATION**

Taxing to Discourage Smoking and Raise Revenue

I phoned my dad to tell him I had stopped smoking.
He called me a quitter. —Steven Pearl

Governments tax cigarettes to discourage socially harmful behavior and to raise tax revenue. The reason to reduce smoking is that it is costly to society in many ways. In 2002, the U.S. Center for Disease Control (CDC) reported the annual economic cost of smoking for U.S. adults at $158 billion (including $82 billion in lost productivity and $75 billion in medical expenses). Neonatal medical care adds another $366 million in costs. The CDC estimated that 442,000 people die annually due to smoking. As a result, 5.6 million potential years of life are lost (13.2 years of life per adult male smoker and 14.5 years per adult female).

Despite the risk, 29.8% of the U.S. population 12 years and older smokes, or 70.8 million people in 2003. If the government really wants to stop people—especially teenagers and pregnant women—from smoking, how should it do so? It could spend millions on education programs and public service ads. Alternatively, the government can tax cigarettes, a measure that reduces smoking and raises revenues rather than costing money.

See Problem 33.

A tax discourages more cigarette smoking but raises less tax revenue, the more elastic is the demand curve. Several economic studies estimate that the elasticity of demand is between –0.3 and –0.6 for the U.S. population and between –0.6 and –0.7 for children. Estimated elasticities are larger for developing countries, but demand is still generally inelastic—because nicotine is an addictive drug.

When the price of cigarettes in Canada increased 158% from 1979 to 1991 (after adjusting for inflation and including taxes), teenage smoking dropped by 61% and overall smoking by 38%. The U.S. Tobacco Settlement between the major tobacco companies and 46 states caused the price of cigarettes to jump by 45¢ (21%) in November 1998. Keeler et al. (2004) estimate that this price increase reduced overall per capita cigarette consumption by 8.3%.[10]

The United States has the lowest cigarette tax burden of all industrialized countries. As of 2005, the federal tax, 39¢, plus the average state tax totaled 84.5¢ per pack. The average state tax per pack is 19.8¢ in tobacco-growing states and 93.1¢ in nontobacco states. The state tax ranges from 5¢ in North Carolina to $1.50 in New York state (plus a city tax of $1.50 in New York City), $1.60 in Alaska, $2.40 in New Jersey, and $2.46 in Rhode Island.

As of 2005, cigarette taxes were much higher in many other countries. For example, the tax per pack was $1.76 in Hong Kong, $2.76 in New Zealand,

---

[10]Cigarette manufacturers are competitive firms. Unfortunately, the cigarette companies responded to the settlement's price increase with an increase in advertising, which drove up cigarette consumption by 2.7% to 4.7%, thus reducing the pure price effect by 33% to 57%.

$2.92 in Australia, $3.13 in Sweden, $4.02 in Denmark, $4.16 in Ireland, $4.30 in the United Kingdom, and $5.23 in Norway.

As long as the demand curve is not completely inelastic, raising the tax discourages additional smokers. By raising the federal cigarette tax to international levels, we would substantially reduce smoking. In 2003, the U.S. Congress considered a proposal to raise the federal cigarette tax from 39¢ to $2.39 per pack. In 2005, Dr. Richard Horton, editor of the medical journal *Lancet,* urged governments around the globe to reduce smoking by raising cigarette taxes by 50% every year.

Even at current tax rates, cigarette tax revenue is substantial. The U.S. government collected cigarette tax revenues of $7.9 billion (2004 fiscal year), and state governments raised $12.6 billion (2004 calendar year). Given an inelastic demand, raising the tax causes government revenue to increase. Indeed, if one person had a completely inelastic demand for cigarettes, the government could raise any amount of revenue it wanted by pushing the tax high enough.

THE SAME EQUILIBRIUM NO MATTER WHO IS TAXED

Our third question is, "Does the equilibrium or the incidence of the tax depend on whether the tax is collected from suppliers or demanders?" Surprisingly, in the supply-and-demand model, the equilibrium and the incidence of the tax are the same regardless of whether the government collects the tax from consumers or producers.

We've already seen that firms are able to pass on some or all of the tax collected from them to consumers. We now show that, if the tax is collected from consumers, they can pass the producer's share back to the firms.

Suppose the specific tax τ = $1.05 on pork is collected from consumers rather than from sellers. Because the government takes τ from each p consumers spend, sellers receive only $p - \tau$. Thus the demand curve as seen by firms shifts downward by $1.05 from D^1 to D^2 in Figure 3.6.

The intersection of D^2 and the supply curve S determines the after-tax equilibrium, e_2, where the equilibrium quantity is Q_2 and the price received by producers is $p_2 - \tau$. The price paid by consumers, p_2 (on the original demand curve D^1 at Q_2), is τ above the price received by producers.

Comparing Figure 3.6 to Figure 3.5, we see that the after-tax equilibrium is the same regardless of whether the tax is imposed on the consumers or the sellers. The price to consumers rises by the same amount, Δp, so the incidence of the tax, $\Delta p / \Delta \tau$, is also the same.

A specific tax, regardless of whether the tax is collected from consumers or producers, creates a *wedge* equal to the per-unit tax of τ between the price consumers pay, p, and the price suppliers receive, $p - \tau$. Indeed, we can insert a wedge—the vertical line labeled τ = $1.05 in the figure—between the original supply and demand curves to determine the after-tax equilibrium.

In short, regardless of whether firms or consumers pay the tax to the government, you can solve tax problems by shifting the supply curve, shifting the demand curve, or using a wedge. All three approaches give the same answer.

THE SIMILAR EFFECTS OF *AD VALOREM* AND SPECIFIC TAXES

In contrast to specific sales taxes, governments levy *ad valorem* taxes on a wide variety of goods. Most states apply an *ad valorem* sales tax to most goods and services,

See Problem 32.

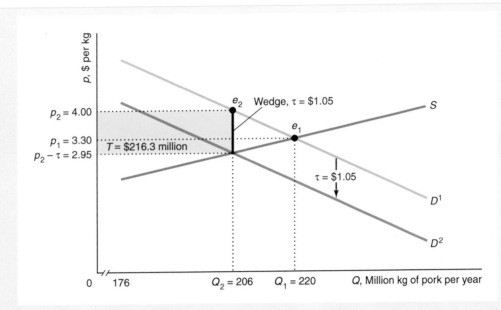

Figure 3.6 **Effect of a $1.05 Specific Tax on Pork Collected from Consumers.** The tax shifts the demand curve down by $\tau = \$1.05$ from D^1 to D^2. The new equilibrium is the same as when the tax is applied to suppliers in Figure 3.5. We can also determine the after-tax equilibrium by sticking a wedge with length $\tau = \$1.05$ between S and D^1.

exempting only a few staples such as food and medicine. There are 6,400 different *ad valorem* sales tax rates across the United States, which can go as high as 8.5% (Besley and Rosen, 1999).

Suppose that the government imposes an *ad valorem* tax of α, instead of a specific tax, on the price that consumers pay for processed pork. We already know that the equilibrium price is $4 with a specific tax of $1.05 per kg. At that price, an *ad valorem* tax of $\alpha = \$1.05/\$4 = 26.25\%$ raises the same amount of tax per unit as a $1.05 specific tax.

It is usually easiest to analyze the effects of an *ad valorem* tax by shifting the demand curve. Figure 3.7 shows how a specific tax and an *ad valorem* tax shift the processed pork demand curve. The specific tax shifts the pretax demand curve, D, down to D^s, which is parallel to the original curve. The *ad valorem* tax shifts the demand curve to D^a. At any given price p, the gap between D and D^a is αp, which is greater at high prices than at low prices. The gap is $1.05 (= 0.2625 \times \$4)$ per unit when the price is $4, and $2.10 when the price is $8.

Imposing an *ad valorem* tax causes the after-tax equilibrium quantity, Q_2, to fall below the original quantity, Q_1, and the after-tax price, p_2, to rise above the original price, p_1. The tax collected per unit of output is $\tau = \alpha p_2$. The incidence of the tax that falls on consumers is the change in price, $\Delta p = (p_2 - p_1)$, divided by the change in the per unit tax, $\Delta \tau = \alpha p_2 - 0$, collected, $\Delta p/(\alpha p_2)$. The incidence of an *ad valorem* tax is generally shared between consumers and suppliers. Because the *ad valorem* tax of $\alpha = 26.25\%$ has exactly the same impact on the equilibrium pork price and raises the same amount of tax per unit as the $1.05 specific tax, the incidence is the same for both types of taxes. (As with specific taxes, the incidence of the *ad valorem* tax depends on the elasticities of supply and demand, but we'll spare you going through that in detail.)

See Questions 17 and 18.

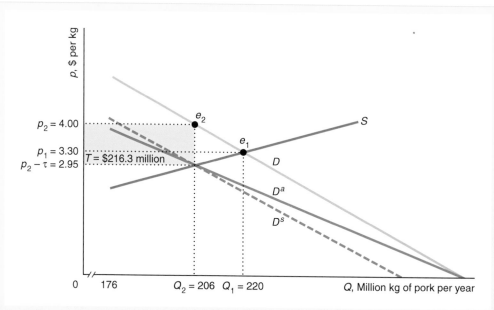

Figure 3.7 **Comparison of an *Ad Valorem* and a Specific Tax on Pork.** Without a tax, the demand curve is *D* and the supply curve is *S*. The *ad valorem* tax of $\alpha = 26.25\%$ shifts the demand curve facing firms to D^a. The gap between *D* and D^a, the per-unit tax, is larger at higher prices. In contrast, the demand curve facing firms given a specific tax of $1.05 per kg, D^s, is parallel to *D*. The after-tax equilibrium is the same with both of these taxes.

SOLVED PROBLEM   3.3

If the short-run supply curve for fresh fruit is perfectly inelastic and the demand curve is a downward-sloping straight line, what is the effect of an ad valorem tax on equilibrium price and quantity, and what is the incidence on consumers? Why?

Answer

1. *Determine the before-tax equilibrium:* The perfectly inelastic supply curve, *S*, is vertical at Q^* in the graph. The pretax demand curve, D^1, intersects *S* at e_1, where the equilibrium price to both consumers and producers is p^* and the equilibrium quantity is Q^*.

2. *Show how the tax shifts the demand curve, and determine the after-tax equilibrium:* When the government imposes an ad valorem tax with a rate of α, the demand curve as seen by the firms rotates down to D^2, where the gap between the two demand curves is αp. The intersection of *S* and D^2 determines the after-tax equilibrium, e_2. The equilibrium quantity remains unchanged at Q^*. Consumers continue to pay p^*. The government collects αp^* per unit, so firms receive less, $(1 - \alpha)p^*$, than the p^* they received before the tax.

3. *Determine the incidence of the tax on consumers:* The consumers continue to pay the same price, so $\Delta p = 0$ when the tax increases by αp^* (from 0), and the incidence of the tax that falls on consumers is $0/(\alpha p^*) = 0\%$.

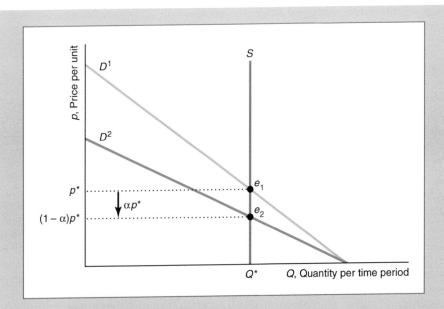

4. *Explain why the incidence of the tax falls entirely on firms:* The reason why firms absorb the entire tax is that firms supply the same amount of fruit, Q^*, no matter what tax the government sets. If firms were to raise the price, consumers would buy less fruit and suppliers would be stuck with the essentially worthless excess quantity, which would spoil quickly. Thus because suppliers prefer to sell their produce at a positive price rather than a zero price, they absorb any tax-induced drop in price.

Summary

1. **How shapes of the demand and supply curves matter:** The degree to which a shock (such as an increase in the price of a factor) shifts the supply curve and affects the equilibrium price and quantity depends on the shape of the demand curve. Similarly, the degree to which a shock (such as an increase in the price of a substitute) shifts the demand curve and affects the equilibrium depends on the shape of the supply curve.

2. **Sensitivity of quantity demanded to price:** The price elasticity of demand (or elasticity of demand), ε, summarizes the shape of a demand curve at a particular point. The elasticity of demand is the percentage change in the quantity demanded in response to a given percentage change in price. For example, a 1% increase in price causes the quantity demanded to fall by $\varepsilon\%$. Because demand curves slope downward according to the Law of Demand, the elasticity of demand is always negative.

The demand curve is perfectly inelastic if $\varepsilon = 0$, inelastic if $0 > \varepsilon > -1$, unitary elastic if $\varepsilon = -1$, elastic if $\varepsilon < -1$, and perfectly elastic when ε approaches negative infinity. A vertical demand curve is perfectly inelastic at every price. A horizontal demand curve is perfectly elastic.

The income elasticity of demand is the percentage change in the quantity demanded in response to a given percentage change in income. The cross-price elasticity of demand is the percentage change in the quantity demanded of one good when the price of a related good increases by a given percentage.

3. **Sensitivity of quantity supplied to price:** The price elasticity of supply (or elasticity of supply), η, is the percentage change in the quantity supplied in response to a given percentage change in price. The elasticity of supply is positive if the supply curve has an upward slope. A vertical supply curve is perfectly inelastic. A horizontal supply curve is perfectly elastic.

4. **Long run versus short run:** Long-run elasticities of demand and supply may differ from the corresponding short-run elasticities. Where consumers can substitute between goods more readily in the long run, long-run demand curves are more elastic than short-run demand curves. However, if goods can be stored easily, short-run demand curves are more elastic than long-run curves. If producers can increase output at lower extra cost in the long run than in the short run, the long-run elasticity of supply is greater than the short-run elasticity.

5. **Effects of a sales tax:** The two common types of sales taxes are *ad valorem* taxes, by which the government collects a fixed percent of the price paid per unit, and specific taxes, by which the government collects a fixed amount of money per unit sold. Both types of sales taxes typically raise the equilibrium price and lower the equilibrium quantity. Both usually raise the price consumers pay and lower the price suppliers receive, so consumers do not bear the full burden or incidence of the tax. The effects on quantity, price, and the incidence of the tax that falls on consumers depend on the demand and supply elasticities. In competitive markets, for which supply-and-demand analysis is appropriate, the effect of a tax on equilibrium quantities, prices, and the incidence of the tax is unaffected by whether the tax is collected from consumers or producers.

Questions

* = answer at the back of this book; **A** *= an application or other real-world material in the text;* **C** *= use of calculus may be necessary.*

1. According to Agcaoli-Sombilla (1991), the elasticity of demand for rice is –0.47 in Austria; –0.8 in Bangladesh, China, India, Indonesia, and Thailand; –0.25 in Japan; –0.55 in the European Union and the United States; and –0.15 in Vietnam. In which countries is the demand for rice inelastic? In which country is it the least elastic?   **A**

*2. According to Duffy-Deno (2003), when the price of broadband access capacity (the amount of information one can send over an Internet connection) increases 10%, commercial customers buy about 3.8% less capacity. What is the elasticity of demand for broadband access capacity for firms? Is demand at the current price inelastic? How does the elasticity of demand of firms compare to those of households reported in the application "Willingness to Surf"?   **A**

3. The United States Tobacco Settlement between the major tobacco companies and 46 states caused the price of cigarettes to jump 45¢ (21%) in November 1998. Levy and Meara (2005) find only a 2.65% drop in prenatal smoking 15 months later. What is the elasticity of demand for this group? Is demand for this group more or less elastic than that of other groups discussed in the application, "Taxing to Discourage Smoking and Raise Revenue"?   **A**

4. What section of a straight-line demand curve is elastic?   **A**

5. The application "Substitution May Save Endangered Species" describes how the equilibrium changed in the market for seal genitalia (used as an aphrodisiac in Asia) when Viagra was introduced. Use a supply and demand diagram to illustrate what happened. Show whether the following is possible: A positive quantity is demanded at various prices, yet nothing is sold in the market.   **A**

6. The 9/11 terrorist attacks caused the U.S. airline travel demand curve to shift left by an estimated 30% (Ito and Lee, 2005). Use a supply-and-demand diagram to show the likely effect on price and quantity (assuming that the market is competitive). Indicate the magnitude of the likely equilibrium price and quantity effects—for example, would you expect that equilibrium quantity changes by about 30%? Show how the answer depends on the shape and location of the supply and demand curves.

7. Suppose that the demand curve for wheat in each country is inelastic up to some "choke" price p^*—a price so high that nothing is bought—so that the demand curve is vertical at Q^* at prices below p^* and horizontal at p^*. If p^* and Q^* vary across countries, what does the world's demand curve look like? Discuss how the elasticity of demand varies with price along the world's demand curve.

8. According to Borjas (2003), immigration into the United States increased the labor supply of working men by 11.0% from 1980 to 2000 and reduced the wage of the average native worker by 3.2 percent. From these results, can we make any inferences about the elasticity of supply or demand? Which curve (or curves) changed, and why? Draw a supply-and-demand diagram and label the axes to illustrate what happened.

9. The U.S. Bureau of Labor Statistics reports that the average salary for postsecondary economics teachers in the Raleigh-Durham-Chapel Hill metropolitan area, which has many top universities, rose to $105,200

(based on a 52-week work year) in 2003. According to the *Wall Street Journal* (Timothy Aeppel, "Economists Gain Star Power," February 22, 2005, A2), the salary increase resulted from an outward shift in the demand curve for academic economists due to the increased popularity of the economics major, while the supply curve of Ph.D. economists did not shift.

    a. If this explanation is correct, what is the short-run price elasticity of supply of academic economists?

    b. If these salaries are expected to remain high, will more people enter doctoral programs in economics? How would such entry affect the long-run price elasticity of supply? **W**

10. According to industry experts, low-priced conventional TVs are generic commodities, and the market is not affected by any single manufacturer (Saul Hansell and Eric A. Taub, "No End in Sight to Supply of Cheap TVs," *New York Times*, January 4, 2005, C1, C4). Typically, 20" sets sell for from $89 to $100. The low end of the television market will be shaken as the U.S. government phases in a requirement by 2007 that all new sets over 13" have a tuner that can receive digital broadcasts. Some predict that this digital tuner, mainly meant for high-definition televisions, will add several hundred dollars in cost, at least at first, to sets so small that they cannot display high-definition signals effectively.

    a. Why? (*Hint:* Answer in terms of cross-elasticities of demand with higher-quality sets.)

    b. Use supply and demand curves to show the likely effect of this new requirement on small televisions. Explain how your prediction depends on the shapes of the supply and demand curves. Speculate about those shapes.

11. Give some examples of evidence that would convince you that the demand curve for a given product was inelastic. Similarly, what evidence would convince you that a supply curve was elastic? (*Hint:* Consider shocks caused by changes in factors that affect demand or by taxes.)

12. In 1997, the shares of consumers who had cable television service were 59% for people with incomes of $25,000 or less; 66%, $25,000–$34,999; 67%, $35,000–$49,999; 71%, $50,000–$74,999; and 78%, $75,000 or more. What can you say about the income elasticity for cable television?

13. What is the effect of a $1 specific tax on equilibrium price and quantity if demand is perfectly inelastic? What is the incidence on consumers? Explain.

14. What is the effect of a $1 specific tax on equilibrium price and quantity if demand is perfectly elastic? What is the incidence on consumers? Explain.

15. What is the effect of a $1 specific tax on equilibrium price and quantity if supply is perfectly inelastic? What is the incidence on consumers? Explain.

16. What is the effect of a $1 specific tax on equilibrium price and quantity if demand is perfectly elastic and supply is perfectly inelastic? What is the incidence on consumers? Explain.

17. On July 1, 1965, the federal *ad valorem* taxes on many goods and services were eliminated. Comparing prices before and after this change, we can determine how much the price fell in response to the tax's elimination. When the tax was in place, the tax per unit on a good that sold for p was αp. If the price fell by αp when the tax was eliminated, consumers must have been bearing the full incidence of the tax. Consequently, consumers got the full benefit of removing the tax from those goods. The entire amount of the tax cut was passed on to consumers for all commodities and services they studied for which the taxes were collected at the retail level (except admissions and club dues) and most commodities for which excise taxes were imposed at the manufacturer level, including face powder, sterling silverware, wristwatches, and handbags (Brownlee and Perry, 1967). List the conditions (in terms of the elasticities or shapes of supply or demand curves) that are consistent with 100% pass-through of the taxes. Use graphs to illustrate your answer. **A**

18. Essentially none of the savings from removing the federal *ad valorem* tax were passed on to consumers for motion picture admissions and club dues (Brownlee and Perry, 1967; see Question 16). List the conditions (in terms of the elasticities or shapes of supply or demand curves) that are consistent with 0% pass-through of the taxes. Use graphs to illustrate your answer. **A**

*19. Do you care whether a 15¢ tax per gallon of milk is collected from milk producers or from consumers at the store? Why?

20. California supplies the United States with 80% of its eating oranges. In late 1998, four days of freezing temperatures in the state's Central Valley substantially damaged the orange crop. In early 1999, Food Lion, with 1,208 grocery stores mostly in the Southeast, said its prices for fresh oranges would rise by 20% to 30%, which was less than the 100% increase it had to pay for the oranges. Explain why the price to consumers did not rise by the full amount of Food Lion's price increase. What can you conclude about the elasticities of demand and supply for oranges? (*Hint:* Remember what determines the incidence of a tax.)

21. Consider the market for labor services. The state collects a tax of α (where $0 < \alpha < 1$) cents of every

dollar a worker earns. If the state raises its minimum wage, what happens to the amount of tax revenues it collects? Must tax revenue necessarily rise or fall?

22. Traditionally, the perfectly round, white saltwater pearls from oysters have been prized above small, irregularly shaped, and strangely colored freshwater pearls from mussels. By 2002, scientists in China (where 99% of freshwater pearls originate) had perfected a means of creating bigger, rounder, and whiter freshwater pearls. These superior mussel pearls now sell well at Tiffany's and other prestigious jewelry stores (though at slightly lower prices than saltwater pearls). What is the likely effect of this innovation on the cross-elasticity of demand for salt-water pearls given a change in the price of freshwater pearls?   **A**

Problems

23. When the U.S. government announced that a domestic mad cow was found in December 2003, analysts estimated that domestic supplies would increase in the short run by 10.4% as many other countries barred U.S. beef. An estimate of the price elasticity of beef demand is –1.6 (Henderson, 2003). Assuming that only the domestic supply curve shifted, how much would you expect the price to change? Compare your analysis and result with those in Solved Problem 2.4.   **A**

24. In a commentary piece on the rising cost of health insurance ("Healthy, Wealthy, and Wise, *Wall Street Journal,* May 4, 2004, A20), economists John Cogan, Glenn Hubbard, and Daniel Kessler state, "Each percentage-point rise in health-insurance costs increases the number of uninsured by 300,000 people." Assuming that their claim is correct, demonstrate that the price elasticity of demand for health insurance depends on the number of people who are insured. What is the price elasticity if 200 million people are insured? What is the price elasticity if 220 million people are insured?   **W**

25. In the application in Chapter 2, "Aggregating the Demand for Broadband Service" (based on Duffy-Deno, 2003), the demand function is $Q_s = 15.6p^{-0.563}$ for small firms and $Q_l = 16.0p^{-0.296}$ for larger ones. As the graph in the application shows, the two demand functions cross. What can you say about the elasticities of demand on the two demand curves at the point where they cross? What can you say about the elasticities of demand more generally (at other prices)? (*Hint:* The question about the crossing point may be a red herring.)   **A**

26. Use calculus to prove that the elasticity of demand is ε everywhere along the demand curve whose demand function is $Q = Ap^\varepsilon$.   **A, C**

*27. Calculate the price and cross-price elasticities of demand for coconut oil. The coconut oil demand function (Buschena and Perloff, 1991) is

$$Q = 1,200 - 9.5p + 16.2p_p + 0.2Y,$$

where Q is the quantity of coconut oil demanded in thousands of metric tons per year, p is the price of coconut oil in cents per pound, p_p is the price of palm oil in cents per pound, and Y is the income of consumers. Assume that p is initially 45¢ per pound, p_p is 31¢ per pound, and Q is 1,275 thousand metric tons per year.   **A**

28. Using the coconut oil demand function from Problem 27, calculate the income elasticity of demand for coconut oil. (If you do not have all the numbers necessary to calculate numerical answers, write your answers in terms of variables.)   **A**

*29. The supply curve is $Q = g + hp$. Derive a formula for the elasticity of supply in terms of p (and not Q). Now give one entirely in terms of Q.   **A**

30. Solved Problem 3.1 claims that a new war in the Persian Gulf could shift the world supply curve to the left by 3 million barrels a day or more, causing the world price of oil to soar regardless of whether we drill in ANWR. How accurate is that claim? Use the same type of analysis as in the solved problem to calculate how much such a shock would cause the price to rise with and without the ANWR production.   **A**

31. In Figure 3.5, applying a $1.05 specific tax causes the equilibrium price to rise by 70¢ and the equilibrium quantity to fall by 14 million kg of pork per year. Using the pork demand function and the original and after-tax supply functions, derive these results.   **A**

32. In Figure 3.6, applying a $1.05 specific tax causes the equilibrium price to rise by 70¢ and the equilibrium quantity to fall by 14 million kg of pork per year. Using the pork supply function and the original and after-tax demand functions, derive these results.   **A**

33. Besley and Rosen (1998) find that a 10¢ increase in the federal tax on a pack of cigarettes leads to an average 2.8¢ increase in state cigarette taxes. What implications does their result have for calculating the effects of an increase in the federal cigarette tax on the quantity demanded? Given the current federal tax (see the application "Taxing to Discourage Smoking

and Raise Revenue") and an elasticity of demand for the U.S. population of –0.3, what is the effect of a 10¢ increase in the federal tax? How would your answer change if the state tax does not change? **A**

34. Green et al. (2005) estimate that the demand elasticity is –0.47 and the long-run supply elasticity is 12.0 for almonds. The corresponding elasticities are –0.68 and 0.73 for cotton and –0.26 and 0.64 for processing tomatoes. If the government were to apply a specific tax to each of these commodities, what incidence would fall on consumers? **A**

35. Suppose that the demand function for apple cider is $Q = 100 - p$, where p is the price paid by consumers in cents per bottle and Q is the quantity demanded in hundreds of thousands of bottles per day. The supply curve for cider is estimated to be $Q = \frac{1}{4}p$. Calculate the equilibrium price for bottles of cider and the equilibrium quantity sold. Illustrate using a diagram. An environmental group suggests that the government impose a specific tax per bottled beverage of 20¢, to be paid when consumers buy cider and to be used by the government to defray the costs of cleaning up bottle litter. Determine the effects of a 20¢ tax per bottle on the equilibrium price paid by consumers and on the equilibrium quantity sold. What price do the cider-producing firms receive? Discuss how the tax may improve the environment.

36. A constant elasticity supply curve, $Q = Bp^{\eta}$, intersects a constant elasticity demand curve, $Q = Ap^{\varepsilon}$, where A, B, η, and ε are constants. What is the incidence of a \$1 specific tax? Does your answer depend on where the supply curve intersects the demand curve? Interpret your result.

*37. Use math to show that, as the supply curve at the equilibrium becomes nearly perfectly elastic, the entire incidence of the tax falls on consumers.

*38. Use calculus to show that an increase in a specific sales tax τ reduces quantity by less and tax revenue more, the less elastic the demand curve. [*Hint:* The quantity demanded depends on its price, which in turn depends on the specific tax, $Q(p(\tau))$, and tax revenue is $R = pQ(p(\tau))$.] **A, C**

39. If the inverse demand function is $p = a - bQ$ and the inverse supply function is $p = c + dQ$, show that the incidence of a specific tax of τ per unit falling on consumers is $b/(b + d) = \eta/(\eta - \varepsilon)$. **C**

40. Various governments subsidize child-care service (see the Cross-Chapter Analysis "Child-Care Subsidies"). Suppose that the subsidy is s per hour of child-care service and the market is competitive. What formula can you use to calculate the incidence of the subsidy in terms of elasticities of supply and demand? (*Hint:* A subsidy is a negative tax.)

Monopoly

Monopoly: one parrot.

A **monopoly** is the only supplier of a good for which there is no close substitute. Monopolies have been common since ancient times. In the fifth century B.C., the Greek philosopher Thales gained control of most of the olive presses during a year of exceptionally productive harvests. Similarly, the ancient Egyptian pharaohs controlled the sale of food. In England, until Parliament limited the practice in 1624, kings granted monopoly rights called royal charters or patents to court favorites. Today, virtually every country grants a *patent*—an exclusive right to sell that lasts for a limited period of time—to an inventor of a new product, process, substance, or design. Until 1999, the U.S. government gave one company the right to be the sole registrar of Internet domain names.

A monopoly can *set* its price—it is not a price taker like a competitive firm. A monopoly's output is the market output, and the demand curve a monopoly faces is the market demand curve. Because the market demand curve is downward sloping, the monopoly (unlike a competitive firm) doesn't lose all its sales if it raises its price. As a consequence, the monopoly sets its price above marginal cost to maximize its profit. Consumers buy less at this high monopoly price than they would at the competitive price, which equals marginal cost.

**In this chapter,
we examine
eight main topics**

1. Monopoly profit maximization: Like all firms, a monopoly maximizes its profit by setting its price or output so that its marginal revenue equals its marginal cost.

2. Effects of a shift of the demand curve: A shift of the demand curve may have a wider range of effects on a monopoly than on a competitive market.

3. Market power: How much the monopoly's price is above its marginal cost depends on the shape of the demand curve it faces.

4. Welfare effects of monopoly: By setting its price above marginal cost, a monopoly creates a deadweight loss.

5. Cost advantages that create monopolies: A firm can use a cost advantage over other firms (due, say, to control of a key input or economies of scale) to become a monopoly.

6. Government actions that create monopolies: Governments create monopolies by establishing government monopoly firms, limiting entry of other firms to create a private monopoly, and issuing patents, which are temporary monopoly rights.

7. Government actions that reduce market power: The welfare loss of a monopoly can be reduced or eliminated if the government regulates the price the monopoly charges or allows other firms to enter the market.

8. Monopoly decisions over time: If its current sales affect a monopoly's future demand curve, a monopoly that maximizes its long-run profit may choose not to maximize its short-run profit.

4.1 | Monopoly Profit Maximization

All firms, including competitive firms and monopolies, maximize their profits by setting *marginal revenue equal to marginal cost*. We already know how to derive the marginal cost curve of a monopoly from its cost curve. We now derive the monopoly's marginal revenue curve and then use the marginal revenue and marginal cost curves to examine the monopoly's profit-maximizing behavior.

MARGINAL REVENUE

A firm's marginal revenue curve depends on its demand curve. We will show that a monopoly's marginal revenue curve lies below its demand curve at any positive quantity because its demand curve is downward sloping.

Marginal Revenue and Price. A firm's demand curve shows the price, p, it receives for selling a given quantity, q. The price is the *average revenue* the firm receives, so a firm's revenue is $R = pq$.

A firm's *marginal revenue*, MR, is the change in its revenue from selling one more unit. A firm that earns ΔR more revenue when it sells Δq extra units of output has a marginal revenue of

$$MR = \Delta R/\Delta q.$$

If the firm sells exactly one more unit, $\Delta q = 1$, its marginal revenue is $MR = \Delta R$.

The marginal revenue of a monopoly differs from that of a competitive firm because the monopoly faces a downward-sloping demand curve unlike the competitive firm. The competitive firm in panel a of Figure 4.1 faces a horizontal demand curve at the market price, p_1. Because its demand curve is horizontal, the competitive firm can sell another unit of output without dropping its price. As a result, the marginal revenue it receives from selling the last unit of output is the market price.

Initially, the competitive firm sells q units of output at the market price of p_1, so its revenue, R_1, is area A, which is a rectangle that is $p_1 \times q$. If the firm sells one more unit, its revenue is $R_2 = A + B$, where area B is $p_1 \times 1 = p_1$. The competitive firm's marginal revenue equals the market price:

$$\Delta R = R_2 - R_1 = (A + B) - A = B = p_1.$$

A monopoly faces a downward-sloping market demand curve, as in panel b of Figure 4.1. (We've called the number of units of output a firm sells q and the output of all the firms in a market, or market output, Q. Because a monopoly is the only firm in the market, there is no distinction between q and Q, so we use Q to describe both the firm's and the market's output.) The monopoly, which is initially selling Q units at p_1, can sell one extra unit only if the price falls to p_2.

The monopoly's initial revenue, $p_1 \times Q$, is $R_1 = A + C$. When it sells the extra unit, its revenue, $p_2 \times (Q + 1)$, is $R_2 = A + B$. Thus its marginal revenue is

$$\Delta R = R_2 - R_1 = (A + B) - (A + C) = B - C.$$

The monopoly sells the extra unit of output at the new price, p_2, so its extra revenue is $B = p_2 \times 1 = p_2$. The monopoly loses the difference between the new price and the original price, $\Delta p = (p_2 - p_1)$, on the Q units it originally sold: $C = \Delta p \times Q$. Thus the monopoly's marginal revenue, $B - C = p_2 - C$, is less than the price it charges by an amount equal to area C.

The competitive firm in panel a does not lose an area C from selling an extra unit because its demand curve is horizontal. It is the downward slope of the monopoly's demand curve that causes its marginal revenue to be less than its price.

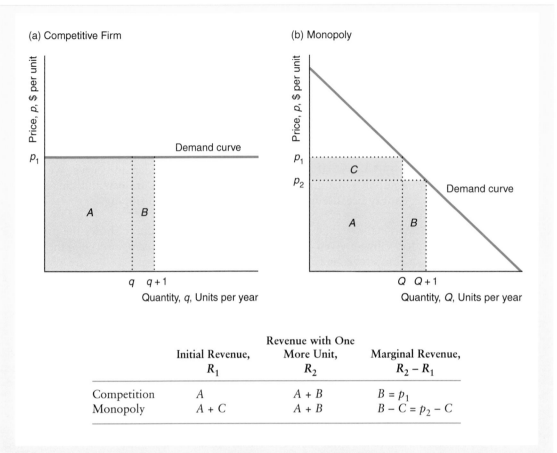

| | | Revenue with One | |
| | Initial Revenue, | More Unit, | Marginal Revenue, |
	R_1	R_2	$R_2 - R_1$
Competition	A	$A + B$	$B = p_1$
Monopoly	$A + C$	$A + B$	$B - C = p_2 - C$

Figure 4.1 **Average and Marginal Revenue.** The demand curve shows the average revenue or price per unit of output sold. (a) The competitive firm's marginal revenue, area B, equals the market price, p_1. (b) The monopoly's marginal revenue is less than the price p_2 by area C (the revenue lost due to a lower price on the Q units originally sold).

Marginal Revenue Curve. Thus *the monopoly's marginal revenue curve lies below the demand curve* at every positive quantity. In general, the relationship between the marginal revenue and demand curves depends on the shape of the demand curve.

For all *linear* demand curves, the relationship between the marginal revenue and demand curve is the same. The marginal revenue curve is a straight line that starts at the same point on the vertical (price) axis as the demand curve but has twice the slope of the demand curve, so the marginal revenue curve hits the horizontal (quantity) axis at half the quantity as the demand curve (see Appendix 4A). In Figure 4.2, the demand curve has a slope of –1 and hits the horizontal axis at 24 units, while the marginal revenue curve has a slope of –2 and hits the horizontal axis at 12 units.

Deriving the Marginal Revenue Curve. To derive the monopoly's marginal revenue curve, we write an equation summarizing the relationship between price and marginal revenue that panel b of Figure 4.1 illustrates. (Because we want this equation to hold at all prices, we drop the subscripts from the prices.) For a monopoly to increase its output by ΔQ, the monopoly lowers its price per unit by $\Delta p / \Delta Q$,

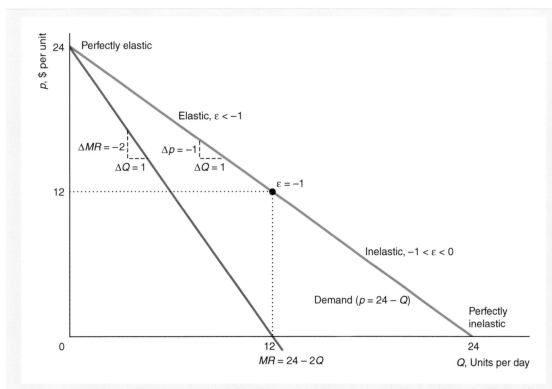

Figure 4.2 **Elasticity of Demand and Total, Average, and Marginal Revenue.** The demand curve (or average revenue curve), $p = 24 - Q$, lies above the marginal revenue curve, $MR = 24 - 2Q$. Where the marginal revenue equals zero, $Q = 12$, the elasticity of demand is $\varepsilon = -1$.

which is the slope of the demand curve. By lowering its price, the monopoly loses $(\Delta p/\Delta Q) \times Q$ on the units it originally sold at the higher price (area C), but it earns an additional p on the extra output it now sells (area B). Thus the monopoly's marginal revenue is[1]

$$MR = p + \frac{\Delta p}{\Delta Q} Q. \qquad (4.1)$$

Because the slope of the monopoly's demand curve, $\Delta p/\Delta Q$, is negative, the last term in Equation 4.1, $(\Delta p/\Delta Q)Q$, is negative. Equation 4.1 confirms that the price is greater than the marginal revenue, which equals p plus a negative term.

We now use Equation 4.1 to derive the marginal revenue curve when the monopoly faces the linear inverse demand function,

$$p = 24 - Q, \qquad (4.2)$$

in Figure 4.2. Equation 4.2 shows that the price consumers are willing to pay falls $1 if quantity increases by one unit. More generally, if quantity increases by ΔQ, price falls by $\Delta p = -\Delta Q$. Thus the slope of the demand curve is $\Delta p/\Delta Q = -1$.

---

[1]Revenue is $R(Q) = p(Q)Q$, where $p(Q)$, the inverse demand function, shows how price changes as quantity increases along the demand curve. Differentiating, we find that the marginal revenue is

$$MR = dR(Q)/dQ = p(Q) + [dp(Q)/dQ]Q.$$

We obtain the marginal revenue function for this monopoly by substituting into Equation 4.1 the actual slope of the demand function, $\Delta p/\Delta Q = -1$, and replacing p with $24 - Q$ (using Equation 4.2):

$$MR = p + \frac{\Delta p}{\Delta Q}Q = (24 - Q) + (-1)Q = 24 - 2Q. \qquad (4.3)$$

Figure 4.2 plots Equation 4.3. The slope of this marginal revenue curve is $\Delta MR/\Delta Q = -2$, so the marginal revenue curve is twice as steeply sloped as is the demand curve.

Marginal Revenue and Price Elasticity of Demand. The marginal revenue at any given quantity depends on the demand curve's height (the price) and shape. The shape of the demand curve at a particular quantity is described by the price elasticity of demand (Chapter 3), $\varepsilon = (\Delta Q/Q)/(\Delta p/p) < 0$, which tells us the percentage by which quantity demanded falls as the price increases by 1%.

At a given quantity, the marginal revenue equals the price times a term involving the elasticity of demand:[2]

$$MR = p\left(1 + \frac{1}{\varepsilon}\right). \qquad (4.4)$$

According to Equation 4.4, marginal revenue is closer to price as demand becomes more elastic. Where the demand curve hits the price axis ($Q = 0$), the demand curve is perfectly elastic, so the marginal revenue equals price: $MR = p$.[3] Where the demand elasticity is unitary, $\varepsilon = -1$, marginal revenue is zero: $MR = p[1 + 1/(-1)] = 0$. Marginal revenue is negative where the demand curve is inelastic, $-1 < \varepsilon \leq 0$.

With the demand function in Equation 4.2, $\Delta Q/\Delta p = -1$, so the elasticity of demand is $\varepsilon = (\Delta Q/\Delta p)(p/Q) = -p/Q$. Table 4.1 shows the relationship among quantity, price, marginal revenue, and elasticity of demand for this linear example. As Q approaches 24, ε approaches 0, and marginal revenue is negative. As Q approaches zero, the demand becomes increasingly elastic, and marginal revenue approaches the price.

CHOOSING PRICE OR QUANTITY

Any firm maximizes its profit by operating where its marginal revenue equals its marginal cost. Unlike a competitive firm, a monopoly can adjust its price, so it has a choice of setting its price *or* its quantity to maximize its profit. (A competitive firm sets its quantity to maximize profit because it cannot affect market price.)

The monopoly is constrained by the market demand curve. Because the demand curve slopes downward, the monopoly faces a trade-off between a higher price and

---

[2]By multiplying the last term in Equation 4.1 by p/p ($=1$) and using algebra, we can rewrite the expression as

$$MR = p + p\frac{\Delta p}{\Delta Q}\frac{Q}{p} = p\left[1 + \frac{1}{(\Delta Q/\Delta p)(p/Q)}\right].$$

The last term in this expression is $1/\varepsilon$, because $\varepsilon = (\Delta Q/\Delta p)(p/Q)$.

[3]As ε approaches $-\infty$ (perfectly elastic demand), the $1/\varepsilon$ term approaches zero, so $MR = p(1 + 1/\varepsilon)$ approaches p.

TABLE 4.1 Quantity, Price, Marginal Revenue, and Elasticity
for the Linear Inverse Demand Curve $p = 24 - Q$

Quantity, Q	Price, p	Marginal Revenue, MR	Elasticity of Demand, $\varepsilon = -p/Q$	
0	24	24	$-\infty$	more elastic→
1	23	22	−23	
2	22	20	−11	
3	21	18	−7	
4	20	16	−5	
5	19	14	−3.8	
6	18	12	−3	
7	17	10	−2.43	
8	16	8	−2	
9	15	6	−1.67	
10	14	4	−1.4	
11	13	2	−1.18	
12	12	0	−1	←less elastic
13	11	−2	−0.85	
. . .	. . .	. . .	. . .	
23	1	−22	−0.043	
24	0	−24	0	

a lower quantity or a lower price and a higher quantity. The monopoly chooses the point on the demand curve that maximizes its profit. Unfortunately for the monopoly, it cannot set both its quantity and its price—thereby picking a point that is above the demand curve. If it could do so, the monopoly would choose an extremely high price and an extremely high output level and would become exceedingly wealthy.

If the monopoly sets its price, the demand curve determines how much output it sells. If the monopoly picks an output level, the demand curve determines the price. Because the monopoly wants to operate at the price and output at which its profit is maximized, it chooses the same profit-maximizing solution whether it sets the price or output. In the following, we assume that the monopoly sets quantity.

GRAPHICAL APPROACH

All firms, including monopolies, use a two-step analysis to determine the output level that maximizes their profit. First, the firm determines the output, Q^*, at which it makes the highest possible profit—the output at which its marginal revenue equals its marginal cost. Second, the firm decides whether to produce Q^* or shut down.

Profit-Maximizing Output. To illustrate how a monopoly chooses its output to maximize its profit, we continue to use the same linear demand and marginal revenue curves but add a linear marginal cost curve in panel a of Figure 4.3. Panel b shows the corresponding profit curve. The profit curve reaches its maximum at 6 units of output, where marginal profit—the slope of the profit curve—is zero. Because *marginal profit is marginal revenue minus marginal cost*, marginal profit is zero where marginal revenue equals marginal cost. In panel a, marginal revenue equals marginal cost at 6 units. The price on the demand curve at that quantity is $18.

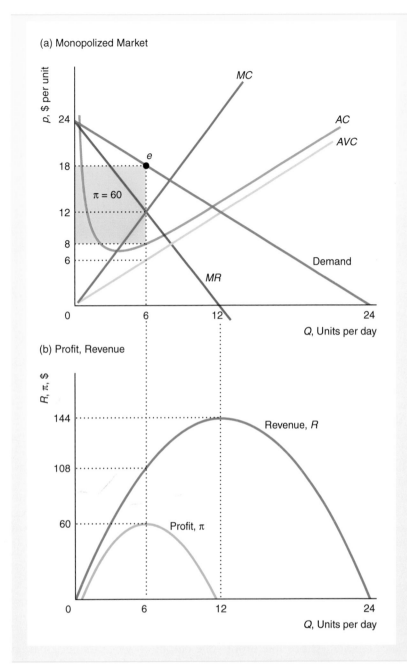

Figure 4.3 **Maximizing Profit.**
(a) At $Q = 6$, where marginal revenue, *MR*, equals marginal cost, *MC*, profit is maximized. The rectangle showing the maximum profit $60 is average profit per unit, $p - AC = \$18 - \$8 = \$10$, times the number of units, 6. (b) Profit is maximized at a smaller quantity, $Q = 6$ (where marginal revenue equals marginal cost), than is revenue, $Q = 12$ (where marginal revenue is zero).

Thus the monopoly maximizes its profit at point *e*, where it sells 6 units per day for $18 each.

Why does the monopoly maximize its profit by producing 6 units where its marginal revenue equals its marginal cost? At smaller quantities, the monopoly's marginal revenue is greater than its marginal cost, so its marginal profit is positive. By increasing its output, it raises its profit. Similarly, at quantities greater than 6 units, the monopoly's marginal cost is greater than its marginal revenue, so it can increase its profit by reducing its output.

The profit-maximizing quantity is smaller than the revenue-maximizing quantity. The revenue curve reaches its maximum at $Q = 12$, where the slope of the revenue curve, the marginal revenue, is zero (panel a). In contrast, the profit curve reaches its maximum at $Q = 6$, where marginal revenue equals marginal cost. Because marginal cost is positive, marginal revenue must be positive where profit is maximized. Because the marginal revenue curve has a negative slope, marginal revenue is positive at a smaller quantity than where it equals zero. Thus the profit curve must reach a maximum at a smaller quantity, 6, than the revenue curve, 12.

As we already know, marginal revenue equals zero at the quantity where the demand curve has a unitary elasticity. Because a linear demand curve is more elastic at smaller quantities, *monopoly profit is maximized in the elastic portion of the demand curve*. (Here profit is maximized at $Q = 6$ where the elasticity of demand is −3.) Equivalently, *a monopoly never operates in the inelastic portion of its demand curve*.

Shutdown Decision. A monopoly shuts down to avoid making a loss in the long run if the monopoly-optimal price is below its average cost. In the short run, the monopoly shuts down if the monopoly-optimal price is less than its average variable cost. In our short-run example in Figure 4.3, the average variable cost, $AVC = \$6$, is less than the price, $p = \$18$, at the profit-maximizing output, $Q = 6$, so the firm chooses to produce.

Price is also above average cost at $Q = 6$, so the monopoly makes a positive profit.[4] At the profit-maximizing quantity of 6 units, the price is $p(6) = \$18$ and the average cost is $AC(6) = \$8$. As a result, the profit, $\pi = \$60$, is the shaded rectangle with a height equal to the average profit per unit, $p(6) - AC(6) = \$18 - \$8 = \$10$, and a width of 6 units.

MATHEMATICAL APPROACH

We can also solve for the profit-maximizing quantity mathematically. We already know the demand and marginal revenue functions for this monopoly. We need to determine its marginal cost curve. The monopoly's cost is a function of its output, $C(Q)$. In Figure 4.3, we assume that the monopoly faces a short-run cost function of

$$C(Q) = Q^2 + 12, \tag{4.5}$$

where Q^2 is the monopoly's variable cost as a function of output and $\$12$ is its fixed cost. Given this cost function, the monopoly's marginal cost function is[5]

$$MC = 2Q. \tag{4.6}$$

This marginal cost curve is a straight line through the origin with a slope of 2 in panel a. The average variable cost is $AVC = Q^2/Q = Q$, so it is a straight line through the origin with a slope of 1. The average cost is $AC = C/Q = (Q^2 + 12)/Q = Q + 12/Q$, which is U-shaped.

We determine the profit-maximizing output by equating the marginal revenue (Equation 4.3) and marginal cost (Equation 4.6) functions:

$$MR = 24 - 2Q = 2Q = MC.$$

---

[4]Because profit is $\pi = p(Q)Q - C(Q)$, average profit is $\pi/Q = p(Q) - C(Q)/Q = p(Q) - AC$. Thus average profit (and hence profit) is positive only if price is above average cost.

[5]By differentiating Equation 4.5 with respect to output, we find that the marginal cost is $MC = dC(Q)/dQ = 2Q$.

Solving for Q, we find that $Q = 6$. Substituting $Q = 6$ into the inverse demand function (Equation 4.2), we find that the profit-maximizing price is

$$p = 24 - Q = 24 - 6 = \$18.$$

At that quantity, the average variable cost is $AVC = \$6$, which is less than the price, so the firm does not shut down. The average cost is $AC = \$(6 + 12/6) = \$8$, which is less than the price, so the firm makes a profit.

★4.2 Effects of a Shift of the Demand Curve

Shifts in the demand curve or marginal cost curve affect the monopoly optimum and can have a wider variety of effects in a monopolized market than in a competitive market. In a competitive market, the effect of a shift in demand on a competitive firm's output depends only on the shape of the marginal cost curve. In contrast, the effect of a shift in demand on a monopoly's output depends on the shapes of both the marginal cost curve and the demand curve.

A competitive firm's marginal cost curve tells us everything we need to know about the amount that firm will supply at any given market price. The competitive firm's supply curve is its upward-sloping marginal cost curve (above its minimum average variable cost). A competitive firm's supply behavior does not depend on the shape of the market demand curve because it always faces a horizontal demand curve at the market price. Thus if you know a competitive firm's marginal cost curve, you can predict how much that firm will produce at any given market price.

In contrast, a monopoly's output decision depends on the shapes of its marginal cost curve and its demand curve. Unlike a competitive firm, *a monopoly does not have a supply curve*. Knowing the monopoly's marginal cost curve is not enough for us to predict how much a monopoly will sell at any given price.

Figure 4.4 illustrates that the relationship between price and quantity is unique in a competitive market but not in a monopoly market. If the market is competitive, the initial equilibrium is e_1 in panel a, where the original demand curve D^1 intersects the supply curve, MC, which is the sum of the marginal cost curves of a large number of competitive firms. When the demand curve shifts to D^2, the new competitive equilibrium, e_2, has a higher price and quantity. A shift of the demand curve maps out competitive equilibria along the marginal cost curve, so for every equilibrium quantity, there is a single corresponding equilibrium price.

See Question 1.

Now suppose there is a monopoly. As demand shifts from D^1 to D^2, the monopoly optimum shifts from E_1 to E_2 in panel b, so the price rises but the quantity stays constant, $Q_1 = Q_2$. Thus *a given quantity can correspond to more than one monopoly-optimal price*. A shift in the demand curve may cause the monopoly-optimal price to stay constant and the quantity to change or both price and quantity to change.

4.3 Market Power

market power
the ability of a firm to charge a price above marginal cost and earn a positive profit

A monopoly has **market power**: the ability of a firm to charge a price above marginal cost and earn a positive profit. We now examine the factors that determine how much above its marginal cost a monopoly sets its price.

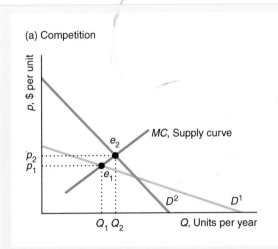

Figure 4.4 **Effects of a Shift of the Demand Curve.** (a) A shift of the demand curve from D^1 to D^2 causes the competitive equilibrium to move from e_1 to e_2 along the supply curve (the horizontal sum of the marginal cost curves of all the competitive firms): Because the competitive equilibrium lies on the supply curve, each quantity corresponds to only one possible equilibrium price. (b) With a monopoly, this same shift of demand causes the monopoly optimum to change from E_1 to E_2. The monopoly quantity stays the same, but the monopoly price rises. Thus a shift in demand does not map out a unique relationship between price and quantity in a monopolized market: The same quantity, $Q_1 = Q_2$, is associated with two different prices, p_1 and p_2.

MARKET POWER AND THE SHAPE OF THE DEMAND CURVE

The degree to which the monopoly raises its price above its marginal cost depends on the shape of the demand curve at the profit-maximizing quantity. If the monopoly faces a highly elastic—nearly flat—demand curve at the profit-maximizing quantity, it would lose substantial sales if it raised its price by even a small amount. Conversely, if the demand curve is not very elastic (relatively steep) at that quantity, the monopoly would lose fewer sales from raising its price by the same amount.

We can derive the relationship between market power and the elasticity of demand at the profit-maximizing quantity using the expression for marginal revenue in Equation 4.4 and the firm's profit-maximizing condition that marginal revenue equals marginal cost:

$$MR = p\left(1 + \frac{1}{\varepsilon}\right) = MC. \tag{4.7}$$

By rearranging terms, we can rewrite Equation 4.7 as

$$\frac{p}{MC} = \frac{1}{1 + (1/\varepsilon)}. \tag{4.8}$$

Equation 4.8 says that the ratio of the price to marginal cost depends *only* on the elasticity of demand at the profit-maximizing quantity.

In our linear demand example in panel a of Figure 4.3, the elasticity of demand is $\varepsilon = -3$ at the monopoly optimum where $Q = 6$. As a result, the ratio of price to marginal cost is $p/MC = 1/[1 + 1/(-3)] = 1.5$, or $p = 1.5MC$. The profit-maximizing price, $18, in panel a is 1.5 times the marginal cost of $12.

TABLE 4.2   Elasticity of Demand, Price, and Marginal Cost

Elasticity of Demand, ε	Price/Marginal Cost Ratio, $p/MC = 1/[1 + (1/\varepsilon)]$	Lerner Index, $(p - MC)/p = -1/\varepsilon$
−1.01	101	0.99
−1.1	11	0.91
−2	2	0.5
−3	1.5	0.33
−5	1.25	0.2
−10	1.11	0.1
−100	1.01	0.01
−∞	1	0

(less elastic → ; ← more elastic)

Table 4.2 illustrates how the ratio of price to marginal cost varies with the elasticity of demand. When the elasticity is −1.01, only slightly elastic, the monopoly's profit-maximizing price is 101 times larger than its marginal cost: $p/MC = 1/[1 + 1/(-1.01)] \approx 101$. As the elasticity of demand approaches negative infinity (becomes perfectly elastic), the ratio of price to marginal cost shrinks to $p/MC = 1$.[6]

This table illustrates that not all monopolies can set high prices. A monopoly that faces a horizontal, perfectly elastic demand curve, sets its price equal to its marginal cost—just like a price-taking, competitive firm. If this monopoly were to raise its price, it would lose all its sales, so it maximizes its profit by setting its price equal to its marginal cost.

The more elastic the demand curve, the less a monopoly can raise its price without losing sales. All else the same, the more close substitutes for the monopoly's good there are, the more elastic the demand the monopoly faces. For example, Addison-Wesley has the monopoly right to produce and sell this textbook. Many other publishers, however, have the rights to produce and sell similar microeconomics textbooks (though you wouldn't like them as much). The demand Addison-Wesley faces is much more elastic than it would be if no substitutes were available. If you think this textbook is expensive, imagine the cost if no substitutes were published!

LERNER INDEX

Lerner Index
the ratio of the difference between price and marginal cost to the price: $(p - MC)/p$

Another way to show how the elasticity of demand affects a monopoly's price relative to its marginal cost is to look at the firm's **Lerner Index** (or *price markup*):[7] the ratio of the difference between price and marginal cost to the price: $(p - MC)/p$. This measure is zero for a competitive firm because a competitive firm cannot raise its price above its marginal cost. The greater the difference between price and marginal cost, the larger the Lerner Index and the greater the monopoly's ability to set price above marginal cost.

[6]As the elasticity approaches negative infinity, $1/\varepsilon$ approaches zero, so $1/(1 + 1/\varepsilon)$ approaches $1/1 = 1$.

[7]This index is named after its inventor, Abba Lerner.

If the firm is maximizing its profit, we can express the Lerner Index in terms of the elasticity of demand by rearranging Equation 4.8:

$$\frac{p - MC}{p} = -\frac{1}{\varepsilon}. \tag{4.9}$$

Because $MC \geq 0$ and $p \geq MC$, $0 \leq p - MC \leq p$, so the Lerner Index ranges from 0 to 1 for a profit-maximizing firm.[8] Equation 4.9 confirms that a competitive firm has a Lerner Index of zero because its demand curve is perfectly elastic.[9] As Table 4.2 illustrates, the Lerner Index for a monopoly increases as the demand becomes less elastic. If $\varepsilon = -5$, the monopoly's markup (Lerner Index) is $1/5 = 0.2$; if $\varepsilon = -2$, the markup is $1/2 = 0.5$; and if $\varepsilon = -1.01$, the markup is 0.99. Monopolies that face demand curves that are only slightly elastic set prices that are multiples of their marginal cost and have Lerner Indexes close to 1.

● APPLICATION

Apple's iPod

Apple introduced its iPod on October 23, 2001. Although the iPod was not the first hard-drive music player, it was the most elegant one to date. Endowed with a tiny hard drive, it was about a quarter the size of its competitors, fit in one's pocket, and weighed only 6.5 ounces. Moreover, it was the only player to use a high-speed FireWire interface to transfer files. It held a thousand songs. Perhaps most importantly, iPod offered an intuitive interface and an attractive white case with unusual ear buds.

People loved the iPod. Even at its extremely high price of $399, Apple has had a virtual monopoly for several years. In 2004, the iPod had 95.6% of the hard-drive player market, and Apple believed that it still had more than 90% in 2005.

To keep ahead of potential competitors, Apple introduced subsequent generations of iPods in quick succession (though it always sells its top-of-the-line model for $399). Its iTune proprietary media player software and its iTunes Music Store help Apple maintain its stranglehold on the market. At iTunes Music Store, users can easily download tracks for 99¢, burn them to a CD, play them using iTunes, or sync them with their MP3 player. However, iTunes supports copying music to the iPod and not from it, and songs purchased from the iTunes Music Store are copy protected with Apple's FairPlay digital rights management scheme, which prevents iTunes customers from using the purchased music on some portable digital music player other than the Apple iPod. Consequently, some current owners of iPods and iTunes are hesitant to switch to potential competitors because they will have to learn new software and may be unable to transfer some of their previously purchased songs to the new equipment.

See Problem 31.

---

[8]For the Lerner Index to be above 1, ε would have to be a negative fraction, indicating that the demand curve was inelastic at the monopoly optimum. However, a profit-maximizing monopoly never operates in the inelastic portion of its demand curve.

[9]As the elasticity of demand approaches negative infinity, the Lerner Index, $-1/\varepsilon$, approaches zero.

SOLVED PROBLEM   **4.1**

Apple's constant marginal cost of producing its top-of-the-line iPod is $200, its fixed cost is $736 million, and its inverse demand function is $p = 600 - 25Q$, where Q is units measured in millions.[10] What is Apple's average cost function? Assuming that Apple is maximizing short-run monopoly profit, what is its marginal revenue function? What are its profit-maximizing price and quantity, profit, and Lerner Index? What is the elasticity of demand at the profit-maximizing level? Show Apple's profit-maximizing solution in a figure.

Answer

1. *Derive the average cost function using the information about Apple's marginal and fixed costs:* Given that Apple's marginal cost is constant, its average variable cost equals its marginal cost, $200. Its average fixed cost is its fixed cost divided by the quantity produced, $736/Q$. Thus, its average cost is $AC = 200 + 736/Q$.

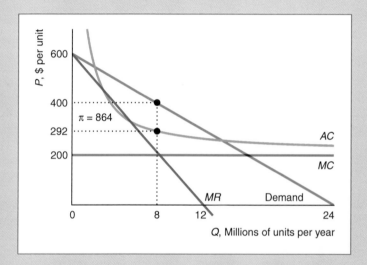

2. *Derive Apple's marginal revenue function using the information about its demand function:* Given that its demand function is linear, we know that its marginal revenue function is twice as steep as the demand function and has the same intercept on the price axis: $MR = 600 - 50Q$, as the figure shows.

3. *Derive Apple's profit-maximizing price and quantity by equating the marginal revenue and marginal cost functions and solving:* Apple maximizes its profit where

$$MR = 600 - 50Q = 200MC.$$

---

[10]The marginal cost estimate comes from **www.eetimes.com/news/latest/showArticle.jhtml?articleID=18306938**. Though we assume that the marginal cost curve is constant, there is some evidence from Apple's other lines that it might be downward sloping. The quantity in 2004 is from In-Stat market research, **www.tomshardware.com/hardnews/20050621_123943.html**. We assumed that the company's gross profit margin for 2004, **www.apple.com/pr/library/2004/oct/13results.html**, held for the iPod line and used that to calculate the fixed cost. We derived the linear demand curve by assuming Apple maximizes profit and using the information on price, marginal cost, and quantity. Assuming that Apple maximizes its short-run profit may not be completely realistic, as we discuss in the last section of this chapter.

Solving this equation for the profit-maximizing output, we find that Q = 8 million units. By substituting this quantity into the inverse demand equation, we determine that the profit-maximizing price is p = \$400 per unit, as the figure shows.

4. *Calculate Apple's profit using the profit-maximizing price and quantity and the average cost:* The firm's profit is $\pi = (p - AC)Q = (400 - [200 + 736/8])8$ = \$864 million. The figure shows that the profit is a rectangle with a height of $(p - AC)$ and a length of Q.

5. *Determine the Lerner Index using the formula:* Apple's Lerner Index is $(p - MC)/p = (400 - 200)/400 = \frac{1}{2}$.

6. *Use Equation 4.9 to infer the elasticity:* According to that equation, a profit-maximizing monopoly operates where $(p - MC)p = -1/\varepsilon$. Substituting into this expression from the previous step, we learn that $\frac{1}{2} = -1/\varepsilon$, or $\varepsilon = -2$.

See Problem 32.

SOURCES OF MARKET POWER

When will a monopoly face a relatively elastic demand curve and hence have little market power? Ultimately, the elasticity of demand of the market demand curve depends on consumers' tastes and options. The more consumers want a good—the more willing they are to pay "virtually anything" for it—the less elastic is the demand curve.

All else the same, the demand curve a firm (not necessarily a monopoly) faces becomes more elastic as *better substitutes* for the firm's product are introduced, *more firms* enter the market selling the same product, or firms that provide the same service *locate closer* to this firm. The demand curves for Xerox, the U.S. Postal Service, and McDonald's have become more elastic in recent decades for these three reasons.

When Xerox started selling its plain-paper copier, no other firm sold a close substitute. Other companies' machines produced copies on special slimy paper that yellowed quickly. As other firms developed plain-paper copiers, the demand curve that Xerox faced became more elastic.

The U.S. Postal Service (USPS) has a monopoly in first-class mail service. Today, phone calls, faxes, and e-mail are excellent substitutes for many types of first-class mail. The USPS had a monopoly in overnight delivery services until 1979. Now Federal Express, United Parcel Service, and many other firms compete with the USPS in providing overnight deliveries. Because of this new competition, the USPS's share of business and personal correspondence fell from 77% in 1988 to 59% in 1996, and its overnight-mail market fell to 4%.[11] Thus over time the demand curves the USPS faces for first-class mail and overnight service have shifted downward and become more elastic.

As you drive down a highway, you may notice that McDonald's restaurants are spaced miles apart. The purpose of this spacing is to reduce the likelihood that two McDonald's outlets will compete for the same customer. Although McDonald's can prevent its own restaurants from competing with each other, it cannot prevent Wendy's or Burger King from locating near its restaurants. As other fast-food restaurants open near a McDonald's, that restaurant faces a more elastic demand.

What happens as a profit-maximizing monopoly faces more elastic demand? It has to lower its price.

---

[11]Peter Passell, "Battered by Its Rivals," *New York Times*, May 15, 1997:C1.

4.4 Welfare Effects of Monopoly

Welfare, W (here defined as the sum of consumer surplus, CS, and producer surplus, PS), is lower under monopoly than under competition. Competition maximizes welfare because price equals marginal cost. By setting its price above its marginal cost, a monopoly causes consumers to buy less than the competitive level of the good, so a deadweight loss to society occurs.

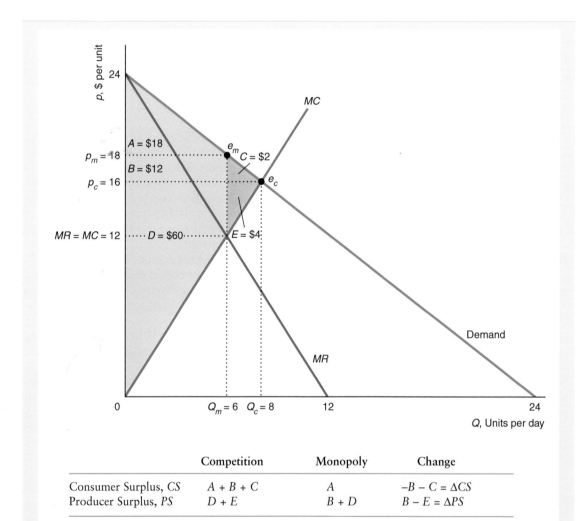

	Competition	Monopoly	Change
Consumer Surplus, CS	$A + B + C$	A	$-B - C = \Delta CS$
Producer Surplus, PS	$D + E$	$B + D$	$B - E = \Delta PS$
Welfare, $W = CS + PS$	$A + B + C + D + E$	$A + B + D$	$-C - E = \Delta W = DWL$

Figure 4.5 **Deadweight Loss of Monopoly.** A competitive market would produce $Q_c = 8$ at $p_c = \$16$, where the demand curve intersects the marginal cost (supply) curve. A monopoly produces only $Q_m = 6$ at $p_m = \$18$, where the marginal revenue curve intersects the marginal cost curve. Under monopoly, consumer surplus is A, producer surplus is $B + D$, and the lost welfare or deadweight loss of monopoly is $-C - E$.

GRAPHING THE WELFARE LOSS

We illustrate this loss using our continuing example. If the monopoly were to act like a competitive market and operate where its inverse demand curve, Equation 4.2, intersects its marginal cost (supply) curve, Equation 4.6,

$$p = 24 - Q = 2Q = MC,$$

it would sell $Q_c = 8$ units of output at a price of $16, as in Figure 4.5. At this competitive price, consumer surplus is area $A + B + C$ and producer surplus is $D + E$.

If the firm acts like a monopoly and operates where its marginal revenue equals its marginal cost, only 6 units are sold at the monopoly price of $18, and consumer surplus is only A. Part of the lost consumer surplus, B, goes to the monopoly; but the rest, C, is lost.

By charging the monopoly price of $18 instead of the competitive price of $16, the monopoly receives $2 more per unit and earns an extra profit of area $B = \$12$ on the $Q_m = 6$ units it sells. The monopoly loses area E, however, because it sells less than the competitive output. Consequently, the monopoly's producer surplus increases by $B - E$ over the competitive level. We know that its producer surplus increases, $B - E > 0$, because the monopoly had the option of producing at the competitive level and chose not to do so.

Monopoly welfare is lower than competitive welfare. The deadweight loss of monopoly is $-C - E$, which represents the consumer surplus and producer surplus lost because less than the competitive output is produced. The deadweight loss is due to the gap between price and marginal cost at the monopoly output. At $Q_m = 6$, the price, $18, is above the marginal cost, $12, so consumers are willing to pay more for the last unit of output than it costs to produce it.

SOLVED PROBLEM 4.2

In the linear example in Figure 4.3, how does charging the monopoly a specific tax of $\tau = \$8$ per unit affect the monopoly optimum and the welfare of consumers, the monopoly, and society (where society's welfare includes the tax revenue)? What is the incidence of the tax on consumers?

Answer

1. *Determine how imposing the tax affects the monopoly optimum*: In the accompanying graph, the intersection of the marginal revenue curve, MR, and the before-tax marginal cost curve, MC^1, determines the monopoly optimum quantity, $Q_1 = 6$. At the before-tax optimum, e_1, the price is $p_1 = \$18$. The specific tax causes the monopoly's before-tax marginal cost curve, $MC^1 = 2Q$, to shift upward by $8 to $MC^2 = MC^1 + 8 = 2Q + 8$. After the tax is applied, the monopoly operates where $MR = 24 - 2Q = 2Q + 8 = MC^2$. In the after-tax monopoly optimum, e_2, the quantity is $Q_2 = 4$ and the price is $p_2 = \$20$. Thus output falls by $\Delta Q = 2$ units and the price increases by $\Delta p = \$2$.

2. *Calculate the change in the various welfare measures*: The graph shows how the welfare measures change. Area G is the tax revenue collected by the government, $\tau Q = \$32$, because its height is the distance between the two marginal cost curves, $\tau = \$8$, and its width is the output the monopoly produces after the tax is imposed, $Q = 4$. The tax reduces consumer and producer surplus and increases the deadweight loss. We know that producer surplus

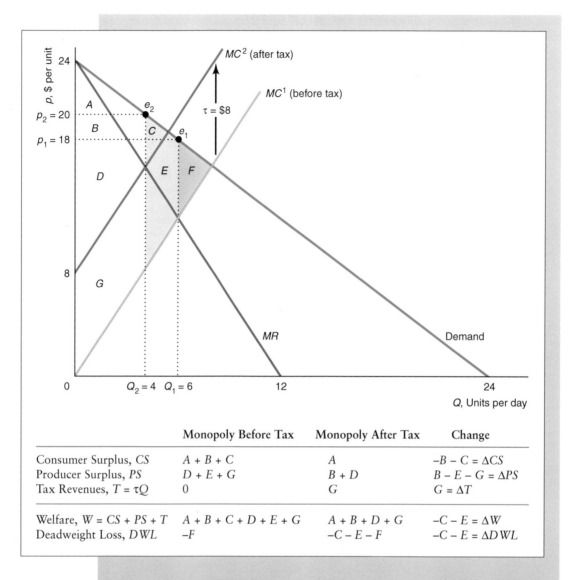

	Monopoly Before Tax	Monopoly After Tax	Change
Consumer Surplus, CS	$A + B + C$	A	$-B - C = \Delta CS$
Producer Surplus, PS	$D + E + G$	$B + D$	$B - E - G = \Delta PS$
Tax Revenues, $T = \tau Q$	0	G	$G = \Delta T$
Welfare, $W = CS + PS + T$	$A + B + C + D + E + G$	$A + B + D + G$	$-C - E = \Delta W$
Deadweight Loss, DWL	$-F$	$-C - E - F$	$-C - E = \Delta DWL$

falls because (a) the monopoly could have produced this reduced output level in the absence of the tax but did not because it was not the profit-maximizing output, so its before-tax profit falls, and (b) the monopoly must now pay taxes. The before-tax deadweight loss from monopoly is $-F$. The after-tax deadweight loss is $-C - E - F$, so the increase in deadweight loss due to the tax is $-C - E$. The table below the graph shows that consumer surplus changes by $-B - C$ and producer surplus by $B - E - G$.

3. *Calculate the incidence of the tax*: Because the tax goes from $0 to $8, the change in the tax is $\Delta \tau = \$8$. The incidence of the tax (Chapter 3) on consumers is $\Delta p / \Delta \tau = \$2/\$8 = \frac{1}{4}$. (The monopoly absorbs $6 of the tax and passes on only $2.)[12]

See Problems 28 and 38.

---

[12]In contrast to a competitive market, when a monopoly is taxed, the incidence of the tax on consumers can exceed 100%, as Appendix 4B demonstrates.

★ WELFARE EFFECTS OF *AD VALOREM* VERSUS SPECIFIC TAXES

Solved Problem 4.1 illustrates that a specific sales tax (the monopoly pays the government τ dollars per unit sold) provides tax revenue but reduces welfare below even the monopoly level. Governments use *ad valorem* taxes more often than specific taxes. Is there an advantage to using an *ad valorem* sales tax (the monopoly pays αp per unit of output, where α is a fraction and p is the price charged)? The answer is that a government raises more tax revenue with an *ad valorem* tax applied to a monopoly than with a specific tax when α and τ are set so that the after-tax output is the same with either tax, as we now show.[13]

In Figure 4.6, the before-tax market demand curve is D, and the corresponding marginal revenue is MR. The before-tax monopoly optimum is e_1. The MR curve intersects the MC curve at Q_1 units, which sell at a price of p_1.

If the government imposes a specific tax τ, the monopoly's after-tax demand curve is D^s, which is the market demand curve D shifted downward by τ dollars.[14]

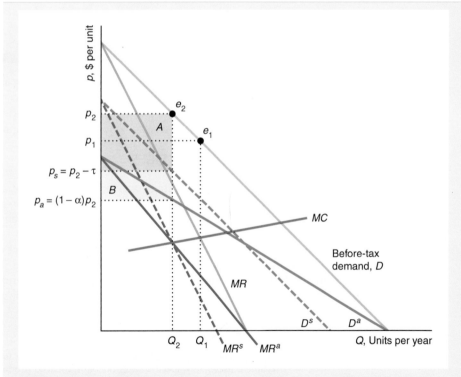

Figure 4.6 *Ad Valorem* Versus Specific Tax. A specific tax (τ) and an *ad valorem* tax (α) that reduce the monopoly output by the same amount (from Q_1 to Q_2) raise different amounts of tax revenues for the government. The tax revenue from the specific tax is area $A = \tau Q_2$. The tax revenue from the *ad valorem* tax is $A + B = \alpha p_2 Q_2$.

---

[13]Chapter 3 shows that both taxes raise the same tax revenue in a competitive market. The taxes raise different amounts when applied to monopolies or other noncompetitive firms. See Delipalla and Keen (1992), Skeath and Trandel (1994), and Hamilton (1999).

[14]Instead, we could capture the effect of a specific tax by shifting the marginal cost curve upward by τ, as in our answer to Solved Problem 4.2.

The corresponding marginal revenue curve, MR^s, intersects the marginal cost curve at Q_2. In this after-tax equilibrium, e_2, consumers pay p_2 and the monopoly receives $p_s = p_2 - \tau$ per unit. The government's revenue from the specific tax is area $A = \tau Q_2$.

If the government imposes an *ad valorem* tax α, the demand curve facing the monopoly is D^a. The gap between D^a and D, which is the tax per unit, αp, is greater at higher prices. By setting α appropriately, the corresponding marginal revenue curve, MR_a, intersects the marginal cost curve at Q_2, where consumers again pay p_2. Although the *ad valorem* tax reduces output by the same amount as the specific tax, the *ad valorem* tax raises more revenue, areas $A + B = \alpha p_2 Q_2$.

Both sales taxes harm consumers by the same amount because they raise the price consumers pay from p_1 to p_2 and reduce the quantity purchased from Q_1 to Q_2. The *ad valorem* tax transfers more revenue from the monopoly to the government, so the government prefers the *ad valorem* tax and the monopoly prefers the specific tax. (Equivalently, if the government set τ and α so that they raised the same amount of tax revenue, the *ad valorem* tax would reduce output and consumer surplus less than the specific tax.) Amazingly, it makes sense for government to employ an *ad valorem* tax, and most state and local governments use *ad valorem* taxes for most goods.[15]

4.5 | Cost Advantages that Create Monopolies

Why are some markets monopolized? Two key reasons are that a firm has a cost advantage over other firms or that a government created the monopoly.[16] If a low-cost firm profitably sells at a price so low that other potential competitors with higher costs would make losses, no other firm enters the market.

SOURCES OF COST ADVANTAGES

A firm can have a cost advantage over potential rivals for a number of reasons. One reason is that the firm controls a key input. For example, a firm that owns the only quarry in a region is the only firm that can profitably sell gravel to local construction firms.

A second important reason why a firm may have lower costs is that the firm uses a superior technology or has a better way of organizing production. Henry Ford's methods of organizing production using assembly lines and standardization allowed him to produce cars at lower cost than rival firms until they copied his organizational techniques.

---

[15]However, as Professor Stearns and his students at the University of Maryland inform me, the federal government uses many specific taxes (alcohol, tobacco products, gasoline and other fuels, international air travel, tires, vaccines, ship passengers, ozone-depleting chemicals) as well as *ad valorem* taxes (telephone service, transportation of property by air, sports fishing equipment, bows and arrow components, gas-guzzler autos, foreign insurance, and firearms).

[16]In later chapters, we discuss three other means by which monopolies are created. One method is the merger of several firms into a single firm (Chapter 6). This method creates a monopoly if new firms fail to enter the market. A second method is for firms to coordinate their activities and set their prices as a monopoly would (Chapter 6). Firms that act collectively in this way are called a *cartel*. A third method is for a monopoly to use strategies that discourage other firms from entering the market.

When a firm develops a better production method that provides an advantage—possibly enough of an advantage for the firm to be a monopoly—the firm must either keep the information secret or obtain a patent, which provides government protection from imitation. According to a survey of 650 research and development managers of U.S. firms (Levin, Klevorick, Nelson, and Winter, 1987), secrecy is more commonly used than patents to prevent duplication of new or improved processes by other firms but less commonly used to protect new products.

NATURAL MONOPOLY

natural monopoly situation in which one firm can produce the total output of the market at lower cost than several firms could

A market has a **natural monopoly** if one firm can produce the total output of the market at lower cost than several firms could. If the cost for any firm to produce q is $C(q)$, the condition for a natural monopoly is

$$C(Q) < C(q_1) + C(q_2) + \cdots + C(q_n), \tag{4.10}$$

where $Q = q_1 + q_2 + \cdots + q_n$ is the sum of the output of any $n \geq 2$ firms. With a natural monopoly, it is more efficient to have only one firm produce than more firms.[17] Believing that they are natural monopolies, governments frequently grant monopoly rights to *public utilities* to provide essential goods or services such as water, gas, electric power, or mail delivery.

If a firm has economies of scale at all levels of output, its average cost curve falls as output increases for any observed level of output. If all potential firms have the same strictly declining average cost curve, this market has a natural monopoly, as we now illustrate.[18]

A company that supplies water to homes incurs a high fixed cost, F, to build a plant and connect houses to the plant. The firm's marginal cost, m, of supplying water is constant, so its marginal cost curve is horizontal and its average cost, $AC = m + F/Q$, declines as output rises. (An example is the iPod in Solved Problem 4.1.)

Figure 4.7 shows such marginal and average cost curves where $m = \$10$ and $F = \$60$. If the market output is 12 units per day, one firm produces that output at an average cost of \$15, or a total cost of \$180 (= \$15 × 12). If two firms each produce 6 units, the average cost is \$20 and the cost of producing the market output is \$240 (= \$20 × 12), which is greater than the cost with a single firm.

If the two firms divided total production in any other way, their cost of production would still exceed the cost of a single firm (as the following question asks you to prove). The reason is that the marginal cost per unit is the same no matter how many firms produce, but each additional firm adds a fixed cost, which raises the cost of producing a given quantity. If only one firm provides water, the cost of building a second plant and a second set of pipes is avoided.

---

[17]A natural monopoly is the most efficient market structure only in the sense that the single firm produces at lowest cost. However, society's welfare may be greater with more than one firm in the industry producing at higher cost, because competition drives down the price from the monopoly level. A solution that allows society to maximize welfare is to have only one firm produce, but the government regulates that firm to charge a price equal to marginal cost (as we discuss later in this chapter).

[18]A firm may be a natural monopoly even if its cost curve does not fall at all levels of output. If a U-shaped average cost curve reaches its minimum at 100 units of output, it may be less costly for only one firm to produce an output of 101 units even though average cost is rising at that output. Thus a cost function with economies of scale everywhere is a sufficient but not a necessary condition for natural monopoly.

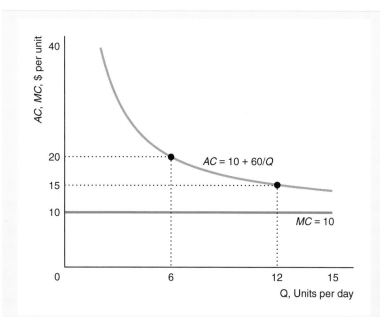

Figure 4.7 **Natural Monopoly.** This natural monopoly has a strictly declining average cost.

SOLVED PROBLEM   4.3

A firm that delivers Q units of water to households has a total cost of $C(Q) = mQ + F$. If any entrant would have the same cost, does this market have a natural monopoly?

Answer

Determine whether costs rise if two firms produce a given quantity: Let q_1 be the output of Firm 1 and q_2 be the output of Firm 2. The combined cost of these two firms producing $Q = q_1 + q_2$ is

$$C(q_1) + C(q_2) = (mq_1 + F) + (mq_2 + F) = m(q_1 + q_2) + 2F = mQ + 2F.$$

If a single firm produces Q, its cost is $C(Q) = mQ + F$. Thus the cost of producing any given Q is greater with two firms than with one firm, so this market has a natural monopoly.

● **APPLICATION**

Electric Power Utilities

According to the estimates of Christensen and Greene (1976), the average cost curve for U.S. electric-power-producing firms in 1970 was U-shaped, reaching its minimum at 33 billion kilowatt-hours (kWh) per year (see graph). Thus whether an electric power utility was a natural monopoly depended on the demand it faced.

For example, if the demand curve for an electric utility was D on the graph, the quantity demanded was less than 33 billion kWh per year at any price, so the electric utility operated in the strictly declining section of its average cost curve and was a natural monopoly. In 1970, most electric companies were

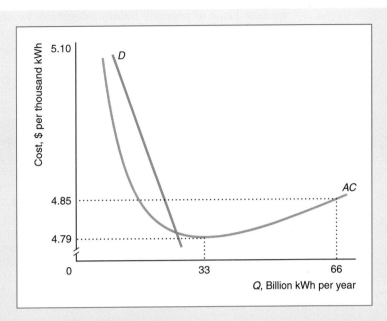

operating in regions of substantial economies of scale. Newport Electric produced only 0.5 billion kWh per year, and Iowa Southern Utilities produced 1.3 billion kWh per year.

A few of these firms operated in the upward-sloping section of the average cost curve and were not natural monopolies. The largest electric utility in 1970, Southern, produced 54 billion kWh per year. It was not a natural monopoly because two firms could produce that quantity at 3¢ less per thousand kWh than a single firm could. As the graph shows, two firms producing 33 billion kWh each have an average cost of $4.79 per thousand kWh, while one firm producing 66 billion kWh has an average cost of $4.85, or 6¢ more per thousand kWh.

See Questions 6, 7, and 8.

4.6 Government Actions that Create Monopolies

Governments create many monopolies. Sometimes governments own and manage monopolies. In the United States, as in most countries, the postal service is a government monopoly. Indeed, the U.S. Constitution explicitly grants the government the right to establish a postal service. Many local governments own and operate public utility monopolies that provide garbage collection, electricity, water, gas, phone services, and other utilities.

Frequently, however, governments create monopolies by preventing competing firms from entering a market. For example, when a government grants a patent, it limits entry and allows the patent-holding firm to earn a monopoly profit from an invention—a reward for developing the new product.

BARRIERS TO ENTRY

By preventing other firms from entering a market, governments create monopolies. Typically, governments create monopolies in one of three ways: by making it difficult for new firms to obtain a license to operate, by granting a firm the rights to be a monopoly, or by auctioning the rights to be a monopoly.

Frequently, firms need government licenses to operate. If governments make it difficult for new firms to obtain licenses, the first firm may maintain its monopoly. Until recently, many U.S. cities required that new hospitals or other inpatient facilities demonstrate the need for a new facility to obtain a certificate of need, which allowed them to enter the market.

Government grants of monopoly rights have been common for public utilities. Instead of running a public utility itself, a government gives a private company the monopoly rights to operate the utility. A government may capture some of the monopoly profits by charging a high rent to the monopoly. Alternatively, government officials may capture the rents for monopoly rights by means of bribes.

Governments around the world have privatized many state-owned monopolies in the past several decades. By selling its monopolies to private firms, a government can capture the value of future monopoly earnings today. However, for political or other reasons, governments frequently sell at a lower price that does not capture all future profits. (See **www.myeconlab.com/perloff**, Chapter 4, "Iceland's Government Creates Genetic Monopoly.")

PATENTS

patent
an exclusive right granted to the inventor to sell a new and useful product, process, substance, or design for a fixed period of time

If a firm cannot prevent imitation by keeping its discovery secret, it may obtain government protection to prevent other firms from duplicating its discovery and entering the market. Virtually all countries provide such protection through a **patent**: an exclusive right granted to the inventor to sell a new and useful product, process, substance, or design for a fixed period of time. A patent grants an inventor the right to be the monopoly provider of the good for a number of years.

Patent Length. The length of a patent varies across countries. The U.S. Constitution explicitly gives the government the right to grant authors and inventors exclusive rights to their writings (copyrights) and to their discoveries (patents) for limited periods of time. Traditionally, U.S. patents lasted *17 years* from the date they were *granted*, but the United States agreed in 1995 to change its patent law as part of a GATT agreement. Now U.S. patents last for *20 years* after the date the inventor *files* for patent protection. The length of protection is likely to be shorter under the new rules, because it frequently takes more than three years after filing to obtain final approval of a patent.

Patents Stimulate Research. A firm with a patent monopoly sets a high price that results in deadweight loss. Why, then, do governments grant patent monopolies? The main reason is that inventive activity would fall if there were no patent monopolies or other incentives to inventors. The costs of developing a new drug or new computer chip are often hundreds of millions or even billions of dollars. If anyone could copy a new drug or chip and compete with the inventor, few individuals or firms would undertake costly research. Thus the government is explicitly trading off the long-run benefits of additional inventions against the shorter-term harms of monopoly pricing during the period of patent protection.

APPLICATION

Botox Patent Monopoly

Ophthalmologist Dr. Alan Scott turned the deadly poison botulinum toxin into a miracle drug to treat two eye conditions: strabismus, which affects about 4% of children; and blepharospasm, an uncontrollable closure of the eyes. Blepharospasm left about 25,000 Americans functionally blind before Scott's discovery. His patented drug, Botox, is sold by Allergan, Inc.

Dr. Scott has been amused to see several of the unintended beneficiaries of his research at the Academy Awards. Even before it was explicitly approved for cosmetic use, many doctors were injecting Botox into the facial muscles of actors, models, and others to smooth out their wrinkles. (The drug paralyzes the muscles, so those injected with it also lose the ability to frown—and, some would say, to act.) The treatment is only temporary, lasting up to 120 days, so repeated injections are necessary. Allergan had expected to sell $400 million worth of Botox in 2002. However, in April of that year, the Federal Food and Drug Administration approved of the use of Botox for cosmetic purposes, a ruling that allows the company to advertise the drug widely.

Allergan had sales of $800 million in 2004 and expects to sell $1 billion worth of Botox in 2005. Allergan has a near-monopoly in the treatment of wrinkles, although plastic surgery and collagen, Restylane, hyaluronic acids, and other filler injections provide limited competition. Between 2002 and 2004, the number of facelifts dropped 3% to about 114,000 according to the American Society of Plastic Surgeons, while the number of Botox injections skyrocketed 166% to nearly 3 million.

Dr. Scott says that he can produce a vial of Botox in his lab for about $25. Allergan then sells the potion to doctors for about $400. Assuming that the firm is setting its price to maximize its short-run profit, we can rearrange Equation 4.9 to determine the elasticity of demand for Botox:

$$\varepsilon = -\frac{p}{p - MC} = -\frac{400}{400 - 25} \approx -1.067.$$

Thus the demand that Allergan faces is only slightly elastic: A 1% increase in price causes quantity to fall by only a little more than 1%.

If we assume that the demand curve is linear and that the elasticity of demand is −1.067 at the 2002 monopoly optimum, e_m (one million vials sold at $400 each, producing revenue of $400 million), then Allergan's inverse demand function is

$$p = 775 - 375Q.$$

This demand curve (see graph) has a slope of −375 and hits the price axis at $775 and the quantity axis at about 2.07 million vials per year. The corresponding marginal revenue curve,

$$MR = 775 - 750Q,$$

strikes the price axis at $775 and has twice the slope, −750, as the demand curve. The intersection of the marginal revenue and marginal cost curves,

$$MR = 775 - 750Q = 25 = MC,$$

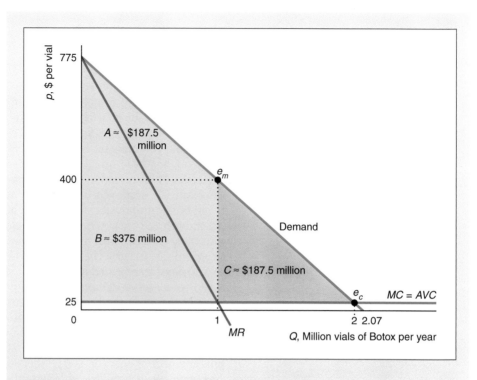

determines the monopoly equilibrium at the profit-maximizing quantity of 1 million vials per year and a price of $400 per vial.

Were the company to sell Botox at a price equal to its marginal cost of $25 (as a competitive industry would), consumer surplus would equal areas $A + B + C = \$750$ million per year. At the higher monopoly price of $400, the consumer surplus is $A = \$187.5$ million. Compared to the competitive solution, e_c, buyers lose consumer surplus of $B + C = \$562.5$ million per year. Part of this loss, $B = \$375$ million per year, is transferred from consumers to Allergan. The rest, $C = \$187.5$ million per year, is the deadweight loss from monopoly pricing. Allergan's profit is its producer surplus, B, minus its fixed costs.

See Problems 28 and 29.

Alternatives to Patents. Instead of using patents to spur research, the government could give research grants or offer prizes. Rather than trying these alternative approaches, Congress has modified the patent system. In the 1960s and 1970s, the effective life of a patent on a drug shrank because of the additional time it took to get FDA approval to sell the drug. By 1978, the average drug had patent protection for fewer than 10 years. The Drug Price Competition and Patent Term Restoration Act of 1984 restored up to three years of the part of the patent life that was lost while the firm demonstrated efficacy and safety to the FDA. At the same time, the act made it easier for generic products to enter at the end of the patent period. Thus the law aimed both to encourage the development of new drugs by increasing the reward—the monopoly period—and to stimulate price competition at the end of the period.

Internet and Other Pirates: Protecting Intellectual Property Rights

A patent grants its owner the exclusive or monopoly right to sell a new and useful product, process, substance, or design for a fixed period. Similarly, a copyright gives its owner the exclusive production, publication, or sales rights to artistic, dramatic, literary, or musical works. The main purpose of providing these intellectual property rights is to encourage research and artistic creativity.

However, patents and copyrights are of little value to their owners if these rights are not enforced. Protecting intellectual property such as music and computer software from unauthorized copying has proved increasingly difficult over the past several years. The growth of piracy over the Internet has threatened traditional copyright protection for books, music, and films. Authors, artists, and publishers are no longer assured of being paid for their work.

Many users download music, movies, and books over the Internet without paying. Condemning these actions as piracy, music and software publishers have sued Napster and other firms that facilitate copying, and have instituted copy protection schemes. These attempts to prevent copying have had limited success. In China, illegal copies of movies, music, and software openly sell for a fraction—a fifth for many new DVDs—of the price of the original.

Worldwide use of music-sharing services such as Napster, KaZaA, and others has flourished—particularly before a series of lawsuits by publishers in 2003. Lawsuits and the threat of them initially discouraged some downloading in the United States. According to one survey, the share of computer users who employed file-sharing programs to download music fell from 29% in the spring of 2003 to 14% by late 2003. Since then, the number of global file-sharing users doubled. The U.S. Supreme Court ruled in June 2005 that Internet file-trading networks such as Grokster and Morpheus can be held liable when their users copy music, movies, and other protected works without permission, so more U.S. prosecutions are likely.

The Business Software Alliance's annual survey for 2005 claims that legal software is the exception in many developing countries. It reports that the rate of software piracy is 92% in Vietnam, 91% in the Ukraine, 90% in China and Zimbabwe, 87% in Indonesia, 53% in the Asia-Pacific region, 35% in Europe, and "only" 22% in North America, which has the toughest penalties for illegal software usage. The alliance claims that the value of illegal software was $32.7 billion in 2005—though evaluating the loss using list price leads to an overestimate. Moreover, consumers who use pirated copies of a work may eventually decide to purchase legitimate copies of it or other related works. Thus, the effect of piracy on legitimate demand is an empirical question.

In the short run, artists and producers are harmed by piracy. If consumers benefit by being able to buy music or software for less or by stealing it, the overall short-run welfare effect of piracy is ambiguous. For example, in the extreme case where downloaders would not have bought the product, piracy raises welfare and harms no one.

Rob and Waldfogel (2004) surveyed college students at the University of Pennsylvania and elsewhere. They found that each album download reduces purchases by at least 0.2 of an album. Students reported downloading almost as many albums as they purchased and admitted that, if downloading had not been possible, they would have purchased 26% of the albums they down-loaded. Among Penn undergrads, the researchers found that downloading reduced their personal expenditures on hit albums from $126 to $100 but raised their per capita consumer surplus by $70. Thus, for this group, the increase in consumer surplus more than offset the loss in revenues.

Regardless of the short-run welfare effects, the more serious harm occurs in the long run. Reduced copyright and patent protection lowers the drive to cre-ate or to innovate.

4.7   Government Actions that Reduce Market Power

Some governments act to reduce or eliminate monopolies' market power. Most Western countries have laws forbidding a firm from driving other firms out of the market so as to monopolize it. Many governments either regulate monopolies—especially those that the government has created—or destroy monopolies by breaking them up into smaller, independent firms or encouraging other firms to enter the market.

REGULATING MONOPOLIES

Governments limit monopolies' market power in a number of ways. Most utilities, for example, are subject to direct regulation. One method governments use to limit the harms of monopoly is to place a ceiling on the price that a monopoly charges.

Optimal Price Regulation. In some markets, the government can eliminate the dead-weight loss of monopoly by requiring that a monopoly charge no more than the competitive price. We use our earlier linear example to illustrate this type of regula-tion in Figure 4.8.

If the government doesn't regulate the profit-maximizing monopoly, the monopoly optimum is e_m, at which 6 units are sold at the monopoly price of $18. Suppose that the government sets a ceiling price of $16, the price at which the marginal cost curve intersects the market demand curve. Because the monopoly cannot charge more than $16 per unit, the monopoly's regulated demand curve is horizontal at $16 (up to 8 units) and is the same as the market demand curve at lower prices. The marginal rev-enue, MR_r, corresponding to the regulated demand curve is horizontal where the reg-ulated demand curve is horizontal (up to 8 units) and equals the marginal revenue curve, MR, corresponding to the market demand curve at larger quantities.

The regulated monopoly sets its output at 8 units, where MR_r equals its marginal cost, MC, and charges the maximum permitted price of $16. The regulated firm still makes a profit, because its average cost is less than $16 at 8 units. The optimally regulated monopoly optimum, e_o, is the same as the competitive equilibrium, where marginal cost (supply) equals the market demand curve.[19] Thus setting a price ceiling where the MC curve and market demand curve intersect eliminates the deadweight loss of monopoly.

---

[19]The monopoly produces at e_o only if the regulated price is greater than its average variable cost. Here the regulated price, $16, exceeds the average variable cost at 8 units of $8. Indeed, the firm makes a profit because the average cost at 8 units is $9.50.

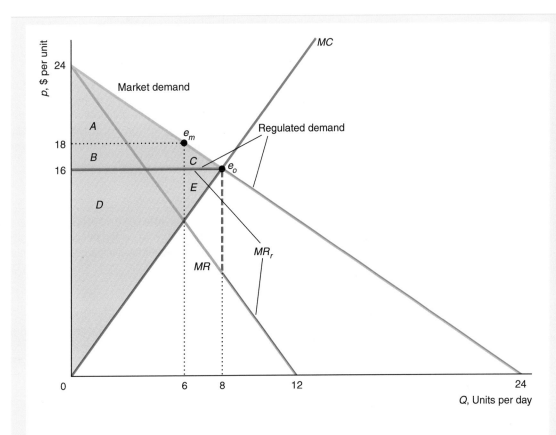

	Monopoly Without Regulation	Monopoly with Optimal Regulation	Change
Consumer Surplus, *CS*	*A*	*A + B + C*	$B + C = \Delta CS$
Producer Surplus, *PS*	*B + D*	*D + E*	$E - B = \Delta PS$
Welfare, *W = CS + PS*	*A + B + D*	*A + B + C + D + E*	$C + E = \Delta W$
Deadweight Loss, *DWL*	*−C − E*	0	$C + E = \Delta DWL$

Figure 4.8 Optimal Price Regulation. If the government sets a price ceiling at $16, where the monopoly's marginal cost curve hits the demand curve, the new demand curve the monopoly faces has a kink at 8 units, and the corresponding marginal revenue curve, MR_r, "jumps" at that quantity. The regulated monopoly sets its output where $MR_r = MC$, selling the same quantity, 8 units, at the same price, $16, as a competitive industry would. The regulation eliminates the monopoly deadweight loss, $C + E$. Consumer surplus, $A + B + C$, and producer surplus, $D + E$, are the same as under competition.

How do we know that this regulation is optimal? The answer is that this regulated outcome is the same as would occur if this market were competitive, where welfare is maximized. As the table accompanying Figure 4.8 shows, the deadweight loss of monopoly, $C + E$, is eliminated by this optimal regulation.

Nonoptimal Price Regulation. Welfare is reduced if the government does not set the price optimally. Suppose that the government sets the regulated price below the optimal level, which is $16 in our example. If it sets the price below the firm's minimum average cost, the firm shuts down. If that happens, the deadweight loss equals the sum of the consumer plus producer surplus under optimal regulation, $A + B + C + D + E$.

If the government sets the price ceiling below the optimally regulated price but high enough that the firm does not shut down, consumers who are lucky enough to buy the good are better off because they can buy goods at a lower price than with optimal regulation. Some customers, however, are frustrated because the monopoly will not sell them the good, as we show next. There is a deadweight loss because less output is sold than with optimal regulation. (Question 11 at the end of the chapter asks you to determine the effects of a regulated price that is above the optimal level.)

SOLVED PROBLEM   4.4

Suppose that the government sets a price, p_2, that is below the socially optimal level, p_1, but above the monopoly's minimum average cost. How do the price, the quantity sold, the quantity demanded, and welfare under this regulation compare to those under optimal regulation?

Answer

1. *Describe the optimally regulated outcome*: With optimal regulation, e_1, the price is set at p_1, where the market demand curve intersects the monopoly's

	Monopoly with Optimal Regulation	Monopoly with a Low Regulated Price	Change
Consumer Surplus, CS	$A + B$	$A + C$	$C - B = \Delta CS$
Producer Surplus, PS	$C + D + E$	E	$-C - D = \Delta PS$
Welfare, $W = CS + PS$	$A + B + C + D + E$	$A + C + E$	$-B - D = \Delta W = DWL$

marginal cost curve on the accompanying graph. The optimally regulated monopoly sells Q_1 units.

2. *Describe the outcome when the government regulates the price at p_2*: Where the market demand is above p_2, the regulated demand curve for the monopoly is horizontal at p_2 (up to Q_d). The corresponding marginal revenue curve, MR_r, is horizontal where the regulated demand curve is horizontal and equals the marginal revenue curve corresponding to the market demand curve, MR, where the regulated demand curve is downward sloping. The monopoly maximizes its profit by selling Q_2 units at p_2. The new regulated monopoly optimum is e_2, where MR_r intersects MC. The firm does not shut down when regulated as long as its average variable cost at Q_2 is less than p_2.

See Question 11.

3. *Compare the outcomes*: The quantity that the monopoly sells falls from Q_1 to Q_2 when the government lowers its price ceiling from p_1 to p_2. At that low price, consumers want to buy Q_d, so there is excess demand equal to $Q_d - Q_2$. Compared to optimal regulation, welfare is lower by at least $B + D$.

Comment: The welfare loss is greater if unlucky consumers waste time trying to buy the good unsuccessfully or if goods are not allocated optimally among consumers. A consumer who values the good at only p_2 may be lucky enough to buy it, while a consumer who values the good at p_1 or more may not be able to obtain it.

Problems in Regulating. Governments face several problems in regulating monopolies. First, because they do not know the actual demand and marginal cost curves, governments may set the price at the wrong level. Second, many governments use regulations that are less efficient than price regulation. Third, regulated firms may bribe or otherwise influence government regulators to help the firms rather than society as a whole.

Because of limited information about the demand and marginal cost curves, governments may set a price ceiling above or below the competitive level. Moreover, a regulatory agency may have to set the price higher than is optimal because it cannot offer a subsidy.

If the regulatory agency were to set the price equal to a natural monopoly's marginal cost, the price would be below the firm's average cost. The monopoly would threaten to shut down unless the regulatory agency were to subsidize it or raise the price.

To illustrate this problem, we calculate how setting the price too low would affect a phone monopoly in Macon, Georgia (before deregulation in 1995 that allowed additional firms into the market).[20] In the absence of regulation and in light of the curves in Figure 4.9, this firm maximizes its profit by operating where its marginal cost equals its marginal revenue, e_1, where it provides 31,000 telephone lines at $710 each annually. At that quantity, its average cost is $248, so its profit is ($710 - $248)31,000 = $14,322,000, area A.

Alternatively, the government may regulate the utility to behave like a price taker, e_3. The firm would lose money if it faced a price ceiling of $160 annually, where the

---

[20]This example is based on Gasmi et al. (2002, Appendix A). We replaced their exponential demand curve with a linear demand curve, where both curves have a price elasticity of demand of −0.2 at point e_2.

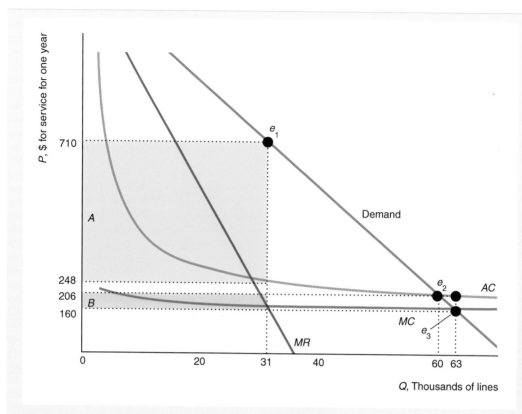

Figure 4.9 **Regulating a Telephone Utility.** If the phone utility is an unregulated, profit-maximizing monopoly, e_1, it provides 31,000 telephone lines at $710 each annually and makes a profit of $14,322,000, equal to area A. The government may regulate the price so that the utility breaks even, e_2. Alternatively, the government may regulate the utility to behave like a price taker, e_3. If so, the government must subsidize the utility by area $B = $2,583,000$ to keep it from shutting down.

demand curve intersects the marginal cost curve at 63,000 lines. At that quantity, its average cost is $204, so it loses ($204 − $160)63,000 = $2,722,000, area B.

Typically, it is politically infeasible for a government regulatory agency to subsidize a firm. Instead, the agency might set the price at $248, where the demand curve intersects the average cost curve and the monopoly breaks even. There is still a deadweight loss because that price is above marginal cost, but the deadweight loss is smaller than it would be if the monopoly were unregulated. The government may regulate the price so that the utility breaks even, e_2. If so, the government must subsidize the utility by area $B = $2,772,000$ to keep it from shutting down.

Unfortunately, regulation is often not effective when regulators are *captured*: influenced by the firms they regulate. Typically, this influence is more subtle than an outright bribe. Many American regulators have worked in the industry before they became regulators and hence are sympathetic to those firms. Many regulators hope to obtain good jobs in the industry eventually, so they don't want to offend potential employers. Other regulators, relying on industry experts for their information, may be misled or at least heavily influenced by the industry. For example, the California Public Utilities Commission urged telephone and cable companies to negotiate among themselves as to how they wanted to open local phone markets to competition by 1997. Arguing that these influences are inherent, some economists contend that price and other types of regulation are unlikely to result in efficiency.

INCREASING COMPETITION

Encouraging competition is an alternative to regulation as a means of reducing the harms of monopoly. When a government has created a monopoly by preventing entry, it can quickly reduce the monopoly's market power by allowing other firms to enter. As new firms enter the market, the former monopoly must lower its price to compete, so welfare rises. Many governments are actively encouraging entry into telephone, electricity, and other utility markets that were formerly monopolized.

Similarly, a government may end a ban on imports so that a domestic monopoly faces competition from foreign firms. If costs for the domestic firm are the same as costs for the foreign firms and there are many foreign firms, the former monopoly becomes just one of many competitive firms. As the market becomes competitive, consumers pay the competitive price, and the deadweight loss of monopoly is eliminated.

Governments around the world are increasing competition in formerly monopolized markets. For example, many U.S. and European governments are forcing former telephone and energy monopolies to compete. See **www.myeconlab.com/ perloff**, "Ending the Monopoly in Telephone Service" and "Deregulating Energy."

Similarly, under pressure from the World Trade Organization, many countries are reducing or eliminating barriers that protected domestic monopolies. The entry of foreign competitive firms into a market can create a new, more competitive market structure.

● **APPLICATION**

Creating and Destroying an Auto Monopoly

In the early 1980s, Mahathir Mohamad, Malaysia's prime minister, fulfilled his dream and created a national car. Putting the Islamic star-and-crescent badge on the front of what was even then an aging Mitsubishi Lancer, Mahathir called the vehicle the Proton Saga. By 1986, the Saga hit the road. Today, Protons are about two-thirds of all of the cars in Malaysia.

The government aided the company by having taxpayers foot the bill for building its plants (about $2 billion). More important, it set import tariffs of between 140% and 300% that served as a major barrier to entry for foreign-made cars. Such barriers were necessary for the Proton to survive because the car's production costs were nearly three times those of Japanese and Korean competitors (partially because Proton production lacked economies of scale).

More recently, the government has undermined this monopoly. It created a second national car, the Perodua, to add variety for consumers. It also introduced a locally assembled multipurpose vehicle sold by Naza Kia Sdn, the Malaysian distributor of South Korea's Kia Motors Corp. Most important, the government reduced the trade barrier. Under the Association of Southeast Asia Nations (ASEAN) Free Trade Area rules, Malaysia slashed its tariff on cars imported from ASEAN countries from 190% to 20% in 2005 and will cut it

See Problem 21.

to 5% by 2008. Partially offsetting this change, the Malaysian government hiked excise duties on all cars sold in Malaysia. Although Proton must pay those duties, it receives a 50% rebate. Nonetheless, Proton's share of the market fell from 65% a couple of years before to 44% in 2005.

4.8 Monopoly Decisions over Time

We have examined how a monopoly behaves in the current period, ignoring the future. For many markets, such an analysis is appropriate. However, in some markets, decisions today affect demand or cost in a future period. In such markets, the monopoly may maximize its long-run profit by making a decision today that does not maximize its short-run profit. For example, frequently a firm introduces a new product—such as a candy bar—by initially charging a low price or giving away free samples to generate word-of-mouth publicity or to let customers learn about its quality in hopes of getting their future business. We now consider an important reason why consumers' demand in the future may depend on a monopoly's actions in the present.

NETWORK EXTERNALITIES

network externality
the situation where one person's demand for a good depends on the consumption of the good by others

The number of customers a firm has today may affect the demand curve it faces in the future. A good has a **network externality** if one person's demand depends on the consumption of a good by others. If a good has a *positive* network externality, its value to a consumer grows as the number of units sold increases.

When a firm introduces a new good with a network externality, it faces a chicken-and-egg problem: It can't get Max to buy the good unless Sofia will buy it, but it can't get Sofia to buy it unless Max will. The firm wants its customers to coordinate or to make their purchase decisions simultaneously.

The telephone provides a classic example of a positive network externality. When the phone was introduced, potential adopters had no reason to get phone service unless their family and friends did. Why buy a phone if there's no one to call? For Bell's phone network to succeed, it had to achieve a *critical mass* of users—enough adopters that others wanted to join. Had it failed to achieve this critical mass, demand would have withered and the network would have died. Similarly, the market for fax machines grew very slowly until a critical mass was achieved where many firms had them.

Direct Size Effect. Many industries exhibit positive network externalities where the customer gets a *direct* benefit from a larger network. The larger an ATM network such as the Plus network, the greater the odds that you will find an ATM machine when you want one, so the more likely it is that you will want to use that network. The more people who use a particular computer operating system, the more attractive it is to someone who wants to exchange files or programs with other users.

Behavioral Economics. These examples of the direct effect of network externalities depend on the size of the network because customers want to interact with each other. However, sometimes consumers' behavior depends on beliefs or tastes that can be explained by psychological and sociological theories. These explanations are called *behavioral economics*.

One alternative explanation for a direct network externality effect is based on tastes. Harvey Leibenstein (1950) suggested that consumers sometimes want a good because "everyone else has it." A fad or other popularity-based explanation for a positive network externality is called a **bandwagon effect**: A person places greater value on a good as more and more other people possess it.[21] The success of the iPod today may be partially due to its early popularity. Ugg boots seem to be another example of a bandwagon effect.

The opposite, negative network externality is called a **snob effect**: A person places greater value on a good as fewer and fewer other people possess it. Some people prefer an original painting by an unknown artist to a lithograph by a star because no one else can possess that painting. (As Yogi Berra said, "Nobody goes there anymore; it's too crowded.")

bandwagon effect
the situation in which a person places greater value on a good as more and more other people possess it

snob effect
the situation in which a person places greater value on a good as fewer and fewer other people possess it

Indirect Effect. In some markets, positive network externalities are indirect and stem from complementary goods that are offered when a product has a critical mass of users. Why buy a computer if no software programs are available? The more extra devices and software that work with a particular computer, the more people want to buy that computer; but these extra devices are available only if a critical mass of customers buys the computer. Similarly, the more people who drive diesel-powered cars, the more likely it is that gas stations will sell diesel fuel; and the more stations that sell the fuel, the more likely it is that someone will want to drive a diesel car. As a final example, once a critical mass of customers has broadband Internet service, more services will provide downloadable music and movies and more high-definition Web pages will become available; and once those killer apps appear, more people will sign up for broadband service.

NETWORK EXTERNALITIES AS AN EXPLANATION FOR MONOPOLIES

Because of the need for a critical mass of customers in a market with a positive network externality, we frequently see only one large firm surviving, as in the case of eBay. Several online auctions started a few years ago, including eBay and Yahoo. However, all else the same, sellers want to use the site that has the most potential buyers, and buyers want the largest choice of sellers. Thus, after eBay reached a critical mass, it grew rapidly, its rivals lost customers, and eventually eBay became a virtual monopoly.

Visa's ad campaign tells consumers that Visa cards are accepted "everywhere you want to be," including at stores that "don't take American Express." One could view its ad campaign as an attempt to convince consumers that its card has a critical mass and therefore everyone should switch to it.

But having achieved a monopoly, a firm does not necessarily keep it. History is filled with examples where one product knocks off another: "The king is dead, long live the king." Google replaced Yahoo as the predominant search engine. Explorer displaced Netscape as the big-dog browser (and Firefox lurks in the wings). Levi Strauss is no longer the fashion leader among the jeans set.

---

[21]*Jargon alert:* Some economists use *bandwagon effect* to mean any positive network externality—not just those that are based on popularity.

A TWO-PERIOD MONOPOLY MODEL

A monopoly may be able to solve the chicken-and-egg problem of getting a critical mass for its product by initially selling the product at a low introductory price. By so doing, the firm maximizes its long-run profit but not its short-run profit.

Suppose that a monopoly sells its good—say, root-beer-scented jeans—for only two periods (after that, the demand goes to zero as a new craze hits the market). If the monopoly sells less than a critical quantity of output, Q, in the first period, its second-period demand curve lies close to the price axis. However, if the good is a success in the first period—at least Q units are sold—the second-period demand curve shifts substantially to the right.

If the monopoly maximizes its short-run profit in the first period, it charges p^* and sells Q^* units, which is fewer than Q. To sell Q units, it would have to lower its first-period price to $\underline{p} < p^*$, which would reduce its first-period profit from π^* to $\underline{\pi}$.

In the second period, the monopoly maximizes its profit given its second-period demand curve. If the monopoly sold only Q^* units in the first period, it earns a relatively low second-period profit of π_l. However, if it sells Q units in the first period, it makes a relatively high second-period profit, π_h.

See Problem 41.

Should the monopoly charge a low introductory price in the first period? Its objective is to maximize its long-run profit: the sum of its profit in the two periods.[22] It maximizes its long-run profit by charging a low introductory price in the first period if the extra profit in the second period $\pi_h - \pi_l$ from achieving a critical mass in the first period is greater than its forgone profit in the first period, $\pi^* - \underline{\pi}$. This policy must pay for some firms: A Google search found a quarter of a million cites to Web pages touting introductory prices.

[22]For now, we assume that the monopoly places equal value on profit in either period.

Summary

1. **Monopoly profit maximization:** Like any firm, a monopoly—a single seller—maximizes its profit by setting its output so that its marginal revenue equals its marginal cost. The monopoly makes a positive profit if its average cost is less than the price at the profit-maximizing output.

2. **Effects of a shift of the demand curve:** Because a monopoly does not have a supply curve, the effect of a shift in demand on a monopoly's output depends on the shapes of both its marginal cost curve and its demand curve. As a monopoly's demand curve shifts, price and output may change in the same direction or different directions.

3. **Market power:** Market power is the ability of a firm to charge a price above marginal cost and earn a positive profit. The more elastic the demand the monopoly faces at the quantity at which it maximizes its profit, the closer its price to its marginal cost and the closer the Lerner Index or price markup, $(p - MC)/p$, to zero, the competitive level.

4. **Welfare effects of monopoly:** Because a monopoly's price is above its marginal cost, too little output is produced, and society suffers a deadweight loss. The monopoly makes higher profit than it would if it acted as a price taker. Consumers are worse off, buying less output at a higher price.

5. **Cost advantages that create monopolies:** A firm may be a monopoly if it controls a key input, has superior knowledge about producing or distributing a good, or has substantial economies of scale. In markets with substantial economies of scale, the single seller is called a natural monopoly because total production costs would rise if more than one firm produced.

6. **Government actions that create monopolies:** Governments may establish government-owned and -operated monopolies. They may also create private monopolies by establishing barriers to entry that prevent other firms from competing. Nations grant patents, which give inventors monopoly rights for a limited period of time.

7. **Government actions that reduce market power:** A government can eliminate the welfare harm of a monopoly by forcing the firm to set its price at the competitive level. If the government sets the price at a different level or otherwise regulates nonoptimally, welfare at the regulated monopoly optimum is lower than in the competitive equilibrium. A government can eliminate or reduce the harms of monopoly by allowing or facilitating entry.

8. **Monopoly decisions over time:** If a good has a positive network externality so that its value to a consumer grows as the number of units sold increases, then current sales affect a monopoly's future demand curve. A monopoly may maximize its long-run profit—its profit over time—by setting a low introductory price in the first period that it sells the good and then later raising its price as its product's popularity assures large future sales at a higher price. Consequently, the monopoly is not maximizing its short-run profit in the first period but is maximizing the sum of its profits over all periods.

Questions

* = answer at the back of this book; **A** *= an application or other real-world material in the text;* **C** *= use of calculus may be necessary.*

1. Show that after a shift in the demand curve, a monopoly's price may remain constant but its output may rise. **A**

2. What is the effect of a franchise (lump-sum) tax on a monopoly? (*Hint*: Consider the possibility that the firm may shut down.)

*3. Only Indian tribes can run casinos in California. These casinos are spread around the state so that each is a monopoly in its local community. California governor Arnold Schwarzenegger negotiated with the state's tribes, getting them to agree to transfer a fraction of their profits to the state in exchange for concessions (Dan Morain and Evan Halper, "Casino Deals Said to Be Near," *Los Angeles Times*, June 16, 2004:1). In 2004, he started with a proposal that the state get 25% of casino profits and then dropped the level to 15%. He announced a deal with two tribes at 10% in 2005. How does a profit tax affect a monopoly's output and price? How would a monopoly change its behavior if the profit tax were 10% rather than 25%? (*Hint:* You may assume that the profit tax refers to the tribe's economic profit.)

4. When is a monopoly unlikely to be profitable? (*Hint*: Discuss the relationship between market demand and average cost.)

5. A monopoly has a constant marginal cost of production of $1 per unit and a fixed cost of $10. Draw the firm's MC, AVC, and AC curves. Add a downward-sloping demand curve, and show the profit-maximizing quantity and price. Indicate the profit as an area on your diagram. Show the deadweight loss.

*6. Can a firm be a natural monopoly if it has a U-shaped average cost curve? Why or why not?

7. Can a firm operating in the upward sloping portion of its average cost curve be a natural monopoly? Explain.

8. Using the information in the "Electric Power Utilities" application, if a utility produced 34 billion kWh per year—which is on the upward-sloping section of the average cost curve—would it be a natural monopoly? **A**

9. Show why a monopoly may operate in the upward- or downward-sloping section of its long-run average cost curve but a competitive firm will operate only in the upward-sloping section.

10. When will a monopoly set its price equal to its marginal cost?

11. Describe the effects on output and welfare if the government regulates a monopoly so that it may not charge a price above $\bar{p}$, which lies between the unregulated monopoly price and the optimally regulated price (determined by the intersection of the firm's marginal cost and the market demand curve).

12. Suppose that many similar price-taking consumers have a single good (candy bars). Jane has a monopoly in wood so she can set prices. Assume that no production is possible. Using an Edgeworth box, illustrate the monopoly optimum and show that it does not lie on the contract curve (isn't Pareto efficient).

13. A monopoly drug company produces a lifesaving medicine at a constant cost of $10 per dose. The demand for this medicine is perfectly inelastic at prices less than or equal to the $100 (per day) income of the 100 patients who need to take this drug daily. At a higher price, nothing is bought. Show the equilibrium price and quantity and the consumer and

producer surplus in a graph. Now the government imposes a price ceiling of $30. Show how the equilibrium, consumer surplus, and producer surplus change. What is the deadweight loss, if any, from this price control?

14. The price of wholesale milk dropped by 30.3% in 1999 as the Pennsylvania Milk Marketing Board lowered the regulated price. The price to consumers fell by substantially less than 30.3% in Philadelphia. Why? (*Hint*: Show that a monopoly will not necessarily lower its price by the same percentage as its constant marginal cost drops.)

15. Today, drug companies spend large sums to determine additional uses for their existing drugs. For example, GlaxoWellcome PLC, a pharmaceutical giant, learned that its drug bupropion hydrochloride is more effective than the nicotine patch for people trying to quit smoking. That drug is now sold as Zyban, but it was introduced in 1997 as an antidepressant, Wellbutrin. Projected 1999 sales were $250 million for Zyban and $590 million for Wellbutrin. Using a graph, show the demand curves for Wellbutrin and Zyban and the aggregate demand for this drug, bupropion hydrochloride. On the graph, indicate the quantity of pills sold for each use and total use at the current price. Why does Glaxo, the monopoly producer, set the same price, $1.16 a pill, for both drugs?

16. Once the copyright runs out on a book or music, it can legally be placed on the Internet for anyone to download. However, the U.S. Congress recently extended the copyright law to 95 years after the original publication. But in Australia and Europe, the copyright holds for only 50 years. Thus, an Australian Web site could post *Gone With the Wind*, a 1936 novel, or Elvis Presley's 1954 single "That's All Right," while a U.S. site could not. Obviously, this legal nicety won't stop American fans from downloading from Australian or European sites. Discuss how limiting the length of a copyright would affect the pricing used by the publisher of a novel. **A**

17. Are major-league baseball clubs profit-maximizing monopolies? Some observers of this market have contended that baseball club owners want to maximize attendance or revenue. Alexander (2001) says that one test of whether a firm is a profit-maximizing monopoly is to check whether the firm is operating in the elastic portion of its demand curve (which he finds is true). Why is that a relevant test? What would the elasticity be if a baseball club were maximizing revenue?

18. Hotels tend to charge a lot for phone calls from their rooms. Cell phones endangered this nice little "monopoly" business to the point that average telephone profit per available room at hotels in the United States fell from $637 in 2000 to $152 in 2003 (Christopher Elliott, "Mystery of the Cellphone That Doesn't Work at the Hotel," *New York Times*, September 7, 2004: C6). But now many travelers complain that their cell phones don't work in hotels. Though hotels deny that they are doing anything so nefarious as blocking signals, Netline Communications Technologies in Tel Aviv says that it has sold hundreds of cell phone jammers to hotels around the world. A Federal Communications Commission rule prohibits cell phone jammers, but it is unenforced. By one estimate, a device that could block all cell phone transmissions would cost $25,000 for a small hotel and $35,000 to $50,000 for a big chain hotel. Assume that the blocker lasts for one year. Under what conditions (in terms of profit per room, number of rooms, and so forth) would it pay for a hotel to install a jammer, assuming the law permits it? Explain your answer.

19. Bleyer Industries Inc., the only U.S. manufacturer of plastic Easter eggs, manufactures 250 million eggs each year. Over the past seven years, imports from China have cut into its business. In 2005, Bleyer filed for bankruptcy because the Chinese firms could produce the eggs at much lower costs ("U.S. Plastic Egg Industry a Shell of Its Former Self," *San Francisco Chronicle*, January 14, 2005). Use graphs to show how a competitive import industry could drive a monopoly out of business.

20. Draw an example of a monopoly with a linear demand curve and a constant marginal cost curve.

   a. Show the profit-maximizing price and output, p^* and Q^*, and identify the areas of consumer surplus, producer surplus, and deadweight loss. Also show the quantity, Q_c, that would be produced if the monopoly were to act like a price taker.

   b. Now suppose that the demand curve is a smooth concave-to-the-origin curve (whose ends hit the axes) that is tangent to the original demand curve at the point (Q^*, p^*). Explain why the monopoly equilibrium will be the same as with the linear demand curve. Show how much output the firm would produce if it acted like a price taker. Show how the welfare areas change.

   c. Repeat the exercises in part b if the demand curve is a smooth convex-to-the-origin curve (whose ends hit the axes) that is tangent to the original demand curve at the point (Q^*, p^*).

21. A country has a monopoly that is protected by a specific tariff, τ, on imported goods. The monopoly's profit-maximizing price is p^*. The world price of the

good is p_w, which is less than p^*. Because the price of imported goods with the tariff is $p_w + \tau$, no foreign goods are imported. Under WTO pressure the government removes the tariff so that the supply of foreign goods to the country's consumers is horizontal at p_w. Show how much the former monopoly produces and what price it charges. Show who gains and who loses from removing the tariff. (*Hint:* Look at the effect of government price regulation on a monopoly's demand curve in Section 4.7.) **A**

22. A monopoly chocolate manufacturer faces two types of consumers. The larger group, the hoi polloi, loves desserts and has a relatively flat, linear demand curve for chocolate. The smaller group, the snobs, is interested in buying chocolate only if the hoi polloi do not buy it. Given that the hoi polloi do not buy the chocolate, the snobs have a relatively steep, linear demand curve. Show the monopoly's possible outcomes—high price, low quantity, low price, high quantity—and explain the condition under which the monopoly chooses to cater to the snobs rather than to the hoi polloi. **A**

Problems

*23. Show mathematically that a monopoly may raise the price to consumers by more than the specific tax imposed on it. (*Hint:* One approach is to consider a monopoly facing a constant-elasticity demand curve and a constant marginal cost, m.)

24. The inverse demand curve a monopoly faces is

$$p = 100 - Q.$$

The firm's cost curve is $C(Q) = 10 + 5Q$. What is the profit-maximizing solution? How does your answer change if $C(Q) = 100 + 5Q$?

25. The inverse demand curve a monopoly faces is

$$p = 10Q^{-\frac{1}{2}}.$$

The firm's cost curve is $C(Q) = 5Q$. What is the profit-maximizing solution? **C**

26. If the inverse demand function facing a monopoly is $P(Q)$ and its cost function is $C(Q)$, show the effect of a specific tax, τ, on its profit-maximizing output. How does imposing τ affect its profit? **C**

27. In the Botox application, consumer surplus, triangle A, equals the deadweight loss, triangle C. Show that this equality is a result of the linear demand and constant marginal cost assumptions. **A**

28. Based on the information in the "Botox Patent Monopoly" application, what would happen to the equilibrium price and quantity if the government had collected a specific tax of $75 per vial of Botox? What welfare effects would such a tax have? **A**

29. Based on the information in the "Botox Patent Monopoly" application, what would happen to the equilibrium price and quantity if the government had set a price ceiling of $200 per vial of Botox? What welfare effects would such a tax have? **A**

30. The Commonwealth of Pennsylvania is the monopoly retailer of wine in the state. Suppose that Quaker Cabernet has no close substitutes and that the statewide inverse demand function for this wine is $p = 5 - 0.001Q$. The state purchases the wine on the wholesale market for $2 per bottle, and the state-operated liquor stores incur no other expenses to sell this wine.

   a. What are the state's profit-maximizing price and quantity?

   b. Neighboring New Jersey permits private retailers to sell wine. They face the same statewide demand curve as in Pennsylvania. No interstate wine trade is permitted. Suppose the New Jersey market for Quaker Cabernet is perfectly competitive. What is the equilibrium price and quantity?

   c. New Jersey taxes wine sales. While the retailers pay the taxes on wine sales, by raising prices they may pass on some or all of these taxes to consumers. Identify the specific tax (tax per bottle sold) for which New Jersey's equilibrium market price and quantity equal the Pennsylvania monopoly price and quantity. Given the quantity tax, show that New Jersey's tax revenue equals Pennsylvania's profit. **W**

31. Suppose all iPod owners consider only two options for downloading music to their MP3 players: purchase songs from iTunes or copy songs from friends' CDs. With these two options, suppose the weekly inverse market demand for the Rolling Stones' song "Satisfaction" is $p = 1.98 - 0.00198Q$. The marginal cost to Apple Inc. of downloading a song is zero.

   a. What is Apple's optimal price of "Satisfaction"? How many downloads of "Satisfaction" does Apple sell each week?

b. Now suppose that Apple sells a version of the iPod equipped with software in which songs played on the iPod must be downloaded from iTunes. For this iPod, the inverse market demand for "Satisfaction" is $p = 2.58 - 0.0129Q$. What is Apple's optimal price of downloads of "Satisfaction" for this new player? How many downloads of "Satisfaction" does Apple sell each week? **A, W**

32. In addition to the hard-drive-based iPod, Apple produces a flash-based audio player. Its 512MB iPod Shuffle (which does not have a hard drive) sold for $99 in 2005. According to iSuppli, Apple's per-unit cost of manufacturing the Shuffle is $45.37 (Brian Dipert, "Song Wars: Striking Back Against the iPod Empire," **www.reed-electronics.com**, June 9, 2005). What is Apple's price/marginal cost ratio? What is its Lerner Index? If we assume (possibly incorrectly) that Apple acts like a short-run profit-maximizing monopoly in pricing its iPod Shuffle, what elasticity of demand does Apple believe it faces? **A**

*33. Humana hospitals in 1991 charged very high prices relative to their marginal costs. For example, Humana's Suburban Hospital in Louisville charged patients $44.90 for a container of saline solution (salt water) that cost the hospital 81¢ (Douglas Frantz, "Congress Probes Hospital Costs—$9 Tylenols, $118 Heat Pads," *San Francisco Chronicle*, October 18, 1991: A2). Calculate the hospital's price/marginal cost ratio, its Lerner Index, and the demand elasticity, ε, that it faces for saline solution (assuming that it maximizes its profit).

34. According to the California Nurses Association, Tenet Healthcare hospitals mark up drugs substantially. At Tenet's Sierra Vista Regional Medical Center, drug prices are 1,840.80% of the hospital's costs (Chuck Squatriglia and Tyche Hendricks, "Tenet Hiked Drug Prices, Study Finds More Than Double U.S. Average," *San Francisco Chronicle*, November 24, 2002: A1, A10). Assuming Tenet is maximizing its profit, what is the elasticity of demand that Tenet believes it faces? What is its Lerner Index for drugs?

35. According to one estimate, the parts for a Segway Human Transporter—which has five gyroscopes, two tilt sensors, dual redundant motors, 10 microprocessors, and can travel up to 12.5 mph—cost at least $1,500 (Eric A. Taub, "Segway Transporter Slow to Catch On," *San Francisco Chronicle*, August 11, 2003: E4). Suppose that Segway's marginal cost is $2,000. Given that the Segway's price is $5,000, calculate the firm's price/marginal cost ratio, its Lerner Index, and

the elasticity of demand it believes it faces (assuming that it is trying to maximize its short-run profit).

36. In 2005, Apple introduced the Mac mini G4, a miniature computer that weighs only 2.9 pounds but comes fully loaded with lots of memory and a large hard disk. According to one estimate, the cost of production was $258 (Toni Duboise, "Low-cost Apple Mini Packs Punch, but BYO Peripherals," **www.eetimes.com**), while its suggested price was $499. Although other firms produce computers, the Mac is viewed as a different product by aficionados. What is Apple's price/marginal cost ratio? What is its Lerner Index? If we assume that Apple is a profit-maximizing monopoly, what elasticity of demand does it believe it faces for this tiny computer?

37. The U.S. Postal Service (USPS) has a constitutionally guaranteed monopoly on first-class mail. It currently charges 37¢ for a stamp, which is probably not the profit-maximizing price, as the USPS goal, allegedly, is to break even rather than to turn a profit. Following the postal services in Australia, Britain, Canada, Switzerland, and Ireland, the USPS has allowed Stamps.com to sell a sheet of twenty 37¢ stamps with a photo of your dog, your mommy, or whatever for $16.99 (that's 84.95¢ per stamp, or a nearly 230% markup). Stamps.com keeps the extra beyond the 37¢ it pays the USPS (Mary Fitzgerald, "Customized Stamps May Lick Postal Service's Finance Woes," *Boston Sunday Globe*, September 12, 2004: A23). What is the firm's Lerner Index? If Stamps.com is a profit-maximizing monopoly, what elasticity of demand does it face for a customized stamp?

38. In 1996, Florida voted on (and rejected) a 1¢-per-pound excise tax on refined cane sugar in the Florida Everglades Agricultural Area. Swinton and Thomas (2001) used linear supply and demand curves (based on elasticities estimated by Marks, 1993) to calculate the incidence from this tax given that the market is competitive. Their inverse demand curve was $p = 1.787 - 0.0004641Q$, and their inverse supply curve was $p = -0.4896 + 0.00020165Q$. Calculate the incidence of the tax that falls on consumers (Chapter 3) for a competitive market. If producers joined together to form a monopoly, and the supply curve is actually the monopoly's marginal cost curve, what is the incidence of the tax? (*Hint:* The incidence that falls on consumers is the difference between the equilibrium price with and without the tax divided by the tax. You should find that the incidence is 70% in a competitive market and 41% with a monopoly.) **A**

39. A monopoly manufactures its product in two factories with marginal cost functions $MC_1(Q_1)$ and

$MC_2(Q_2)$, where Q_1 is the quantity produced in the first factory and Q_2 is the quantity manufactured in the second factory. The monopoly's total output is $Q = Q_1 + Q_2$. Use a graph (or math) to determine how much total output the monopoly produces and how much it produces at each factory. (*Hint*: Consider the cases where the factories have constant marginal costs—not necessarily equal—and where they have upward-sloping marginal cost curves.)

40. A monopoly sells music CDs. It has a constant marginal and average cost of 20. It faces two groups of potential customers: honest and dishonest people. The dishonest and the honest consumers' demand functions are the same: $p = 120 - Q$.

    a. If it is not possible for the dishonest customers to steal the music, what are the monopoly's profit-maximizing price and quantity? What is its profit? What are the consumer surplus, producer surplus, and welfare?

    b. Answer the same questions as in the previous part if the dishonest customers can pirate the music.

    c. How do consumer surplus, producer surplus, and welfare change if piracy occurs?   **A**

*41. A monopoly produces a good with a network externality at a constant marginal and average cost of 2. In the first period, its inverse demand curve is $p = 10 - Q$. In the second period, its demand is $p = 10 - Q$ unless it sells at least $Q = 8$ units in the first period. If it meets or exceeds this target, then the demand curve rotates out by α (it sells α times as many units for any given price), so that its inverse demand curve is $p = 10 - Q/\alpha$. The monopoly knows that it can sell no output after the second period. The monopoly's objective is to maximize the sum of its profits over the two periods. In the first period, should the monopoly set the output that maximizes its profit in that period? How does your answer depend on α? (*Hint*: See the discussion of the two-period monopoly model in Section 4.8 of this chapter.)   **A**

42. A monopoly's production function is Cobb-Douglas: $Q = L^{\frac{1}{2}}K^{\frac{1}{2}}$, where L is labor and K is capital. As a result, the marginal product functions are $MP_L = \frac{1}{2}K^{\frac{1}{2}}/L^{\frac{1}{2}}$ and $MP_K = \frac{1}{2}L^{\frac{1}{2}}/K^{\frac{1}{2}}$. The demand function is $p = 100 - Q$. The wage, w, is \$1 per hour, and the rental cost of capital, r, is \$4.

    a. What is the equation of the (long-run) expansion path? Illustrate in a graph.

    b. Derive the long-run total cost curve equation as a function of q.

    c. What quantity maximizes this firm's profit?

    d. Find the optimal input combination that produces the profit-maximizing quantity. Illustrate with a graph.

Chapter 5

Pricing

Everything is worth what its purchaser will pay for it. —Publilius Syrus (1st century B.C.)

Why does Disneyland charge local residents $149 for one-year admissions but out-of-towners $209? Why are airline fares less if you book in advance and stay over a Saturday night? Why are some goods, among them computers and software, sold bundled together at a single price? To answer these questions, we need to examine how monopolies set prices.

Monopolies (and other noncompetitive firms) can use information about individual consumers' demand curves to increase their profits. Instead of setting a single price, such firms use **nonuniform pricing**: charging consumers different prices for the same product or charging a single customer a price that depends on the number of units the customer buys. By replacing a single price with nonuniform pricing, the firm raises its profit.

Why can a monopoly earn a higher profit from using a nonuniform pricing scheme than from setting a single price? A monopoly that uses nonuniform prices can capture some or all of the consumer surplus and deadweight loss that results if the monopoly sets a single price. As we saw in Chapter 4, a monopoly that sets a high single price only sells to the customers who value the good the most, and those customers retain some consumer surplus. The monopoly loses sales to other customers who value the good less than the single price. These lost sales are a *deadweight loss*: the value of these potential sales in excess of the cost of producing the good. A monopoly that uses nonuniform pricing captures additional consumer surplus by raising the price to customers that value the good the most. By lowering its price to other customers, the monopoly makes additional sales, thereby changing what would otherwise be deadweight loss into profit.

We examine several types of nonuniform pricing including price discrimination, two-part tariffs, and tie-in sales. The most common form of nonuniform pricing is **price discrimination**, whereby a firm charges consumers different prices for the same good. Many magazines price discriminate by charging college students less for subscriptions than they charge older adults. If a magazine were to start setting a high price for everyone, many college student subscribers—who are sensitive to price increases (have relatively elastic demands)—would cancel their subscriptions. If the magazine were to let everyone buy at the college student price, it would gain few additional subscriptions because most potential older adult subscribers are relatively insensitive to the price, and it would earn less from those older adults who are willing to pay the higher price. Thus the magazine makes more profit by price discriminating.

Some noncompetitive firms that cannot practically price discriminate use other forms of nonuniform pricing to increase profits. One method is for a firm to charge a *two-part tariff*, whereby a customer pays one fee for the right to buy the good and another price for each unit purchased. Health club members pay an annual fee to join the club and then shell out an additional amount each time they use the facilities.

Another type of nonlinear pricing is a *tie-in sale*, whereby a customer may buy one good only if also agreeing to buy another good or service. Vacation package deals may include airfare and a hotel room for a single price. Some restaurants provide only full-course dinners: A single price buys an appetizer, a main dish, and dessert. A firm may

nonuniform pricing charging consumers different prices for the same product or charging a single customer a price that depends on the number of units the customer buys

price discrimination practice in which a firm charges consumers different prices for the same good sell copiers under the condition that customers agree to buy all future copier service and supplies from it.

In this chapter, we examine six main topics	1. **Why and how firms price discriminate:** A firm can increase its profit by price discriminating if it has market power, can identify which customers are more price sensitive than others, and can prevent customers who pay low prices from reselling to those who pay high prices.
	2. **Perfect price discrimination:** If a monopoly can charge the maximum each customer is willing to pay for each unit of output, the monopoly captures all potential consumer surplus, and the efficient (competitive) level of output is sold.
	3. **Quantity discrimination:** Some firms profit by charging different prices for large purchases than for small ones, which is a form of price discrimination.
	4. **Multimarket price discrimination:** Firms that cannot perfectly price discriminate may charge a group of consumers with relatively elastic demands a lower price than other groups of consumers.
	5. **Two-part tariffs:** By charging consumers a fee for the right to buy any number of units and a price per unit, firms earn higher profits than they do by charging a single price per unit.
	6. **Tie-in sales:** By requiring a customer to buy a second good or service along with the first, firms make higher profits than they do by selling the goods or services separately.

5.1 Why and How Firms Price Discriminate

A prince was once lost in the forest for many hours. Finally, he came upon an inn, where he was recognized immediately. He ordered a light meal of fried eggs. When he finished, the prince asked the innkeeper, "How much do I owe you for the eggs?"

The innkeeper replied, "Twenty-five rubles."

"Why such an exorbitant price?" asked the prince. "Is there a shortage of eggs in this area?"

"No, there is no shortage of eggs," the innkeeper replied. "We have plenty of eggs. But, there is a shortage of princes."[1]

Until now, we've examined how a monopoly sets its price if it charges all its customers the same price. However, many noncompetitive firms increase their profits by charging *nonuniform prices*, which vary across customers. We start by studying the most common form of nonuniform pricing: price discrimination.

WHY PRICE DISCRIMINATION PAYS

For almost any good or service, some consumers are willing to pay more than others. A firm that sets a single price faces a trade-off between charging consumers who really want the good as much as they are willing to pay and charging a low

---

[1]Thanks to Steve Salop.

enough price that the firm doesn't lose sales to less enthusiastic customers. As a result, the firm usually sets an intermediate price. A price-discriminating firm that varies its prices across customers avoids this trade-off.

A firm earns a higher profit from price discrimination than from uniform pricing for two reasons. First, a price-discriminating firm charges a higher price to customers who are willing to pay more than the uniform price, capturing some or all of their consumer surplus—the difference between what a good is worth to a consumer and what the consumer paid—under uniform pricing. Second, a price-discriminating firm sells to some people who were not willing to pay as much as the uniform price.

We use a pair of extreme examples to illustrate the two benefits of price discrimination to firms—capturing more of the consumer surplus and selling to more customers. These examples are extreme in the sense that the firm sets a uniform price at the price the most enthusiastic consumers are willing to pay or at the price the least enthusiastic consumers are willing to pay, rather than at an intermediate level.

Suppose that the only movie theater in town has two types of patrons: college students and senior citizens. The college student will see the Saturday night movie if the price is $10 or less, and the senior citizens will attend if the price is $5 or less. For simplicity, we assume that there is no cost in showing the movie, so profit is the same as revenue. The theater is large enough to hold all potential customers, so the marginal cost of admitting one more customer is zero. Table 5.1 shows how pricing affects the theater's profit.

In panel a, there are 10 college students and 20 senior citizens. If the theater charges everyone $5, its profit is $150 = $5 × (10 college students + 20 senior citizens). If it charges $10, the senior citizens do not go to the movie, so the theater makes only $100. Thus if the theater is going to charge everyone the same price, it maximizes its profit by setting the price at $5. Charging less than $5 makes no sense because the same number of people go to the movie as go when $5 is charged. Charging between $5 and $10 is less profitable than charging $10 because no extra seniors go and the college students are willing to pay $10. Charging more than $10 results in no customers.

TABLE 5.1   A Theater's Profit Based on the Pricing Method Used

(a) No Extra Customers from Price Discrimination

Pricing	Profit from 10 College Students	Profit from 20 Senior Citizens	Total Profit
Uniform, $5	$50	$100	$150
Uniform, $10	$100	$0	$100
Price discrimination*	$100	$100	$200

(b) Extra Customers from Price Discrimination

Pricing	Profit from 10 College Students	Profit from 5 Senior Citizens	Total Profit
Uniform, $5	$50	$25	$75
Uniform, $10	$100	$0	$100
Price discrimination*	$100	$25	$125

*The theater price discriminates by charging college students $10 and senior citizens $5.

Notes: College students go to the theater if they are charged no more than $10. Senior citizens are willing to pay up to $5. The theater's marginal cost for an extra customer is zero.

At a price of $5, the seniors have no consumer surplus: They pay exactly what seeing the movie is worth to them. Seeing the movie is worth $10 to the college students, but they have to pay only $5, so each has a consumer surplus of $5, and their total consumer surplus is $50.

If the theater can price discriminate by charging senior citizens $5 and college students $10, its profit increases to $200. Its profit rises because the theater makes as much from the seniors as before but gets an extra $50 from the college students. By price discriminating, the theater sells the same number of seats but makes more money from the college students, capturing all the consumer surplus they had under uniform pricing. Neither group of customers has any consumer surplus if the theater price discriminates.

In panel b, there are 10 college students and 5 senior citizens. If the theater must charge a single price, it charges $10. Only college students see the movie, so the theater's profit is $100. (If it charges $5, both students and seniors go to the theater, but its profit is only $75.) If the theater can price discriminate and charge seniors $5 and college students $10, its profit increases to $125. Here the gain from price discrimination comes from selling extra tickets to seniors (not from making more money on the same number of tickets, as in panel a). The theater earns as much from the students as before and makes more from the seniors, and neither group enjoys consumer surplus. These examples illustrate that firms can make a higher profit by price discriminating, either by charging some existing customers more or by selling extra units. Leslie (1997) finds that Broadway theaters increase their profits 5% by price discriminating rather than using uniform prices.

● **APPLICATION**

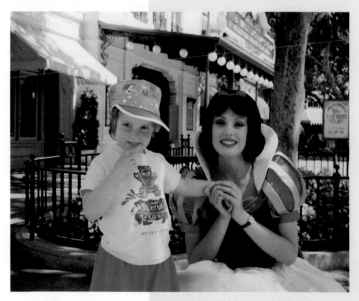

Disneyland Pricing

Disneyland, in southern California, is a well-run operation that rarely misses a trick when it comes to increasing profits. (Indeed, Disneyland mints money: When you enter the park, you can exchange U.S. currency for Disney dollars, which can be spent only in the park.)[2]

In 2005, Disneyland charged most adults $76 for a park hopper ticket (good for both Disneyland and Disney's California Adventure park) but charged southern Californians only $71. This policy of giving locals discounts makes sense if visitors from afar are willing to pay more than locals and if Disneyland can prevent locals from selling discount tickets to non-locals. Imagine a Midwesterner who's never been to Disneyland before and wants to visit. Travel accounts for most of the cost of the trip, so an extra $5 for entrance to Disneyland makes little percentage difference in the total cost of a

---

[2]According to **www.babycenter.com**, it costs $832,056 to raise a child from cradle through college. Parents can cut that total in half, however: They don't *have* to take their kids to Disneyland.

visit and hence doesn't greatly affect that person's decision whether or not to go. In contrast, for a local who has gone to Disneyland many times and for whom the entrance price is a larger share of the cost of the visit, a slightly higher price might prevent a visit.

Charging both groups the same price is not in Disney's best interest. If Disney were to charge the higher price to everyone, many locals would stay away. If Disney were to use the lower price for everyone, it would be charging nonresidents much less than they are willing to pay.

See Question 6.

By setting different prices for the two groups, Disney increases its profit if it can prevent the locals from selling discount tickets to others. Disney prevents resales by checking a purchaser's driver's license and requiring that the ticket be used for same-day entrance.[3]

WHO CAN PRICE DISCRIMINATE

Not all firms can price discriminate. For a firm to price discriminate successfully, three conditions must be met.

First, a firm must have *market power*; otherwise, it cannot charge any consumer more than the competitive price. A monopoly, an oligopoly firm, a monopolistically competitive firm, or a cartel may be able to price discriminate. A competitive firm cannot price discriminate.

Second, consumers must *differ* in their sensitivity to price (demand elasticities), and a firm must be able to *identify* how consumers differ in this sensitivity.[4] The movie theater knows that college students and senior citizens differ in their willingness to pay for a ticket, and Disneyland knows that tourists and natives differ in their willingness to pay for admission. In both cases, the firms can identify members of these two groups by using driver's licenses or other forms of identification. Similarly, if a firm knows that each individual's demand curve slopes downward, it may charge each customer a higher price for the first unit of a good than for subsequent units.

Third, a firm must be able to *prevent or limit resales* to higher-price-paying customers by customers whom the firm charges relatively low prices. Price discrimination doesn't work if resales are easy because the firm would be able to make only low-price sales. A movie theater can charge different prices because senior citizens, who enter the theater as soon as they buy the ticket, do not have time to resell it.

Except for competitive firms, the first two conditions—market power and ability to identify groups with different price sensitivities—frequently hold. Usually, the biggest obstacle to price discrimination is a firm's inability to prevent resales. In

---

[3]Shivani Sopory, one of my students, said that the Disneyland example "reminded me of the last time I was in India. At all the tourist attractions, they charge foreigners more than Indians. At the Taj Mahal, Indians pay 20 rupees (45¢) and foreigners are charged 750 rupees ($17.40). I remember two sites distinctly, Jantar Mantar and Red Fort in New Delhi, because the guards stopped me to ask me to pay more on my last trip to India about a year ago."

[4]Even if consumers are identical, price discrimination is possible if each consumer has a downward-sloping demand curve for the monopoly's product. To price discriminate over the units purchased by a consumer, the monopoly has to know how the elasticity of demand varies with the number of units purchased.

some markets, however, resales are inherently difficult or impossible, firms can take actions that prevent resales, or government actions or laws prevent resales.

PREVENTING RESALES

Resales are difficult or impossible for most *services* and when *transaction costs are high*. If a plumber charges you less than your neighbor for clearing a pipe, you cannot make a deal with your neighbor to resell this service. The higher the transaction costs a consumer must incur to resell a good, the less likely that resales will occur. Suppose that you are able to buy a jar of pickles for $1 less than the usual price. Could you practically find and sell this jar to someone else, or would the transaction costs be prohibitive? The more valuable a product or the more widely consumed it is, the more likely it is that transaction costs are low enough that resales occur.

Some firms act to raise transaction costs or otherwise make resales difficult. If your college requires that someone with a student ticket must show a student identification card with a picture on it before being admitted to a sporting event, you'll find it difficult to resell your low-price tickets to nonstudents, who must pay higher prices. When students at some universities buy computers at lower-than-usual prices, they must sign a contract that forbids them to resell the computer.

Similarly, a firm can prevent resales by *vertically integrating*: participating in more than one successive stage of the production and distribution chain for a good or service. Alcoa, the former aluminum monopoly, wanted to sell aluminum ingots to producers of aluminum wire at a lower price than was set for producers of aluminum aircraft parts. If Alcoa did so, however, the wire producers could easily resell their ingots. By starting its own wire production firm, Alcoa prevented such resales and was able to charge high prices to firms that manufactured aircraft parts (Perry, 1980).

Governments frequently aid price discrimination by preventing resales. State and federal governments require that milk producers, under penalty of law, price discriminate by selling milk at a higher price for fresh use than for processing (cheese, ice cream) and forbid resales. Government *tariffs* (taxes on imports) limit resales by making it expensive to buy goods in a low-price country and resell them in a high-price country. In some cases, laws prevent such reselling explicitly. Under U.S. trade laws, certain brand-name perfumes may not be sold in the United States except by their manufacturers.

NOT ALL PRICE DIFFERENCES ARE PRICE DISCRIMINATION

Not every seller who charges consumers different prices is price discriminating. Hotels charge newlyweds more for bridal suites. Is that price discrimination? Some hotel managers say no. They contend that honeymooners, unlike other customers, always steal mementos, so the price differential reflects an actual cost differential.

The price for all issues of *TV Guide* magazine for a year is $103.48 if you buy it at the newsstand, $56.68 for a standard subscription, and $39.52 for a college student subscription. The difference between the newsstand cost and the standard subscription cost reflects, at least in part, the higher cost of selling at a newsstand rather than mailing the magazine directly to customers, so this price difference does not reflect pure price discrimination. The price difference between the standard subscription rate and the college student rate reflects pure price discrimination because the two subscriptions are identical in every respect except price.

perfect price discrimination (*first-degree price discrimination*) situation in which a firm sells each unit at the maximum amount any customer is willing to pay for it, so prices differ across customers and a given customer may pay more for some units than for others

quantity discrimination (*second-degree price discrimination*) situation in which a firm charges a different price for large quantities than for small quantities but all customers who buy a given quantity pay the same price

TYPES OF PRICE DISCRIMINATION

There are three main types of price discrimination. With **perfect price discrimination**—also called *first-degree price discrimination*—the firm sells each unit at the maximum amount any customer is willing to pay for it, so prices differ across customers, and a given customer may pay more for some units than for others.

With **quantity discrimination** (*second-degree price discrimination*), the firm charges a different price for large quantities than for small quantities, but all customers who buy a given quantity pay the same price. With **multimarket price discrimination** (*third-degree price discrimination*), the firm charges different groups of customers different prices, but it charges a given customer the same price for every unit of output sold. Typically, not all customers pay different prices—the firm sets different prices only for a few groups of customers. Because this last type of discrimination is the most common, the phrase *price discrimination* is often used to mean *multimarket price discrimination*.

In addition to price discriminating, many firms use other, more complicated types of nonuniform pricing. Later in this chapter, we examine two other frequently used nonuniform pricing methods—two-part tariffs and tie-in sales—that are similar to quantity discrimination.

multimarket price discrimination (*third-degree price discrimination*) a situation in which a firm charges different groups of customers different prices but charges a given customer the same price for every unit of output sold

reservation price the maximum amount a person would be willing to pay for a unit of output

5.2   Perfect Price Discrimination

If a firm with market power knows exactly how much each customer is willing to pay for each unit of its good and it can prevent resales, the firm charges each person his or her **reservation price**: the maximum amount a person would be willing to pay for a unit of output. Such an all-knowing firm *perfectly price discriminates*. By selling each unit of its output to the customer who values it the most at the maximum price that person is willing to pay, the perfectly price-discriminating monopoly captures all possible consumer surplus. For example, the managers of the Suez Canal set tolls on an individual basis, taking into account many factors such as weather and each ship's alternative routes.

We first show how a firm uses its information about consumers to perfectly price discriminate. We then compare the perfectly price-discriminating monopoly to competition and single-price monopoly. By showing that the same quantity is produced as would be produced by a competitive market and that the last unit of output sells for the marginal cost, we demonstrate that perfect price discrimination is efficient. We then illustrate how the perfect price discrimination equilibrium differs from single-price monopoly by using the Botox application from Chapter 4. Finally, we discuss how firms obtain the information they need to perfectly price discriminate.

HOW A FIRM PERFECTLY PRICE DISCRIMINATES

Suppose that a monopoly has market power, can prevent resales, and has enough information to perfectly price discriminate. The monopoly sells each unit at its reservation price, which is the height of the demand curve: the maximum price consumers will pay for a given amount of output.

Figure 5.1 illustrates how this perfectly price-discriminating firm maximizes its profit (see Appendix 5A for a mathematical treatment). The figure shows that the first customer is willing to pay $6 for a unit, the next is willing to pay $5, and so forth. This perfectly price-discriminating firm sells its first unit of output for $6.

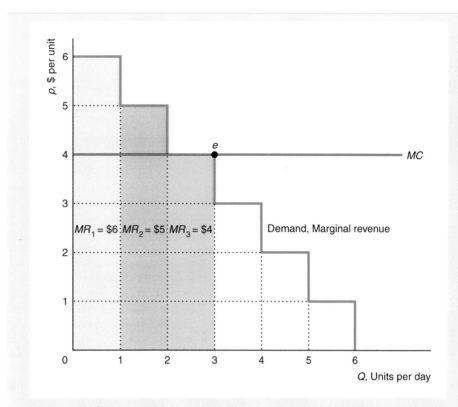

Figure 5.1 **Perfect Price Discrimination.** The monopoly can charge $6 for the first unit, $5 for the second, and $4 for the third, as the demand curve shows. Its marginal revenue is $MR_1 = \$6$ for the first unit, $MR_2 = \$5$ for the second unit, and $MR_3 = \$4$ for the third unit. Thus the demand curve is also the marginal revenue curve. Because the firm's marginal and average cost is $4 per unit, it is unwilling to sell at a price below $4, so it sells 3 units, point *e*, and breaks even on the last unit.

Having sold the first unit, the firm can get at most $5 for its second unit. The firm must drop its price by $1 for each successive unit it sells.

A perfectly price-discriminating monopoly's marginal revenue is the same as its price. As the figure shows, the firm's marginal revenue is $MR_1 = \$6$ on the first unit, $MR_2 = \$5$ on the second unit, and $MR_3 = \$4$ on the third unit. As a result, *the firm's marginal revenue curve is its demand curve.*

This firm has a constant marginal cost of $4 per unit. It pays for the firm to produce the first unit because the firm sells that unit for $6, so its marginal revenue exceeds its marginal cost by $2. Similarly, the firm certainly wants to sell the second unit for $5, which also exceeds its marginal cost. The firm breaks even when it sells the third unit for $4. The firm is unwilling to sell more than 3 units because its marginal cost would exceed its marginal revenue on all successive units. Thus like any profit-maximizing firm, a perfectly price-discriminating firm produces at point *e*, where its marginal revenue curve intersects its marginal cost curve. (If you find it upsetting that the firm is indifferent between producing two and three units, assume that the firm's marginal cost is $3.99 so that it definitely wants to produce three units.)

This perfectly price-discriminating firm earns revenues of $MR_1 + MR_2 + MR_3 =$ $6 + $5 + $4 = $15, which is the area under its marginal revenue curve up to the number of units, 3, it sells. If the firm has no fixed cost, its cost of producing 3 units is $12 = 4×3, so its profit is $3.

APPLICATION

Amazon Is Watching You

Amazon, a giant among e-commerce vendors, collects an enormous amount of information about its 23 million customers' tastes and willingness to buy. If you've shopped at Amazon, you've probably noticed that its Web site now greets you by name (thanks to a *cookie* it leaves on your computer, which provides information about you to Amazon's Web site).

In 2000, the firm decided to use this information to engage in *dynamic pricing*, where the price it charges its customers today depends on these customers' actions in the recent past—including what they bought, how much they paid, and whether they paid for high-speed shipping—and personal data such as where they live. Several Amazon customers discovered this practice. One man reported on the Web site DVDTalk.com that he had bought Julie Taylor's "Titus" for $24.49. The next week, he returned to Amazon and saw that the price had jumped to $26.24. As an experiment, he removed the cookie that identified him, and found that the price dropped to $22.74.

Presumably, Amazon reasoned that a returning customer was less likely to compare prices across Web sites than was a new customer, and was pricing accordingly. Other DVDTalk.com visitors reported that regular Amazon customers were charged 3% to 5% more than new customers.

Amazon announced that its pricing variations stopped as soon as it started receiving complaints from DVDTalk members. It claimed that the variations were random and designed only to determine price elasticities. A spokesperson explained "This was a pure and simple price test. This was not dynamic pricing. We don't do that and have no plans ever to do that." Right. An Amazon customer service representative called it dynamic pricing in an e-mail to a DVDTalk member, allowing that dynamic pricing was a common practice among firms. A 2003 experiment, **www.managingchange.com/dynamic/survey/analysis.htm**, suggests that Amazon did not continue to use dynamic pricing.

See Question 8.

PERFECT PRICE DISCRIMINATION: EFFICIENT BUT HURTS CONSUMERS

A perfect price discrimination equilibrium is efficient and maximizes total welfare, where welfare is defined as the sum of consumer surplus and producer surplus. As such, this equilibrium has more in common with a competitive equilibrium than with a single-price-monopoly equilibrium.

If the market in Figure 5.2 is competitive, the intersection of the demand curve and the marginal cost curve, MC, determines the competitive equilibrium at e_c, where price is p_c and quantity is Q_c. Consumer surplus is $A + B + C$, producer surplus is $D + E$, and there is no deadweight loss. The market is efficient because the price, p_c, equals the marginal cost, MC_c.

With a single-price monopoly (which charges all its customers the same price because it cannot distinguish among them), the intersection of the MC curve and the single-price monopoly's marginal revenue curve, MC_s, determines the output, Q_s. The monopoly operates at e_s, where it charges p_s. The deadweight loss from

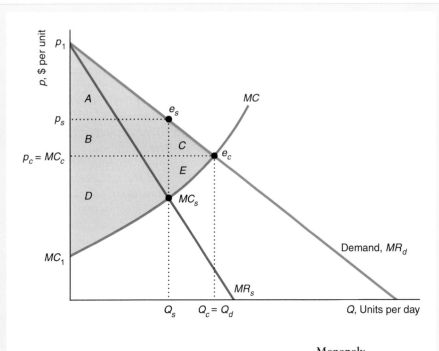

| | | Monopoly | |
| | | | |
	Competition	Single Price	Perfect Price Discrimination
Consumer surplus, CS	$A + B + C$	A	0
Producer surplus, PS	$D + E$	$B + D$	$A + B + C + D + E$
Welfare, $W = CS + PS$	$A + B + C + D + E$	$A + B + D$	$A + B + C + D + E$
Deadweight loss	0	$C + E$	0

Figure 5.2 **Competitive, Single-Price, and Perfect Discrimination Equilibria.** In the competitive market equilibrium, e_c, price is p_c, quantity is Q_c, consumer surplus is $A + B + C$, producer surplus is $D + E$, and there is no deadweight loss. In the single-price monopoly equilibrium, e_s, price is p_s, quantity is Q_s, consumer surplus falls to A, producer surplus is $B + D$, and deadweight loss is $C + E$. In the perfect discrimination equilibrium, the monopoly sells each unit at the customer's reservation price on the demand curve. It sells Q_d $(= Q_c)$ units, where the last unit is sold at its marginal cost. Customers have no consumer surplus, but there is no deadweight loss.

monopoly is $C + E$. This efficiency loss is due to the monopoly's charging a price, p_s, that's above its marginal cost, MC_s, so less is sold than in a competitive market.

A perfectly price-discriminating monopoly sells each unit at its reservation price, which is the height of the demand curve. As a result, the firm's marginal revenue curve, MR_d, is the same as its demand curve. The firm sells the first unit for p_1 to the consumer who will pay the most for the good. The firm's marginal cost for that unit is MC_1, so it makes $p_1 - MC_1$ on that unit. The firm receives a lower price and has a higher marginal cost for each successive unit. It sells the Q_d unit for p_c, where its marginal revenue curve, MR_d, intersects the marginal cost curve, MC, so it just covers its marginal cost on the last unit. The firm is unwilling to sell additional units because its marginal revenue would be less than the marginal cost of producing them.

The perfectly price-discriminating monopoly's total producer surplus on the Q_d units it sells is the area below its demand curve and above its marginal cost curve, $A + B + C + D + E$. Its profit is the producer surplus minus its fixed cost, if any. Consumers receive no consumer surplus because each consumer pays his or her reservation price. The perfectly price-discriminating monopoly's equilibrium has *no deadweight loss* because the last unit is sold at a price, p_c, that equals the marginal cost, MC_c, as in a competitive market. Thus both a perfect price discrimination equilibrium and a competitive equilibrium are efficient.

The perfect price discrimination equilibrium differs from the competitive equilibrium in two ways. First, in the competitive equilibrium, everyone is charged a price equal to the equilibrium marginal cost, $p_c = MC_c$; however, in the perfect price discrimination equilibrium, only the last unit is sold at that price. The other units are sold at customers' reservation prices, which are greater than p_c. Second, consumers receive some welfare (consumer surplus, $A + B + C$) in a competitive market, whereas a perfectly price-discriminating monopoly captures all the welfare. Thus perfect price discrimination doesn't reduce efficiency—the output and total welfare are the same as under competition—but it does redistribute income away from consumers: consumers are much better off under competition.

Is a single-price or perfectly price-discriminating monopoly better for consumers? The perfect price discrimination equilibrium is more efficient than the single-price monopoly equilibrium because more output is produced. A single-price monopoly, however, takes less consumer surplus from consumers than a perfectly price-discriminating monopoly. Consumers who put a very high value on the good are better off under single-price monopoly, where they have consumer surplus, than with perfect price discrimination, where they have none. Consumers with lower reservation prices who purchase from the perfectly price-discriminating monopoly but not from the single-price monopoly have no consumer surplus in either case. All the social gain from the extra output goes to the perfectly price-discriminating firm. Consumer surplus is greatest with competition, lower with single-price monopoly, and eliminated by perfect price discrimination.

APPLICATION

Botox Revisited

We illustrate how perfect price discrimination differs from competition and single-price monopoly using the application on Allergan's Botox from Chapter 4. The graph shows a linear demand curve for Botox and a constant marginal cost (and average variable cost) of $25 per vial. If the market had been competitive (price equal to marginal cost at e_c), consumer surplus would have been triangle $A + B + C = \$750$ million per year, and there would have been no producer surplus or deadweight loss. In the single-price monopoly equilibrium, e_s, the Botox vials sell for $400, and one million vials are sold. The corresponding consumer surplus is triangle $A = \$187.5$ million per year, producer surplus is rectangle $B = \$375$ million, and the deadweight loss is triangle $C = \$187.5$ million.

If Allergan could perfectly price discriminate, its producer surplus would double to $A + B + C = \$750$ million per year, and consumers would obtain no consumer surplus. The marginal consumer would pay the marginal cost of $25, the same as in a competitive market.

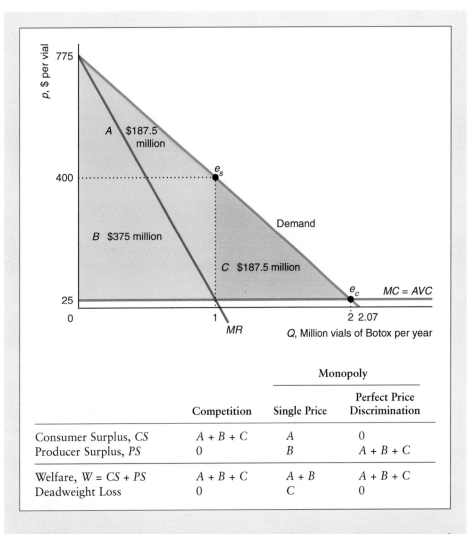

		Monopoly	
	Competition	Single Price	Perfect Price Discrimination
Consumer Surplus, *CS*	A + B + C	A	0
Producer Surplus, *PS*	0	B	A + B + C
Welfare, W = CS + PS	A + B + C	A + B	A + B + C
Deadweight Loss	0	C	0

Allergan's inability to perfectly price discriminate costs the company and society dearly. The profit of the single-price monopoly, B = $187.5 million per day, is lower than that of a perfectly price-discriminating monopoly by A + C = $562.5 million per year. Similarly society's welfare under single-price monopoly is lower than from perfect price discrimination by the deadweight loss, C, of $187.5 million per year.

See Question 12.

SOLVED PROBLEM 5.1

How does welfare change if the movie theater described in Table 5.1 goes from charging a single price to perfectly price discriminating?

Answer

1. *Calculate welfare for panel a (a) if the theater sets a single price and (b) if it perfectly price discriminates, and (c) compare them:* (a) If the theater sets the profit-maximizing single price of $5, it sells 30 tickets and makes a profit of

$150. The 20 senior citizen customers are paying their reservation price, so they have no consumer surplus. The 10 college students have reservation prices of $10, so their consumer surplus is $50. Thus welfare is $200: the sum of the profit, $150, and the consumer surplus, $50. (b) If the firm perfectly price discriminates, it charges seniors $5 and college students $10. Because the theater is charging all customers their reservation prices, there is no consumer surplus. The firm's profit rises to $200. (c) Thus *welfare is the same under both pricing systems where output stays the same.*

2. *Calculate welfare for panel b (a) if the theater sets a single price and (b) if it perfectly price discriminates, and (c) compare them:* (a) If the theater sets the profit-maximizing single price of $10, only college students attend and have no consumer surplus. The theater's profit is $100, so total welfare is $100. (b) With perfect price discrimination, there is no consumer surplus, but profit increases to $125, so welfare rises to $125. (c) Thus *welfare is greater with perfect price discrimination where output increases.* (The result that welfare increases if and only if output rises holds generally.)

TRANSACTION COSTS AND PERFECT PRICE DISCRIMINATION

Although some firms come close to perfect price discrimination, many more firms set a single price or use another nonlinear pricing method. Transaction costs are a major reason why these firms do not perfectly price discriminate: It is too difficult or costly to gather information about each customer's price sensitivity. Recent advances in computer technologies, however, have lowered these costs, causing hotels, car and truck rental companies, cruise lines, and airlines to price discriminate more often.

Private colleges request and receive financial information from students, which allows the schools to nearly perfectly price discriminate. The schools give partial scholarships as a means of reducing tuition to relatively poor students.

Many auto dealerships try to increase their profit by perfectly price discriminating, charging each customer the most that customer is willing to pay. These firms hire salespeople to ascertain potential customers' willingness to pay for a car and to bargain with them. Not all car companies believe that it pays to price discriminate in this way, however. As we saw in Chapter 1, Saturn charges all customers the same price, believing that the transaction costs (including wages of salespeople) of such information gathering and bargaining exceed the benefits to the firm of charging customers differential prices.

Many other firms believe that, taking the transaction costs into account, it pays to use quantity discrimination, multimarket price discrimination, or other nonlinear pricing methods rather than try to perfectly price discriminate. We now turn to these alternative approaches.

SOLVED PROBLEM 5.2

Competitive firms are the customers of a union, which is the monopoly supplier of labor services. Show the union's "producer surplus" if it perfectly price discriminates. Then suppose that the union makes the firms a take-it-or-leave-it offer: They must guarantee to hire a minimum of H^* hours of work at a wage of w^*, or they can hire no one. Show that by setting w* and H* appropriately, the union can achieve the same outcome as if it could perfectly price discriminate.

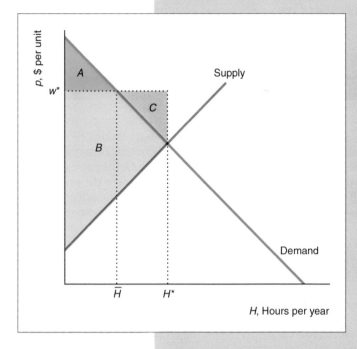

Answer

1. *Show the outcome and welfare areas if the union can perfectly price discriminate:* The figure shows the labor supply curve if the market were competitive. The union views this curve as its marginal cost curve. For each successive hour of labor service, the union sets the wage equal to the height of the demand curve and sells H* total hours of labor services (see the discussion of Figure 5.2). Its producer surplus equals the total welfare: A + B.

2. *Show that the firms will agree to hire H* at w*, and the union will capture all the surplus:* If the union gives the firms a take-it-or-leave-it offer of hiring H* hours at w* or of hiring no one, the firms will accept the offer because area C is the same size as area A in the figure. At a wage of w*, the firms have "consumer surplus" (the amount they are willing to pay above the wage for a given amount of labor services) of A for the first $\bar{H}$ hours of work, but they have negative consumer surplus of C for the remaining $H^* - \bar{H}$ hours of work. Thus, they have no consumer surplus overall, so they are indifferent between hiring the workers or not. The union's producer surplus is B + C, which equals its surplus if it perfectly price discriminated: A + B. Similarly, the number of hours of labor service provided, H*, is the same under both pricing schemes.

See Question 13.

● APPLICATION

Unions that Have It All

Most unions act as a single-price monopoly of labor services. They set a wage and allow their customers to determine how many units of labor services to purchase. However, a few unions set both wages and a minimum number of work hours that employers must provide. Such contracts are common only in the transportation industry (excluding railroads and airplanes).

The International Longshore and Warehouse Union (ILWU) negotiates with the companies represented by the Pacific Maritime Association. The 10,500 union workers at West Coast ports handle $300 billion worth of goods per year. The registered union workers earn at least $80,000 (and some estimates set the figure at $100,000) per year with benefits and other perks worth about $42,000. The union contract in effect through 2008 guarantees a weekly income for each worker (it effectively sets the minimum number of hours). However, the number of dockworkers has shrunk over the years as firms have automated to become more efficient. Consequently, the union has insisted that the lost positions be replaced with new clerical positions.

5.3   Quantity Discrimination

Many firms are unable to determine which customers have the highest reservation prices. Such firms may know, however, that most customers are willing to pay more for the first unit than for successive units: The typical customer's demand curve is downward sloping. Such a firm can price discriminate by letting the price each customer pays vary with the number of units the customer buys. Here the price varies only with quantity: All customers pay the same price for a given quantity.

Not all quantity discounts are a form of price discrimination. Some reflect the reduction in a firm's cost with large-quantity sales. For example, the cost per ounce of selling a soft drink in a large cup is less than that of selling it in a smaller cup; the cost of cups varies little with size, and the cost of pouring and serving is the same. A restaurant offering quantity discounts on drinks may be passing on actual cost savings to larger purchasers rather than price discriminating. However, if the quantity discount is not due to cost differences, the firm is engaging in quantity discrimination. Moreover, a firm may quantity discriminate by charging customers who make large purchases more per unit than those who make small purchases.

Many utilities use *block-pricing* schedules, by which they charge one price for the first few units (a *block*) of usage and a different price for subsequent blocks. Both declining-block and increasing-block pricing are common.

The utility monopoly in Figure 5.3 faces a linear demand curve for each (identical) customer. The demand curve hits the vertical axis at $90 and the horizontal axis at 90 units. The monopoly has a constant marginal and average cost of $m = \$30$. Panel a shows how this monopoly maximizes its profit if it can quantity discriminate by setting two prices. The firm uses declining-block prices to maximize its profit. The monopoly charges a price of $70 on any quantity between 1 and 20—the first block—and $50 on any units beyond the first 20—the second block. (The point that determines the first block, $70 and 20 units, lies on the demand curve.) Given each consumer's demand curve, a consumer decides to buy 40 units and pays $1,400 (= $70 × 20) for the first block and $1,000 (= $50 × 20) for the second block. (See Appendix 5B for a mathematical analysis.)

If the monopoly can set only a single price (panel b), it produces where its marginal revenue equals its marginal cost, selling 30 units at $60 per unit. Thus by quantity discriminating instead of using a single price, the utility sells more units, 40 instead of 30, and makes a higher profit, $B = \$1,200$ instead of $F = \$900$. With quantity discounting, consumer surplus is lower, $A + C = \$400$ instead of $E = \$450$; welfare (consumer surplus plus producer surplus) is higher, $A + B + C = \$1,600$ instead of $E + F = \$1,350$; and deadweight loss is lower, $D = \$200$ instead of $G = \$450$. Thus in this example, the firm and society are better off with quantity discounting, but consumers as a group suffer.

The more block prices that the monopoly can set, the closer the monopoly can get to perfect price discrimination. The deadweight loss results from the monopoly

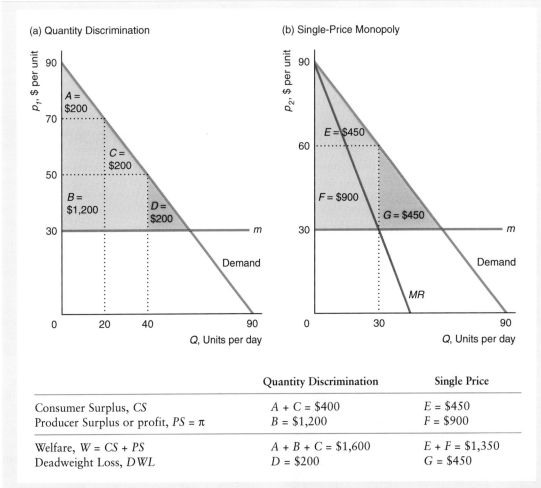

	Quantity Discrimination	Single Price
Consumer Surplus, CS	$A + C = \$400$	$E = \$450$
Producer Surplus or profit, $PS = \pi$	$B = \$1,200$	$F = \$900$
Welfare, $W = CS + PS$	$A + B + C = \$1,600$	$E + F = \$1,350$
Deadweight Loss, DWL	$D = \$200$	$G = \$450$

Figure 5.3 **Quantity Discrimination.** If this monopoly engages in quantity discounting, it makes a larger profit (producer surplus) than it does if it sets a single price, and welfare is greater. (a) With quantity discounting, profit is $B = \$1,200$ and welfare is $A + B + C = \$1,600$. (b) If it sets a single price (so that its marginal revenue equals its marginal cost), the monopoly's profit is $F = \$900$, and welfare is $E + F = \$1,350$.

See Problems 31–33.

setting a price above marginal cost so that too few units are sold. The more prices the monopoly sets, the lower the last price and hence the closer it is to marginal cost.

5.4   Multimarket Price Discrimination

Typically, a firm does not know the reservation price for each of its customers. But the firm may know which groups of customers are likely to have higher reservation prices than others. The most common method of multimarket price discrimination is to divide potential customers into two or more groups and set a different price for each group. All units of the good sold to customers within a group are sold at a single price. As with perfect price discrimination, to engage in multimarket price discrimination, a firm must have market power, be able to identify groups with different demands, and prevent resales.

For example, first-run movie theaters with market power charge senior citizens a lower price than they charge younger adults because senior citizens are not willing to pay as much as others to see a movie. By admitting people as soon as they demonstrate their age and buy tickets, the theater prevents resales.

MULTIMARKET PRICE DISCRIMINATION WITH TWO GROUPS

How does a monopoly set its prices if it sells to two (or more) groups of consumers with different demand curves and if resales between the two groups are impossible? We examine this question for a firm that sells to groups of consumers in different countries.

A copyright gives Warner Home Entertainment the legal monopoly to produce and sell the *Harry Potter and the Prisoner of Azkaban* 2-DVD movie set, which it released in November 2004. Warner engages in multimarket price discrimination by charging different prices in various countries because it believes that the elasticities

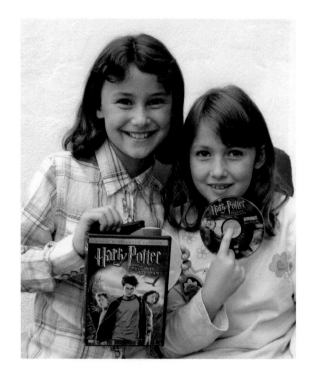

of demand differ. Compared to the U.S. price, it sold this DVD set for 20% more in the United Kingdom, 33% more in Canada, and 66% more in Japan in 2005.[5] Presumably the cost to consumers of reselling across countries is so prohibitively high that Warner can ignore the problem of resales.[6]

For simplicity, we consider how Warner prices in just the United States and the United Kingdom. Warner charges its American consumers p_A for Q_A units, so its revenue is $p_A Q_A$. If Warner has the same constant marginal and average cost, m, in both countries, its profit (ignoring any sunk development cost and other fixed costs) from selling the DVD sets is $\pi_A = p_A Q_A - m Q_A$, where $m Q_A$ is its cost of producing Q_A units. Warner wants to maximize its combined profit, π, which is the sum of its American and British profits, π_A and π_B:

$$\pi = \pi_A + \pi_B = [p_A Q_A - m Q_A] + [p_B Q_B - m Q_B].$$

How should Warner set its prices p_A and p_B—or equivalently Q_A and Q_B—so that it maximizes its combined profit? Appendix 5C gives a mathematical answer. Here we use our understanding of a single-price monopoly's behavior to answer this question graphically.

---

[5]Sources of information and data for this section include **www.timewarner.com**, **Amazon.com** Web sites for each country, **www.ukfilmcouncil.org.uk**, **www.dvdexclusive.com**, and **www.leesmovieinfo.com**.

[6]Why don't customers in higher-price countries order the DVDs from a low-price country using Amazon.com or other Internet vendors? Explanations include consumers' lack of an Internet connection, their ignorance, higher shipping costs (though the price differentials slightly exceed this cost), language differences on the DVDs, desire for quick delivery, and legal restrictions.

A multimarket-price-discriminating monopoly with a constant marginal cost maximizes its total profit by maximizing its profit to each group separately. Warner sets its quantities so that the marginal revenue for each group equals the common marginal cost, *m*, which is about $1 per unit.

Warner released the *Azkaban* DVD set in November 2004. Figure 5.4 uses sales data through the end of the year. In panel a, Warner equates its marginal revenue to its marginal cost, $MR_A = m = 1$, at $Q_A = 9.4$ million sets. The resulting price is $p_A = \$15$ per set. In panel b, $MR_B = m = \$1$ at $Q_B = 2.2$ million sets and the price is $p_B = \$18$ per set.

This price-setting rule must be profit maximizing if the firm doesn't want to change its price to either group. Would the monopoly want to lower its price and sell more output in the United States? If it did so, its marginal revenue would be below its marginal cost, so this change would reduce its profit. Similarly, if the monopoly sold less output in the United States, its marginal revenue would be above its marginal cost, which would reduce its profit. The same arguments can be made about its pricing in Britain. Thus, the price-discriminating monopoly maximizes its profit by operating where its marginal revenue for each country equals its common marginal cost.

Because the monopoly equates the marginal revenue for each group to its common marginal cost, $MC = m$, the marginal revenues for the two countries are equal:

$$MR_A = m = MR_B. \tag{5.1}$$

Figure 5.4

Multimarket Pricing of Harry Potter DVD.
Warner Home Entertainment, the monopoly producer of the *Harry Potter and the Prisoner of Azkaban* DVD set, charges more in the United Kingdom, $p_B = \$18$, than in the United States, $p_A = \$15$, because the elasticity of demand is greater in the United States. Warner sets the quantity independently in each country where its relevant marginal revenue equals its common, constant marginal cost, $m = \$1$. As a result, it maximizes its profit by equating the two marginal revenues: $MR_A = 1 = MR_B$.

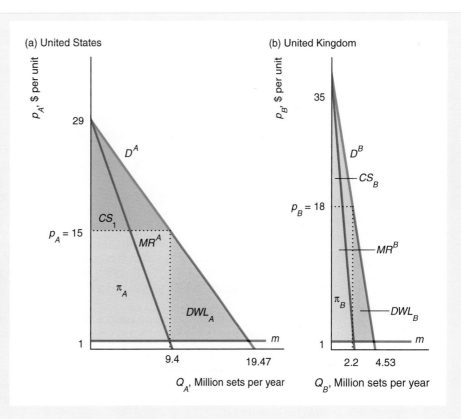

We can use Equation 5.1 to determine how the prices to the two groups vary with the price elasticities of demand at the profit-maximizing outputs. Each marginal revenue is a function of the corresponding price and the price elasticity of demand: $MR_A = p_A(1 + 1/\varepsilon_A)$, where ε_A is the price elasticity of demand for U.S. consumers, and $MR_B = p_B(1 + 1/\varepsilon_B)$, where ε_B is the price elasticity of demand for British consumers. Rewriting Equation 5.1 using these expressions for marginal revenue, we find that

$$MR_A = p_A\left(1 + \frac{1}{\varepsilon_A}\right) = m = p_B\left(1 + \frac{1}{\varepsilon_B}\right) = MR_B. \tag{5.2}$$

If $m = \$1$, $p_A = \$15$, and $p_B = \$18$ in Equation 5.2, Warner must believe that $\varepsilon_A = -15/14 \approx -1.07$ and $\varepsilon_B = -18/17 \approx -1.06$.[7]

By rearranging Equation 5.2, we learn that the ratio of prices in the two countries depends only on demand elasticities in those countries:

$$\frac{p_C}{p_{US}} = \frac{1 + 1/\varepsilon_{US}}{1 + 1/\varepsilon_C}. \tag{5.3}$$

Substituting the prices and the demand elasticities into Equation 5.3, we determine that

$$\frac{p_B}{p_A} = \frac{\$18}{\$15} = 1.2 = \frac{1 + 1/(-15/14)}{1 + 1/(-18/17)} = \frac{1 + 1/\varepsilon_A}{1 + 1/\varepsilon_B}.$$

See Problems 29 and 30.   Thus, because Warner believes that the British demand curve is more elastic at its profit-maximizing prices, it charges British consumers 20% more than U.S. customers.

APPLICATION

Smuggling Prescription Drugs into the United States

A federal law forbids U.S. citizens from importing pharmaceuticals from Canada and other countries, but many U.S. citizens, city governments, and state governments openly flout this law. U.S. senior citizens have taken well-publicized bus trips across the Canadian and Mexican borders to buy their drugs at lower prices; and many Canadian, Mexican, and other Internet sites offer to ship drugs to U.S. customers. In a 2004 poll, two-thirds of Americans favored making importation of drugs easier. (European countries permit such imports.)

A U.S. citizen's incentive to import is great, as the prices of many popular drugs are substantially lower in virtually every other country. Zoloft, an antidepression drug, sells for one-third the U.S. price in Mexico and about one-half in Luxembourg and Austria. U.S. citizens paid an average of 81% more for brand-name drugs than buyers in Canada and six western European countries according to a 2004 Boston University study. U.S. citizens pay 75% more than Canada, which sets its prices at the median level of the countries it surveys.

However, most U.S. citizens are not buying outside the country. According to Espicom, the U.S. expenditures on pharmaceuticals were $270 billion in

---

[7] Rearranging the left side of Equation 5.2, we can obtain expressions of the form of Equation 4.9, which we can use to solve for the elasticity of demand. For example, $(p_A - m)/p_A = (15 - 1)/15 = -1/\varepsilon_A$, so $\varepsilon_A = -15/14$.

2004, of which Canadian drug Internet imports were only $1.2 billion. Thus, the ban appears to be relatively effective.

The Bush administration opposes changing the importation law. The U.S. Food and Drug Administration (FDA) has raised the specter that imported brand-name drugs are not as safe as those purchased in the United States, although the FDA has not identified a single American injured by defective imported drugs.

Not surprisingly, U.S. pharmaceutical companies support the FDA's opposition to imports. They fear the possibility of resales, by which the drugs they sell at lower prices in other countries are then shipped to the United States. Such resales would drive down the drug firms' U.S. prices. The lower prices in other countries may reflect price discrimination by pharmaceutical firms, more competition due to differences in patent laws, price regulation by governments, or other causes.

Some drug companies, among them GlaxoSmithKline and Pfizer, are trying to reduce imports by cutting off Canadian pharmacies that ship south of the border. Wyeth and AstraZeneca report that they watch Canadian pharmacies and wholesale customers for spikes in sales volume that could indicate exports, and then restrict supplies to the Canadian pharmacies.

To date, the FDA has not enforced restrictions on purchases by individuals. Many states, including Minnesota, North Dakota, New Hampshire, Rhode Island, and Wisconsin, as well as many local governments, have provided Web site information about Canadian sources and plan to import the drugs. However, starting in 2003, the FDA sent threatening letters to various state attorneys general advising that state agencies that import Canadian prescription drugs would be violating federal law—a practice the agency continued in 2005 (**www.fda.gov/importeddrugs**). In 2003, the FDA completed a sting operation targeting the supplier of Canadian drugs to the employee insurance program of the city of Springfield, Massachusetts, which had reported that it could save $4 million to $9 million a year by ordering drugs through Canada. The FDA also took actions to close a Canadian drugstore chain that ships drugs to the United States (Rx Depot has 85 stores in 26 states and operates other stores in Canada under the name Rx of Canada).

The interesting question is not why many Democrats, Republicans, seniors, and most other U.S. citizens favor permitting such imports, but whether Canadians should oppose them. The following solved problem addresses these questions.

SOLVED PROBLEM 5.3

A monopoly drug producer with a constant marginal cost of $m = 1$ sells in only two countries and faces a linear demand curve of $Q_1 = 12 - 2p_1$ in Country 1 and $Q_2 = 9 - p_2$ in Country 2. What price does the monopoly charge in each country, how much does it sell in each, and what profit does it earn in each with and without a ban against shipments between the countries?

Answer

If resales across borders are banned so that price discrimination is possible:

1. *Determine the profit-maximizing price that the monopoly sets in each country by setting the relevant marginal revenue equal to the marginal cost:* If the

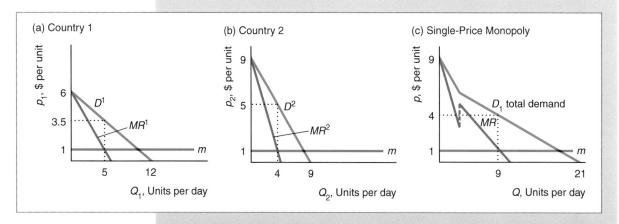

monopoly can price discriminate, it sets a monopoly price independently in each country (as Section 4.1 shows). By rearranging the demand function for Country 1, we find that the inverse demand function is $p_1 = 6 - \frac{1}{2}Q_1$ for quantities less than 6, and zero otherwise, as panel a shows. The marginal revenue curve is twice as steeply sloped as is the linear inverse demand curve (see Chapter 4): $MR_1 = 6 - Q_1$. The monopoly maximizes its profit where its marginal revenue equals its marginal cost,

$$MR_1 = 6 - Q_1 = 1 = m.$$

Solving, we find that its profit-maximizing output is $Q_1 = 5$. Substituting this expression back into the monopoly's inverse demand curve, we learn that its profit-maximizing price is $p_1 = 3.50$—see panel a. In Country 2, the inverse demand curve is $p_2 = 9 - Q_2$, so the monopoly chooses Q_2 such that $MR_2 = 9 - 2Q_2 = 1 = m$. Thus, it maximizes its profit in Country 2 where $Q_2 = 4$ and $p_2 = 5$, as panel b shows.

2. *Calculate the profits:* The monopoly's profit in each country is the output times the difference between the price and its constant average cost, 1. The monopoly's profit in Country 1 is $\pi_1 = (3.50 - 1)5 = 12.50$. Its profit in Country 2 is $\pi_2 = (5 - 1)4 = 16$. Thus, its total profit is $\pi = \pi_1 + \pi_2 = 12.50 + 16 = 28.50$.

If imports are permitted so that price discrimination is impossible:

3. *Derive the total demand curve:* If the monopoly cannot price discriminate, it charges the same price, p, in both countries. We can determine the aggregate demand curve it faces by horizontally summing the demand curves in each country at a given price (see Chapter 2). The total demand curve in panel c is the horizontal sum of the demand curves for each of the two countries in panels a and b. In the range of price where positive quantities are sold in each country $(p < 6)$, the total demand function is $Q = (12 - 2p) + (9 - p) = 21 - 3p$, where $Q = q_1 + q_2$ is the total quantity that the monopoly sells.

4. *Determine the marginal revenue curve corresponding to the total demand curve:* Because no drugs are sold in Country 1 at prices above $p = 6$, the total demand curve (panel c) equals Country 2's demand curve (panel b) at prices above 6, and the total demand curve is the horizontal sum of the two countries' demand curves (panels a and b) at lower prices. Thus, the total demand curve has a kink at $p = 6$. Consequently, the corresponding marginal revenue

curve has two sections. At prices above 6, the marginal revenue curve is that of Country 2. At prices below 6, where the total demand curve is the horizontal sum of the two countries' demand curves, the inverse demand curve is $p = 7 - (\frac{1}{3})Q$, so the marginal revenue curve is $MR = 7 - (\frac{2}{3})Q$. Panel c shows that the marginal revenue curve "jumps" (is discontinuous) at the point where we connect the two sections.

5. *Solve for the single-price monopoly solution:* The monopoly maximizes its profit where its marginal revenue equals its marginal cost. From inspecting panel c, we learn that the intersection occurs in the section where both countries are buying the good: $MR = 7 - (\frac{2}{3})Q = 1 = m$. Thus, the profit-maximizing output is $Q = 9$. Substituting that quantity into the inverse total demand function, we find that the monopoly charges $p = 4$.

See Problem 20.

6. *Calculate the profits:* The monopoly's profits are $\pi_1 = (4 - 1)4 = 12$, $\pi_2 = (4 - 1)5 = 15$, and $\pi = 12 + 15 = 27$.

Comments: The monopoly's profit falls from 28.50 to 27 if it loses the ability to price discriminate. The price of the nondiscriminating monopoly, 4, lies between the two prices it would charge if it could price discriminate: $3.50 < 4 < 5$. The nondiscriminating monopoly charges a single price that is effectively the average of the prices it would charge in the two countries if it could discriminate. Consequently, if a monopoly wants to charge a relatively high price in the United States, and the U.S. market is large relative to the market in the other country, the single (average) price will be close to the price the monopoly would charge in the United States if it could price discriminate. U.S. consumers would benefit (slightly) and consumers in the other country would suffer. Hence, it is understandable why a low-price country might ban pharmaceutical exports, as Canadian officials announced in 2005 that they were considering.

IDENTIFYING GROUPS

Firms use two approaches to divide customers into groups. One method is to divide buyers into groups based on *observable characteristics* of consumers that the firm believes are associated with unusually high or low price elasticities. For example, movie theaters price discriminate using the age of customers. Similarly, some firms charge customers in one country higher prices than those in another country.[8] In 2005, Windows XP Home Edition sells for $95 in the United States but $315 in Britain, $213 in Japan, $307 in France, and $141 in Canada (based on Amazon.com sites in each country). A 2-liter bottle of Coca-Cola costs 50% more in Britain than in other European Union nations. These differences are much greater than can be explained by shipping costs and reflect multimarket price discrimination.

Another approach is to identify and divide consumers on the basis of their *actions*: The firm allows consumers to self-select the group to which they belong. For example, customers may be identified by their willingness to spend time to buy a good at a lower price or to order goods and services in advance of delivery.

---

[8]A firm can charge a higher price for customers in one country than in another if the price differential is too small for many resales between the two countries to occur or if governments enforce import or export restrictions to prevent resales between countries.

Firms use differences in the value customers place on their time to discriminate by using queues (making people wait in line) and other time-intensive methods of selling goods. Store managers who believe that high-wage people are unwilling to "waste their time shopping" may run sales by which consumers who visit the store and pick up the good themselves get a low price while consumers who order over the phone or by mail pay a higher price. This type of price discrimination increases profit if people who put a high value on their time also have less elastic demands for the good.

● **APPLICATION**

Consumers Pay for Lower Prices

Firms draw on a variety of methods to induce consumers to indicate whether they have relatively high or low elasticities of demand. Each of these methods requires that, to receive a discount, consumers incur some cost, such as their time. Otherwise, all consumers would get the discount. By spending extra time to obtain a discount, price-sensitive consumers are able to differentiate themselves from others.

Coupons Many firms use discount coupons to multimarket price discriminate. By doing so, they divide customers into two groups, charging those who are willing to use coupons less than those who won't clip coupons. Providing coupons makes sense if people who don't use coupons are less price sensitive on average than those who clip.[9] People who are willing to spend their time clipping coupons buy cereals and other goods at lower prices than those who value their time more. More than three-quarters (77%) of U.S. consumers redeemed more than 3.5 billion coupons and "saved" about $3 billion on their purchases in 2003. However, manufacturers offered more than $250 billion in coupon savings that year. In addition, almost $487 million was issued in consumer rebates in 2004.

Airline Tickets By choosing between two different types of tickets, airline customers indicate whether they are likely to be business travelers or vacationers. Airlines give customers a choice between high-price tickets with no strings attached and low-price fares that must be purchased long in advance and require the traveler to stay over a Saturday night.

Airlines know that many business travelers have little advance warning before they book a flight and are usually unwilling to stay away over a Saturday night. These business travelers have relatively inelastic demand curves: They want to travel at a specific time even if the price is relatively high. In contrast, vacation travelers can usually plan in advance and stay over a Saturday night. Because vacation travelers can drive, take trains or buses, or postpone trips, they have relatively high elasticities of demand for air travel. The choice that airlines give customers ensures that vacationers with relatively elastic demands obtain cheap seats while most business travelers with relatively inelastic demands buy high-price tickets (often more than four times higher than the plan-ahead rate). The expected absolute difference in fares between two passengers on a route is 36% of the airline's average ticket price.

---

[9]Firms post coupons on the Internet, and coupon clippers trade or sell their coupons to others, using sites such as **www.rebatenet.com** and **www.coolsavings.com**.

Reverse Auctions Priceline.com and other online merchants use a name-your-own-price or reverse auction to identify price-sensitive customers. A customer enters a relatively low-price bid for a good or service, such as airline tickets. Then merchants decide whether to accept that bid or not. To keep their less price-sensitive customers from using those methods, airlines force successful Priceline bidders to be flexible: to fly at off hours, to make one or more connections, and to accept any type of aircraft. Similarly, when bidding on groceries, a customer must list "one or two brands you like." As Jay Walker, Priceline's founder explained, "The manufacturers would rather not give you a discount, of course, but if you prove that you're willing to switch brands, they're willing to pay to keep you."

WELFARE EFFECTS OF MULTIMARKET PRICE DISCRIMINATION

Multimarket price discrimination results in inefficient production and consumption. As a result, welfare under multimarket price discrimination is lower than that under competition or perfect price discrimination. Welfare may be lower or higher with multimarket price discrimination than with a single-price monopoly, however.

Multimarket Price Discrimination Versus Competition. Consumer surplus is greater and more output is produced with competition (or perfect price discrimination) than with multimarket price discrimination. In Figure 5.4, consumer surplus with multimarket price discrimination is CS_1 (for Group 1 in panel a) and CS_2 (for Group 2 in panel b). Under competition, consumer surplus is the area below the demand curve and above the marginal cost curve: $CS_1 + \pi_1 + DWL_1$ in panel a and $CS_2 + \pi_2 + DWL_2$ in panel b.

Thus multimarket price discrimination transfers some of the competitive consumer surplus, π_1 and π_2, to the monopoly as additional profit and causes the deadweight loss, DWL_1 and DWL_2, of some of the rest of the competitive consumer surplus. The deadweight loss is due to the multimarket-price-discriminating monopoly's charging prices above marginal cost, which results in reduced production from the optimal competitive level.

Multimarket Price Discrimination Versus Single-Price Monopoly. From theory alone, we can't tell whether welfare is higher if the monopoly uses multimarket price discrimination or if it sets a single price. Both types of monopolies set price above marginal cost, so too little is produced relative to competition. Output may rise as the firm starts discriminating if groups that did not buy when the firm charged a single price start buying. In the movie theater example in panel b of Table 5.1, welfare is higher with discrimination than with single-price monopoly because more tickets are sold when the monopoly discriminates (see Solved Problem 5.1).

The closer the multimarket-price-discriminating monopoly comes to perfectly price discriminating (say, by dividing its customers into many groups rather than just two), the more output it produces, so the less the production inefficiency there is. However, unless a multimarket-price-discriminating monopoly sells significantly more output than it would if it had to set a single price, welfare is likely to be lower with discrimination because of consumption inefficiency and time wasted shopping. These two inefficiencies don't occur with a monopoly that charges all consumers the same price. As a result, consumers place the same marginal value (the single sales price) on the good, so they have no incentive to trade with each other. Similarly, if everyone pays the same price, consumers have no incentive to search for low prices.

5.5   Two-Part Tariffs

We now turn to two other forms of second-degree price discrimination: *two-part tariffs* in this section and *tie-in sales* in the next one. Both are similar to the type of second-degree price discrimination we examined earlier because the average price per unit varies with the number of units consumers buy.

two-part tariff
a pricing system in which the firm charges a customer a lump-sum fee (the first tariff or price) for the right to buy as many units of the good as the consumer wants at a specified price (the second tariff)

See Problem 21.

With a **two-part tariff**, the firm charges a consumer a lump-sum fee (the first tariff) for the right to buy as many units of the good as the consumer wants at a specified price (the second tariff). Because of the lump-sum fee, consumers pay more per unit if they buy a small number of goods than if they buy a larger number.

To get telephone service, you may pay a monthly connection fee and a price per minute of use. Some car rental firms charge a per-day fee and a price per mile driven. To buy season tickets to Oakland Raiders football games, a fan pays a fee of $250 to $4,000 for a *personal seat license* (PSL), which gives the fan the right to buy season tickets for the next 11 years at a ticket price per game ranging between $40 and $60. The Carolina Panthers introduced the PSL in 1993, and at least 11 NFL teams used a PSL by 2002. By one estimate, more than $700 million has been raised by the PSL portion of this two-part tariff.

To profit from two-part tariffs, a firm must have market power, know how demand differs across customers or with the quantity that a single customer buys, and successfully prevent resales. We now examine two results. First, we consider how a firm uses a two-part tariff to extract consumer surplus (as in our previous price discrimination examples). Second, we see how, if the firm cannot vary its two-part tariff across its customers, its profit is greater the more similar the demand curves of its customers are.

We illustrate these two points for a monopoly that knows its customers' demand curves. We start by examining the monopoly's two-part tariff where all its customers have identical demand curves and then look at one where its customers' demand curves differ.

A TWO-PART TARIFF WITH IDENTICAL CONSUMERS

If all the monopoly's customers are identical, a monopoly that knows its customers' demand curve can set a two-part tariff that has the same two properties as the perfect price discrimination equilibrium. First, the efficient quantity, Q_1, is sold because the price of the last unit equals marginal cost. Second, all consumer surplus is transferred from consumers to the firm.

Suppose that the monopoly has a constant marginal and average cost of $m = \$10$ (no fixed cost), and every consumer has the demand curve D^1 in panel a of Figure 5.5. To maximize its profit, the monopoly charges a price, p, equal to the constant marginal and average cost, $m = \$10$, and just breaks even on each unit sold. By setting price equal to marginal cost, it maximizes the *potential consumer surplus*: the consumer surplus if no lump-sum fee is charged. It charges the largest possible lump-sum fee, $\mathcal{L}$, which is the potential consumer surplus $A_1 + B_1 + C_1 = \$2,450$. Thus its profit is $2,450 times the number of customers.

Had the firm charged a higher per-unit price, it would sell fewer units and hence make a smaller profit. For example, if the monopoly charges $p = \$20$, it sells 60 units, making a profit from its unit sales of $B_1 = (\$20 - \$10)60 = \$600$. It must

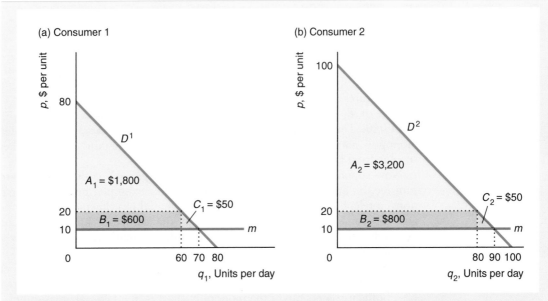

Figure 5.5 **Two-Part Tariff.** If all consumers have the demand curve in panel a, a monopoly can capture all the consumer surplus with a two-part tariff by which it charges a price, p, equal to the marginal cost, $m = \$10$, for each item and a lump-sum membership fee of $\mathscr{L} = A_1 + B_1 + C_1 = \$2,450$. Now suppose that the monopoly has two customers, Consumer 1 in panel a and Consumer 2 in panel b. If the monopoly can treat its customers differently, it maximizes its profit by setting $p = m = \$10$ and charging Consumer 1 a fee equal to its potential consumer surplus, $A_1 + B_1 + C_1 = \$2,450$, and Consumer 2 a fee of $A_2 + B_2 + C_2 = \$4,050$, for a total profit of $6,500$. If the monopoly must charge all customers the same price, it maximizes its profit at $5,000$ by setting $p = \$20$ and charging both customers a lump-sum fee equal to the potential consumer surplus of Consumer 1, $\mathscr{L} = A_1 = \$1,800$.

lower its fee to equal the new potential consumer surplus of $A_1 = \$1,800$, so its total profit per customer is only $2,400$. It loses area $C_1 = \$50$ by charging the higher price. Similarly, had the monopoly charged a lower per-unit price, its profit would be lower: It would sell too many units and make a loss on each unit because its price would be below its marginal cost.

Because the monopoly knows the demand curve, it could instead perfectly price discriminate by charging each customer a different price for each unit purchased: the price along the demand curve. Thus this knowledgeable monopoly can capture all potential consumer surplus either by perfectly price discriminating or by setting its optimal two-part tariff.

If the monopoly does not know its customers' demand curve, it must guess how high a lump-sum fee to set. This fee will almost certainly be less than the potential consumer surplus. If the firm sets its fee above the potential consumer surplus, it loses all its customers.

A TWO-PART TARIFF WITH NONIDENTICAL CONSUMERS

Now suppose that there are two customers, Consumer 1 and Consumer 2, with demand curves D_1 and D_2 in panels a and b of Figure 5.5. If the monopoly knows each customer's demand curve and can prevent resales, it can capture all the consumer surplus by varying its two-part tariffs across customers. However, if the monopoly is unable to distinguish among the types of customers or cannot charge consumers different prices, efficiency and profitability fall.

Suppose that the monopoly knows its customers' demand curves. By charging each customer $p = m = \$10$ per unit, the monopoly makes no profit per unit but sells the number of units that maximizes the potential consumer surplus. The monopoly then captures all this potential consumer surplus by charging Consumer 1 a lump-sum fee of $\mathcal{L}_1 = A_1 + B_1 + C_1 = \$2,450$ and Consumer 2 a fee of $\mathcal{L}_2 = A_2 + B_2 + C_2 = \$4,050$. The monopoly's total profit is $\mathcal{L}_1 + \mathcal{L}_2 = \$6,500$. By doing so, the monopoly maximizes its total profit by capturing the maximum potential consumer surplus from both customers.

Now suppose that the monopoly has to charge each consumer the same lump-sum fee, $\mathcal{L}$, and the same per-unit price, p. For example, because of legal restrictions, a telephone company charges all residential customers the same monthly fee and the same fee per call, even though the company knows that consumers' demands vary. As with multimarket price discrimination, the monopoly does not capture all the consumer surplus.

The monopoly charges a lump-sum fee, $\mathcal{L}$, equal to either the potential consumer surplus of Consumer 1, CS_1, or of Consumer 2, CS_2. Because CS_2 is greater than CS_1, both customers buy if the monopoly charges $\mathcal{L} = CS_1$, whereas only Consumer 2 buys if the monopoly charges $\mathcal{L} = CS_2$. The monopoly sets either the low lump-sum fee or the higher one, depending on which produces the greater profit.

Any other lump-sum fee would lower its profit. The monopoly has no customers if it charges more than $\mathcal{L} = CS_2$. If it charges between CS_1 and CS_2, it loses money on Consumer 2 compared to what it could earn by charging CS_2, and it still does not sell to Consumer 1. By charging less than $\mathcal{L} = CS_1$, it earns less per customer and does not gain any additional customers.

In our example, the monopoly maximizes its profit by setting the lower lump-sum fee and charging a price $p = \$20$, which is above marginal cost (see Appendix 5D). Consumer 1 buys 60 units, and Consumer 2 buys 80 units. The monopoly makes $(p - m) = (\$20 - \$10) = \$10$ on each unit, so it earns $B_1 + B_2 = \$600 + \$800 = \$1,400$ from the units it sells. In addition, it gets a fee from both consumers equal to the consumer surplus of Consumer 1, $A_1 = \$1,800$. Thus its total profit is $2 \times \$1,800 + \$1,400 = \$5,000$, which is $\$1,500$ less than if it could set different lump-sum fees for each customer. Consumer 1 has no consumer surplus, but Consumer 2 enjoys a consumer surplus of $\$1,400$ (= $\$3,200 - \$1,800$).

Why does the monopoly charge a price above marginal cost when using a two-part tariff? By raising its price, the monopoly earns more per unit from both types of customers but lowers its customers' potential consumer surplus. Thus if the monopoly can capture each customer's potential surplus by charging different lump-sum fees, it sets its price equal to marginal cost. However, if the monopoly cannot capture all the potential consumer surplus because it must charge everyone the same lump-sum fee, the increase in profit from Customer 2 from the higher price more than offsets the reduction in the lump-sum fee (the potential consumer surplus of Customer 1).[10]

---

[10]If the monopoly lowers its price from $\$20$ to the marginal cost of $\$10$, it loses B_1 from Customer 1, but it can raise its lump-sum fee from A_1 to $A_1 + B_1 + C_1$, so its total profit from Customer 1 increases by $C_1 = \$50$. The lump-sum fee it collects from Customer 2 also rises by $B_1 + C_1 = \$650$, but its profit from unit sales falls by $B_2 = \$800$, so its total profit decreases by $\$150$. The loss from Customer 2, $-\$150$, more than offsets the gain from Customer 1, $\$50$. Thus the monopoly makes $\$100$ more by charging a price of $\$20$ rather than $\$10$.

5.6 | Tie-In Sales

tie-in sale
a type of nonlinear pricing in which customers can buy one product only if they agree to buy another product as well

requirement tie-in sale
a tie-in sale in which customers who buy one product from a firm are required to make all their purchases of another product from that firm

bundling (*package tie-in sale*)
a type of tie-in sale in which two goods are combined so that customers cannot buy either good separately

Another type of nonlinear pricing is a **tie-in sale**, in which customers can buy one product only if they agree to purchase another product as well. There are two forms of tie-in sales.

The first type is a **requirement tie-in sale**, in which customers who buy one product from a firm are required to make all their purchases of another product from that firm. Some firms sell durable machines such as copiers under the condition that customers buy copier services and supplies from them in the future. Because the amount of services and supplies each customer buys differs, the per-unit price of copiers varies across customers.

The second type of tie-in sale is **bundling** (or a *package tie-in sale*), in which two goods are combined so that customers cannot buy either good separately. For example, a Whirlpool refrigerator is sold with shelves, and a Hewlett-Packard ink-jet printer comes in a box that includes both black and color printer cartridges.

Most tie-in sales increase efficiency by lowering transaction costs. Indeed, tie-ins for efficiency purposes are so common that we hardly think about them. Presumably, no one would want to buy a shirt without buttons, so selling shirts with buttons attached lowers transaction costs. Because virtually everyone wants certain basic software, most companies sell computers with this software already installed. Firms also often use tie-in sales to increase profits, as we now illustrate.

REQUIREMENT TIE-IN SALES

Frequently, a firm cannot tell which customers are going to use its product the most and hence are willing to pay the most for the good. These firms may be able to use a requirement tie-in sale to identify heavy users of the product and charge them more.

APPLICATION

IBM

In the 1930s, IBM increased its profit by using a requirement tie-in. IBM produced card punch machines, sorters, and tabulating machines (precursors of modern computers) that computed by using punched cards. Rather than selling its card punch machines, IBM leased them under the condition that the lease would terminate if any card not manufactured by IBM were used. (By leasing the equipment, IBM avoided resale problems and forced customers to buy cards from it.) IBM charged customers more per card than other firms would have charged. If we think of this extra payment per card as part of the cost of using the machine, this requirement tie-in resulted in heavy users' paying more for the machines than others did. This tie-in was profitable because heavy users were willing to pay more.[11]

---

[11]The U.S. Supreme Court held that IBM's actions violated the antitrust laws because they lessened competition in the (potential) market for tabulating cards. IBM's defense was that its requirement was designed to protect its reputation. IBM claimed that badly made tabulating cards might cause its machines to malfunction and that consumers would falsely blame IBM's equipment. The Court did not accept IBM's argument. The Court apparently did not understand—or at least care about—the price discrimination aspect of IBM's actions.

BUNDLING

Firms that sell two or more goods may use bundling to raise profits. Bundling allows firms that can't directly price discriminate to charge customers different prices. Whether bundling is profitable depends on customers' tastes and the ability to prevent resales.

Imagine that you are in charge of selling season tickets for the local football team. Your stadium can hold all your potential customers, so the marginal cost of selling one more ticket is zero.

Should you bundle tickets for preseason (exhibition) and regular-season games, or should you sell books of tickets for the preseason and the regular season separately?[12] To answer this question, you have to determine how the fans differ in their desires to see preseason and regular-season games.

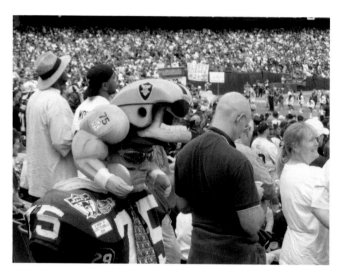

For simplicity, suppose that there are two customers (or types of customers). These football fans are so fanatical that they are willing to pay to see preseason exhibition games: There's no accounting for tastes!

Whether you should bundle depends on your customers' tastes. It does not pay to bundle in panel a of Table 5.2, in which Fan 1 is willing to pay more for both regular and preseason tickets than Fan 2. Bundling does pay in panel b, in which Fan 1 is willing to pay more for regular-season but less for exhibition tickets than Fan 2.

To determine whether it pays to bundle, we have to calculate the profit-maximizing unbundled and bundled prices. We start by calculating the profit-maximizing unbundled prices in panel a. If you charge $2,000 for the regular-season tickets, you earn only $2,000 because

TABLE 5.2　Bundling of Tickets to Football Games

(a) Unprofitable Bundle

	Regular Season	Preseason	Bundle
Fan 1	$2,000	$500	$2,500
Fan 2	$1,400	$100	$1,500
Profit-maximizing price	$1,400	$500	$1,500

(b) Profitable Bundle

	Regular Season	Preseason	Bundle
Fan 1	$1,700	$300	$2,000
Fan 2	$1,500	$500	$2,000
Profit-maximizing price	$1,500	$300	$2,000

[12]We assume that you don't want to sell tickets to each game separately. One reason for selling only season tickets is to reduce transaction costs. A second explanation is the same type of bundling argument that we discuss in this section.

Fan 2 won't buy tickets. It is more profitable to charge $1,400, sell tickets to both customers, and earn $2,800 for the regular season. By similar reasoning, the profit-maximizing price for the exhibition tickets is $500, at which you sell only to Fan 1 and earn $500. As a result, you earn $3,300 (= $2,800 + $500) if you do not bundle.

If you bundle and charge $2,500, you sell only to Fan 1. Your better option if you bundle is to set a bundle price of $1,500 and sell to both fans, earning $3,000. Nonetheless, you earn $300 more if you sell the tickets separately than if you bundle.

In this first example, in which it doesn't pay to bundle, the same customer who values the regular-season tickets the most also values the preseason tickets the most. In contrast, in panel b, the fan who values the regular-season tickets more values the exhibition season tickets less than the other fan does. Here your profit is higher if you bundle. If you sell the tickets separately, you charge $1,500 for regular-season tickets, earning $3,000 from the two customers, and $300 for preseason tickets, earning $600, for a total of $3,600. By selling a bundle of tickets for all games at $2,000 each, you'd earn $4,000. Thus you earn $400 more by bundling than by selling the tickets separately.

By bundling, you can charge the fans different prices for the two components of the bundle. Fan 1 is paying $1,700 for regular-season tickets and $300 for exhibition tickets, while Fan 2 is paying $1,500 and $500, respectively.[13] If you could perfectly price discriminate, you'd charge each consumer his or her reservation price for the preseason and regular-season tickets and would make the same amount as you do by bundling.

These examples illustrate that bundling a pair of goods pays only if their demands are *negatively correlated*: Customers who are willing to pay relatively more for regular-season tickets are not willing to pay as much as others for preseason tickets, and vice versa. When a good or service is sold to different people, the price is determined by the purchaser with the *lowest* reservation price. If reservation prices differ substantially across consumers, a monopoly has to charge a relatively low price to make many sales. By bundling when demands are negatively correlated, the monopoly reduces the dispersion in reservation prices, so it can charge more and still sell to a large number of customers.

---

[13]As with price discrimination, you have to prevent resales for bundling to increase your profit. Someone could make a $198 profit by purchasing the bundle for $2,000, selling Fan 1 the regular-season tickets for $1,699, and selling Fan 2 the preseason tickets for $499. Each fan would prefer attending only one type of game at those prices to paying $2,000 for the bundle.

Summary

1. **Why and how firms price discriminate:** A firm can price discriminate if it has market power, knows which customers will pay more for each unit of output, and can prevent customers who pay low prices from reselling to those who pay high prices. A firm earns a higher profit from price discrimination than from uniform pricing because (a) the firm captures some or all of the consumer surplus of customers who are willing to pay more than the uniform price and (b) the firm sells to some people who would not buy at the uniform price.

2. **Perfect price discrimination:** To perfectly price discriminate, a firm must know the maximum amount each customer is willing to pay for each unit of output. If a firm charges customers the maximum each is willing to pay for each unit of output, the monopoly captures all potential consumer surplus and sells the efficient (competitive) level of output. Compared to competition, total welfare is the same, consumers are worse off, and firms are better off under perfect price discrimination.

3. **Quantity discrimination:** Some firms charge customers different prices depending on how many units they purchase. If consumers who want more water have less elastic demands, a water utility can increase its profit by using declining-block pricing, in which the price for the first few gallons of water is higher than that for additional gallons.

4. **Multimarket price discrimination:** A firm that does not have enough information to perfectly price discriminate may know the relative elasticities of demand of groups of its customers. Such a profit-maximizing firm charges groups of consumers prices in proportion to their elasticities of demand, the group of consumers with the least elastic demand paying the highest price. Welfare is less under multimarket price discrimination than under competition or perfect price discrimination but may be greater or less than that under single-price monopoly.

5. **Two-part tariffs:** By charging consumers one fee for the right to buy and a separate price per unit, firms may earn higher profits than from charging only for each unit sold. If a firm knows its customers' demand curves, it can use two-part tariffs (instead of perfectly price discriminating) to capture all the consumer surplus. Even if the firm does not know each customer's demand curve or cannot vary the two-part tariffs across customers, it can use a two-part tariff to make a larger profit than it can get if it set a single price.

6. **Tie-in sales:** A firm may increase its profit by using a tie-in sale that allows customers to buy one product only if they also purchase another one. In a requirement tie-in sale, customers who buy one good must make all of their purchases of another good or service from that firm. With bundling (a package tie-in sale), a firm sells only a bundle of two goods together. Prices differ across customers under both types of tie-in sales.

Questions

*= answer at the back of this book; **A** = an application or other real-world material in the text; **C** = use of calculus may be necessary; **W** = audio-slide show answers by James Dearden at www.myeconlab.com/perloff.

1. Alexx's monopoly currently sells its product at a single price. What conditions must be met so that he can profitably price discriminate?

*2. Spenser's Superior Stoves advertises a one-day sale on electric stoves. The ad specifies that no phone orders are accepted and that the purchaser must transport the stove. Why does the firm include these restrictions?

*3. Many colleges provide students from low-income families with scholarships, subsidized loans, and other programs so that they pay lower tuitions than students from high-income families. Explain why universities behave this way.

4. In 2002, seven pharmaceutical companies announced a plan to provide low-income elderly people with a card guaranteeing them discounts of 20% or more on dozens of prescription medicines. Why did the firms institute this program?

5. In the examples in Table 5.1, if the movie theater does not price discriminate, it charges either the highest price the college students are willing to pay or the one that the senior citizens are willing to pay. Why doesn't it charge an intermediate price? (*Hint*: Discuss how the demand curves of these two groups are unusual.)

6. Disneyland price discriminates by charging lower entry fees for children than adults and for local residents than for other visitors. Why does it not have a resales problem? **A**

7. The 2002 production run of 25,000 new Thunderbirds included only 2,000 cars for Canada. Yet potential buyers besieged Ford dealers there. Many buyers hoped to make a quick profit by reselling the cars in the United States. Reselling was relatively easy, and shipping costs were comparatively low. When the Thunderbird with the optional hardtop first became available at the end of 2001, Canadians paid $56,550 Cdn. for the vehicle, while U.S. customers spent up to $73,000 Cdn. in the United States. Why? Why would a Canadian want to ship a T-Bird south? Why did Ford require that Canadian dealers sign an agreement with Ford that prohibited moving vehicles to the United States?

8. As described in the "Amazon Is Watching You" application, some Amazon customers contended that Amazon used a dynamic pricing approach where the price offered depended on a customer's past purchases. What type of price discrimination is this? **A**

9. On August 2, 2005, Hertz charged $141.06 a day to rent a Taurus in New York City but only $66.68 a day in Miami. Is this price discrimination? Why or why not?

10. College students could once buy a computer at a substantial discount through a campus buying program. The discounts largely disappeared in the late 1990s, when PC companies dropped their prices. "The industry's margins just got too thin to allow for those [college discounts]," said the president of Educause,

a group that promotes and surveys using technology on campus (David LaGesse, "A PC Choice: Dorm or Quad?" *U.S. News & World Report,* May 5, 2003: 64). Using the concepts and terminology discussed in this chapter, explain why shrinking profit margins are associated with the reduction or elimination of student discounts.

11. Ticketmaster Corp. used an Internet auction to sell tickets for a Sting concert (Leslie Walker, "Auctions Could Set Ticket Prices for Future Events," *San Francisco Chronicle,* October 13, 2003: E5).

    a. The floor seats were auctioned in a uniform price format where all winning bidders paid the same amount: the lowest bid ($90) at which all the seats were sold. Is this price discrimination? If so, what type?
    b. Suppose, instead, that each ticket was sold at the bid price to the highest bidder. Is this price discrimination? If so, what type?

12. Using the information in the "Botox Revisited" application, determine how much Allergan loses by being a single-price monopoly rather than a perfectly price-discriminating monopoly. Explain your answer. **A**

13. Consider a third pricing scheme that the union in Solved Problem 5.2 might use. It sets a wage, w^*, and lets the firms hire as many workers as they want (that is, the union does not set a minimum number of hours), but requires a lump-sum contribution to each worker's retirement fund. What is such a pricing scheme called? Can the union achieve the same outcome as it would if it perfectly price discriminated? (*Hint:* It could set the wage where the supply curve hits the demand curve.) Does your answer depend on whether the union workers are identical? **A**

14. A firm is a natural monopoly. (See Chapter 4.) Its marginal cost curve is flat, and its average cost curve is downward sloping (because it has a fixed cost). The firm can perfectly price discriminate.

    a. In a graph, show how much the monopoly produces, Q^*. Will it produce to where price equals its marginal cost?
    b. Show graphically (and explain) what its profit is.

15. Are all the customers of the quantity-discriminating monopoly in panel a of Figure 5.3 worse off than they would be if the firm set a single price (panel b)?

16. A monopoly has a marginal cost of zero and faces two groups of consumers. At first, the monopoly could not prevent resales, so it maximized its profit by charging everyone the same price, $p = \$5$. No one from the first group chose to purchase. Now the monopoly can prevent resales, so it decides to price

discriminate. Will total output expand? Why or why not? What happens to profit and consumer surplus?

17. Each week, a department store places a different item of clothing on sale. Give an explanation based on price discrimination for why the store conducts such regular sales.

18. Does a monopoly's ability to price discriminate between two groups of consumers depend on its marginal cost curve? Why or why not? [Consider two cases: (a) the marginal cost is so high that the monopoly is uninterested in selling to one group; (b) the marginal cost is low enough that the monopoly wants to sell to both groups.]

19. A monopoly sells two products, of which consumers want only one. Assuming that it can prevent resales, can the monopoly increase its profit by bundling them, forcing consumers to buy both goods?

20. How would the analysis in Solved Problem 5.3 change if $m = 7$ or if $m = 4$? (*Hint:* Where $m = 4$, the marginal cost curve crosses the *MR* curve three times—if we include the vertical section. The single-price monopoly will choose one of these three points where its profit is maximized.) **A**

21. Abbott Laboratories, the patent holder of the anti-AIDS drug Norvir, raised the price from $1.71 to $8.57 a day in 2003 (Lauran Neergaard, "No Price Rollback on Costly AIDS Drug," *San Francisco Chronicle,* August 5, 2004: A4). The price was increased in the United States only when low doses of Norvir are used to boost the effects of other anti-HIV medicines—not in Abbott's own Kaletra, a medicine that includes Norvir. Why did Abbott raise one price but not others?

22. In the spring of 2005, General Motors shifted its auto discounting policy to regionally targeted rebates in which the manufacturer offers varying discounts to different parts of the United States. Suppose that GM dealers offer all consumers in a given region the same posted price for a specific model (which is GM's pricing policy for its Saturn automobiles). Assume that it is unprofitable for a consumer to purchase an automobile in a low-price area and then to resell it in a high-price area.

    a. What form of price discrimination is GM's new policy?
    b. What is the relationship between a region's price and its price elasticity of demand?
    c. GM also eliminated a high-profile discount program "in an apparent effort to damp consumer expectation of big price cuts" (Lee Hawkins Jr., "GM Alters U.S. Discount Program with a Region-Specific Strategy," *Wall Street Journal,* March 7,

2005: A2). How do expected future prices of an automobile affect the current demand? Is a national discount program that is targeted to reduce slumping sales a form of price discrimination? Explain. **W**

23. In the 2003 Major League Baseball season, the New York Mets began charging fans up to twice as much to watch games involving the cross-town Yankees or other popular teams than less popular or less competitive teams. Other professional teams have adopted the same pricing strategy. While the Yankees increased the prices of popular games, they dropped the price of upper-deck seats for some weekday games against weak opponents.

   a. A Mets-Yankees game is more popular than a Mets-Marlins game. Is the Mets' policy of charging fans more to see the Yankees than the Marlins a form of price discrimination? If so, which type?
   b. What is the effect on the quantity of tickets demanded for the Yankees-Mets games if the Mets drop the price of the cheap seats for unpopular games? How do the Mets take this effect into account when setting ticket prices? In answering the question, assume that the Mets choose two ticket prices—one for the Mets-Yankees game and the other for the Mets-Marlins game—to maximize the sum of revenues of the two games. **W**

24. Grocery stores often set consumer-specific prices by issuing frequent-buyer cards to willing customers and collecting information on their purchases. Grocery chains can use that data to offer customized discount coupons to individuals.

   a. Which type of price discrimination—first-degree, second-degree, or third-degree—are these personalized discounts?
   b. How should a grocery store use past-purchase data to set individualized prices to maximize its profit? (*Hint:* Refer to a customer's price elasticity of demand.) **W**

25. The publisher Reed Elsevier uses what economists call a mixed-bundling pricing strategy. The publisher sells a university access to a bundle of 930 of its journals for $1.7 million for one year. It also offers the

journals separately at individual prices. Because Elsevier offers the journals online (with password access), universities can track how often their students and faculty access journals and then cancel those journals that are seldom read. Suppose that a publisher offers a university only three journals—A, B, and C—at the unbundled, individual annual subscription prices of $p_A = \$1,600$, $p_B = \$800$, and $p_C = \$1,500$. Suppose a university's willingness to pay for each of the journals is $v_A = \$2,000$, $v_B = \$1,100$, and $v_C = \$1,400$.

   a. If the publisher offers the journals only at the individual subscription prices, to which journals does the university subscribe?
   b. Given these individual prices, what is the highest price that the university is willing to pay for the three journals bundled together?
   c. Now suppose that the publisher offers the same deal to a second university with willingness-to-pay $v_A = \$1,800$, $v_B = \$100$, and $v_C = \$2,100$. With the two universities, calculate the revenue-maximizing individual and bundle prices. **W**

26. To promote her platinum-selling CD, *Feels Like Home* in 2005, singer Norah Jones toured the country for live performances. However, she sold an average of only two-thirds of the tickets available for each show, T^* (Robert Levine, "The Trick of Making a Hot Ticket Pay," *New York Times*, June 6, 2005: C1, C4).

   a. Suppose that the local promoter is the monopoly provider of each concert. Each concert hall has a fixed number of seats. Assume that the promoter's cost is independent of the number of people who attend the concert (Ms. Jones received a guaranteed payment). Graph the promoter's marginal cost curve for the concert hall, where the number of tickets sold is on the horizontal axis (be sure to show T^*).
   b. If the monopoly can charge a single market price, does the concert's failure to sell out prove that the monopoly set too high a price? Explain.
   c. Would your answer in part b be the same if the monopoly can perfectly price discriminate? Use a graph to explain.

Problems

*27. A patent gaves Sony a legal monopoly to produce a robot dog called Aibo ("eye-BO"). The Chihuahua-size pooch robot can sit, beg, chase balls, dance, and play an electronic tune. When Sony started selling the toy in July 1999, it announced that it would sell 3,000 Aibo robots in Japan for about $2,000 each and a

limited litter of 2,000 in the United States for $2,500 each. Suppose that Sony's marginal cost of producing Aibos is $500. Its inverse demand curve is $p_J = 3,500 - \frac{1}{2}Q_J$ in Japan and $p_A = 4,500 - 4,500Q_A$ in the United States. Solve for the equilibrium prices and quantities (assuming that U.S. customers cannot buy robots from Japan). Show how the profit-maximizing price ratio depends on the elasticities of demand in the two countries. What are the deadweight losses in each country, and in which is the loss from monopoly pricing greater?

*28. A monopoly sells its good in the U.S. and Japanese markets. The American inverse demand function is $p_A = 10 - Q_A$, and the Japanese inverse demand function is $p_J = 80 - 2Q_J$, where both prices, p_A and p_J, are measured in dollars. The firm's marginal cost of production is $m = 20$ in both countries. If the firm can prevent resales, what price will it charge in both markets? (*Hint:* The monopoly determines its optimal (monopoly) price in each country separately because customers cannot resell the good.)

29. Warner Home Entertainment sells the *Harry Potter and the Prisoner of Azkaban* 2-DVD movie set around the world. Warner charges 33% more in Canada and 66% more in Japan than in the United States. Using the information about Warner's marginal cost and U.S. sales in Section 5.4, determine what the elasticities of demand must be in Canada and in Japan if Warner is profit maximizing. **A**

*30. Warner Home Entertainment sells the *Harry Potter and the Prisoner of Azkaban* 2-DVD movie set in China for about $3, which is only one-fifth the U.S. price, and has sold nearly 100,000 units. The price is extremely low in China because Chinese consumers are less wealthy than those in the other countries and because (lower-quality) pirated versions are available in China for 72¢–$1.20, compared to the roughly $3 required for the legal version (Jin Baicheng, "Powerful Ally Joins Government in War on Piracy," *China Daily*, March 11, 2005: 13). Assuming a marginal cost of $1, what is the Chinese elasticity of demand? Derive the demand function for China and illustrate Warner's policy in China using a figure similar to panel a in Figure 5.4. **A**

31. In panel b of Figure 5.3, the single-price monopoly faces a demand curve of $p = 90 - Q$ and a constant marginal (and average) cost of $m = 30$. Find the profit-maximizing quantity (or price) using math (Chapter 4). Determine the profit, consumer surplus, welfare, and deadweight loss. **A**

32. The quantity-discriminating monopoly in panel a of Figure 5.3 can set three prices, depending on the quantity a consumer purchases. The firm's profit is

$$\pi = p_1 Q_1 + p_2(Q_2 - Q_1) + p_3(Q_3 - Q_2) - mQ_3,$$

where p_1 is the high price charged on the first Q_1 units (first block), p_2 is a lower price charged on the next $Q_2 - Q_1$ units, and p_3 is the lowest price charged on the $Q_3 - Q_2$ remaining units, Q_3 is the total number of units actually purchased, and $m = \$30$ is the firm's constant marginal and average cost. Use calculus to determine the profit-maximizing p_1, p_2, and p_3. **A, C**

33. In the quantity discrimination analysis in panel a of Figure 5.3, suppose that the monopoly can make consumers a take-it-or-leave-it offer (similar to the union in Solved Problem 5.2).

   a. Suppose the monopoly sets a price, p^*, and a minimum quantity, Q^*, that a consumer must pay to be able to purchase any units at all. What price and minimum quantity should it set to achieve the same outcome as it would if it perfectly price discriminated?

   b. Now suppose the monopolist charges a price of $90 for the first 30 units and a price of $30 for all subsequent units, but requires that a consumer must buy at least 30 units to be allowed to buy any. Compare this outcome to the one in part a and to the perfectly price discriminating outcome.

34. A monopoly sells its good in the United States, where the elasticity of demand is –2, and in Japan, where the elasticity of demand is –5. Its marginal cost is $10. At what price does the monopoly sell its good in each country if resales are impossible?

35. A monopoly sells in two countries, and resales between the countries are impossible. The demand curves in the two countries are

$$p_1 = 100 - Q_1,$$
$$p_2 = 120 - 2Q_2.$$

The monopoly's marginal cost is $m = 30$. Solve for the equilibrium price in each country.

36. Using math, show why a two-part tariff causes customers who purchase few units to pay more per unit than customers who buy more units. **C**

Chapter 6

Oligopoly and Monopolistic Competition

Anyone can win unless there happens to be a second entry. —George Ade

When deciding how to price its cars, General Motors (GM) takes into account the pricing of Ford, Chrysler, and other automobile manufacturers. In June 2005, GM announced that anyone could receive the discount previously reserved for its employees—an average of $4,458 per vehicle. GM sales that month zoomed up 41%. Ford and Chrysler quickly offered the same type of discount. In August, GM announced that it was ending the discount, but when Ford and Chrysler didn't follow, GM reversed itself and extended the program through September, when all the companies cancelled the discount. These firms closely monitor their rivals' actions to predict their future behavior. Indeed, they pay large sums to hire executives and engineers from their rivals in part to gain insights into their decision making and planning.

oligopoly
a small group of firms in a market with substantial barriers to entry

Firms pay attention to each other's behavior in an **oligopoly**: a small group of firms in a market with substantial barriers to entry. Because relatively few firms compete in such a market, each can influence the price, and hence each affects rival firms. The need to consider the behavior of rival firms makes an oligopoly firm's profit-maximization decision more difficult than that of a monopoly or a competitive firm. A monopoly has no rivals, and a competitive firm ignores the behavior of individual rivals—it considers only the market price and its own costs in choosing its profit-maximizing output.

An oligopoly firm that ignores or inaccurately predicts its rivals' behavior is likely to suffer a loss of profit. For example, as its rivals produce more cars, the price Ford can get for its cars falls. If Ford underestimates how many cars its rivals will produce, Ford may produce too many automobiles and lose money.

cartel
a group of firms that explicitly agree to coordinate their activities

Oligopolistic firms may act independently or coordinate their actions. A group of firms that explicitly agree to coordinate their activities is called a **cartel**. These firms may agree on how much each firm will sell or on a common price. By cooperating and behaving like a monopoly, the members of a cartel collectively earn the monopoly profit—the maximum possible profit.

If oligopolistic firms do not collude, they earn lower profits. Nonetheless, because there are relatively few firms in the market, oligopolistic firms that act independently may earn positive economic profits in the long run, unlike competitive firms.

A barrier to entry keeps the number of firms small in an oligopolistic market. If a market has no barriers to entry, firms enter the market until profits are driven to zero. In perfectly competitive markets, enough entry occurs that firms face a horizontal demand curve and are price takers. However, in other markets, even after entry has driven profits to zero, each firm faces a downward-sloping demand curve. Because of this slope, the firm can charge a price above its marginal cost, creating a *market failure*: inefficient (too little) consumption. **Monopolistic competition** is a market structure in which firms have market power (the ability to raise price profitably above marginal cost) but no additional firm can enter and earn positive profits.

monopolistic competition
a market structure in which firms have market power but no additional firm can enter and earn positive profits

In this chapter, we examine cartelized, oligopolistic, and monopolistically competitive markets in which firms set quantities or prices. As noted in Chapter 4, the monopoly equilibrium is the same whether a monopoly sets price or quantity. Similarly, if colluding oligopolies sell identical products, the cartel equilibrium is the same whether they set quantity or price. The oligopolistic and monopolistically competitive equilibria differ, however, if firms set prices instead of quantities.

In this chapter, we examine eight main topics

1. **Market structures:** The number of firms, price, profits, and other properties of markets vary, depending on whether the market is monopolistic, oligopolistic, monopolistically competitive, or competitive.

2. **Game theory:** When there are relatively few firms in a market, firms take into account how their actions affect other firms and how other firms' actions affect them. Economists use a set of tools called *game theory* to analyze conflicts and cooperation between such firms.

3. **Cooperative oligopoly models:** If firms successfully coordinate their actions, they can collectively behave like a monopoly.

4. **Cournot model of noncooperative oligopoly:** In a Cournot model, in which firms choose their output levels without colluding, the market output and firms' profits lie between the competitive and monopoly levels.

5. **Stackelberg model of noncooperative behavior:** In a Stackelberg model, in which a *leader* firm chooses its output level before its identical-cost rivals, market output is greater than if all firms choose their output simultaneously, and the leader makes a higher profit than the other firms.

6. **Comparison of collusive, Cournot, Stackelberg, and competitive equilibria:** Total market output declines from the competitive level to the Stackelberg level to the Cournot level and reaches a minimum with monopoly or collusion.

7. **Monopolistic competition:** When firms can freely enter the market but, in equilibrium, face downward-sloping demand curves, firms charge prices above marginal cost but make no profit.

8. **Bertrand price-setting model:** The oligopoly equilibrium in which firms set prices differs from the quantity-setting equilibrium and depends on the degree of product differentiation.

6.1 | Market Structures

Markets differ according to the number of firms in the market, the ease with which firms may enter and leave the market, and the ability of firms in a market to differentiate their products from those of their rivals. Table 6.1 lists characteristics and properties of competition, monopoly, oligopoly, and monopolistic competition. For each of these market structures, we assume that the firms face many price-taking buyers.

Regardless of market structures, a firm maximizes its profit by setting quantity so that marginal revenue equals marginal cost (row 1 of Table 6.1). The

TABLE 6.1   Properties of Monopoly, Oligopoly, Monopolistic Competition, and Competition

	Monopoly	Oligopoly	Monopolistic Competition	Competition
1. Profit-maximization condition	$MR = MC$	$MR = MC$	$MR = MC$	$p = MR = MC$
2. Ability to set price	Price setter	Price setter	Price setter	Price taker
3. Market power	$p > MC$	$p > MC$	$p > MC$	$p = MC$
4. Entry conditions	No entry	Limited entry	Free entry	Free entry
5. Number of firms	1	Few	Few or many	Many
6. Long-run profit	≥ 0	≥ 0	0	0
7. Strategy dependent on individual rival firms' behavior	No (has no rivals)	Yes	Yes	No (cares about market price only)
8. Products	Single product	May be differentiated	May be differentiated	Undifferentiated
9. Example	Local natural gas utility	Automobile manufacturers	Plumbers in a small town	Apple farmers

four market structures differ in terms of the market power of firms (ability to set price above marginal cost), ease of entry of new firms, and strategic behavior on the part of firms (taking account of rivals' actions). Monopolies, oligopolies, and monopolistically competitive firms are price setters rather than price takers (row 2) because they face downward-sloping demand curves. As a consequence, market failures occur in each of these market structures because price is above marginal revenue and hence above marginal cost (row 3). In contrast, a competitive firm faces a horizontal demand curve, so its price equals its marginal cost.

A monopoly or an oligopoly does not fear entry (row 4) because of insurmountable barriers to entry such as government licenses or patents. These barriers to entry restrict the number of firms so that there is only one firm (*mono-*) in a monopoly and, usually, a few (*oligo-*) in an oligopoly (row 5). The key difference between oligopolistic and monopolistically competitive markets is that firms are free to enter only in a monopolistically competitive market.

In both competitive and monopolistically competitive markets, entry occurs until no new firm can profitably enter (so the marginal firm earns zero profit, row 6). Monopolistically competitive markets have fewer firms than perfectly competitive markets do. Because they have relatively few rivals and hence are large relative to the market, each monopolistically competitive firm faces a downward-sloping demand curve.

Oligopolistic and monopolistically competitive firms pay attention to rival firms' behavior, in contrast to monopolistic or competitive firms (row 7). A monopoly has no rivals. A competitive firm ignores the behavior of individual rivals in choosing its output because the market price tells the firm everything it needs to know about its competitors.

Oligopolistic and monopolistically competitive firms may produce differentiated products (row 8). For example, Camry and Taurus automobiles differ in size, weight, and various other dimensions. In contrast, competitive apple farmers sell undifferentiated (homogeneous) products.

6.2 Game Theory

Business is a good game—lots of competition and a minimum of rules. You keep score with money. —Nolan Bushnell (founder of Atari, an electronic game company)

strategy
a battle plan of the actions a firm plans to take to compete with other firms

game
any competition between players (firms) in which strategic behavior plays a major role

game theory
a set of tools that economists, political scientists, military analysts, and others use to analyze decision-making by players that use strategies

Nash equilibrium
a set of strategies such that, holding the strategies of all other firms constant, no firm can obtain a higher profit by choosing a different strategy

best response
the strategy that maximizes a firm's profit, given its beliefs about its rivals' strategies

duopoly
an oligopoly with two firms

Unlike a monopoly or a competitive firm, an oligopolistic or monopolistically competitive firm considers how its actions affect its rivals and how rivals' actions will affect it. Each firm forms a **strategy**, which is a battle plan of the actions (such as setting a price or quantity) that it will take to compete with other firms. A fairly simple strategy is to produce 100 units of output regardless of what anyone else does. A more complex strategy is for a firm to produce a small quantity as long as its rival produces a small amount and a large quantity otherwise.

We can think of oligopolies as engaging in a **game**, which is any competition between players (such as firms) in which strategic behavior plays a major role. **Game theory** is a set of tools that economists, political scientists, military analysts, and others use to analyze decision making by players (such as firms) who use strategies. These same tools can be used to analyze oligopolistic games, poker, coin-matching games, tic-tac-toe, elections, and wars.

Although we call the conflict between oligopolists a game, firms do not view this competition as frivolous. These games are serious business. Each firm is interested in achieving the largest possible profit (or payoff) at the end of the game. Typically, one firm's gain comes at the expense of the other firm. Each firm's profit depends on the actions taken by all the firms. For example, if one oligopolistic firm increases its output, the price falls for all firms, affecting the profits of all firms.

When is an oligopolistic market in equilibrium? In describing competitive and monopolistic markets, we said that the market is in equilibrium if no firm has a desire to change its output level given what everyone else is doing. John Nash (1951), a Nobel Prize–winning economist and mathematician, defined an oligopolistic equilibrium similarly: No firm wants to change its strategy given what everyone else is doing. Formally, a set of strategies is a **Nash equilibrium** if, holding the strategies of all other players (firms) constant, no player (firm) can obtain a higher payoff (profit) by choosing a different strategy. In a Nash equilibrium, no firm wants to change its strategy because each firm is using its **best response**—the strategy that maximizes its profit, given its beliefs about its rivals' strategies.

A SINGLE-PERIOD, TWO-FIRM, QUANTITY-SETTING GAME

We illustrate game theory and determine the Nash equilibrium for a **duopoly**: an oligopoly with two (*duo-*) firms. We examine how American Airlines and United Airlines actually compete for customers on flights between Chicago and Los Angeles.[1]

The total number of passengers flown by these two firms, Q, is the sum of the number of passengers flown on American, q_A, and those flown on United, q_U. These airlines have a great deal of latitude in setting the number of flights and the number of seats per flight. For simplicity in this section, however, we assume that the airlines can pick only a relatively large quantity, 64 units (one unit being 1,000 passengers) per quarter, or a relatively small quantity, 48 units per quarter.

---

[1]This example is based on Brander and Zhang (1990). They reported data for economy and discount passengers taking direct flights between the two cities in the third quarter of 1985. In calculating the profits, we assume that Brander and Zhang's estimate of the firms' constant marginal cost is the same as the firms' relevant long-run average cost.

TABLE 6.2   Profit Matrix for a Quantity-Setting Game

		American Airlines	
		$q_A = 64$	$q_A = 48$
United Airlines	$q_U = 64$	$4.1 / $4.1	$5.1 / $3.8
	$q_U = 48$	$3.8 / $5.1	$4.6 / $4.6

Note: Quantities are in thousands of passengers per quarter; profits are in millions of dollars per quarter.

A *profit matrix* (or *payoff matrix*), such as in Table 6.2, shows the strategies the firms may choose and the resulting profits. If American chooses a large quantity, $q_A = 64$ units per quarter, and United chooses a small quantity, $q_U = 48$ units per quarter, the firms' profits are in the cell in the lower left-hand corner of the matrix. In that cell, American's profit (upper-right number) is $5.1 million per quarter, and United's profit (bottom-left number) is $3.8 million per quarter.

Because the firms choose their strategies simultaneously, each firm selects a strategy that maximizes its profit *given what it believes the other firm will do.* Thus the firms are playing a *noncooperative game of imperfect information* in which each firm must choose an action before observing the simultaneous action by its rival.

How can a firm decide its best response to the other firm's strategy if it doesn't know what the other firm will do? The firm rejects any strategy that is strictly dominated by another strategy. Strategy 1 *strictly dominates* Strategy 2 if Strategy 1 produces a profit at least as high as Strategy 2 does, *regardless of the action taken by the rival firm.* If one strategy strictly dominates *all* other strategies, regardless of the actions chosen by rival firms, the firm should choose this **dominant strategy**. Where a firm has a dominant strategy, its belief about its rivals' behavior is irrelevant.

Although firms do not always have dominant strategies, they do have them in this game. To determine American's dominant strategy, American's managers can use the following reasoning:

dominant strategy
a strategy that strictly dominates (gives higher profits than) all other strategies, regardless of the actions chosen by rival firms

■ *If United chooses the high-output strategy* ($q_U = 64$), *American's high-output strategy maximizes its profit:* Given United's strategy, American's profit is $4.1 million (top-right number in the upper-left cell) with its high-output strategy ($q_A = 64$) and only $3.8 million (top-right number in the upper-right cell) with its low-output strategy ($q_A = 48$). Thus American is better off using a high-output strategy if United chooses its high-output strategy.

■ *If United chooses the low-output strategy* ($q_U = 48$), *American's high-output strategy maximizes its profit:* Given United's strategy, American's profit is $5.1 million with its high-output strategy and only $4.6 million with its low-output strategy.

■ *Thus the high-output strategy is American's dominant strategy:* Whichever strategy United uses, American's profit is higher if it uses its high-output strategy.

By the same type of reasoning, United's high-output strategy is also a dominant strategy.

Because the high-output strategy is a dominant strategy for both firms, the pair of high-output strategies, $q_A = q_U = 64$, is a Nash equilibrium. We can use the profit matrix to confirm that this pair of strategies is a Nash equilibrium by showing that neither firm wants to change its strategy if it is certain that the other firm will use its high-output strategy. If American knew that United would use its high-output strategy, it still would not switch to its low-output strategy because its profit would fall from $4.1 million to $3.8 million. Similarly, United wouldn't switch if it knew American would use its high-output strategy. Because neither firm wants to change its strategy given that the other firm is playing its Nash equilibrium strategy, this pair of strategies ($q_A = q_U = 64$) is a Nash equilibrium.

WHY FIRMS DO NOT COOPERATE IN A SINGLE-PERIOD GAME

In this Nash equilibrium, each firm earns $4.1 million, which is less than the $4.6 million it would make if firms restricted their outputs to $q_A = q_U = 48$. Thus *the sum of the firms' profits is not maximized in this simultaneous-choice, one-period game.*

Many people are surprised the first time they hear this result. Why don't the firms cooperate and use the individually and jointly more profitable low-output strategies, by which each earns a profit of $4.6 million, instead of the $4.1 million in the Nash equilibrium? They don't cooperate due to a lack of trust: Each firm uses the low-output strategy only if the firms have a binding agreement.

Suppose that the two firms meet in advance and agree to restrict their outputs to the lower quantity. If the firms are going to engage in this game only once, each has an incentive to cheat on their agreement. If American believes that United will stick to the agreement and produce $q_U = 48$, American can increase its profit from $4.6 million to $5.1 million by violating the agreement and producing $q_A = 64$. Moreover if American thinks that United will also cheat on the agreement by producing $q_U = 64$, American wants to produce the high output (so that it will earn $4.1 million rather than $3.8 million). By this reasoning, each firm has a substantial profit incentive to cheat on the agreement. In this type of game—called a **prisoners' dilemma** game—all players have dominant strategies that lead to a profit (or other payoff) that is inferior to what they could achieve if they cooperated and pursued alternative strategies.[2]

prisoners' dilemma
a game in which all players have dominant strategies that result in profits (or other payoffs) that are inferior to what they could achieve if they used cooperative strategies

COLLUSION IN REPEATED GAMES

If you must play, decide upon three things at the start: the rules of the game, the stakes, and the quitting time. —Chinese Proverb

We've just seen that in a single-period prisoners' dilemma game, the two firms produce more than they would if they colluded. Yet cartels do form. What's wrong with this theory, which says that cartels won't occur? One explanation is that firms frequently engage in multiperiod games, in which collusion is more likely than it is in a single-period game.

In a single-period game, one firm cannot punish the other firm for cheating on a cartel agreement. But if the firms meet period after period, a wayward firm can be punished by the other.

See Question 1.

---

[2]The prisoners' dilemma crops up in virtually every cops-and-robbers show you've seen. The cops arrest Larry and Duncan and put them in separate rooms so that they cannot talk. An assistant district attorney tells Larry, "We have enough evidence to convict you both of a relatively minor crime for which you'll serve a year in prison. If you'll squeal on your partner and he stays silent, we can convict him of a major crime, for which he'll serve five years and you'll go free. If you both confess, you'll each get two years." Meanwhile another assistant district attorney is making Duncan the same offer. By the same reasoning as in the airlines example, both Larry and Duncan confess, even though they are better off if they both keep quiet.

supergame
a game that is played repeatedly, allowing players to devise strategies for one period that depend on rivals' actions in previous periods

Suppose that the single-period prisoners' dilemma game is repeated period after period. In the single-period game, each firm takes its rival's strategy as given and assumes that it cannot affect its rival's strategy. If the same game is played repeatedly, however, firms engage in a **supergame** in which players may devise strategies for this period that depend on rivals' actions in previous periods. For example, a firm may set a low-output level this period only if its rival set a low-output level in the previous period.

In a repeated game, a firm can influence its rival's behavior by *signaling* and *threatening to punish*. One airline could use a low-quantity strategy for a couple of periods to signal to the other firm its desire that the two firms cooperate and produce that low quantity in the future. If the other firm does not respond by lowering its output in future periods, the first firm suffers lower profits for only a couple of periods. However, if the other firm responds to this signal and lowers its quantity, both firms can profitably produce at the low quantity thereafter.

In addition to or instead of signaling, a firm can punish a rival for not restricting output. We can illustrate how firms punish rivals to ensure collusion by using the profit matrix in Table 6.2. Suppose that American announces or somehow indicates to United that it will use the following two-part strategy:

- American will produce the smaller quantity each period as long as United does the same.
- If United produces the larger quantity in period t, American will produce the larger quantity in period $t + 1$ and all subsequent periods.

If United believes that American will follow this strategy, United knows that it will make $4.6 million each period if it produces the lower quantity. Although United can make a higher profit, $5.1 million, in period t by producing the larger quantity, by doing so it lowers its potential profit to $4.1 million in each following period. Thus United's best policy is to produce the lower quantity in each period unless it cares greatly about current profit and little about future profits. If United values future profits nearly as much as current ones, the one-period gain from deviating from the collusive output level does not compensate for the losses from reduced profits in future periods, which is the punishment American will impose. United may take this threat by American seriously because American's best response is to produce the larger quantity if it believes it can't trust United to produce the smaller quantity.[3] Thus if firms play the same game *indefinitely*, they should find it easier to collude.

Playing the same game many times, however, doesn't necessarily help the firms collude. Suppose, for example, that the firms know that they are going to play the game for T periods. In the last period, they know that they're not going to play again, so they know they can cheat—produce a lot of output—without fear of punishment. As a result, the last period is like a single-period game, and all firms cheat. That makes the $T - 1$ period the last interesting period. By the same reasoning, they'll cheat in $T - 1$. Continuing this type of argument, we conclude that maintaining a cartel will be difficult if the game has a known stopping point. If the players know that the game will end but aren't sure when, cheating is less likely to occur. Collusion is therefore more likely in a game that will continue forever or that will end at an uncertain time.

---

[3]American does not have to punish United forever to induce it to cooperate. All it has to do is punish it for a long enough period that it does not pay for United to deviate from the low-quantity strategy in any period.

6.3 Cooperative Oligopoly Models

We have seen that firms have an incentive to form a cartel in which each firm reduces its output so that firms' individual and collective profits rise. As Adam Smith observed more than two centuries ago, "People of the same trade seldom meet together, even for merriment and diversion, but the conversation ends in a conspiracy against the public, or some contrivance to raise prices." Luckily for consumers, cartels often fail because a government forbids them and because each firm in a cartel has an incentive to cheat on the cartel agreement by producing extra output.

LAWS AGAINST CARTELS

In the late nineteenth century, cartels (or, as they were called then, *trusts*) were legal and common in the United States. Oil, railroad, sugar, and tobacco trusts raised prices substantially above competitive levels.

In response to the trusts' high prices, the U.S. Congress passed the Sherman Antitrust Act in 1890 and the Federal Trade Commission Act of 1914, which prohibit firms from *explicitly* agreeing to take actions that reduce competition. In particular, cartels that are formed for the purpose of jointly setting price are strictly prohibited. These laws reduce the probability that cartels form by imposing penalties on firms caught colluding. Virtually all industrialized nations have *antitrust laws*—or, as they are known in other countries, *competition policies*—that limit or forbid some or all cartels.

Some cartels persist despite these laws, for three reasons. First, international cartels and cartels within certain countries operate legally. Second, some illegal cartels operate believing that they can avoid detection or that the punishment will be insignificant. Third, some firms are able to coordinate their activity without explicitly colluding and thereby running afoul of competition laws.

Some international cartels organized by countries rather than firms are legal. The Organization of Petroleum Exporting Countries (OPEC) is an international cartel that was formed in 1960 by five major oil-exporting countries: Iran, Iraq, Kuwait, Saudi Arabia, and Venezuela. In 1971, OPEC members agreed to take an active role in setting oil prices.

Many illegal cartels flout the competition laws in major industrial countries. These firms apparently believe that they are unlikely to get caught or that the punishments they face are so negligible that it pays to collude anyway. Small fines fail to discourage cartel behavior. In a cartel case involving the $9 billion American carpet industry, a firm with $150 million annual sales agreed with the U.S. Justice Department to plead guilty and pay a fine of $150,000. It is hard to imagine that a fine of one-tenth of 1% of annual sales significantly deters cartel behavior.

Even larger fines fail to discourage repeated collusion. In 1996, Archer Daniels Midland (ADM) paid to settle three civil price-fixing-related cases: $35 million in a case involving citric acid (used in many consumer products), $30 million to shareholders as compensation for lost stock value after the citric acid price-fixing scandal became public, and $25 million in a lysine (a feed additive) case. ADM paid a $100 million fine in a federal criminal case for fixing the price of lysine and citric acid in 1996. ADM settled a fructose corn syrup price-fixing case for $400 million in 2004.

American antitrust laws use evidence of conspiracy (such as explicit agreements) rather than the economic effect of monopoly to determine guilt. Charging monopoly-level prices is not necessarily illegal—only the "bad behavior" of explicitly agreeing to raise prices is illegal. As a result, some groups of firms charge monopoly-level prices without violating the competition laws. These firms may *tacitly collude* without meeting by signaling to each other through their actions. Although the firms' actions may not be illegal, they behave much like cartels. For example, MacAvoy (1995) concluded that the major U.S. long-distance telephone companies tacitly colluded; as a result, each firm's Lerner Index (Chapter 4), $(p - MC)/p$, exceeded 60%, which is well above competitive levels.

Over the past dozen years, the European Commission has been pursuing antitrust (competition) cases under laws that are similar to U.S. statutes. Recently the European Commission, the DOJ, and the FTC have become increasingly aggressive, prosecuting many more cases. Following the lead of the United States, which imposes both civil and criminal penalties, the British government introduced legislation in 2002 to criminalize certain cartel-related conduct. The European Union uses only civil penalties, but its fines have mounted dramatically, as have U.S. fines.

In 1993, the DOJ introduced a new Corporate Leniency Program guaranteeing that participants in cartels who blow the whistle will receive immunity from federal prosecution. As a consequence, the DOJ has caught, prosecuted, and fined several gigantic cartels. On Valentine's Day, 2002, the European Commission adopted a similar policy. In 2004, Japan started more aggressively pursuing antitrust cases.

WHY CARTELS FORM

We now consider why cartels form, why cartel members have an incentive to deviate from the cartel agreement, and why some cartels succeed where others fail. A cartel forms if members of the cartel believe that they can raise their profits by coordinating their actions. Although cartels usually involve oligopolies, cartels may form in a market that would otherwise be competitive.

If a competitive firm is maximizing its profit, why should joining a cartel increase its profit? The answer involves a subtle argument. When a competitive firm chooses its profit-maximizing output level, it considers how varying its output affects its own profit only. The firm ignores the effect that changing its output level has on other firms' profits. A cartel, by contrast, takes into account how changes in any one firm's output affect the profits of all members of the cartel.

If a competitive firm lowers its output, it raises the market price very slightly—so slightly that the firm ignores the effect not only on other firms' profits but also on its own. If all the identical competitive firms in an industry lower their output by this same amount, however, the market price will change noticeably. Recognizing this effect of collective action, a cartel chooses to produce a smaller market output than is produced by a competitive market.

Figure 6.1 illustrates this difference between a competitive market and a cartel. There are n firms in this market, and no further entry is possible. Panel a shows the marginal and average cost curves of a typical firm. If all firms are price takers, the market supply curve, S, is the horizontal sum of the individual marginal cost curves above minimum average cost, as shown in panel b. At the competitive price, p_c, each price-taking firm produces q_c units of output (where MC intersects the line at p_c in panel a). The market output is $Q_c = nq_c$ (where S intersects the market demand curve in panel b).

Now suppose that the firms form a cartel. Should they reduce their output? At the competitive output, the cartel's marginal cost (which is the competitive industry supply curve, S in panel b) is greater than its marginal revenue, so the cartel's profit rises if it reduces output. The cartel's collective profit rises until output is reduced by enough that its marginal revenue equals its marginal cost at Q_m, the monopoly output. If the profit of the cartel increases, the profit of each of the n members of

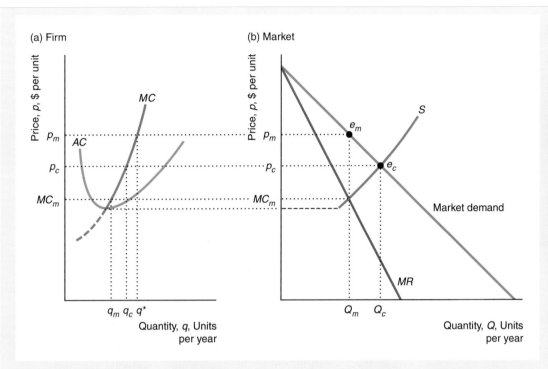

Figure 6.1 Competition Versus Cartel. (a) The marginal cost and average cost of one of the n firms in the market are shown. A competitive firm produces q_c units of output, whereas a cartel member produces $q_m < q_c$. At the cartel price, p_m, each cartel member has an incentive to increase its output from q_m to q^* (where the dotted line at p_m intersects the MC curve). (b) The competitive equilibrium, e_c, has more output and a lower price than the cartel equilibrium, e_m.

See Question 2.

the cartel also increases. To achieve the cartel output level, each firm must reduce its output to $q_m = Q_m/n$, as panel a shows.

Why must the firms form a cartel to achieve these higher profits? A competitive firm produces q_c, where its marginal cost equals the market price. If only one firm reduces its output, it loses profit because it sells fewer units at essentially the same price. By getting all the firms to lower their output together, the cartel raises the market price and hence individual firms' profits. The less elastic the market demand the potential cartel faces, all else the same, the higher the price the cartel sets (Chapter 4) and the greater the benefit from cartelizing. If the penalty for forming an illegal cartel is relatively low, some unscrupulous businesspeople may succumb to the lure of extra profits and join.

APPLICATION

Catwalk Cartel

Being thin, rich, and beautiful doesn't make you immune to exploitation. Some of the world's most successful models charged 10 of New York's top modeling agencies—including Wilhelmina, Ford, Next, IMG, and Elite—with operating a sleazy cartel that cheated them out of millions of dollars in commissions.

Carolyn Fears—a 5'11", redheaded former model who had earned up to $200,000 a year—initiated the suit when she learned that her agency not only charged her a 20% commission every time she was booked, but also extracted a 20% commission from her employers (mostly magazines). Her class-action lawsuit alleged that the agencies collectively fixed commissions for Claudia Schiffer, Heidi Klum, Gisele Bundchen, and thousands of other models over many years.

The agencies had formed an industry group, International Model Managers Association, Inc. (IMMA), which held repeated meetings. Monique Pillard, an executive at Elite Model Management, fired off a memo concerning one IMMA meeting, in which she "made a point . . . that we are all committing suicide, if we do not stick together. Pauline's agreed with me but as usual, Bill Weinberg [of Wilhelmina] cautioned me about price fixing. . . . Ha! Ha! Ha! . . . the usual (expletive)." As the trial judge, Harold Baer Jr., observed, while "Wilhelmina objects to the outward discussion of price fixing, it is plausible from Pillard's reaction that Wilhelmina's objection was to the dissemination of information, not to the underlying price-fixing agreement."

The models argue that the association was little more than a front for helping agency heads keep track of each other's pricing policies. Documents show that, shortly after association meetings, the agencies uniformly raised their commission rates from 10% to 15% and then to 20%. For example, at a meeting before the last increase, an Elite executive gave his competitors a heads up—but had not informed his clients—that Elite planned to raise its commissions to 20%. He said that at Elite, "we were also favorable to letting everyone know as much as possible about our pricing policies."

The trial started in 2004. Most of the parties settled in 2005. IMG alone paid the models $11 million.

WHY CARTELS FAIL

A thing worth having is a thing worth cheating for. —W. C. Fields

Cartels fail if noncartel members can supply consumers with large quantities of goods. For example, copper producers formed an international cartel that controlled only about a third of the noncommunist world's copper production and faced additional competition from firms that recycle copper from scrap materials. Because of this competition from noncartel members, the cartel was not successful in raising and keeping copper prices high.

In addition, *each member of a cartel has an incentive to cheat on the cartel agreement.* The owner of a firm may reason, "I joined the cartel to encourage others to reduce their output and increase profits for everyone. I can make more, however, if I cheat on the cartel agreement by producing extra output. I can get away with cheating if the other firms can't tell who's producing the extra output because I'm just one of many firms and because I'll hardly affect the market price." By this reasoning, it is in each firm's best interest for all *other* firms to honor the cartel agreement—thus driving up the market price—while it ignores the agreement and makes extra, profitable sales at the high price.

Figure 6.1 illustrates why firms want to cheat. At the cartel output, q_m in panel a, each cartel member's marginal cost is MC_m. The marginal revenue of a firm that violates the agreement is p_m because it is acting like a price taker with respect to the market price. Because the firm's marginal revenue (price) is above its marginal cost, the firm wants to increase its output. If the firm decides to violate the cartel agreement, it maximizes its profit by increasing its output to q^*, where its marginal cost equals p_m.

As more and more firms leave the cartel, the cartel price falls. The colluding firms act like a dominant firm facing a competitive fringe (Chapter 4). Eventually, if enough firms quit, the cartel collapses.

MAINTAINING CARTELS

To keep firms from violating the cartel agreement, the cartel must be able to detect cheating and punish violators. Further, the members of the cartel must keep their illegal behavior hidden from customers and government agencies.

Detection. Cartels use many techniques to detect cheating. Some cartels, for example, give members the right to inspect each other's books. Similarly, governments often help cartels by reporting bids on government contracts, so that other firms learn if a cartel member bids below the agreed-on cartel price.

Cartels may divide the market by region or by customers, so that a firm that tries to steal another firm's customer is more likely to be detected. The two-country mercury cartel (1928–1972) allocated the Americas to Spain and Europe to Italy.

Other cartels use industry organizations to detect cheating. These organizations collect data on market share by firm and circulate their results. If a firm cheats on a cartel, its share would rise and other firms would know that it cheated.

You may have seen "low price" ads in which local retail stores guarantee to meet or beat the prices of any competitors. You may have thought that such a guarantee assured you of a low price. However, it may be a way for the firm to induce its customers to report cheating on a cartel agreement by other firms (Salop, 1986).

Enforcement. Many methods are used to enforce cartel agreements. For example, GE and Westinghouse, the two major sellers of large steam-turbine generators, included "most-favored-nation clauses" in their contracts. These contracts stated that the seller would not offer a lower price to any other current or future buyer without offering the same price decrease to that buyer. This type of rebate clause creates a penalty for cheating on the cartel: If either company cheats by cutting prices, it has to lower prices to all previous buyers as well. Another means of enforcing a cartel agreement is through threats of violence.

Government Support. Sometimes governments help create and enforce cartels. For example, U.S., European, and other governments signed an agreement in 1944 to establish a cartel to fix prices for international airline flights and prevent competition.[4]

---

[4] The European Court of Justice struck down the central provisions of aviation treaties among the United States and eight other countries in 2002. The European Commission plans to try to negotiate new treaties.

Professional baseball teams have been exempted from some U.S. antitrust laws since 1922. As a result, they can use the courts to help enforce certain aspects of their cartel agreement. Major league clubs are able to avoid competing for young athletes by means of a draft and contracts, limited geographic competition between teams, joint negotiations for television and other rights, and by acting collectively in many other ways.

● APPLICATION

A Government-Created Cartel

In recent years, a number of governments have created foreign cartels through their trade policies. In 1981, to protect U.S. auto manufacturers and workers, the Reagan administration negotiated voluntary export restraint (VER) agreements whereby Japanese automobile manufacturers would reduce their exports to the United States. The Japanese manufacturers also signed VER agreements with West Germany and Belgium at about the same time.

Why would the Japanese manufacturers "voluntarily" reduce their exports? One explanation is that they were under pressure from both the U.S. and Japanese governments and feared that quotas would be applied. A more likely explanation is that agreeing to the VERs was in their best interests.

Under these agreements, the Japanese manufacturers were to reduce their exports to the United States, thereby forcing American consumers to pay more for domestic and Japanese cars. The VER agreements achieved this goal: Domestic and foreign manufacturers benefited at the expense of American consumers.

If the Japanese car manufacturers were operating independently before 1981, they could increase their collective profit by reducing the number of cars each exported to the United States. They would face the usual problems in trying to agree between themselves to restrict exports. The VERs, then, provided a mechanism for the firms to reduce exports collectively and profitably. By this argument, the Japanese manufacturers wanted firm-specific quotas (if not set too low), which would ensure that no manufacturer cheated on the agreement. Indeed, when the United States allowed the VER agreements to lapse in 1985, the Japanese government—presumably reflecting the sentiments of the car manufacturers—said that it wanted to continue to restrict exports.

Ries (1993) reported that the stock market value of firms in the Japanese automobile industry increased during the VER period by $6.6 billion, of which $2.2 billion was due to the American VER announcement. Scott (1994) estimated that the VERs raised the price of American cars by 5.4% between 1981 and 1983. Using a general-equilibrium trade model, de Melo and Tarr (1996) estimated that the welfare cost of the VER was about $9 billion and that the annual costs per job protected in the auto sector (at the expense of employment elsewhere) ranged from $164,000 to $296,000. Berry et al. (1999) estimated that the VER increased U.S. auto firms' profits by $10.2 billion but cost U.S. consumers $13.1 billion.

See Question 11.

The U.S. government's use of quantity restrictions is bizarre. Foreign and domestic auto manufacturers capture the extra "cartel" profits from the higher prices caused by the VER. Had the U.S. government used tariffs instead, the domestic price would have risen, helping domestic firms, but the extra profits from the increase in price would have gone to the U.S. government through tariff revenues instead of to foreign manufacturers.

The longstanding Multi-fiber Arrangement on Textiles, which ended in 2005, is a more recent VER. Under the WTO's rules, governments are prohibited from negotiating VERs but may negotiate price undertakings that set import price minimums. For example, the United States currently has such restrictions on tomato imports from Mexico.

ENTRY AND CARTEL SUCCESS

Barriers to entry that limit the number of firms help the cartel detect and punish cheating. The fewer the firms in a market, the more likely it is that other firms will know if a given firm cheats and the easier it is to impose costs on that firm. Cartels with a large number of firms are relatively rare, except those involving professional associations. Hay and Kelley (1974) examined Department of Justice price-fixing cases from 1963 to 1972 and found that only 6.5% involved 50 or more conspirators, the average number of firms was 7.25, and nearly half the cases (48%) involved 6 or fewer firms.

When new firms enter their market, cartels frequently fail. For example, when only Italy and Spain sold mercury, they were able to establish and maintain a stable cartel. When a larger group of countries joined them, their attempts to cartelize the world mercury market repeatedly failed (MacKie-Mason and Pindyck, 1986).

● APPLICATION

Bail Bonds

The state of Connecticut sets a maximum fee that bail-bond businesses can charge for posting a given size bond (Ayres and Waldfogel, 1994). The bail-bond fee is set at virtually the maximum amount allowed by law in cities with only one active firm (Plainville, 99% of the maximum; Stamford, 99%; and Wallingford, 99%). The price is as high in cities with a duopoly (Ansonia, 99.6%; Meriden, 98%; and New London, 98%). In cities with three or more firms, however, the price falls well below the maximum permitted price, possibly because the difficulty of maintaining a cartel or tacit collusion rises with the number of firms. The fees are only 54% of the maximum in Norwalk with 3 firms, 64% in New Haven with 8 firms, and 78% in Bridgeport with 10 firms.

See Question 8.

MERGERS

If antitrust or competition laws prevent firms from colluding, they may try to merge instead. Recognizing this potential problem, U.S. laws restrict the ability of firms to merge if the effect would be anticompetitive. Whether the Department of Justice or the Federal Trade Commission (FTC) challenges a proposed merger turns on a large number of issues. Similarly, for the last 12 years, the European Commission has been active in reviewing and, when it felt it was necessary, blocking mergers. With only one exception (in 2002), none of the commission's decisions have been rejected by the courts. One reason why governments limit mergers is that all the firms in a market could combine and form a monopoly.

Then would it not be a good idea to ban all mergers? No, because some mergers result in more efficient production. Formerly separate firms may become more efficient because of greater scale, sharing trade secrets, or closing duplicative retail outlets. For example, when Chase and Chemical banks merged, they closed or combined seven branches in Manhattan that were located within two blocks of other branches.

● **APPLICATION**

Airline Mergers: Market Power Versus Flight Frequency

When duopoly airlines merge, the resulting monopoly may raise its price—due to its greater market power—and change its flight schedule. Consumers value both low prices and frequent, convenient flights. If the duopoly firms had similar departure times for their flights, the monopoly could schedule fewer but more convenient flights that would reduce costly travel delays for consumers.

Richard (2003) empirically examined United Airlines and American Airlines routes out of Chicago's O'Hare Airport. He concluded that airline mergers reduce passenger volume and cause consumer surplus to fall 20% on average, taking account of schedules. However, in one in nine markets, a gain from better schedules would increase consumer surplus by 19%.

6.4   Cournot Model of Oligopoly

We just used our monopoly and dominant-firm models to analyze markets where oligopoly firms collude. We need new models, however, to explain how oligopolies behave if they act independently.

Although there is only one model of competition and one model of monopoly, there are many models of noncooperative oligopoly behavior. Because strategies matter for oligopolies, many market outcomes are possible. Here we examine two oligopoly models in which firms choose quantities: the Cournot and Stackelberg models.

Which model is appropriate to use depends on the institutional features of a market. If firms set output simultaneously and let the market determine the price, a Cournot model works well. If one firm can set output before other firms, a Stackelberg model is appropriate. Similarly, if oligopolies set price instead of quantity, a Bertrand oligopoly model is relevant. Where the institutional features of a market are not well understood, an economist may try each model to see which best predicts actual behavior in that market.

Antoine-Augustin Cournot introduced the first formal model of oligopoly in 1838. Cournot asked how oligopoly firms behave if they choose how much to produce at the same time. As in the prisoners' dilemma game, the firms are playing a noncooperative game of imperfect information; each firm must choose its output level before knowing what the other firm will choose. Now, however, the firms may choose any output level they want.

To simplify our analysis of the Cournot oligopoly model, we examine a market in which

■   There are two firms, and no other firms can enter.
■   The firms sell identical (undifferentiated, homogeneous) products.
■   The firms compete in a market that lasts for only one period, and the product or service that they sell cannot be stored and sold later.

How much one firm produces directly affects the profit of the other firms, because market price depends on total output. Thus in choosing its strategy to maximize its profit, each firm takes into account its beliefs about the output other firms will sell.

COURNOT MODEL OF AN AIRLINE MARKET

We again examine the duopoly market in which United Airlines and American Airlines fly passengers between Chicago and Los Angeles. We assume that no other companies can enter, perhaps because they cannot obtain landing rights at both airports.[5]

How many passengers does each airline choose to carry? To answer this question, we determine the Nash equilibrium for this model. This Nash equilibrium, in which firms choose quantities, is also called a **Cournot equilibrium**: a set of quantities sold by firms such that, holding the quantities of all other firms constant, no firm can obtain a higher profit by choosing a different quantity.

> **Cournot equilibrium**
> (*Nash equilibrium in quantities*)
> a set of quantities sold by firms such that, holding the quantities of all other firms constant, no firm can obtain a higher profit by choosing a different quantity

To determine the Cournot equilibrium, we need to establish how each firm chooses its strategy: the quantity it produces. We start by using the total demand curve for the Chicago–Los Angeles route and a firm's belief about how much its rival will sell to determine the residual demand curve this firm faces. Next, we examine how a firm uses its residual demand curve to determine its best response: the output level that maximizes its profit, given its belief about how much its rival will produce. Finally, we apply this information about both firms' best responses to determine the Cournot equilibrium.

Graphical Approach. The strategy that each firm uses depends on the demand curve it faces and its marginal cost. American Airline's profit-maximizing output depends on how many passengers it believes United will fly. Figure 6.2 illustrates two possibilities.

If American were a monopoly, it wouldn't have to worry about United's strategy. American's demand would be the market demand curve, *D* in panel a. To maximize its profit, American would set its output so that its marginal revenue curve, *MR*, intersected its marginal cost curve, *MC*, which is constant at $147 per passenger. Panel a shows that the monopoly output is 96 units (thousands of passengers) per quarter and the monopoly price is $243 per passenger (one way).

Because American competes with United, American must take account of United's behavior when choosing its profit-maximizing output. American's demand is not the entire market demand. Rather, American is concerned with its **residual demand curve**: the market demand that is not met by other sellers at any given price. (This concept is analogous to the *residual supply curve*.) In general, if the market demand function is $D(p)$, and the supply of other firms is $S^o(p)$, then the residual demand function, $D^r(p)$, is

> **residual demand curve**
> the market demand that is not met by other sellers at any given price

$$D^r(p) = D(p) - S^o(p).$$

Thus, if United flies q_U passengers regardless of the price, American transports only the residual demand, $Q = D(p)$, minus the q_U passengers, so $q_A = Q - q_U$.

Suppose that American believes that United will fly $q_U = 64$. Panel b shows that American's residual demand curve, D^r, is the market demand curve, D, moved to the left by $q_U = 64$. For example, if the price is $211, the total number of passengers who want to fly is $Q = 128$. If United transports $q_U = 64$, American flies $Q - q_U = 128 - 64 = 64 = q_A$.

---

[5]With the end of deregulation, existing firms were given the right to buy, sell, or rent landing slots. By controlling landing slots, existing firms can make entry difficult.

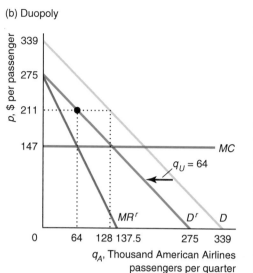

Figure 6.2 American Airlines' Profit-Maximizing Output. (a) If American is a monopoly, it picks its profit-maximizing output, $q_A = 96$ units (thousand passengers) per quarter, so that its marginal revenue, MR, equals its marginal cost, MC. (b) If American believes that United will fly $q_U = 64$ units per quarter, its residual demand curve, D^r, is the market demand curve, D, minus q_U. American maximizes its profit at $q_A = 64$, where its marginal revenue, MR^r, equals MC.

What is American's best-response, profit-maximizing output if its managers believe that United will fly q_U passengers? American can think of itself as having a monopoly with respect to the people who don't fly on United, which its residual demand curve, D^r, shows. To maximize its profit, American sets its output so that its marginal revenue corresponding to this residual demand, MR^r, equals its marginal cost. Panel b shows that if $q_U = 64$, American's best response is $q_A = 64$.

By shifting its residual demand curve appropriately, American can calculate its best response to any given q_U using this type of analysis. Figure 6.3 plots American Airlines' best-response curve, which shows how many tickets American sells for each possible q_U.[6] As this curve shows, American will sell the monopoly number of tickets, 96, if American thinks United will fly no passengers, $q_U = 0$. The negative slope of the best-response curve shows that American sells fewer tickets, the more people American thinks that United will fly. American sells $q_A = 64$ if it thinks q_U will be 64. American shuts down, $q_A = 0$, if it thinks q_U will be 192 or more, because operating wouldn't be profitable.

Similarly, United's best-response curve shows how many tickets United sells if it thinks American will sell q_A. For example, United sells $q_U = 0$ if it thinks American will sell $q_A = 192$, $q_U = 48$ if $q_A = 96$, $q_U = 64$ if $q_A = 64$, and $q_U = 96$ if $q_A = 0$.

A firm wants to change its behavior if it is selling a quantity that is not on its best-response curve. In a Cournot equilibrium, neither firm wants to change its behavior. Thus in a Cournot equilibrium, each firm is on its best-response curve: Each firm is maximizing its profit, given its correct belief about its rival's output.

---

[6]*Jargon alert:* Some economists refer to the *best-response curve* as the *reaction curve*.

Figure 6.3 **American and United's Best-Response Curves.** The best-response curves show the output each firm picks to maximize its profit, given its belief about its rival's output. The Cournot equilibrium occurs at the intersection of the best-response curves.

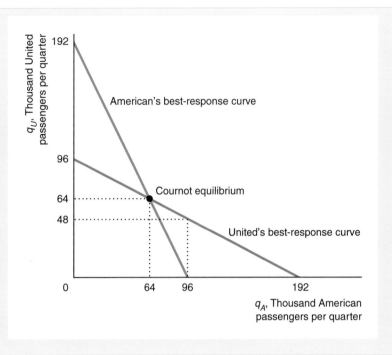

These firms' best-response curves intersect at $q_A = q_U = 64$. If American expects United to sell $q_U = 64$, American wants to sell $q_A = 64$. Because this point is on its best-response curve, American doesn't want to change its output from 64. Similarly, if United expects American to sell $q_A = 64$, United doesn't want to change q_U from 64. Thus this pair of outputs is a Cournot (Nash) equilibrium: Given its correct belief about its rival's output, each firm is maximizing its profit, and neither firm wants to change its output.

Any pair of outputs other than the pair at an intersection of the best-response functions is *not* a Cournot equilibrium. If either firm is not on its best-response curve, it changes its output to increase its profit. For example, the output pair $q_A = 96$ and $q_U = 0$ is not a Cournot equilibrium. American is perfectly happy producing the monopoly output if United doesn't operate at all: American is on its best-response curve. United, however, would not be happy with this outcome because it is not on United's best-response curve. As its best-response curve shows, if it knows that American will sell $q_A = 96$, United wants to sell $q_U = 48$. Only at $q_A = q_U = 64$ does neither firm want to change its behavior.

Algebraic Approach. We can also use algebra to solve for the Cournot equilibrium for these two airlines. (See Appendix 6A for the general case.) We use estimates of the market demand and firms' marginal costs to determine the equilibrium.

Our estimate of the market demand function is

$$Q = 339 - p, \qquad (6.1)$$

where price, p, is the dollar cost of a one-way flight, and total quantity of the two airlines combined, Q, is measured in thousands of passengers flying one way per quarter. Panels a and b of Figure 6.2 show that this market demand curve, D, is a straight line that hits the price axis at \$339 and the quantity axis at 339 units (thousands of passengers) per quarter. Each airline has a constant marginal cost, MC, and average cost, AC, of \$147 per passenger per flight. Using only this information and our economic model, we can find the Cournot equilibrium for the two airlines.

If American believes that United will fly q_U passengers, American expects to fly only the total market demand minus q_U passengers. At a price of p, the total number of passengers, $Q(p)$, is given by the market demand function, Equation 6.1. Thus the residual demand American faces is

$$q_A = Q(p) - q_U = (339 - p) - q_U.$$

Using algebra, we can rewrite this inverse residual demand function as

$$p = 339 - q_A - q_U. \tag{6.2}$$

In panel b, the linear residual demand, D^r, is parallel to the market demand, D, and lies to the left of D by $q_U = 64$.

If a demand curve is linear, the corresponding marginal revenue curve is twice as steep (Chapter 4). The slope of the residual demand curve, Equation 6.2, is $\Delta p / \Delta q_A = -1$, so the slope of the corresponding marginal revenue curve, MR^r in panel b, is -2. Thus the marginal revenue function is[7]

$$MR^r = 339 - 2q_A - q_U. \tag{6.3}$$

American Airlines' best response—its profit-maximizing output, given q_U—is the output that equates its marginal revenue, Equation 6.3, and its marginal cost:

$$MR^r = 339 - 2q_A - q_U = 147 = MC. \tag{6.4}$$

By rearranging Equation 6.4, we can write American's best-response output, q_A, as a function of q_U:

$$q_A = 96 - \tfrac{1}{2}q_U. \tag{6.5}$$

Figure 6.3 shows American's best-response function, Equation 6.5. According to this best-response function, $q_A = 96$ if $q_U = 0$ and $q_A = 64$ if $q_U = 64$. By the same reasoning, United's best-response function is

$$q_U = 96 - \tfrac{1}{2}q_A. \tag{6.6}$$

A Cournot equilibrium is a pair of quantities, q_A and q_U, such that Equations 6.5 and 6.6 both hold: Each firm is on its best-response curve. This statement is equivalent to saying that the Cournot equilibrium is a point at which the best-response curves cross.

One way to determine the Cournot equilibrium is to substitute Equation 6.6 into Equation 6.5,

$$q_A = 96 - \tfrac{1}{2}(96 - \tfrac{1}{2}q_A),$$

See Problem 24.

and solve for q_A. Doing so, we find that $q_A = 64$ is the Cournot equilibrium quantity for American. Substituting $q_A = 64$ into Equation 6.6, we find that $q_U = 64$ is the Cournot equilibrium quantity for United. As a result, the total output in the Cournot equilibrium is $Q = q_A + q_U = 128$. Setting $Q = 128$ in the market demand Equation 6.1, we learn that the Cournot equilibrium price is \$211. (Appendix 6A discusses the Cournot equilibrium where firms have different marginal costs.)

---

[7]American's revenue is $R = pq_A = (339 - q_A - q_U)q_A$. If American treats q_U as a constant and differentiates R with respect to its output, it finds that its marginal revenue is $MR = \partial R / \partial q_A = 339 - 2q_A - q_U$.

COMPARING THE COURNOT AND CARTEL MODELS

The Cournot equilibrium is the only plausible Nash outcome if oligopoly firms set quantities independently in a one-period game. It is possible, however, that the firms could collude—especially if the game is repeated over many periods.

How would American and United behave if they colluded? They would maximize joint profits by producing the monopoly output, 96 units, at the monopoly price, $243 per passenger (panel a of Figure 6.2).

If the airlines collude, they could split the monopoly quantity in many ways. American could act as a monopoly and serve all the passengers, $q_A = 96$ and $q_U = 0$, and possibly give United some of the profits. Or they could reverse roles so that United served everyone: $q_A = 0$ and $q_U = 96$. Or the two airlines could share the passengers in any combination such that the sum of the airlines' passengers equals the monopoly number:

$$q_A + q_U = 96. \tag{6.7}$$

Panel a of Figure 6.4 shows the possible collusive output combinations in Equation 6.7 as a line labeled "Contract curve." Collusive firms could agree (contract) to produce at any of the points along this curve. In the figure, we assume that the collusive firms split the market equally so that $q_A = q_U = 48$.

If the firms were to act as price takers, they would each produce where their residual demand curve intersects their marginal cost curve, so price equals marginal cost of $147. The price-taking equilibrium is $q_A = q_U = 96$. (The Stackelberg equilibrium in the figure is discussed later in this chapter.)

The cartel profits are the highest-possible level of profits the firms can earn. The contract curve shows how the firms split the total monopoly-level profit. Panel b of

(a) Equilibrium Quantities

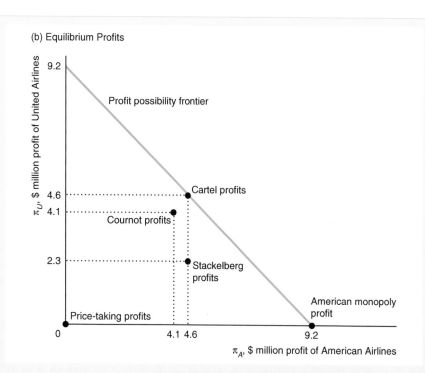

(b) Equilibrium Profits

Figure 6.4 **Duopoly Equilibria.** (a) The intersection of the best-response curves determines the Cournot equilibrium. The possible cartel equilibria lie on the contract curve. If the firms act as price takers, each firm produces where its residual demand equals its marginal cost. (b) The highest possible profit for the two firms combined is given by the profit possibility frontier. It reflects all the possible collusive equilibria, including the one indicated where the firms split the market equally. All equilibria except collusive ones lie within the profit possibility frontier.

Figure 6.4 shows the profit possibility frontier, which corresponds to the contract curve. At the upper left of the profit possibility frontier, United is a monopoly and earns the entire monopoly profit of approximately $9.2 million per quarter.[8] At the lower right, American earns the entire monopoly profit. At points in between, they split the profit. Where they split the profit equally, each earns approximately $4.6 million.

In contrast, if the firms act independently, each earns the Cournot profit of approximately $4.1 million. Because the Cournot price, $211, is lower than the cartel price, $243, consumers are better off if the firms act independently than if they collude.

The Cournot equilibrium market quantity predicted by this model, 128, is closer to the actual observed output, 128.6, than is the predicted cartel quantity, 96. Brander and Zhang (1990) reported that they could not reject the hypothesis that American and United are engaged in a Cournot game based on statistical tests.[9]

THE COURNOT EQUILIBRIUM AND THE NUMBER OF FIRMS

We've just seen that the price to consumers is lower if two firms set output independently than if they collude. The price to consumers is even lower if there are more than two firms acting independently in the market. We now show how the Cournot equilibrium varies with the number of firms.

---

[8]Each firm's profit per passenger is price minus average cost, $p - AC$, so the firm's profit is $\pi = (p - AC)q$, where q is the number of passengers the firm flies. The monopoly price is $243 and the average cost is $147, so the monopoly profit is $\pi = (243 - 147) \times 96$ units per quarter = $9.216 million per quarter.

[9]Because the model described here is a simplified version of the Brander and Zhang (1990) model, the predicted output levels, $q_A = q_U = 64$, differ slightly from theirs. Nonetheless, our predictions are very close to the actual observed outcome, $q_A = 65.9$ and $q_U = 62.7$.

Each Cournot firm maximizes its profit by operating where its marginal revenue equals its marginal cost. Chapter 4 shows that a firm's marginal revenue depends on the price and the elasticity of demand it faces where it maximizes its profit. The marginal revenue for a typical Cournot firm is $MR = p(1 + 1/\varepsilon_r)$, where ε_r is the elasticity of the residual demand curve the firm faces. Appendix 6A shows that $\varepsilon_r = n\varepsilon$, where ε is the market elasticity of demand and n is the number of firms with identical costs. Thus we can write a typical Cournot firm's profit-maximizing condition as

$$MR = p\left(1 + \frac{1}{n\varepsilon}\right) = MC. \tag{6.8}$$

If $n = 1$, the Cournot firm is a monopoly, and Equation 6.8 is the same as the profit-maximizing monopoly condition, Equation 4.7. The more firms there are, the larger the residual demand elasticity, $n\varepsilon$, a single firm faces. As n grows very large, the residual demand elasticity approaches negative infinity ($-\infty$), and Equation 6.8 becomes $p = MC$, which is the profit-maximizing condition of a price-taking competitive firm.

The Lerner Index, $(p - MC)/p$, is a measure of market power: the firm's ability to raise price above marginal cost. By rearranging the terms in Equation 6.8, we find that a Cournot firm's Lerner Index depends on the elasticity the firm faces:

$$\frac{p - MC}{p} = -\frac{1}{n\varepsilon}. \tag{6.9}$$

Thus a Cournot firm's Lerner Index equals the monopoly level, $-1/\varepsilon$, if there is only one firm: Setting $n = 1$ in Equation 6.9, we obtain the monopoly expression (Equation 4.9). Again, as the number of firms grows large, the residual demand elasticity a firm faces approaches $-\infty$, so the Lerner Index approaches zero, which is the same as with price-taking, competitive firms.

We can illustrate these results using our airlines example. Suppose that other airlines with identical marginal cost, $MC = \$147$, were to fly between Chicago and Los Angeles. Table 6.3 shows how the Cournot equilibrium price and the Lerner Index vary with the number of firms.[10]

TABLE 6.3 Cournot Equilibrium Varies with the Number of Firms

Number of Firms, n	Firm Output, q	Market Output, Q	Price, p, \$	Market Elasticity, ε	Residual Demand Elasticity, $n\varepsilon$	Lerner Index, $(p - m)/p = -1/(n\varepsilon)$
1	96	96	243	−2.53	−2.53	0.40
2	64	128	211	−1.65	−3.30	0.30
3	48	144	195	−1.35	−4.06	0.25
4	38.4	154	185.40	−1.21	−4.83	0.21
5	32	160	179	−1.12	−5.59	0.18
10	17.5	175	164.45	−0.94	−9.42	0.11
50	3.8	188	150.76	−0.80	−40.05	0.02
100	1.9	190	148.90	−0.78	−78.33	0.01
200	1.0	191	147.96	−0.77	−154.89	0.01

See Question 7 and Problem 21.

---

[10]In Appendix 6A, we derive the Cournot equilibrium quantity and price for a general linear demand. Given our particular demand curve, Equation 6.1, and marginal cost, \$147, each firm's Cournot equilibrium output is $q = (339 - 147)/(n + 1) = 192/(n + 1)$ and the Cournot market price is $p = (339 + 147n)/(n + 1)$.

As we already know, if there were only one "Cournot" firm, it would produce the monopoly quantity, 96, at the monopoly price, $243. We also know that each duopoly firm's output is 64, so market output is 128 and price is $211. The duopoly market elasticity is $\varepsilon = 1.65$, so the residual demand elasticity each duopolist faces is twice as large as the market elasticity, $2\varepsilon = -3.3$.

As the number of firms increases, each firm's output falls toward zero, but total output approaches 192, the quantity on the market demand curve where price equals marginal cost of $147. Although the market elasticity of demand falls as the number of firms grows, the residual demand curve for each firm becomes increasingly horizontal (perfectly elastic). As a result, the price approaches the marginal cost, $147. Similarly, as the number of firms increases, the Lerner Index approaches the price-taking level of zero.[11]

The table shows that having extra firms in the market benefits consumers. When the number of firms rises from 1 to 4, the price falls by a quarter and the Lerner Index is cut nearly in half. At 10 firms, the price is one-third less than the monopoly level, and the Lerner Index is a quarter of the monopoly level.

APPLICATION

Air Ticket Prices and Rivalry

The markup of price over marginal cost is much greater on routes in which one airline carries most of the passengers than on other routes. Unfortunately, a single firm is the only carrier or the dominant carrier on 58% of all U.S. domestic routes (Weiher et al., 2002).

The first column of the table identifies the market structure for U.S. air routes. The last column shows the share of routes. A single firm (monopoly) serves 18% of all routes. Duopolies control 19% of the routes, three-firm markets are 16%, four-firm markets are 13%, and five or more firms fly on 35% of the routes.

Although nearly two-thirds of all routes have three or more carriers, one or two firms dominate virtually all routes. We call a carrier a *dominant firm* if it has at least 60% of ticket sales by value but is not a monopoly. We call two carriers a *dominant pair* if they collectively have at least 60% of the market but neither firm is a dominant firm and three or more firms fly this route. All but 0.1% of routes have a monopoly (18%), a dominant firm (40%), or a dominant pair (42%).

The first row of the table shows that the price is slightly more than double (2.1 times) marginal cost on average across all U.S. routes and market structures. (This average price includes "free" frequent flier tickets and other below-cost tickets.) The price is 3.3 times marginal cost for monopolies and 3.1 times marginal cost for dominant firms. In contrast, over the sample period, the average price is only 1.2 times marginal cost for dominant pairs.

---

[11]As the number of firms goes to infinity, the Cournot equilibrium goes to perfect competition only if average cost is nondecreasing (Ruffin, 1971).

Type of Market	*p/MC*	Share of All Routes (%)
All market types	2.1	100
Dominant firm	3.1	40
Dominant pair	1.2	42
One firm (monopoly)	3.3	18
Two firms (duopoly)	2.2	19
Dominant firm	2.3	14
No dominant firm	1.5	5
Three firms	1.8	16
Dominant firm	1.9	9
No dominant firm	1.3	7
Four firms	1.8	13
Dominant firm	2.2	6
Dominant pair	1.3	7
No dominant firm or pair	2.1	~0
Five or more firms	1.3	35
Dominant firm	3.5	11
Dominant pair	1.4	23
No dominant firm or pair	1.1	0.1

The markup of price over marginal cost depends much more on whether there is a dominant firm or dominant pair than on the total number of firms in the market. If there is a dominant pair, whether there are four or five firms, the price is between 1.3 times marginal cost for a four-firm route and 1.4 times marginal cost for a route with five or more firms. If there is a dominant firm, price is 2.3 times marginal cost on duopoly routes, 1.9 times on three-firm routes, 2.2 on four-firm routes, and 3.5 times on routes with five or more firms.

Thus, preventing a single firm from dominating a route may substantially lower prices. Even if two firms dominate the market, the markup of price over marginal cpost is substantially lower than if a single firm dominates.

6.5   Stackelberg Model of Noncooperative Behavior

In the Cournot model, both firms make their output decisions at the same time. Suppose, however, that one of the firms, called the *leader*, can set its output before its rival, the *follower*, sets its output. This type of game, in which the players make decisions sequentially, arises naturally if one firm enters a market before another.

Would the firm that got to act first have an advantage? Heinrich von Stackelberg showed how to modify the Cournot model to answer this question.

How does the leader decide to set its output? The leader realizes that once it sets its output, the rival firm will use its Cournot best-response curve to pick a best-response output. Thus the leader predicts what the follower will do before the follower acts. Using this knowledge, the leader manipulates the follower, thereby benefiting at the follower's expense.

We illustrate this model using our airlines market example (Appendix 6B analyzes the model mathematically). Although it is difficult to imagine that either American Airlines or United Airlines actually has an advantage that would allow it to act before its rival, we assume (arbitrarily) that American Airlines can act before United Airlines. We first examine how the airlines would behave if they could pick one of only a few quantities. Then we examine the more general problem, in which they can choose any quantity they want.

STACKELBERG GAME TREE

We illustrate the importance of moving first by using a *game tree*, Figure 6.5. The game tree shows the order of the firms' moves, each firm's possible strategies at the time of its move, and the resulting profits. For simplicity, we assume that each airline can choose one of only three quantities, 48, 64, and 96.

Each line in the decision tree represents an action, and each box is a point of decision by one of the firms. American—the leader—starts by picking one of the three output levels (left side of the figure); then United—the follower—chooses one of the three quantities (middle of the figure), which determines the profits that American and United earn (right side of the figure). For instance, if American picks 64 and then United picks 96, American earns $2.0 million profit per quarter and United earns $3.1 million.

How should American, the leader, pick its output? For each possible quantity it can produce, American predicts what United will do and picks the output level that maximizes its profit.

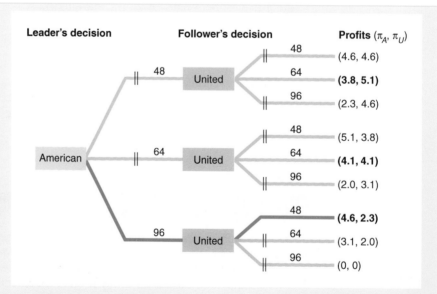

Figure 6.5 **Stackelberg Game Tree.** American, the leader firm, chooses its output level first. Given American's choice, United, the follower, picks an output level. The profits of the two firms that result from these decisions are shown on the right-hand side of the figure. Two lines through an action line show that the firm rejects that action.

To determine the strategies the firms use, we work backward from the follower's decision to the leader's. We first ask what United, the follower, would do, given each possible output choice of American, the leader. Then, using this information about United's reasoning, we determine which strategy American chooses.

United, the follower, does not have a dominant strategy. How much output it produces depends on the quantity that American chose. If American chooses 96, United's profit is $2.3 million if its output is 48, $2 million if it produces 64, and $0 if it picks a quantity of 96. Thus if American chose 96, United's best response is 48. The double lines through the other two action lines show that United will not choose those actions.

Using the same reasoning, American determines how United will respond to each of American's possible actions, as the right-hand side of the figure illustrates. Using its predictions of United's responses, American knows that

- If American chooses 48, United will sell 64, so American's profit will be $3.8 million.
- If American chooses 64, United will sell 64, so American's profit will be $4.1 million.
- If American chooses 96, United will sell 48, so American's profit will be $4.6 million.

Thus to maximize its profit, American chooses 96. United responds by selling 48.

This outcome is a Stackelberg (Nash) equilibrium. Given that American Airlines sets its output at 96, United is using a strategy that maximizes its profit, $q_U = 48$, so it doesn't want to change. Similarly, given how United will respond to each possible American output level, American can't make more profit than selling 96.

American, the Stackelberg leader, sells 50% more than the Cournot quantity, 64, and earns $4.6 million, which is 15% more than the Cournot level of profit, $4.1 million. United, the Stackelberg follower, sells a quantity, 48, and earns a profit, $2.3 million, both of which are less than the Cournot levels.

The value to American of being the leader is $0.5 (= $4.6 − $4.1) million, the amount its profit rises over the Cournot level. However, it is worth $1.8 (= $4.1 − $2.3) million to United Airlines not to be the follower.

Given the option to act first, American chooses a large output level to make it in United's best interest to pick a relatively small output level, 48. In this example, if the firms colluded and both produced 48, both would earn $4.6 million, which is what American earns as the leader. Why doesn't American pick the collusive output level, 48, so that both firms can earn the collusive profit? If American did so, it would be in United's best interest to sell 64 and earn $5.1 million, which would reduce American's profit to $3.8 million. Thus American produces a large output to keep United's output low.

STACKELBERG GRAPHICAL MODEL

Now suppose that the airlines can choose any output level they want and that American Airlines chooses its output first. How does American decide on its optimal policy now?

American uses its residual demand curve to determine its profit-maximizing output. American knows that when it sets q_A, United will use its Cournot best-response function to pick its best-response q_U. Thus American's residual demand curve, D^r (panel a of Figure 6.6), is the market demand curve, D (panel a) minus the output United will produce as summarized by United's best-response curve (panel b). For example, if American sets $q_A = 192$, United's best response is $q_U = 0$ (as shown by

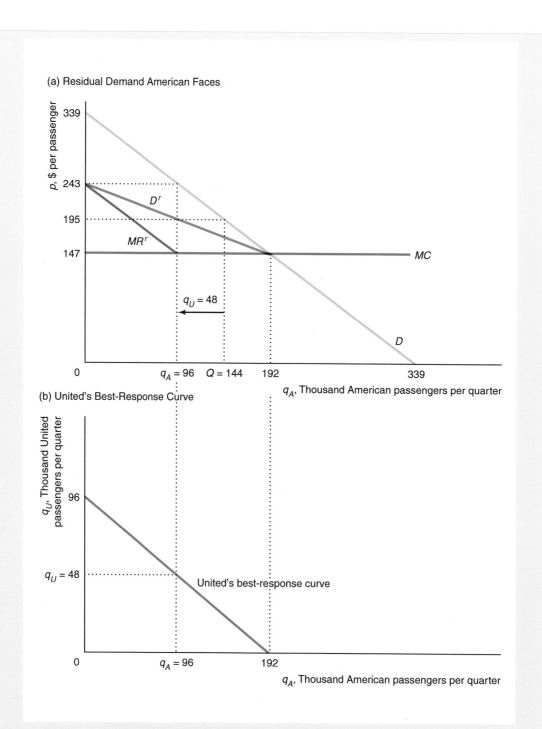

Figure 6.6 Stackelberg Equilibrium. (a) The residual demand the Stackelberg leader faces is the market demand minus the quantity produced by the follower, q_U, given the leader's quantity, q_A. The leader chooses $q_A = 96$ so that its marginal revenue, MR^r, equals its marginal cost. The total output, $Q = 144$, is the sum of the output of the two firms. (b) The quantity the follower produces is its best response to the leader's output, as given by its Cournot best-response curve.

United's best-response curve in panel b). As a result, the residual demand curve and the market demand curve are identical at q_A = 192 (panel a).

Similarly, if American set q_A = 0, United would choose q_U = 96, so the residual demand at q_A = 0 is 96 less than demand. The residual demand curve hits the vertical axis, where q_A = 0, at p = \$243, which is 96 units to the left of demand at that price. When q_A = 96, q_U = 48, so the residual demand at q_A = 96 is 48 units to the left of the demand.

American chooses its profit-maximizing output, q_A = 96, where its marginal revenue curve that corresponds to the residual demand curve, MR^r, equals its marginal cost, \$147. At q_A = 96, the price, which is the height of the residual demand curve, is \$195. Total demand at \$195 is Q = 144. At that price, United produces $q_U = Q - q_A$ = 48, its best response to American's output of q_A = 96.

Thus in this Stackelberg equilibrium, the leader produces twice as much as the follower, as Figure 6.6 and panel a of Figure 6.4 show.[12] The total Stackelberg output, 144, is greater than the total Cournot, 128, and collusive, 96, outputs. As a result, the Stackelberg price, \$195, is less than the Cournot, \$211, and collusive, \$243, prices. Thus consumers prefer the Stackelberg equilibrium to the Cournot equilibrium and the Cournot equilibrium to the collusive equilibrium here (and in any market where all firms have identical cost functions).

The combined Stackelberg profit, \$6.9 million, is less than the combined Cournot, \$8 million, and collusive, \$9.2 million, profits, as panel b of Figure 6.4 shows. The Stackelberg leader, though, earns \$4.6 million, which is more than it could earn in a Cournot game, \$4.1 million. Total Stackelberg profit is less than total Cournot profit because the Stackelberg follower, earning \$2.3 million, is much worse off than in the Cournot equilibrium.

SOLVED PROBLEM 6.1

Use algebra to solve for the Stackelberg equilibrium quantities and market price if American Airlines were a Stackelberg leader and United Airlines were a follower. (*Hint:* As the graphical analysis shows, American Airlines, the Stackelberg leader, maximizes its profit as though it were a monopoly facing a residual demand function.)

Answer

1. *Determine the inverse residual demand function facing American Airlines:* The residual demand function facing American Airlines is the market demand function (Equation 6.1), Q = 330 – p, minus the best-response function of United Airlines (Equation 6.6), $q_U = 96 - \frac{1}{2}q_A$:

$$q_A(p) = Q(p) - q_U(q_A) = 339 - p - [96 - \tfrac{1}{2}q_A] = 243 - p - \tfrac{1}{2}q_A. \qquad (6.10)$$

Using algebra, we can rewrite Equation 6.10 as the inverse residual demand function (which is the D^r line in panel a of Figure 6.6):

$$p = 243 - \tfrac{1}{2}q_A. \qquad (6.11)$$

2. *Solve for American Airlines' profit-maximizing output by equating its marginal revenue and marginal cost:* American Airlines, the Stackelberg leader, acts

---

[12]Here the leader produces the same quantity as a monopoly would, and the follower produces the same quantity as it would in the cartel equilibrium. These relationships are due to the linear demand curve and the constant marginal cost—they do not hold more generally.

like a monopoly with respect to its residual demand. From Chapter 4, we know that its marginal revenue function is the same as its inverse residual demand function, Equation 6.11, except it has twice the slope: $MR_A = 243 - q_A$ (which is the MR^r line in panel a of Figure 6.6). To maximize its profit, American Airlines picks its output so as to equate its marginal revenue to its marginal cost:

$$MR_A = 243 - q_A = 147 = MC. \qquad (6.12)$$

Solving Equation 6.12 for American Airlines' output, we find that $q_A = 96$.

3. *Use United Airlines' best-response function to solve for its quantity and the total output:* Substituting $q_A = 96$ into United Airlines' best-response function, Equation 6.6, we learn that United Airlines sells half as many seats as American Airlines: $q_U = 96 - \frac{1}{2}q_A = 48$. Thus, total output is $Q = q_A + q_U = 96 + 48 = 144$.

4. *Use the market demand function to solve for the market price:* Substituting $Q = 144$, total output, into the market demand function, we determine that the market price is $195.

Comment: See Appendix 6B for the solution to a more general case.

WHY MOVING SEQUENTIALLY IS ESSENTIAL

Why don't we get the Stackelberg equilibrium when both firms move simultaneously? Why doesn't one firm—say, American—announce that it will produce the Stackelberg leader output to induce United to produce the Stackelberg follower output level? The answer is that when the firms move simultaneously, United doesn't view American's warning that it will produce a large quantity as a *credible threat*.

If United believed that threat, it would indeed produce the Stackelberg follower output level. But United doesn't believe the threat because it is not in American's best interest to produce that large a quantity of output. If American were to produce the leader level of output and United produced the Cournot level, American's profit would be lower than if it too produced the Cournot level. Because American cannot be sure that United will believe its threat and reduce its output, American will actually produce the Cournot output level.

Indeed, each firm may make the same threat and announce that it wants to be the leader. Because neither firm can be sure that the other will be intimidated and produce the smaller quantity, both produce the Cournot output level. In contrast, when one firm moves first, its threat to produce a large quantity is credible because it has already *committed* to producing the larger quantity, thereby carrying out its threat.

★ STRATEGIC TRADE POLICY

Suppose that two identical firms in two different countries compete in a world market. Both firms act simultaneously, so neither firm can make itself the Stackelberg leader. A government may be tempted to intervene to make its firm a Stackelberg leader. The Japanese and French governments often help their domestic firms compete with international rivals; so do the U.S., British, Canadian, and many other governments. If only one government intervenes, it can make its domestic firm's threat to produce a large quantity of output credible, so foreign rivals will produce the Stackelberg follower level of output (Spencer and Brander, 1983).

Subsidizing an Airline. We'll modify our airline example to illustrate how one country's government can aid its firm. Suppose that United Airlines were based in one country and American Airlines in another. Initially, United and American are in a Cournot equilibrium. Each firm has a marginal cost of $147 and flies 64 thousand passengers (64 units) per quarter at a price of $211.

Now suppose that United's government gives United a $48-per-passenger subsidy, but the other government doesn't help American. As a result, American's marginal cost remains at $147, but United's marginal cost after the subsidy is only $99.

The firms continue to play Cournot, but the playing field is no longer level.[13] How does the Cournot equilibrium change? Your intuition probably tells you that United's output increases relative to that of American, as we now show.

United still acts at the same time as American, so United acts like any Cournot firm and determines its best-response curve. United's best response to any given American output is the output at which its marginal revenue corresponding to its residual demand, MR^r, equals its marginal cost. The subsidy does not affect United's MR^r curve, but it lowers its MC curve, so United produces more output for any given American output after the cost falls.

Panel a of Figure 6.7 illustrates this reasoning. United's residual demand, D^r, lies 64 units to the left of the market demand, D, if American produces 64. The MR^r curve intersects the original marginal cost, $MC^1 = \$147$, at 64 and the new marginal cost, $MC^2 = \$99$, at 88. Thus if we hold American's output constant at 64, United produces more as its marginal cost falls.

Because this reasoning applies for any level of output American picks, United's best-response function in panel b shifts outward as its marginal cost falls.[14] United's best response to any given quantity that American sells is to sell more than at its previous, higher cost. As a result, the Cournot equilibrium shifts from the original e_1, at which both firms sold 64, to e_2, at which United sells 96 and American sells 48. Thus the $48 subsidy to United causes it to sell the Stackelberg leader quantity and American to sell the Stackelberg follower quantity. The subsidy works by convincing American that United will produce large quantities of output.

Using the market demand curve, Equation 6.1, we find that the market price falls from $211 to $195, benefiting consumers. United's profit increases from $4.1 million to $9.2 million, while American's profit falls to $2.3 million. Thus United and consumers gain and American loses from the fall in United's marginal cost.

This example illustrates that a government subsidy to one firm *can* lead to the same outcome as in a Stackelberg equilibrium. Would a government *want* to give the subsidy that leads to the Stackelberg outcome?

The answer depends on the government's objective. Suppose that the government is interested in maximizing its domestic firm's profit net of (not including) the government's subsidy. The subsidy is a transfer from some citizens (taxpayers) to others

---

[13]Don't you think that anyone who uses the phrase "level playing field" should have to pay a fine?

[14]United sets the marginal revenue that corresponds to its residual demand curve, MR^r, equal to its new marginal cost, MC:

$$MR^r = 339 - 2q_U - q_A = 99 = MC.$$

Using algebra to rearrange this expression, we find that United's best-response function is

$$q_U = 120 - \tfrac{1}{2}q_A.$$

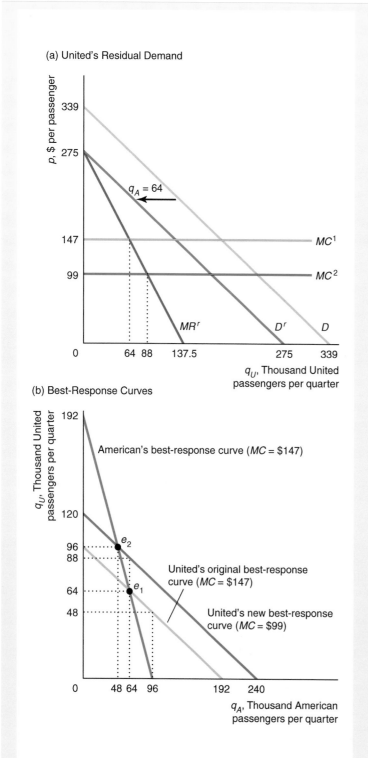

(a) United's Residual Demand

(b) Best-Response Curves

Figure 6.7 Effect of a Government Subsidy on a Cournot Equilibrium.
(a) A government subsidy that lowers United's marginal cost from $MC^1 = \$147$ to $MC^2 = \$99$ causes United's best-response output to American's $q_A = 64$ to rise from $q_U = 64$ to 88. (b) If both airlines' marginal costs are $147, the Cournot equilibrium is e_1. If United's marginal cost falls to $99, its best-response function shifts outward. It now sells more tickets in response to any given American output than previously. At the new Cournot equilibrium, e_2, United sells $q_U = 96$, while American sells only $q_A = 48$.

TABLE 6.4   Effects of a Subsidy Given to United Airlines

Subsidy, s	United				American	
	q_U	π_U	Welfare, $\pi_U - sq_U$		q_A	π_A
60	104	$10.8	$4.58		44	$1.9
48	96	$9.2	$4.61		48	$2.3
30	84	$7.1	$4.50		54	$2.9
0	64	$4.1	$4.10		64	$4.1
−30	44	$1.9	$3.30		74	$5.5

Notes:

The subsidy is in dollars per passenger (and is a tax if negative).

Output units are in thousands of passengers per quarter.

Profits and welfare (defined as United's profits minus the subsidy) are in millions of dollars per quarter.

(the owners of United). We assume that the government doesn't care about consumers—which is certainly true if they live in another country.

Table 6.4 shows the effects of various subsidies and a tax (a negative subsidy). If the subsidy is zero, we have the usual Cournot equilibrium. A $48-per-passenger subsidy leads to the same outcome as in the Stackelberg equilibrium and maximizes the government's welfare measure. At a larger subsidy, such as $60, United's profit rises, but by less than the cost of the subsidy to the government. Similarly, at smaller subsidies or taxes, welfare is also lower.

Problems with Intervention. Thus in theory, a government may want to subsidize its domestic firm to make it produce the same output as it would if it were a Stackelberg leader. If such subsidies are to work as desired, however, five conditions must hold.

First, the government must be able to set its subsidy before the firms choose their output levels. The idea behind this intervention is that one firm cannot act before the other, but its government can act first.

Second, the other government must not retaliate. If both governments intervene, instead of having a game of strategies between firms, we have a game of strategies between governments, in which both countries may lose.

Third, the government's actions must be credible. If the foreign firm's country doesn't believe that the government actually will subsidize its domestic firm, the foreign firm produces the Cournot level. Countries have difficulty in committing to long-term policies. For example, during the 1996 Republican presidential primaries, many candidates said that they would reverse President Clinton's trade policies if they were elected. Similarly, the 2004 Democratic presidential candidates promised to change President Bush's trade policies.

Fourth, the government must know enough about how firms behave to intervene appropriately. If it doesn't know the demand function and the costs of all firms, the government may set its subsidy at the wrong level.

Fifth, the government must know which game the firms are playing. If they are not engaged in a Cournot game, the government would have to intervene in a different way.

Many economists who analyze strategic trade policies strongly oppose them because they are difficult to implement and mean-spirited, "beggar thy neighbor" policies. If only one government intervenes, another country's firm is harmed. If both governments intervene, both countries may suffer. For these reasons, the General Agreement on Tariffs and Trade and the World Trade Organization forbade the use of virtually all explicit export subsidies.

APPLICATION

Government Aircraft Subsidies

Governments consistently intervene in aircraft manufacturing markets. France, Germany, Spain, and the United Kingdom own and heavily subsidize Airbus, which competes in the widebody aircraft market with the U.S. firm Boeing. The U.S. government decries the European subsidies to Airbus, while directing lucrative military contracts to Boeing that the Europeans view as implicit subsidies. In 1992, the governments signed a U.S.–EU agreement on trade in civil aircraft that limits government subsidies (including a maximum direct subsidy limit of 33% of development costs and various limits on variable costs).

Irwin and Pavcnik (2004) found that aircraft prices increased by about 3.7% after the 1992 agreement. This price hike is consistent with a 5% increase in firms' marginal costs after the subsidy cuts.

In 2005, Washington and the European Union traded countercomplaints to the World Trade Organization. Each again charged the other with illegally subsidizing its aircraft manufacturer. And the cycle of subsidies, charges, agreements, and new subsidies continues.

SOLVED PROBLEM   6.2

If governments subsidize identical Cournot duopolies with a specific subsidy of s per unit of output, what is the qualitative effect (direction of change) on the equilibrium quantities and price? Assume that the before-subsidy best-response functions are linear.

Answer

1. *Show the initial, before-subsidy Cournot equilibrium*: We're told that the Cournot firms, labeled Firm A and Firm B on the graph, are identical. As a result, their best-response curves are mirror images of each other, and both firms produce the same quantity, q_1, at the Cournot equilibrium, e_1, where their best-response functions cross.

2. *Show how the best-response curves shift in response to the tax*: We've just seen that a subsidy lowers a firm's marginal cost, causing its best-response curve to shift away from the origin. Because both firms face the same specific subsidy, marginal costs of both firms fall by the same amount. As a result, both after-subsidy best-response curves shift away from the origin by the same amount and remain mirror images of each other.

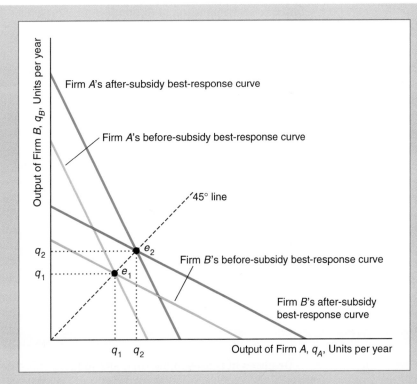

See Question 1.

3. *Compare the two Cournot equilibria*: Each firm produces a larger quantity, q_2, at the new Cournot equilibrium, e_2, than in the original Cournot equilibrium. As a result, total equilibrium quantity rises and the equilibrium price falls.

6.6 Comparison of Collusive, Cournot, Stackelberg, and Competitive Equilibria

The welfare of consumers and firms depends on the market structure, as Table 6.5 shows for our airline example. In this table, the welfare measure is the sum of consumer surplus and the profits of the two firms.

At one extreme, if one firm has a monopoly or if the two firms form a cartel and split the market equally, total output is relatively low, price is high, consumer surplus and welfare are low, and deadweight loss is high. At the other extreme, if American and United act as price takers, output is relatively high, price is low, consumer surplus and welfare are high, and society does not suffer a deadweight loss.

The duopoly Cournot and Stackelberg equilibria (in the table, American is the leader) lie between the extreme cases of monopoly or cartel and price taking. The Stackelberg equilibrium is closer to the price-taking equilibrium than the Cournot equilibrium in terms of total output, price, consumer surplus, welfare, and deadweight loss.

We already know that the Cournot equilibrium approaches the price-taking equilibrium as the number of firms grows. Similarly, we can show that the Stackelberg equilibrium approaches the price-taking equilibrium as the number of Stackelberg followers grows. As a result, the differences between the Cournot, Stackelberg, and price-taking market structures shrink as the number of firms grows.

TABLE 6.5   Comparison of Airline Market Structures

	Monopoly	Cartel	Cournot	Stackelberg	Price Taking
q_A	96	48	64	96	96
q_U	0	48	64	48	96
$Q = q_A + q_U$	96	96	128	144	192
p	\$243	\$243	\$211	\$195	\$147
π_A	\$9.2	\$4.6	\$4.1	\$4.6	\$0
π_U	\$0	\$4.6	\$4.1	\$2.3	\$0
$\Pi = \pi_A + \pi_U$	\$9.2	\$9.2	\$8.2	\$6.9	\$0
Consumer surplus, CS	\$4.6	\$4.6	\$8.2	\$10.4	\$18.4
Welfare, $W = CS + \Pi$	\$13.8	\$13.8	\$16.4	\$17.3	\$18.4
Deadweight loss, DWL	\$4.6	\$4.6	\$2.0	\$1.2	\$0

Notes:

Passengers are in thousands per quarter.

Price is in dollars per passenger.

Profits, consumer surplus, welfare, and deadweight loss are in millions of dollars per quarter.

● **APPLICATION**

Deadweight Losses in the Food and Tobacco Industries

Bhuyan and Lopez (1998) and Bhuyan (2000) estimated the deadweight loss for various U.S. food and tobacco manufacturing oligopolies and monopolistically competitive markets. Most of these industries have deadweight losses that are a relatively small percentage of sales (their prices and quantities are close to competitive levels). However, a few industries, such as cereal and flour and grain mills, have relatively large deadweight losses.

See Problem 21.

Industry	Loss, \$ millions	Share of Sales, %
Cereal	2,192	33
Flour and grain mills	541	26
Poultry and eggs	1,183	8
Roasted coffee	440	7
Cigarettes	1,032	6
All food manufacturing	14,947	5

6.7   Monopolistic Competition

We've assumed that the number of oligopoly firms is fixed because of barriers to entry. As a result, the oligopoly firms (such as the airlines) may earn economic profits. In contrast, monopolistically competitive markets do not have barriers to entry, so firms enter the market until no new firm can enter profitably.

If both competitive and monopolistically competitive firms make zero profits, what distinguishes these two market structures? In contrast to competitive firms (which face horizontal residual demand curves and charge prices equal to marginal cost), monopolistically competitive firms face downward-sloping residual demand curves, so they charge prices above marginal cost. Monopolistically competitive firms face downward-sloping residual demand because they have relatively few rivals or because they sell differentiated products.

The fewer monopolistically competitive firms, the less elastic the residual demand curve each firm faces. As we saw, the elasticity of demand for an individual Cournot firm is $n\varepsilon$, where n is the number of firms and ε is the market elasticity. Thus the fewer the firms in a market, the less elastic the residual demand curve.

When monopolistically competitive firms benefit from economies of scale at high levels of output (the average cost curve is downward sloping), so that each firm is relatively large in comparison to market demand, there is room in the market for only a few firms. In the short run, if fixed costs are large and marginal costs are constant or diminishing, firms have economies of scale at all output levels, so there are relatively few firms in the market. In an extreme case with substantial enough economies of scale, the market may have room for only one firm: a natural monopoly (Chapter 4). The number of firms in equilibrium is smaller the greater the economies of scale and the farther to the left the market demand curve.

Monopolistically competitive firms also face downward-sloping residual demand curves if each firm sells a differentiated product. If some consumers believe that Tide laundry detergent is better than Cheer and other brands, Tide won't lose all its sales even if Tide has a slightly higher price than Cheer. Thus Tide faces a downward-sloping demand curve—not a horizontal one.

MONOPOLISTICALLY COMPETITIVE EQUILIBRIUM

In a monopolistically competitive market, each firm tries to maximize its profit; however, each makes zero economic profit due to entry. Two conditions hold in a monopolistically competitive equilibrium: *Marginal revenue equals marginal cost* (because firms set output to maximize profit), and *price equals average cost* (because firms enter until no further profitable entry is possible).

Figure 6.8 shows a monopolistically competitive market equilibrium. A typical monopolistically competitive firm faces a residual demand curve D^r. To maximize its profit, the firm sets its output, q, where its marginal revenue curve corresponding to the residual demand curve intersects its marginal cost curve: $MR^r = MC$. At that quantity, the firm's average cost curve, AC, is tangent to its residual demand curve. Because the height of the residual demand curve is the price, at the point of tangency, price equals average cost, $p = AC$, and the firm makes zero profit.

If the average cost were less than price at that quantity, firms would make positive profits and entrants would be attracted. If average cost were above price, firms would lose money, so firms would exit until the marginal firm was breaking even.

minimum efficient scale (*full capacity*) the smallest quantity at which the average cost curve reaches its minimum

The smallest quantity at which the average cost curve reaches its minimum is referred to as *full capacity* or **minimum efficient scale**. The firm's full capacity or minimum efficient scale is the quantity at which the firm no longer benefits from economies of scale. Because a monopolistically competitive equilibrium occurs in the downward-sloping section of the average cost curve (where the average cost curve is tangent to the downward-sloping demand curve), a monopolistically competitive firm operates at less than full capacity in the long run.

FIXED COSTS AND THE NUMBER OF FIRMS

The number of firms in a monopolistically competitive equilibrium depends on firms' costs. The larger each firm's fixed cost, the smaller the number of monopolistically competitive firms in the market equilibrium.

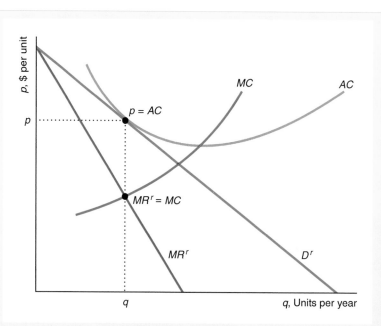

Figure 6.8 **Monopolistically Competitive Equilibrium.** A monopolistically competitive firm, facing residual demand curve D^r, sets its output where its marginal revenue equals its marginal cost: $MR^r = MC$. Because firms can enter this market, the profit of the firm is driven to zero, so price equals the firm's average cost: $p = AC$.

Although entry is free, if the fixed costs are high, few firms may enter. In the automobile industry, just to develop a new fender costs $8 to $10 million.[15] Developing a new pharmaceutical drug may cost $350 million or more.

We can illustrate this relationship using the airlines example, in which we modify our assumptions about entry and fixed costs. American and United are the only airlines providing service on the Chicago–Los Angeles route. Until now, we have assumed that a barrier to entry—such as an inability to obtain landing rights at both airports—prevented entry and that the firms had no fixed costs. If fixed cost is zero and marginal cost is constant at $147 per passenger, average cost is also constant at $147 per passenger. As we showed earlier, each firm in this oligopolistic market flies $q = 64$ per quarter at a price of $p = \$211$ and makes a profit of $4.1 million per quarter.

Now suppose that there are no barriers to entry, but each airline incurs a fixed cost, F, due to airport fees, capital expenditure, or other factors. Each firm's marginal cost remains $147 per passenger, but its average cost,

$$AC = 147 + \frac{F}{q},$$

---

[15]James B. Treece, "Sometimes, You Gotta Have Size," *Business Week*, Enterprise 1993:200–1. Treece illustrates the role of fixed costs on entry in the following anecdote: "In 1946, steel magnate Henry J. Kaiser boasted to a Detroit dinner gathering that two recent stock offerings had raised a huge $50 million to invest in his budding car company. Suddenly, a voice from the back of the room shot out: 'Give that man one white chip.'"

falls as the number of passengers rises, as panels a and b of Figure 6.9 illustrate for F = \$2.3 million.

If there are only two firms in a monopolistically competitive market, what must the fixed costs be so that the two firms earn zero profit? We know that these firms receive a profit of \$4.1 million per firm in the absence of fixed costs. As a result, the fixed cost must be \$4.1 million per firm for the firms to earn zero profit. With this fixed cost, the monopolistically competitive price and quantity are the same as in the oligopolistic equilibrium, q = 64 and p = \$211, and the number of firms is the same, but now each firm's profit is zero.

If the fixed cost is only \$2.3 million and there are only two firms in the market, each firm makes a profit, as panel a shows. Each duopoly firm faces a residual demand curve (labeled "D^r for 2 firms"), which is the market demand minus its rival's Cournot equilibrium quantity, q = 64. Given this residual demand, each firm produces q = 64, which equates its marginal revenue, MR^r, and its marginal cost, MC. At q = 64, the firm's average cost is AC = \$147 + (\$2.3 million)/(64 units) $\approx$ \$183, so each firm makes a profit of $\pi = (p - AC)q \approx$ (\$211 − \$183) × 64 units per quarter $\approx$ \$1.8 million per quarter.

This substantial economic profit attracts an entrant. The entry of a third firm causes the residual demand for any one firm to shift to the left in panel b. In the new equilibrium, each firm sets q = 48 and charges p = \$195. At this quantity, each firm's average cost is \$195, so the firms break even. No other firms enter because if one did, the residual demand curve would shift even farther to the left and all the firms would lose money. Thus if fixed cost is \$2.3 million, there are three firms in the

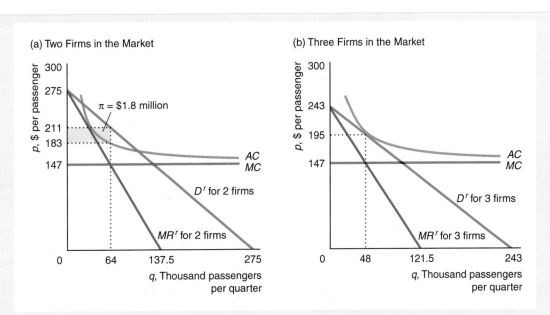

Figure 6.9 Monopolistic Competition Among Airlines. (a) If each identical airline has a fixed cost of \$2.3 million and there are two firms in the market, each firm flies q = 64 units (thousands of passengers) per quarter at a price of p = \$211 per passenger and makes a profit of \$1.8 million. This profit attracts entry. (b) After a third firm enters, the residual demand curve shifts, so each firm flies q = 48 units at p = \$195 and makes zero profit, which is the monopolistically competitive equilibrium.

monopolistically competitive equilibrium. This example illustrates a general result: *The lower the fixed costs, the more firms there are in the monopolistically competitive equilibrium.*

SOLVED PROBLEM 6.3

What is the monopolistically competitive airline equilibrium if each firm has a fixed cost of $3 million?

Answer

1. *Determine the number of firms*: We already know that the monopolistically competitive equilibrium has two firms if the fixed cost is $4.1 million and three firms if the fixed cost is $2.3 million. With a fixed cost of $3 million, if there are only two firms in the market, each makes a profit of $1.1 (= $4.1 − 3) million. If another firm enters, though, each firm's loss equals −$0.7 (= 2.3 − 3) million. Thus the monopolistically competitive equilibrium has two firms, each of which earns a positive profit that is too small to attract another firm. This outcome is a monopolistically competitive equilibrium because no other firm wants to enter.

2. *Determine the equilibrium quantities and prices*: We already know that each duopoly firm produces $q = 64$, so $Q = 128$ and $p = 211.

6.8 Bertrand Price-Setting Model

We have examined how oligopolistic and monopolistically competitive firms set quantities to try to maximize their profits. However, many such firms set prices instead of quantities and allow consumers to decide how much to buy. The market equilibrium is different if firms set prices rather than quantities.

In monopolistic and competitive markets, the issue of whether firms set quantities or prices does not arise. Competitive firms have no choice: They cannot affect price and hence can choose only quantity. The monopoly equilibrium is the same whether the monopoly sets price or quantity (Chapter 4).

In 1883, Joseph Bertrand argued that oligopolies set prices, and then consumers decide how many units to buy. The resulting Nash equilibrium is called a **Bertrand equilibrium**: a set of prices such that no firm can obtain a higher profit by choosing a different price if the other firms continue to charge these prices.

We will show that the price and quantity in a Bertrand equilibrium are different from those in a Cournot equilibrium. We will also show that a Bertrand equilibrium depends on whether firms are producing identical or differentiated products.

BERTRAND EQUILIBRIUM WITH IDENTICAL PRODUCTS

We start by examining a price-setting oligopoly in which firms have identical costs and produce identical goods. The resulting Bertrand equilibrium price equals the marginal cost, as in the price-taking equilibrium. To show this result, we use best-response curves to determine the Bertrand equilibrium, as we did in the Cournot model.

Best-Response Curves. Suppose that each of the two price-setting oligopoly firms in a market produces an identical product and faces a constant marginal and average

Bertrand equilibrium a *Nash equilibrium* in prices; a set of prices such that no firm can obtain a higher profit by choosing a different price if the other firms continue to charge these prices cost of $5 per unit. What is Firm 1's best response—what price should it set—if Firm 2 sets a price of $p_2 = \$10$? If Firm 1 charges more than $10, it makes no sales because consumers will buy from Firm 2. Firm 1 makes a profit of $5 on each unit it sells if it also charges $10 per unit. If the market demand is 200 units and both firms charge the same price, we'd expect Firm 1 to make half the sales, so its profit is $500.

Suppose, however, that Firm 1 slightly undercuts its rival's price by charging $9.99. Because the products are identical, Firm 1 captures the entire market. Firm 1 makes a profit of $4.99 per unit and a total profit of $998. Thus Firm 1's profit is higher if it slightly undercuts its rival's price. By similar reasoning, if Firm 2 charges $8, Firm 1 also charges slightly less than Firm 2.

Now imagine that Firm 2 charges $p_2 = \$5$. If Firm 1 charges more than $5, it makes no sales. The firms split the market and make zero profit if Firm 1 charges $5. If Firm 1 undercuts its rival, it captures the entire market, but it makes a loss on each unit. Thus Firm 1 will undercut only if its rival's price is higher than Firm 1's marginal and average cost of $5. By similar reasoning, if Firm 2 charges less than $5, Firm 1 chooses not to produce.

Figure 6.10 shows that Firm 1's best response is to produce nothing if Firm 2 charges less than $5. Firm 1's best response is $5 if Firm 2 charges $5. If Firm 2 charges prices above $5, Firm 1's best response is to undercut Firm 2's price slightly. Above $5, Firm 1's best-response curve is above the 45° line by the smallest amount possible. (The distance of the best-response curve from the 45° line is exaggerated

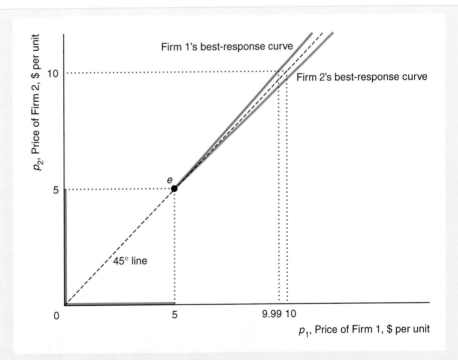

Figure 6.10 Bertrand Equilibrium with Identical Products. With identical products and constant marginal and average costs of $5, Firm 1's best-response curve starts at $5 and then lies slightly above the 45° line. That is, Firm 1 undercuts its rival's price as long as its price remains above $5. The best-response curves intersect at *e*, the Bertrand or Nash equilibrium, where both firms charge $5.

See Question 9.

in the figure for clarity.) By the same reasoning, Firm 2's best-response curve starts at $5 and lies slightly below the 45° line.

The two best-response functions intersect only at e, where each firm charges $5. It does not pay for either firm to change its price as long as the other charges $5, so e is a Nash or Bertrand equilibrium. In this equilibrium, each firm makes zero profit. Thus *the Bertrand equilibrium when firms produce identical products is the same as the price-taking, competitive equilibrium.*

Bertrand Versus Cournot. The Bertrand equilibrium differs substantially from the Cournot equilibrium. We can calculate the Cournot equilibrium price for firms with constant marginal costs of $5 per unit by rearranging Equation 6.8:

$$p = \frac{MC}{1 + 1 / (n\varepsilon)} = \frac{\$5}{1 + 1 / (n\varepsilon)}, \tag{6.13}$$

where n is the number of firms and ε is the market demand elasticity. If the market demand elasticity is $\varepsilon = -1$ and $n = 2$, the Cournot equilibrium price is $\$5/(1 - \frac{1}{2}) = \$10$, which is double the Bertrand equilibrium price.

When firms produce identical products and have a constant marginal cost, the Cournot model is more plausible than the Bertrand. The Bertrand model—unlike the Cournot model—appears inconsistent with real oligopoly markets in at least two ways.

First, the Bertrand model's "competitive" equilibrium price is implausible. If there is only a small number of firms, why would they compete so vigorously that they would make no profit? In contrast, the Cournot equilibrium price with a small number of firms lies between the competitive price and the monopoly price. Because oligopolies typically charge a higher price than competitive firms, the Cournot equilibrium is more plausible.

Second, the Bertrand equilibrium price, which depends only on cost, is insensitive to demand conditions and the number of firms. In contrast, the Cournot equilibrium price, Equation 6.13, depends on the number of firms and demand and cost conditions. In our example, if the number of firms rises from two to three, the Cournot price falls from $10 to $\$5/(1 - \frac{1}{3}) = \$7.50$, but the Bertrand equilibrium price remains $5. Again, the Cournot model is more plausible because we usually observe market price changing with the number of firms and demand conditions, not just with changes in costs.

As a result, it seems more likely that when firms' products are identical, firms set quantities rather than prices. For these reasons, economists are much more likely to use the Cournot model than the Bertrand model to study markets in which firms produce identical goods.

BERTRAND EQUILIBRIUM WITH DIFFERENTIATED PRODUCTS

Chance that a British baby's first word is a brand name: 1 in 4. —Harper's Index 2004

If most markets were characterized by firms producing homogeneous goods, the Bertrand model would probably have been forgotten. Markets with differentiated goods—automobiles, stereos, computers, toothpastes, and spaghetti sauces—however, are extremely common, as is price setting by firms. In such markets, the Bertrand equilibrium is plausible, and the two "problems" of the homogeneous-goods model disappear: Firms set prices above marginal cost, and prices are sensitive to demand conditions.

Indeed, many economists believe that price-setting models are more plausible than quantity-setting models when goods are differentiated. If products are differentiated and firms set prices, then consumers determine quantities. In contrast, if firms set quantities, it is not clear how the prices of the differentiated goods are determined in the market.

We illustrate a Bertrand equilibrium with the differentiated products in the cola market. We use best-response curves in a figure to solve for the equilibrium.

Coke and Pepsi produce similar but not identical products; many consumers prefer one of these products to the other. If the price of Pepsi were to fall slightly relative to that of Coke, some consumers who prefer Coke to Pepsi would not switch. Thus neither firm has to match exactly a price cut by its rival. As a result, neither firm's best-response curve in Figure 6.11 lies along a 45° line through the origin.[16]

The Bertrand best-response curves have different slopes than the Cournot best-response curves in Figure 6.3. The Cournot curves—which plot relationships

Figure 6.11 Bertrand Equilibrium with Differentiated Products. If both firms have a constant marginal cost of $5, the best-response curves of Coke and Pepsi intersect at e_1, where each sets a price of $13 per unit. If Coke's marginal cost rises to $14.50, its best-response function shifts upward. In the new equilibrium, e_2, Coke charges a higher price, $18, than Pepsi, $14.

[16]The figure is based on Bertrand estimates from Gasmi, Laffont, and Vuong (1992). Their estimated model allows the firms to set both prices and advertising. We assume that the firms' advertising is held constant. The Coke equations are the authors' estimates (with slight rounding). The Pepsi equations are rescaled so that the equilibrium prices of Coke and Pepsi are equal. Quantities are in tens of millions of cases (a case consists of 24 twelve-ounce cans) per quarter, and prices (to retailers) and costs are in real 1982 dollars per 10 cases.

between quantities—slope downward, showing that a firm produces less the more its rival produces. In Figure 6.11, the Bertrand best-response curves—which plot relationships between prices—slope upward, indicating that a firm charges a higher price the higher the price its rival charges.

See Question 19.

If both Pepsi and Coke have a constant marginal cost of $MC_p = MC_c = \$5$, the Bertrand equilibrium, e_1 in Figure 6.11, occurs where the price of each firm is $13 per unit (10 cases). In this Nash equilibrium, each firm sets its best-response price *given the price the other firm is charging.* Neither firm wants to change its price because neither firm can increase its profit by so doing. (See Appendix 6C for a mathematical presentation.)

DIFFERENTIATING PRODUCTS

> *Why don't they make mouse-flavored cat food?*   —Steven Wright

The Bertrand model demonstrates that firms can profit from selling differentiated products. If products are homogeneous, Bertrand firms cannot charge above marginal cost. With differentiated products, they can charge prices above marginal cost and make larger profits. Firms aggressively differentiate their products to raise profits. By such differentiation, they affect the average price in a market and welfare.

Economists view products as differentiated if consumers *believe* that they differ. Although few consumers can reliably distinguish Coke from Pepsi in blind taste tests, many consumers strongly prefer buying one product over the other. Conversely, if consumers view products that differ chemically or physically to be identical, the products are homogeneous for the purposes of economic analysis. A firm can differentiate its product from its rivals' by changing a product characteristic consumers view as important (taste or appearance), or the firm can convince consumers that its product differs through advertising and other means, even if the products do not differ physically.

● APPLICATION

Blue Fries, Green Ketchup

How can a food manufacturer differentiate its product to gain market power? Different flavors? New packaging? Easier preparation? That's all been done.

Heinz determined that the world needed colorful Blastin' Green and Funky Purple ketchup. These colors were such a hit that it later added Squirt Mystery Color, which includes "three new colors [Passion Pink, Awesome Orange, and

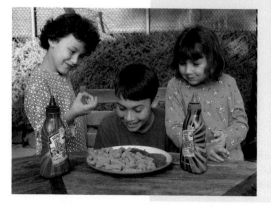

Totally Teal] that kids can mix and match to triple their fun at family meals, but you won't know which color is inside until the very first squeeze." Heinz followed up this marketing coup with Funky Fries, a new line of Ore-Ida frozen potatoes in various colors (including Kool Blue) and flavors (would you believe chocolate?). More fizzle than sizzle with consumers, these fries were unceremoniously yanked out of freezer cases the next year, whereupon Heinz introduced "Stellar Blue" ketchup. In the first two-and-a-half years after the debut of funny-color ketchup, Heinz sold 25 million bottles of the oddly tinted goop. Moreover, its share of all ketchup rose substantially, from 50% in 1999 to more than 60% by 2005.

Not to be outdone, Parkay produced Shocking Pink and Electric Blue butter-tasting spread. And in 2005, Mars Inc., in honor of the release of the movie *Star Wars Revenge of the Sith,* produced its first dark-chocolate M&Ms in black and gray, for those committed to the dark side.

Product Differentiation and Price. Whether the difference is a nonslip handle or a sneaker pump, if a firm can convince some customers that its brand is superior in some fashion, it can charge a higher price than it could if it sold plain or generic products. Clorox and Bayer are just two examples of firms that charge higher prices for products (bleach and aspirin, respectively) that have an active ingredient that is chemically identical to that of generic brands.

The reason differentiation allows a firm to charge a higher price is that the residual demand curve the firm faces (the market demand minus the quantity supplied by rivals at each price) becomes less elastic. That is, a given decrease in the price charged by a rival lowers the demand for this firm's product by *less,* the less substitutable are the two goods. If consumers view the goods as perfect substitutes, a small drop in the rival's price causes this firm to lose all its sales. If some consumers become convinced that this firm's product is superior in some way, they do not switch to the rival if the rival lowers its price slightly.

Product Differentiation and Welfare. Thus prices are likely to be higher when products are differentiated than when they're identical, all else the same. We also know that welfare falls as the gap between price and marginal cost rises. Does it follow that differentiating products lowers welfare? Not necessarily. Although differentiation leads to higher prices, which harm consumers, differentiation is desirable in its own right. Consumers value having a choice, and some may greatly prefer a new brand to existing ones.

One way to illustrate the importance of this second effect is to consider what the value is of introducing a new, differentiated product. This value reflects how much extra income consumers would require to be as well off without the good as with it.

● **APPLICATION**

Welfare Gain from More Toilet Paper

An article in the *Economist* asked, "Why does it cost more to wipe your bottom in Britain than in any other country in the European Union?" The answer given was that British consumers are "extremely fussy" in demanding a soft, luxurious texture—in contrast to barbarians elsewhere. As a consequence, they pay twice as much for toilet paper as the Germans and French, and nearly 2.5 times as much as Americans.

Probably completely uninfluenced by this important cross-country research, Hausman and Leonard (2002) used U.S. data to measure the price effect and the extra consumer surplus from greater variety resulting from Kimberly-Clark's introduction of Kleenex Bath Tissue (KBT). Bath tissue products are divided into premium, economy, and private labels, with premium receiving more than 70% of revenue. Before KBT's entry, the major premium brands were Angel Soft, Charmin, Cottonelle, and Northern. ScotTissue was the leading economy brand.

Firms incur a sizeable fixed cost from capital investments. The marginal cost depends primarily on the price of wood pulp, which varies cyclically. Because KBT was rolled out in various cities at different times, Hausman and Leonard could compare the effects of entry at various times and control for variations in cost and other factors.

The prices of all rival brands fell after KBT entered; the price of the leading brand, Charmin, dropped by 3.5%, while Cottonelle's price plummeted 8.2%. In contrast, the price of ScotTissue, an economy brand, decreased by only 0.6%.

Hausman and Leonard calculated that the additional consumer surplus due to extra variety was $33.4 million, or 3.5% of sales. When they included the gains due to lower prices, the total consumer surplus increase was $69.2 million, or 7.3% of sales. Thus, the gains to consumers were roughly equally divided between the price effect and the benefit from extra variety.

Summary

1. **Market structures:** Prices, profits, and quantities in a market equilibrium depend on the market's structure. Because profit-maximizing firms set marginal revenue equal to marginal cost, price is above marginal revenue—and hence marginal cost—only if firms face downward-sloping demand curves. In monopoly, oligopoly, and monopolistically competitive markets, firms face downward-sloping demand curves, in contrast to firms in a competitive market. When entry is blocked, as with a monopoly or an oligopoly, firms may earn positive profits; however, when entry is free, as in competition or monopolistic competition, profits are driven toward zero. Noncooperative oligopoly and monopolistically competitive firms, in contrast to competitive and monopoly firms, must pay attention to their rivals.

2. **Game theory:** The set of tools that economists use to analyze conflict and cooperation between firms is called game theory. Each oligopolistic or monopolistically competitive firm adopts a strategy or battle plan of action to compete with other firms. The firms' set of strategies is a Nash equilibrium if, holding the strategies of all other firms constant, no firm can obtain a higher profit by choosing a different strategy.

3. **Cooperative oligopoly models:** If firms successfully collude, they produce the monopoly output and collectively earn the monopoly level of profit. Although their collective profits rise if all firms collude, each individual firm has an incentive to cheat on a cartel arrangement so as to raise its own profit even higher. For cartel prices to remain high, cartel members must be able to detect and prevent cheating, and noncartel firms must not be able to supply very much output. When antitrust laws or competition policies prevent firms from colluding, firms may try to merge if permitted by law.

4. **Cournot model of noncooperative oligopoly:** If oligopoly firms act independently, the market output and firms' profits lie between the competitive and monopoly levels. In a Cournot model, each oligopoly firm sets its output at the same time. In the Cournot (Nash) equilibrium, each firm produces its best-response output—the output that maximizes its profit—given the output its rival produces. As the number of Cournot firms increases, the Cournot equilibrium price, quantity, and profits approach the price-taking levels.

5. **Stackelberg model of noncooperative behavior:** If one firm, the Stackelberg leader, chooses its output before its rivals, the Stackelberg followers, the leader produces more and earns a higher profit than each identical-cost follower firm. A government may subsidize a domestic oligopoly firm so that it produces the Stackelberg leader quantity, which it sells in an international market.

6. **Comparison of collusive, Cournot, Stackelberg, and competitive equilibria:** Total market output is maximized and price is minimized under competition. For a given number of firms, the Stackelberg equilibrium output exceeds that of the Cournot equilibrium, which

exceeds that of the collusive equilibrium (which is the same as a monopoly produces). Correspondingly, the Stackelberg price is less than the Cournot price, which is less than the collusive or monopoly price.

7. **Monopolistic competition:** In monopolistically competitive markets, after all profitable entry occurs, there are few enough firms in the market that each firm faces a downward-sloping demand curve. Consequently, the firms charge prices above marginal cost. These markets are not perfectly competitive because there are relatively few firms—possibly because of high fixed costs or economies of scale that are large relative to market demand—or because the firms sell differentiated products.

8. **Bertrand price-setting model:** In many oligopolistic or monopolistically competitive markets, firms set prices instead of quantities. If the product is homogeneous and firms set prices, the Bertrand equilibrium price equals marginal cost (which is lower than the Cournot quantity-setting equilibrium price). If the products are differentiated, the Bertrand equilibrium price is above marginal cost. Typically, the markup of price over marginal cost is greater the more the goods are differentiated.

Questions

** = answer at the back of this book; **A** = an application or other real-world material in the text; **C** = use of calculus may be necessary.*

*1. Show the payoff matrix and explain the reasoning in the prisoners' dilemma example involving criminals given in footnote 2 in this chapter. (*Note:* The payoffs are negative because they represent years in jail, which is a bad.) **A**

2. At each Organization of Petroleum Exporting Countries (OPEC) meeting, Saudi Arabia, the largest oil producer, argues that the cartel should cut production. The Saudis complain that most OPEC countries, including Saudi Arabia (but not Indonesia or Venezuela), produce more oil than they are allotted under their cartel agreement (Simon Romero, "Saudis Push Plan for Cut in Production by OPEC," *New York Times,* March 31, 2004). Use a graph and words to explain why the members of a cartel would produce more than the allotted amount given that they know that overproduction will drive down the price of their product. **A**

3. Two firms are planning to sell 10 or 20 units of their goods and face the following payoff matrix:

		Firm 2	
		10	20
Firm 1	10	30 / 30	50 / 35
	20	40 / 60	20 / 20

a. What is the Nash equilibrium if both firms make their decisions simultaneously? Why? (What strategy does each firm use?)

b. Suppose that Firm 1 can decide first. What is the outcome? Why?

c. Suppose that Firm 2 can decide first. What is the outcome? Why?

4. Southwest Airlines' cost to fly one seat one mile is 7.38¢ compared to 15.20¢ for USAir (*New York Times*, August 20, 2002:C4). Assuming that Southwest and USAir compete on a route, use a graph to show that their equilibrium quantities differ.

*5. Your college is considering renting space in the student union to one or two commercial textbook stores. The rent the college can charge per square foot of space depends on the profit (before rent) of the firms and hence on whether there is a monopoly or a duopoly. Which number of stores is better for the college in terms of rent? Which is better for students? Why?

6. In the initial Cournot duopoly equilibrium, both firms have constant marginal costs, m, and no fixed costs, and there is a barrier to entry. Show what happens to the best-response function of firms if both firms now face a fixed cost of F.

7. In 2005, the prices for 36 prescription painkillers shot up as much as 15% since Merck yanked its once-popular arthritis drug Vioxx from the market due to fears that it caused heart problems ("Prices Climb as Much as 15% for Some Painkillers," *Los Angeles Times,* June 3, 2005: C3). Can this product's exit be the cause of the price increases if the prices reflect a Cournot equilibrium? Explain. **A**

8. In the "Bail Bonds" application, the price tends to fall as the number of firms rises above 2, but prices are higher in New Haven, with 8 firms, and Bridgeport, with 10 firms, than in Norwalk with 3 firms. What are possible explanations for this pattern? **A**

9. What happens to the homogeneous good, Bertrand equilibrium price if the number of firms increases? **A**

10. For the airline example in the chapter, use a graph to show the effect of a specific tax of τ per flight applied to both firms.   **A**

11. The "A Government-Created Cartel" application suggests that it would make more sense for the United States to use a tariff than a voluntary export restraint. Explain why.   **A**

12. What is the effect of a government subsidy that reduces the fixed cost of each firm in an industry in a Cournot monopolistic equilibrium?

13. In the monopolistically competitive airline model, what is the equilibrium if firms face no fixed costs?

14. In a monopolistically competitive market, the government applies a specific tax of $1 per unit of output. What happens to the profit of a typical firm in this market? Does the number of firms in the market change? Why?

15. Does an oligopoly or a monopolistically competitive firm have a supply curve? Why or why not? (*Hint*: See the discussion in Chapter 4 of whether a monopoly has a supply curve.)

*16. Will the price be lower if duopoly firms set price or if they set quantity? Under what conditions can you give a definitive answer to this question?

*17. Why does differentiating its product allow an oligopoly to charge a higher price?

18. In the initial Bertrand equilibrium, two firms with differentiated products charge the same equilibrium prices. A consumer testing agency praises the product of one firm, causing its demand curve to shift to the right as new customers start buying the product. (The demand curve of the other product is not substantially affected.) Use a graph to illustrate how this new information affects the Bertrand equilibrium. What happens to the equilibrium prices of the two firms?

19. In the Coke and Pepsi example, what is the effect of a specific tax, τ, on the equilibrium prices? (*Hint*: What does the tax do to the firm's marginal cost?)

20. In 1998, California became the first state to adopt rules requiring many sport utility vehicles, pickups, and minivans to meet the same pollution standards as regular cars, effective in 2004. A business group (which may have an incentive to exaggerate) estimates that using the new technology to reduce pollution would increase vehicle prices by as much as $7,000. A spokesperson for the California Air Resources Board, which imposed the mandate, says that the additional materials cost is only about $70 to $270 per vehicle. Suppose that the two major producers are Toyota and Ford, and these firms are price setters with differentiated products. Show the effect of the new regulation. Is it possible that the price for these vehicles will rise by substantially more than marginal cost does?

Problems

21. The "Deadweight Losses in the Food and Tobacco Industries" application shows that the deadweight loss as a fraction of sales varies substantially across industries. One possible explanation is that the number of firms (degree of competition) varies across industries. Using the example in Table 6.3, show how the deadweight loss varies in this market as the number of firms increases from one to three.   **A**

22. A duopoly faces a market demand of $p = 120 - Q$. Firm 1 has a constant marginal cost of $MC^1 = 20$. Firm 2's constant marginal cost is $MC^2 = 40$. Calculate the output of each firm, market output, and price if there is (a) a collusive equilibrium or (b) a Cournot equilibrium.

*23. What is the duopoly Cournot equilibrium if the market demand function is

$$Q = 1{,}000 - 1{,}000p,$$

and each firm's marginal cost is $0.28 per unit?

24. How would the Cournot equilibrium change in the airline example if United's marginal cost were $100 and American's were $200?   **A**

25. What is the equilibrium in the airline example in the chapter if both American and United receive a subsidy of $48 per passenger?

*26. The demand the duopoly quantity-setting firms face is

$$p = 90 - 2q_1 - 2q_2.$$

Firm 1 has no marginal cost of production, but Firm 2 has a marginal cost of $30. How much does each firm produce if they move simultaneously? What is the equilibrium price?

27. Show how the Cournot equilibrium for n firms given in Appendix 6A changes if each firm faces a fixed cost of F as well as a constant marginal cost per unit.   **C**

28. Determine the Stackelberg equilibrium with one leader firm and two follower firms if the market

demand curve is linear and each firm faces a constant marginal cost, m, and no fixed cost. (*Hint:* See Appendix 6B for the Stackelberg model with one follower.) **C**

*29. Suppose that identical duopoly firms have constant marginal costs of $10 per unit. Firm 1 faces a demand function of

$$q_1 = 100 - 2p_1 + p_2,$$

where q_1 is Firm 1's output, p_1 is Firm 1's price, and p_2 is Firm 2's price. Similarly, the demand Firm 2 faces is

$$q_2 = 100 - 2p_2 + p_1.$$

Solve for the Bertrand equilibrium.

30. Solve for the Bertrand equilibrium for the firms described in Problem 29 if both firms have a marginal cost of $0 per unit.

31. Solve for the Bertrand equilibrium for the firms described in Problem 29 if Firm 1's marginal cost is $30 per unit and Firm 2's marginal cost is $10 per unit.

*32. The viatical settlement industry enables terminally ill consumers, typically HIV patients, to borrow against equity in their existing life insurance contracts to finance their consumption and medical expenses. The introduction and dissemination of effective anti-HIV medication in 1996 reduced AIDS mortality, extending patients' lives and hence delaying when the viatical settlement industry would receive the insurance payments. However, viatical settlement payments (what patients can borrow) fell more than can be explained by greater life expectancy. The number of viatical settlement firms dropped from 44 in 1995 to 24 in 2001. Sood et al. (2005) found that an increase in market power of viatical settlement firms reduced the value of life insurance holdings of HIV-positive persons by about $1.0 billion. When marginal cost rises and the number of firms falls, what happens to Cournot equilibrium price? Use graphs or math to illustrate your answer. (*Hint:* If you use math, it may be helpful to assume that the market demand curve has a constant elasticity throughout.)

33. Firms in some industries with a small number of competitors earn normal economic profit. The *Wall Street Journal* (Lee Gomes, "Competition Lives On in Just One PC Sector," March 17, 2003, B1) reports that the computer graphics chips industry is one such market. Two chip manufacturers, nVidia and ATI, "both face the prospect of razor-thin profits, largely on account of the other's existence."

a. Consider the Bertrand model in which each firm has a positive fixed and sunk cost and a zero marginal cost. What are the Nash equilibrium prices? What are the Nash equilibrium profits?

b. Does this "razor-thin" profit result imply that the two manufacturers necessarily produce chips that are nearly perfect substitutes?

c. Assume that nVidia and ATI produce differentiated products and are Bertrand competitors. The demand for nVidia's chip is $q_V = \alpha - \beta p_V + \gamma p_A$; the demand for ATI's chip is $q_A = \alpha - \beta p_A + \gamma p_V$, where p_V is nVidia's price, p_A is ATI's price, and α, β, and γ are coefficients of the demand function. Suppose each manufacturer's marginal cost is a constant, m. What are values of α, β, and γ for which the equilibrium profit of each chip manufacturer is zero? In answering this question, show that despite differentiated products, duopolists may earn zero economic profit. **W**

34. The town of Perkasie, Pennsylvania, has two diners: Emil's Diner and Bobby Ray's Diner. Both sell only chicken pies. Everyone who would consider eating at the diners is aware that they sell the same chicken pies, and knows the prices that they charge (p_E, p_{BR}). At precisely 5 P.M., each diner (simultaneously) sets its price of chicken pie for that evening. The market demand function for chicken pie is $Q = 120 - 20p$, where p is the lower of the two diners' prices. If there is a lower-priced diner, then people eat chicken pie at only that diner and the diner sells $120 - 20p$ chicken pies. If the two diners post the same price, then each sells to one-half of the market: $\frac{1}{2}(100 - 20p)$. Suppose that prices can be quoted in dollar units only (0, 1, 2, 3, 4, 5, or 6). Each diner's marginal cost is $2 and fixed cost is $0.

a. Create a 7×7 payoff matrix and fill in the diners' profits.

b. Identify all Nash equilibria.

c. Suppose that Bobby Ray's Diner is out of business and Emil's is a monopoly. Find Emil's profit-maximizing price.

d. Now return to the Emil-versus-Bobby Ray's game. Pick one of the Nash equilibria that you identified in part b. Could Emil and Bobby Ray's collude: set prices different from the particular Nash equilibrium prices and increase both diners' profits? **W**

35. Acura and Volvo offer warranties on their automobiles, where w_A is the number of years of an Acura warranty and w_V is the number of years of a Volvo warranty. The revenue for Firm i, $i = A$ for Acura and V for Volvo, is $R_i = 27{,}000 w_i / (w_A + w_V)$. Its cost of providing the warranty is $C_i = 2{,}000 w_i$. Acura and Volvo participate in a warranty-setting game in which they simultaneously set warranties.

a. What is the profit function for each firm?

b. Suppose Acura and Volvo can set warranties in year lengths only, with a maximum of five years. Fill in a 5×5 payoff matrix with Acura's and Volvo's profits.

c. Determine the Nash equilibrium warranties.

d. Compare the Nash equilibrium warranties. If the two manufacturers offer the same warranty, explain why. If they offer different warranties, explain why.

e. Suppose Acura and Volvo collude in setting warranties. What warranties do they set?

f. Suppose Acura's cost of offering warranties decreases to $C_V = 1,000 w_V$. What is the new Nash equilibrium? Explain the effect of the decrease in Volvo's cost function on the equilibrium warranties. **W**

36. In the competition to attract athletes and produce champion teams, universities increased their spending on college athletics four times faster than overall university spending from 2001 through 2003. Schools have poured money into athletic programs even though studies show that this practice does not increase winning rates or alumni donations ("Review & Outlook," *Wall Street Journal*, May 27, 2005, W15). Nonetheless, suppose that money does matter in producing championships. University A spends m_A on its football team and University B spends m_B. The fraction of the time that University A wins is $w_A = m_A/(m_A + m_B)$, and the fraction that B wins is $w_B = 1 - w_A = m_B/(m_A + m_B)$. Suppose that each university wants to maximize its profit from having sports teams. The expected profit of University i, $i = A, B$, is $\pi_i = v_i m_i/(m_A + m_B)$, where v_i is the value to University i of winning a game.

a. Show that if $v_A = v_B$, in the Nash equilibrium each school wins one-half of its games.

b. Show that if $v_A = v_B$ increases, each school spends more on its teams but continues to win one-half of its games.

c. Explain the result that schools are spending more on sports without affecting their win-loss ratios. **W**

37. In October 2002, the European Union fined Sotheby's auction house more than 20 million euros for operating, along with rival auction house Christie's, a price-fixing cartel. "The Art of Price Fixing"). The two auction houses were jointly setting commission rates that sellers must pay. Let r denote the jointly set auction commission rate, $D_i(r)$ represent the demand for auction house i's services by sellers of auctioned items, p denote the average price of auctioned items, F represent an auction house's fixed cost, and v denote its average variable cost of auctioning an object. At the agreed-upon commission rate r, the profit of an auction house i is $\pi_i = rpD_i(r) - [F + vD_i(r)]$.

a. What is the sum of the profits of the houses i and j?

b. Characterize the commission rate that maximizes the sum of profits. That is, show that the commission rate that maximizes the sum of profits satisfies an equation that looks something like the monopoly's profit-maximizing condition, Equation 4.9.

c. Do the auction houses have an incentive to cheat on their agreement? If Christie's does so while Sotheby's continues to charge r, what will happen to their individual and collective profits? **W**

38. In February 2005, the U.S. Federal Trade Commission (FTC) went to court to undo the January 2000 takeover of Highland Park Hospital by Evanston Northwestern Healthcare Corp. The FTC accused Evanston Northwestern of antitrust violations by using its post-merger market power in the Evanston hospital market to impose 40% to 60% price increases (Bernard Wysocki, Jr., "FTC Targets Hospital Merger in Antitrust Case," *Wall Street Journal*, January 17, 2005, A1). Hospitals, even within the same community, are geographically differentiated as well as possibly quality differentiated. The demand for an appendectomy at Highland Park Hospital is a function of the price of the procedure at Highland Park and Evanston Northwestern Hospital: $q_H = 50 - 0.01p_H + 0.005p_N$. The comparable demand function at Evanston Northwestern is $q_N = 500 - 0.01p_N + 0.005p_H$. At each hospital, the fixed cost of the procedure is $20,000 and the marginal cost is $2,000.

a. Use the product-differentiated Bertrand model to analyze the prices the hospitals set before the merger. Find the Nash equilibrium prices of the producers at the two hospitals.

b. After the merger, find the profit-maximizing monopoly prices of the procedure at each hospital. Include the effect of each hospital's price on the profit of the other hospital.

c. Does the merger result in increased prices? **W**

*39. To examine the trade-off between efficiency and market power from a merger, consider a market with two firms that sell identical products. Firm 1 has a constant marginal cost of 1, and Firm 2 has a constant marginal cost of 2. The market demand is $Q = 15 - p$.

a. Solve for the Cournot equilibrium price, quantities, profits, consumer surplus, and deadweight loss.

b. If the firms merge and produce at the lower marginal cost, how do the equilibrium values change?

c. Discuss the change in efficiency (average cost of producing the output) and welfare—consumer surplus, producer surplus (or profit), and deadweight loss.

Frequent Flier Programs

Imagine that you are working for an airline company just before frequent flier programs take off, and the president of the firm asks you to analyze whether the firm should institute a frequent flier program (FFP). In particular, she asks you to predict how an FFP will affect the price your firm will charge and its profit. She understands that, if only one airline adopts an FFP, it will gain many extra customers. However, she suspects that if all airlines introduce the program, none may gain a substantial number of extra customers and all will incur the extra costs of the program. Is she correct that airlines will necessarily lose money by using FFPs?

Background

In May 1981, American Airlines launched AAdvantage, the first frequent flier program. American Airlines' objective was to retain its best customers by rewarding their loyalty with free tickets and upgrades. American Airlines used its Sabre computer reservation system to compile a database of 150,000 of its top customers. The company searched Sabre bookings for recurring phone numbers, which were then connected to customers' names. These customers were the initial members of AAdvantage.

Had other airlines not responded, American Airlines would have attracted many of its rivals' best customers. Unfortunately for American Airlines, within days after it introduced AAdvantage, United Airlines announced its own FFP, Mileage Plus. Later in that same year, both Delta and TWA introduced FFPs.

Although all major U.S. airlines now have such programs, many adopted them reluctantly. For example, Southwest hesitated due to the costs and its belief that the programs were short-run marketing gimmicks that would soon be dropped. However, after losing passengers to other airlines with such programs, Southwest Airlines belatedly introduced an FFP to stem the losses. Today, its FFP is one of the three top-rated programs. As Herb Kelleher, president of Southwest Airlines, has admitted,

> We didn't want an FFP. But it came to my attention that FFPs were siphoning business travel away from us. We did it defensively, and I think had we not done that we would have been terribly disadvantaged.

In 2005, 49 airlines had a combined FFP membership of 283 million. In 2004, American Airlines' FFP had 48 million members, and United Airlines' had 46 million members. Of critical importance to the airlines is that 94% of business travelers belong to at least one FFP and 60% belong to three or more programs. Airlines adopt these programs because 80% of business travelers—those with the least elastic demands, who are charged the highest prices—report that FFPs influence their travel decisions.

A customer's main incentive to join an FFP is to get free tickets. By one estimate, more than 14.7 million passengers flew on frequent flyer awards during 2004, a 2.1% decrease from 2003. Among the largest airlines, most allocated 5–8% of their seats to award travelers during 2004, but America West and JetBlue gave away 1.5% or less of their available seats to members of their loyalty programs. Moreover, for the seven airlines that report statistics, an average of 30.6% of frequent flyer miles are unused, ranging from 12% for Alaska Airlines to 70% for JetBlue. (In short, good luck using JetBlue miles!)

Because the major airlines usually limit FFP award tickets to flights with unpurchased seats, a seat costs the airline only $10 to $20: the cost of a few additional gallons of jet fuel and an extra bag of peanuts. However, some smaller airlines join alliances with other airlines and must pay their partners if one of their customers uses an FFP reward ticket on another alliance airline.

Task

On your major route, you face only one competitor, American Airlines, which, before the introduction of the FFP, flies the same number of passengers as your airline and has the same costs.

Your firm conducts a marketing study and concludes that this market has a constant elasticity demand curve (Chapter 3) and that, if both firms introduce FFP programs, the elasticity of demand would change from –2 to –1.75. Each firm's FFP would raise its marginal cost (extra meals, extra fuel) per passenger from $150 to $160 per trip.

For simplicity, we assume that both your airline and American Airlines set a single price for tickets—that is, they do not price discriminate (Chapter 5)—they engage in a Cournot, Nash-in-quantities game (Chapter 6), and each customer joins only one FFP. Before making your recommendation, you need to determine how equilibrium prices will change if both firms adopt the FFP.

Analysis

If only one of the airlines adopts an FFP, it gains many extra customers. However, if both airlines introduce the program, it's possible that none gains a substantial number of extra customers, yet both incur the extra costs of the program. Does it follow that airlines are likely to lose money by using FFPs? Not necessarily.

Introducing an FFP allows your firm to differentiate its service (see Chapter 6): All else the same, a customer who belongs only to your FFP will prefer to fly on your airline than on your rival's if both charge the same price for a ticket. The rise in variable cost and the product differentiation both lead to higher equilibrium prices.

In the absence of FFPs, Kathy, a typical customer, flies on whichever airline has the least expensive ticket. If both set the same fare, Kathy chooses randomly between them. If both airlines introduce an FFP and Kathy joins one of these programs, say American Airlines' AAdvantage Program, Kathy now prefers buying a ticket from American Airlines even if she has to pay slightly more than she would have to pay for a ticket from its rival. Thus, due to this product differentiation, Kathy has a less elastic demand for American Airlines' services. All else the same, American Airlines can charge a higher fare, the less elastic is its demand curve. Before, if American raised its price above its rival's even slightly, it would have lost Kathy's business. Consequently, if each airline has its own loyal customers who belong to its FFP, each airline can raise its price in equilibrium because each faces a less elastic demand curve.

We can use Equation 6.13 to determine the Cournot equilibrium price, p, that each airline initially sets:

$$p = \frac{MC}{1 + 1/(n\varepsilon)},$$

where $MC = \$150$ is its marginal cost, $n = 2$ is the number of identical firms, and the market elasticity of demand is $\varepsilon = -2$. Thus, each airline sets its price at

$$p = \frac{\$150}{1 + 1/(2 \times -2)} = \$200.$$

When the airlines introduce FFPs, the elasticity of demand facing each airline falls to $\varepsilon = -1.75$ and the marginal cost rises to $160, so the equilibrium price rises to

$$p = \frac{\$160}{1 + 1/(2 \times -1.75)} = \$224.$$

Thus, the FFPs cause prices to rise both because each firm's demand has become less elastic and because its marginal cost has increased.

Have the airlines benefited? The answer depends on whether their total profits have increased. The airlines benefit from higher revenues because they now face less elastic demand curves. However, their costs (including possibly fixed costs) are also higher. Thus, it is possible, but not certain, that they are better off having frequent flier programs than not. Presumably, the larger airlines, whose costs have not risen substantially due to FFPs, have benefited. Some of the smaller airlines that must pay allies for FFP tickets, such as Alaska, may have suffered.

Questions

Answers appear at the back of the book.

1. How much would the equilibrium price have risen if only the elasticity of demand had changed and not the marginal cost? If only the marginal cost had changed?

2. How has the firm's profit changed? Suppose that the firm's weekly constant elasticity demand curve is $Q = 50,000,000p^{\varepsilon}$.

Chapter Appendixes

Appendix 2A: Regressions

Economists use a *regression* to estimate economic relationships such as demand curves and supply curves. A regression analysis allows us to answer three types of questions:

- How can we best fit an economic relationship to actual data?
- How confident are we in our results?
- How can we determine the effect of a change in one variable on another if many other variables are changing at the same time?

ESTIMATING ECONOMIC RELATIONS

We use a demand curve example to illustrate how regressions can answer these questions. The points in Figure 2A.1 show eight years of data on Nancy's annual purchases of candy bars, q, and the prices, p, she paid.[1] For example, in the year when candy bars cost 20¢, Nancy bought q_2 candy bars.

Because we assume that Nancy's tastes and income did not change during this period, we write her demand for candy bars as a function of the price of candy bars and unobservable random effects. We believe that her demand curve is linear and want to estimate the demand function:

$$q = a + bp + e,$$

where a and b are coefficients we want to determine and e is an error term. This *error term* captures random effects that are not otherwise reflected in our function. For instance, in one year, Nancy broke up with her longtime boyfriend and ate more candy bars than usual, resulting in a relatively large positive error term for that year.

The data points in the figure exhibit a generally downward-sloping relationship between quantity and price, but the points do not lie strictly on a line because of the error terms. There are many possible ways in which we could draw a line through these data points.

The way we fit the line in the figure is to use the standard criterion that our estimates *minimize the sum of squared residuals*, where a residual, $e = q - \hat{q}$, is the difference between an actual quantity, q, and the fitted or predicted quantity on the estimated line, $\hat{q}$. That is, we choose estimated coefficients $\hat{a}$ and $\hat{b}$ so that the estimated quantities from the regression line,

$$\hat{q} = \hat{a} + \hat{b}p,$$

make the sum of the squared residuals, $e_1^2 + e_2^2 + \cdots + e_8^2$, as small as possible. By summing the square of the residuals instead of the residuals themselves, we treat the

---

[1]We use a lowercase q for the quantity demanded for an individual instead of the uppercase Q that we use for a market. Notice that we violated the rule economists usually follow of putting quantity on the horizontal axis and price on the vertical axis. We are now looking at this relationship as statisticians who put the independent or explanatory variable, price, on the horizontal axis and the dependent variable, quantity, on the vertical axis.

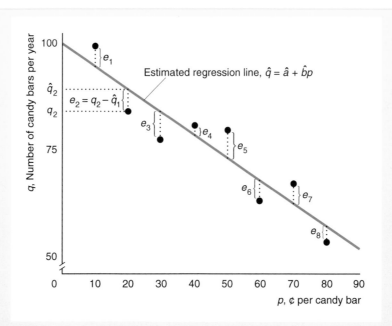

Figure 2A.1 **Regression.** The circles show data on how many candy bars Nancy bought in a year at several different prices. The regression line minimizes the sum of the squared residuals, e_1 through e_8.

effects of a positive or negative error symmetrically and give greater weight to large errors than to small ones.[2] In the figure, the regression line is

$$\hat{q} = 99.4 - 0.49p,$$

where $\hat{a} = 99.4$ is the intercept of the estimated line and $\hat{b} = -0.49$ is the slope of the line.

CONFIDENCE IN OUR ESTIMATES

Because the data reflect random errors, so do the estimated coefficients. Our estimate of Nancy's demand curve depends on the *sample* of data we use. If we were to use data from a different set of years, our estimates, $\hat{a}$ and $\hat{b}$, of the true coefficients, a and b, would differ.

If we had many estimates of the true parameter based on many samples, the estimates would be distributed around the true coefficient. These estimates are *unbiased* in the sense that the average of the estimates would equal the true coefficients.

Computer programs that calculate regression lines report a *standard error* for each coefficient, which is an estimate of the dispersion of the estimated coefficients around the true coefficient. In our example, a computer program reports

$$\hat{q} = \; 99.4 \; - \; 0.49p,$$
$$\qquad (3.99) \quad (0.08)$$

---

[2]Using calculus, we can derive the $\hat{a}$ and $\hat{b}$ that minimize the sum of squared residuals. The estimate of the slope coefficient is a weighted average of the observed quantities, $\hat{b} = \sum_i w_i q_i$, where $w_i = (p_i - \bar{p}) / \sum_i (p_i - \bar{p})^2$, $\bar{p}$ is the average of the observed prices, and $\sum_i$ indicates the sum over each observation i. The estimate of the intercept, $\hat{a}$, is the average of the observed quantities.

where, below each estimated coefficient, its estimated standard error appears between parentheses.

The smaller the estimated standard error, the more precise the estimate, and the more likely it is to be close to the true value. As a rough rule of thumb, there is a 95% probability that the interval that is within two standard errors of the estimated coefficient contains the true coefficient.[3] Using this rule, the *confidence interval* for the slope coefficient, $\hat{b}$, ranges from $-0.49 - (2 \times 0.08) = -0.65$ to $-0.49 + (2 \times 0.08) = -0.33$.

If zero were to lie within the confidence interval for $\hat{b}$, we would conclude that we cannot reject the hypothesis that the price has no effect on the quantity demanded. In our case, however, the entire confidence interval contains negative values, so we are reasonably sure that the higher the price, the less Nancy demands.

MULTIPLE REGRESSION

We can also estimate relationships involving more than one explanatory variable using a *multiple regression*. For example, Moschini and Meilke (1992) estimate a pork demand function, Equation 2.2, in which the quantity demanded is a function of income, Y, and the prices of pork, p, beef, p_b, and chicken, p_c:

$$Q = 171 - 20p + 20p_b + 3p_c + 2Y.$$

The multiple regression is able to separate the effects of the various explanatory variables. The coefficient 20 on the p variable says that an increase in the price of pork by $1 per kg lowers the quantity demanded by 20 million kg per year, holding the effects of the other prices and income constant.

Appendix 3A: Effects of a Specific Tax on Equilibrium

The government collects a specific or unit tax, τ, from sellers, so sellers receive $p - \tau$ when consumers pay p. We now determine the effect of the tax on the equilibrium.

In the new equilibrium, the price that consumers pay is determined by the intersection of supply and demand after taxes:

$$D(p) - S(p - \tau) = 0, \tag{3A.1}$$

where the supply equals demand equation is written in implicit function form (the right-hand side of the equation is zero).

We determine the effect of a small tax on price by totally differentiating Equation 3A.1 with respect to p and τ:

$$\frac{dS}{dp}\,d\tau + \left(\frac{dD}{dp} - \frac{dS}{dp}\right)dp = 0$$

Rearranging terms, it follows that the change in the price that consumers pay with respect to a change in the tax is

---

[3]The confidence interval is the coefficient plus or minus 1.96 times its standard error for large samples (at least hundreds of observations) in which the coefficients are normally distributed. For smaller samples, the confidence interval tends to be larger.

$$\frac{dp}{d\tau} = \frac{dS/dp}{dS/dp - dD/dp} \tag{3A.2}$$

We know that $dD/dp < 0$ from the Law of Demand. If the supply curve slopes up, $dS/dp > 0$, then $dp/d\tau > 0$. The higher the tax, the greater the price consumers pay. If $dS/dp < 0$, the direction of change is ambiguous.

By multiplying both the numerator and denominator of the right-hand side of Equation 3A.2 by p/Q, we can express this derivative in terms of elasticities:

$$\frac{dp}{d\tau} = \frac{(dS/dp)(p/Q)}{(dS/dp)(p/Q) - (dD/dP)(p/Q)} = \frac{\eta}{\eta - \varepsilon}$$

where the last equality follows because dS/dp and dD/dp are the changes in the quantities supplied and demanded as price changes and the consumer and producer prices are identical when $\tau = 0$. The change in price, Δp, equals $[\eta/(\eta - \varepsilon)]\Delta\tau$. This expression holds for any size change in $\Delta\tau$ if both the demand and supply curves are linear. The expression only holds for small changes $\Delta\tau$ for other curves.

To determine the effect on quantity, we can combine the price result from Equation 3A.2 with information from either the demand or supply curve. Differentiating the demand function with respect to τ, we know that

$$\frac{dQ}{d\tau} = \frac{dD}{dp}\frac{dp}{d\tau} = \frac{(dD/dP)(dS/dp)}{dS/dp - dD/dP}$$

which is negative if the supply curve is upward sloping.

Appendix 4A: Relationship Between a Linear Demand Curve and Its Marginal Revenue Curve

When the demand curve is linear, its marginal revenue curve is twice as steep and hits the horizontal axis at half the quantity of the demand curve. A linear demand curve can be written generally as

$$p = a - bQ.$$

The monopoly's revenues are quadratic, $R = pQ = aQ - bQ^2$. Differentiating revenue with respect to quantity, we find that the marginal revenue, $dR(Q)/dQ$, is linear,

$$MR = a - 2bQ.$$

The demand and MR curves hit the price axis at a. The slope of the demand curve, $dp/dQ = -b$, is half (in absolute value) the slope of the marginal revenue curve, $dMR/dQ = -2b$. The MR curve hits the quantity axis at half the distance, $a/(2b)$, of the demand curve, a/b.

Appendix 4B: Incidence of a Specific Tax on a Monopoly

In a monopolized market, the incidence of a specific tax falling on consumers can exceed 100%: The price may rise by an amount greater than the tax. To demonstrate this possibility, we examine a market where the demand curve has a constant elasticity of ε and the marginal cost is constant at $MC = m$.

Suppose that the inverse demand curve the monopoly faces is

$$p = Q^{1/\varepsilon}. \tag{4B.1}$$

The monopoly's revenue is $R = pQ = Q^{1+1/\varepsilon}$. By differentiating, we learn that the monopoly's marginal revenue is $MR = (1 + 1/\varepsilon)Q^{1/\varepsilon}$.

To maximize its profit, the monopoly operates where its marginal revenue equals its marginal cost:

$$MR = (1 + 1/\varepsilon)Q^{1/\varepsilon} = m = MC.$$

Solving this equation for the profit-maximizing output, we find that $Q = [m/(1 + 1/\varepsilon)]^\varepsilon$. Substituting that value of Q into Equation 11B.1, we find that

$$p = m/(1 + 1/\varepsilon)$$

A specific tax of τ per unit raises the marginal cost to $m + \tau$, so that the monopoly price increases to

$$p_t = (m + \tau)/(1 + 1/\varepsilon).$$

Consequently, the increase in price is $\tau/(1 + 1/\varepsilon)$. The incidence of the tax that falls on consumers is $\Delta p/\Delta \tau = [\tau/(1 + 1/\varepsilon)]/\tau = 1/(1 + 1/\varepsilon) > 1$, because $\varepsilon < -1$ (a monopoly never operates in the inelastic portion of its demand curve).

Appendix 5A: Perfect Price Discrimination

A perfectly price-discriminating monopoly charges each customer the reservation price $p = D(Q)$, where $D(Q)$ is the inverse demand function and Q is total output. The discriminating monopoly's revenue, R, is the area under the demand curve up to the quantity, Q, it sells:

$$R = \int_0^Q D(z)\,dz,$$

where z is a placeholder for quantity. Its objective is to maximize its profit through its choice of Q:

$$\max_Q \pi = \int_0^Q D(z)\,dz - C(Q). \tag{5A.1}$$

Its first-order condition for a maximum is found by differentiating Equation 5A.1 to obtain

$$\frac{d\pi}{dQ} = D(Q) - \frac{dC(Q)}{dQ} = 0. \tag{5A.2}$$

According to Equation 5A.2, the discriminating monopoly sells units up to the quantity, Q, where the reservation price for the last unit, $D(Q)$, equals its marginal cost, $dC(Q)/dQ$. (This quantity is $Q_c = Q_d$ in Figure 5.2.)

For this solution to maximize profits, the second-order condition must hold: $d^2\pi/dQ^2 = dD(Q)/dQ - d^2C(Q)/dQ^2 < 0$. Thus the second-order condition holds if the marginal cost curve has a nonnegative slope (because the demand curve has a negative slope). More generally, the second-order condition holds if the demand curve has a greater (absolute) slope than the marginal cost curve.

The perfectly price-discriminating monopoly's profit is

$$\pi = \int_0^Q D(z)\,dz - C(Q).$$

For example, if $D(Q) = a - bQ$,

$$\pi = \int_0^Q (a - bz)\,dz - C(Q) = aQ - \frac{b}{2}Q^2 - C(Q). \tag{5A.3}$$

The monopoly finds the output that maximizes the profit by setting the derivative of the profit in Equation 5A.3 equal to zero:

$$a - bQ - \frac{dC(Q)}{dQ} = 0.$$

By rearranging terms, we find that $D(Q) = a - bQ = dC(Q)/dQ = MC$, as in Equation 5A.2. Thus the monopoly produces the quantity at which the demand curve hits the marginal cost curve.

Appendix 5B: Quantity Discrimination

In the block-pricing example in the chapter, we assume that the utility monopoly faces an inverse demand curve $p = 90 - Q$ and that its marginal and average cost is $m = 30$. Consequently, the quantity-discounting utility's profit is

$$\pi = p(Q_1)Q_1 + p(Q_2)(Q_2 - Q_1) - mQ_2$$
$$= (90 - Q_1)Q_1 + (90 - Q_2)(Q_2 - Q_1) - 30Q_2,$$

where Q_1 is the largest quantity for which the first-block rate, $p_1 = 90 - Q_1$, is charged and Q_2 is the total quantity a consumer purchases. The utility chooses Q_1 and Q_2 to maximize its profit. It sets the derivative of profit with respect to Q_1 equal to zero, $Q_2 - 2Q_1 = 0$, and the derivative of profit with respect to Q_2 equal to zero, $Q_1 - 2Q_2 + 60 = 0$. By solving these two equations, the utility determines its profit-maximizing quantities, $Q_1 = 20$ and $Q_2 = 40$. The corresponding block prices are $p_1 = 90 - 20 = 70$ and $p_2 = 50$.

Appendix 5C: Multimarket Price Discrimination

Suppose that a monopoly can divide its customers into two groups, as in Figure 5.4. It sells Q_1 to the first group and earns revenues of $R_1(Q_1)$, and it sells Q_2 units to the second group and earns $R_2(Q_2)$. Its cost of producing total output $Q = Q_1 + Q_2$ units is $C(Q)$. The monopoly can maximize its profit through its choice of prices or quantities to each group. We examine its problem when it chooses quantities:

$$\max_{Q_1, Q_2} \pi = R_1(Q_1) + R_2(Q_2) - C(Q_1 + Q_2). \tag{5C.1}$$

The first-order conditions corresponding to Equation 5C.1 are obtained by differentiating with respect to Q_1 and Q_2 and setting the partial derivative equal to zero:

$$\frac{\partial \pi}{\partial Q_1} = \frac{dR_1(Q_1)}{dQ_1} - \frac{dC(Q)}{dQ}\frac{\partial Q}{\partial Q_1} = 0, \tag{5C.2}$$

$$\frac{\partial \pi}{\partial Q_2} = \frac{dR_2(Q_2)}{dQ_2} - \frac{dC(Q)}{dQ}\frac{\partial Q}{\partial Q_2} = 0. \tag{5C.3}$$

Equation 5C.2 says that the marginal revenue from sales to the first group, $MR^1 = dR_1(Q_1)/dQ_1$, should equal the marginal cost of producing the last unit of total output, $MC = dC(Q)/dQ$, because $\partial Q/\partial Q_1 = 1$. Similarly, Equation 5C.3 says that the marginal revenue from the second group, MR^2, should also equal the marginal cost. By combining Equations 5C.2 and 5C.3, we find that the two marginal revenues are equal where the monopoly is profit maximizing:

$$MR^1 = MR^2 = MC.$$

Appendix 5D: Two-Part Tariffs

In the example of a two-part tariff with nonidentical consumers, the demand curves for Consumers 1 and 2 are $q_1 = 80 - p$ and $q_2 = 100 - p$. The consumer surplus for Consumer 1 is $CS_1 = \frac{1}{2}(80 - p)q_1 = \frac{1}{2}(80 - p)^2$. Similarly, $CS_2 = \frac{1}{2}(100 - p)^2$. If the monopoly charges the lower fee, $\mathcal{L} = CS_1$, it sells to both consumers and its profit is

$$\pi = 2\mathcal{L} + (p - m)(q_1 + q_2) = (80 - p)^2 + (p - 10)(180 - 2p).$$

Setting the derivative of π with respect to p equal to zero, we find that the profit-maximizing price is $p = 20$. The monopoly charges a fee of $\mathcal{L} = CS_1 = \$1,800$ and makes a profit of $\$5,000$. If the monopoly charges the higher fee, $\mathcal{L} = CS_2$, it sells only to Consumer 2, and its profit is

$$\pi = \mathcal{L} + (p - m)q_2 = \frac{1}{2}(100 - p)^2 + (p - 10)(100 - p).$$

The monopoly's profit-maximizing price is $p = 10$, and its profit is $\mathcal{L} = CS_2 = \$4,050$. Thus the monopoly makes more by setting $\mathcal{L} = CS_1$ and selling to both customers.

Appendix 6A: Cournot Equilibrium

Here we use calculus to determine the Cournot equilibrium for n identical oligopolistic firms. We first solve for the equilibrium using general demand and cost functions, which are identical for all firms. Then we apply this general solution to a linear example. Finally, using the linear example, we determine the equilibrium when two firms have different marginal costs.

GENERAL MODEL

Suppose that the market demand function is $p(Q)$ and that each firm's cost function is the same $C(q_i)$. To analyze a Cournot market of identical firms, we first examine the behavior of a representative firm. Firm 1 tries to maximize its profits through its choice of q_1:

$$\max_{q_1} \pi_1(q_1, q_2, \cdots, q_n) = q_1 p(q_1 + q_2 + \cdots + q_n) - C(q_1), \qquad (6A.1)$$

where $q_1 + q_2 + \cdots + q_n = Q$, the total market output. Firm 1 takes the outputs of the other firms as fixed. If Firm 1 changes its output by a small amount, the price changes by $(dp(Q)/dQ)(dQ/dq_1) = dp(Q)/dQ$. Its necessary condition to maximize profit (first-order condition) is found by differentiating profit in Equation 6A.1 and setting the result equal to zero. After we rearrange terms, this necessary condition is

$$MR = p(Q) + q_1 \frac{dp(Q)}{dQ} = \frac{dC(q_1)}{dq_1} = MC, \qquad (6A.2)$$

or marginal revenue equals marginal cost. Equation 6A.2 specifies the firm's best-response function: the optimal q_1 for any given output of other firms.

The marginal revenue expression can be rewritten as $p[1 + (q_1/p)(dp/dQ)]$. Multiplying and dividing the last term by n, noting that $Q = nq_1$ (given that all firms are identical), and observing that ε, the market elasticity of demand, is $(dQ/dp)(p/Q)$, we can rewrite Equation 6A.2 as

$$p\left(1 + \frac{1}{n\varepsilon}\right) = \frac{dC(q_1)}{dq_1}. \qquad (6A.3)$$

The left-hand side of Equation 6A.3 expresses Firm 1's marginal revenue in terms of the elasticity of demand of its residual demand curve, $n\varepsilon$, which is the number of firms, n, times the market demand elasticity, ε. Holding ε constant, the more firms, the more elastic the residual demand curve, and hence the closer a firm's marginal revenue to the price.

We can rearrange Equation 6A.3 to obtain an expression for the Lerner Index, $(p - MC)/p$, in terms of the market demand elasticity and the number of firms:

$$\frac{p - MC}{p} = -\frac{1}{n\varepsilon}. \qquad (6A.4)$$

The larger the Lerner Index, the greater the firm's market power. As Equation 6A.4 shows, if we hold the market elasticity constant and increase the number of firms, the Lerner Index falls. As n approaches ∞, the elasticity any one firm faces approaches $-\infty$, so the Lerner Index approaches 0 and the market is competitive.

LINEAR EXAMPLE

Now suppose that the market demand is linear,

$$p = a - bQ,$$

and each firm's marginal cost is m, a constant, and it has no fixed cost. Firm 1, a typical firm, maximizes its profits through its choice of q_1:

$$\max_{q_1} \pi_1(q_1, q_2, \cdots, q_n) = q_1[a - b(q_1 + q_2 + \cdots + q_n)] - mq_1. \qquad (6A.5)$$

Setting the derivative of profit with respect to q_1, holding the output levels of the other firms fixed, equal to zero, and rearranging terms, we find that the necessary condition for Firm 1 to maximize its profit is

$$MR = a - b(2q_1 + q_2 + \cdots + q_n) = m = MC. \tag{6A.6}$$

Because all firms have the same cost function, $q_2 = q_3 = \cdots = q_n \equiv q$ in equilibrium. Substituting this expression into Equation 6A.6, we find that the first firm's best-response function is

$$q_1 = R_1(q_2, \ldots, q_n) = \frac{a - m}{2b} - \frac{n - 1}{2} q. \tag{6A.7}$$

The other firms' best-response functions are derived similarly.

All these best-response functions must hold simultaneously. The intersection of the best-response functions determines the Cournot equilibrium. Setting $q_1 = q$ in Equation 6A.7 and solving for q, we find that the Cournot equilibrium output for each firm is

$$q = \frac{a - m}{(n + 1)b}. \tag{6A.8}$$

Total market output, $Q = nq$, equals $n(a - m)/[(n + 1)b]$. The corresponding price is obtained by substituting this expression for market output into the demand function:

$$p = \frac{a + nm}{n + 1}. \tag{6A.9}$$

Setting $n = 1$ in Equations 6A.8 and 6A.9 yields the monopoly quantity and price. As n becomes large, each firm's quantity approaches zero, total output approaches $(a - m)/b$, and price approaches m, which are the competitive levels. In Equation 6A.9, the Lerner Index is

$$\frac{p - MC}{p} = \frac{a - m}{a + nm}.$$

As n grows large, the denominator goes to ∞, so the Lerner Index goes to 0, and there is no market power.

DIFFERENT COSTS

In the linear example with two firms, how does the equilibrium change if the firms have different marginal costs? The marginal cost of Firm 1 is m_1, and that of Firm 2 is m_2. Firm 1 chooses output to maximize its profit:

$$\max_{q_1} \pi_1(q_1, q_2) = q_1[a - b(q_1 + q_2)] - m_1 q_1. \tag{6A.10}$$

Setting the derivative of Firm 1's profit with respect to q_1, holding q_2 fixed, equal to zero, and rearranging terms, we find that the necessary condition for Firm 1 to maximize its profit is $MR_1 = a - b(2q_1 + q_2) = m_1 = MC$. Using algebra, we can rearrange this expression to obtain Firm 1's best-response function:

$$q_1 = \frac{q - m_1 - bq_2}{2b}. \tag{6A.11}$$

By similar reasoning, Firm 2's best-response function is

$$q_2 = \frac{a - m_2 - bq_1}{2b}. \tag{6A.12}$$

To determine the equilibrium, we solve Equations 6A.11 and 6A.12 simultaneously for q_1 and q_2:

$$q_1 = \frac{a - 2m_1 + m_2}{3b}, \qquad (6A.13)$$

$$q_2 = \frac{a - 2m_2 + m_1}{3b}. \qquad (6A.14)$$

By inspecting Equations 6A.13 and 6A.14, we find that the firm with the smaller marginal cost has the larger equilibrium output. Similarly, the low-cost firm has a higher profit. If m_1 is less than m_2, then

$$\pi_1 = \frac{(a + m_2 - 2m_1)^2}{9b} > \frac{(a + m_1 - 2m_2)^2}{9b} = \pi_2.$$

Appendix 6B: Stackelberg Equilibrium

We use calculus to derive the Stackelberg equilibrium for the linear example given in Appendix 6A with two firms that have the same marginal cost, m. Because Firm 1, the Stackelberg leader, chooses its output first, it knows that Firm 2, the follower, will choose its output using its best-response function, which is (see Equation 6A.7, where $n = 2$)

$$q_2 = R_2(q_1) = \frac{a - m}{2b} - \frac{1}{2} q_1. \qquad (6B.1)$$

The Stackelberg leader's profit, $\pi_1(q_1 + q_2)$, can be written as $\pi_1(q_1 + R_2(q_1))$, where we've replaced the follower's output with its best-response function. The Stackelberg leader maximizes its profit by taking the best-response function as given:

$$\max_{q_1} \pi_1(q_1, R_2(q_1)) = q_1 \left[a - b \left(q_1 + \frac{a - m}{2b} - \frac{1}{2} q_1 \right) \right] - mq_1. \qquad (6B.2)$$

Setting the derivative of Firm 1's profit (in Equation 6B.2) with respect to q_1 equal to zero and solving for q_1, we find that the profit-maximizing output of the leader is

$$q_1 = \frac{a - m}{2b}. \qquad (6B.3)$$

Substituting the expression for q_1 in Equation 6B.3 into Equation 6B.1, we obtain the equilibrium output of the follower:

$$q_2 = \frac{a - m}{4b}.$$

Appendix 6C: Bertrand Equilibrium

We can use math to determine the cola market Bertrand equilibrium discussed in the chapter. First, we determine the best-response functions each firm faces. Then we equate the best-response functions to determine the equilibrium prices for the two firms.

Coke's best-response function tells us the price Coke charges that maximizes its profit as a function of the price Pepsi charges. We use the demand curve for Coke to derive the best-response function.

The reason Coke's price depends on Pepsi's price is that the quantity of Coke demanded, q_c, depends on the price of Coke, p_c, and the price of Pepsi, p_p. Coke's demand curve is

$$q_c = 58 - 4p_c + 2p_p. \tag{6C.1}$$

Partially differentiating Equation 6C.1 with respect to p_c (that is, holding the price of Pepsi fixed), we find that the change in quantity for every dollar change in price is $\partial q_c/\partial p_c = -4$, so a \$1-per-unit increase in the price of Coke causes the quantity of Coke demanded to fall by 4 units. Similarly, the demand for Coke rises by 2 units if the price of Pepsi rises by \$1, while the price of Coke remains constant: $\partial q_c/\partial p_p = 2$.

If Coke faces a constant marginal and average cost of m per unit, its profit is

$$\pi_c = (p_c - m)q_c = (p_c - m)(58 - 4p_c + 2p_p), \tag{6C.2}$$

where $p_c - m$ is Coke's profit per unit. To determine Coke's profit-maximizing price (holding Pepsi's price fixed), we set the partial derivative of the profit function, Equation 6C.2, with respect to the price of Coke equal to zero,

$$\frac{\partial \pi_c}{\partial p_c} = q_c + (p_c - m)\frac{\partial q_c}{\partial p_c} = q_c - 4(p_c - m) = 0, \tag{6C.3}$$

and solve for p_c as a function of p_p and m to find Coke's best-response function:

$$p_c = 7.25 + 0.25p_p + 0.5m. \tag{6C.4}$$

Equation 6C.4 shows that Coke's best-response price is 25¢ higher for every extra dollar that Pepsi charges and 50¢ higher for every extra dollar of Coke's marginal cost.

If Coke's average and marginal cost of production is \$5 per unit, its best-response function is

$$p_c = 9.75 + 0.25p_p, \tag{6C.5}$$

as Figure 6.11 shows. If $p_p = \$13$, then Coke's best response is to set $p_c = \$13$.

Pepsi's demand curve is

$$q_p = 63.2 - 4p_p + 1.6p_c. \tag{6C.6}$$

Using the same approach, we find that Pepsi's best-response function (for $m = \$5$) is

$$p_p = 10.4 + 0.2p_c. \tag{6C.7}$$

The intersection of Coke's and Pepsi's best-response functions (Equations 6C.5 and 6C.7) determines the Nash equilibrium. By substituting Pepsi's best-response function, Equation 6C.7, for p_p in Coke's best-response function, Equation 6C.5, we find that

$$p_c = 9.75 + 0.25(10.4 + 0.2p_c).$$

Solving this equation for p_c, we determine that the equilibrium price of Coke is \$13. Substituting $p_c = \$13$ into Equation 6C.6, we discover that the equilibrium price of Pepsi is also \$13.

Answers to Selected Problems

I know the answer! The answer lies within the heart of all mankind! The answer is twelve? I think I'm in the wrong building. —Charles Schultz

Chapter 2

12. The law would create a price ceiling (at 110% of the pre-emergency price). Because the supply curve shifts substantially to the left during the emergency, the price control will create a shortage: A smaller quantity will be supplied at the ceiling price than will be demanded.

13. A ban has no effect if foreigners supply nothing at the pre-ban, equilibrium price. Thus if imports occur only at prices above those actually observed, a ban has no practical effect.

21. The statement "Talk is cheap because supply exceeds demand" makes sense if we interpret it to mean that the *quantity supplied* of talk exceeds the *quantity demanded* at a price of zero. Imagine a downward-sloping demand curve that hits the horizontal, quantity axis to the left of where the upward-sloping supply curve hits the axis. (The correct aphorism is "Talk is cheap until you hire a lawyer.")

22. The demand curve for pork is $Q = 171 - 20p + 20p_b + 3p_c + 2Y$, where quantity is measured in millions of kg per year and income is measured in thousands of dollars per year. As a result, a ΔY change in income causes the quantity demanded to change by $\Delta Q = 2\Delta Y$. That is, a \$1,000 increase in income causes the quantity demanded to increase by 2 million kg per year, and a \$100 increase in income causes the quantity demanded to increase by a tenth as much, 0.2 million kg per year.

27. In equilibrium, the quantity demanded, $Q = a - bp$, equals the quantity supplied, $Q = c + ep$, so

$$a - bp = c + ep.$$

By solving this equation for p, we find that the equilibrium price is $p = (a - c)/(b + e)$. By substituting this expression for p into either the demand curve or the supply curve, we find that the equilibrium quantity is $Q = (ae + bc)/(b + e)$.

29. $Q = Q_1 + Q_2 = (120 - p) + (60 - \frac{1}{2}p) = 180 - 1.5p$.

33. Equating the right-hand sides of the supply and demand functions and using algebra, we find that $\ln(p) = 3.2 + 0.2 \ln(p_t)$. We then set $p_t = 110$, solve for $\ln(p)$, and exponentiate $\ln(p)$ to obtain the equilibrium price: $p \approx \$61.62$/ton. Substituting p into the supply curve and exponentiating, we determine the equilibrium: $Q \approx 11.78$ million short tons/year.

Chapter 3

2. According to Equation 3.1, the elasticity of demand is ε = (percentage change in quantity demanded) ÷ (percentage change in price) = -3.8% ÷ 10% = -0.38, which is inelastic. It is less elastic than household demand.

18. The incidence of the tax on consumers is zero if the demand curve is perfectly elastic or the supply curve is perfectly inelastic (see Questions 14 and 15).

19. We showed that, in a competitive market, the effect of a specific tax is the same whether it is placed on suppliers or demanders. Thus if the market for milk is competitive, consumers will pay the same price in equilibrium regardless of whether the government taxes consumers or stores.

23. If the quantity changes by 10.4% and the price elasticity of demand is -1.6, then we would expect the price to change by $-1.6 \times 10.4\% = -16.64\%$ (which is close to the 15% drop actually observed in the first month after the announcement).

26. Differentiating the demand function as $Q = Ap^\varepsilon$ with respect to p, we find that $dQ/dp = \varepsilon Ap^{\varepsilon-1}$. To get the elasticity, we multiply dQ/dp by $p/Q = p/Ap^\varepsilon = 1/Ap^{\varepsilon-1}$. That is, the elasticity is $\varepsilon Ap^{\varepsilon-1} \times 1/Ap^{\varepsilon-1} = \varepsilon$. Because this result holds for any p, the elasticity is the same, ε, at every point along the demand curve.

27. The elasticity of demand is (slope) $\times$ (p/Q) = $(\Delta Q/\Delta p)(p/Q)$ = (-9.5 thousand metric tons per year per cent) $\times$ (45¢/1,275 thousand metric tons per year) ≈ -0.34. That is, for every 1% fall in the price, a third of a percent more coconut oil is demanded. The cross-price elasticity of demand for coconut oil with respect to the price of palm oil is $(\Delta Q/\Delta p_p)(p_p/Q)$ = 16.2 $\times$ (31/1,275) $\approx$ 0.39.

29. Because the linear supply function is $Q = g + hp$, a change in price of Δp causes a $\Delta Q = h\Delta p$ change in quantity. Thus $\Delta Q/\Delta p = h$, and the elasticity of supply is $\eta = (\Delta Q/\Delta p)(p/Q) = hp/Q$. By substituting for Q using the supply function, we find that $\eta = hp/(g + hp)$. By using the supply function to substitute for p, we learn that $\eta = (Q - g)/Q$.

37. By dividing both the numerator and the denominator of the right-hand side of Equation 3.7 by η, we can rewrite that incidence equation as

$$\frac{\eta}{\eta - \varepsilon} = \frac{1}{1 - \varepsilon / \eta}.$$

As η goes to infinity, ε/η goes to zero, so the incidence approaches 1.

38. Differentiating quantity, $Q(p(\tau))$, with respect to the specific tax τ, we learn that the change in quantity as the tax changes is $dQ/d\tau = (dQ/dp)(dp/d\tau)$. Multiplying and dividing this expression by p/Q, we find that the change in quantity as the tax changes is $\varepsilon(Q/p)(dp/d\tau)$. Thus the closer ε is to zero, the less the quantity falls, all else the same. The tax causes revenue to change by

$$\frac{dR}{d\tau} = \left(Q + p\,\frac{dQ}{dp}\right)\frac{dp}{d\tau} = (1 + \varepsilon)Q\,\frac{dp}{d\tau}.$$

The closer ε is to zero, the larger the tax revenue effect.

Chapter 4

3. A profit tax (of less than 100%) has no effect on a firm's profit-maximizing behavior. Suppose the government's share of the profit is γ. Then the firm wants to maximize its after-tax profit, which is $(1 - \gamma)\pi$. However, whatever choice of Q (or p) maximizes π, will maximize $(1 - \gamma)\pi$. Consequently, the tribe's behavior is unaffected by a change in the share that the government receives. We can also answer this problem using calculus. The before-tax profit is $\pi_B = R(Q) - C(Q)$, and the after-tax profit is $\pi_A = (1 - \gamma)[R(Q) - C(Q)]$. For both, the first-order condition is marginal revenue equals marginal cost: $R'(Q) = C'(Q)$.

6. Yes. As the electric power utility application illustrates, the demand curve could cut the average cost curve only in its downward-sloping section. Consequently, the average cost is strictly downward sloping in the relevant region.

23. Suppose that the monopoly faces a constant-elasticity demand curve, with elasticity ε, and has a constant marginal cost, m, and that the government imposes a specific tax of τ. The monopoly sets its price such that $p = (m + \tau)/(1 + 1/\varepsilon)$. Thus $dp/d\tau = 1/(1 + 1/\varepsilon) > 1$.

32. For saline solution, $p/MC \approx 55.4$ and the Lerner Index is $(p - MC)/p \approx 0.98$. From Equation 4.9, we know that $(p - MC)/p \approx 0.98 = -1/\varepsilon$, so $\varepsilon \approx 1.02$.

41. If the demand curve is $p = 10 - Q$, its marginal revenue curve is $MR = 10 - 2Q$. Thus, the output that maximizes the monopoly's profit is determined by $MR = 10 - 2Q = 2 = MC$, or $Q^* = 4$. At that output level, its price is $p^* = 6$ and its profit is $\pi^* = 16$. If the monopoly chooses to sell 8 units in the first period (it has no incentive to sell more), its price is 2 and it makes no profit. Given that the firm sells 8 units in the first period, its demand curve in the second period is $p = 10 - Q/\alpha$, so its marginal revenue function is $MR = 10 - 2Q/\alpha$. The output that leads to its maximum profit is determined by $MR = 10 - 2Q/\alpha = 2 = MC$, or its output is 4α. Thus, its price is 6 and its profit is 16α. It pays for the firm to set a low price in the first period if the lost profit, 16, is less than the extra profit in the second period, which is $16(\alpha - 1)$. Thus, it pays to set a low price in the first period if $16 < 16(\alpha - 1)$, or $2 < \alpha$.

Chapter 5

2. This policy allows the firm to maximize its profit by price discriminating if people who put a lower value on their time (are willing to drive to the store and move their purchases themselves) have a higher elasticity of demand than people who want to order over the phone and have the goods delivered.

3. The colleges may be providing scholarships as a form of charity, or they may be price discriminating by lowering the final price to less wealthy families (with presumably higher elasticities of demand).

27. The two marginal revenue curves are $MR_J = 3,500 - Q_J$ and $MR_A = 4,500 - 2Q_A$. Equating the marginal revenues with the marginal cost of $500, we find that $Q_J = 3,000$ and $Q_A = 2,000$. Substituting these quantities into the inverse demand curves, we learn that $p_J = \$2,000$ and $p_A = \$2,500$. Rearranging Equation 4.9, we know that the elasticities of demand are $\varepsilon_J = p/(MC - p) = 2,000/(500 - 2,000) = -4/3$ and $\varepsilon_A = 2,500/(500 - 2,500) = -5/4$. Thus, using Equation 5.3, we find that

$$\frac{p_J}{p_A} = \frac{2,000}{2,500} = 0.8 = \frac{1 + 1/(-5/4)}{1 + 1/(-4/3)} = \frac{1 + 1/\varepsilon_A}{1 + 1/\varepsilon_J}.$$

The profit in Japan is $(p_J - m)Q_J = (\$2,000 - \$500) \times 3,000 = \$4.5$ million, and the U.S. profit is $4 million. The deadweight loss is greater in Japan, $2.25 million ($= \frac{1}{2} \times \$1,500 \times 3,000$), than in the United States, $2 million ($= \frac{1}{2} \times \$2,000 \times 2,000$).

28. The marginal revenue function corresponding to a linear inverse demand function has the same intercept and twice as steep a slope (see Chapter 4). Thus, the American marginal revenue function is $MR_A = 100 - 2Q_A$, and the Japanese one is $MR_J = 80 - 4Q_J$. To determine how many units to sell in the United States, the monopoly sets its American marginal revenue equal to its marginal cost, $MR_A = 100 - 2Q_A = 20$, and solves for the optimal quantity, $Q_A = 40$ units. Similarly, because $MR_J = 80 - 4Q_J = 20$, the optimal quantity is $Q_J = 15$ units in Japan. Substituting $Q_A = 40$ into the American demand function, we find that $p_A = 100 - 40 = \$60$. Similarly, substituting $Q_J = 15$ units into the Japanese demand function, we learn that $p_J = 80 - (2 \times 15) = \$50$. Thus, the price-discriminating monopoly charges 20% more in the United States than in Japan. We can also show this result using elasticities. From Equation 3.3, we know that the elasticity of demand is $\varepsilon_A = -p_A/Q_A$ in the United States and $\varepsilon_J = -\frac{1}{2}p_J/Q_J$ in Japan. In the equilibrium, $\varepsilon_A = -60/40 = -3/2$ and $\varepsilon_J = -50/(2 \times 15) = -5/3$. As Equation 5.3 shows, the ratio of the prices depends on the relative elasticities of demand: $p_A/p_J = 60/50 = (1 + 1/\varepsilon_J)/(1 + 1/\varepsilon_A) = (1 - 3/5)/(1 - 2/3) = 6/5$.

31. From the problem, we know that the profit-maximizing Chinese price is $p = 3$ and the quantity is $Q = 0.1$ (million). The marginal cost is $m = 1$. Using Equation 4.9, $(p_C - m)/p_C = (3 - 1)/3 = -1/\varepsilon_C$, so $\varepsilon_C = -3/2$. If the Chinese inverse demand curve is $p = a - bQ$, then the corresponding marginal revenue curve is $MR = a - 2bQ$. Warner maximizes its profit where $MR = a - 2bQ = m = 1$, so its optimal $Q = (a - 1)/(2b)$. Substituting this expression into the inverse demand curve, we find that its optimal $p = (a + 1)/2 = 3$, or $a = 5$. Substituting that result into the output equation, we have $Q = (5 - 1)/(2b) = 0.1$ (million). Thus, $b = 20$, the inverse demand function is $p = 5 - 20Q$, and the marginal revenue function is $MR = 5 - 40Q$. Using this information, you can draw a figure similar to Figure 5.4.

Chapter 6

1. The payoff matrix in this prisoners' dilemma game is

		Duncan	
		Squeal	Stay silent
Larry	Squeal	−2 −2	−5 0
	Stay silent	0 −5	−1 −1

If Duncan stays silent, Larry gets 0 if he squeals and −1 (a year in jail) if he stays silent. If Duncan confesses, Larry gets −2 if he squeals and −5 if he does not. Thus Larry is better off squealing in either case, so squealing is his dominant strategy. By the same reasoning, squealing is also Duncan's dominant strategy. As a result, the Nash equilibrium is for both to confess.

5. The monopoly will make more profit than the duopoly will, so the monopoly is willing to pay the college more rent. Although granting monopoly rights may be attractive to the college in terms of higher rent, students will suffer (lose consumer surplus) because of the higher prices.

16. Given that the duopolies produce identical goods, the equilibrium price is lower if the duopolies set price rather than quantity. If the goods are heterogeneous, we cannot answer this question definitively.

17. By differentiating its product, a firm makes the residual demand curve it faces less elastic everywhere. For example, no consumer will buy from that firm if its rival charges less and the goods are homogeneous. In contrast, some consumers who prefer this firm's product to that of its rival will still buy from this firm even if its rival charges less. As the chapter shows, a firm sets a higher price, the lower the elasticity of demand at the equilibrium.

23. The inverse demand curve is $p = 1 - 0.001Q$. The first firm's profit is $\pi_1 = [1 - 0.001(q_1 + q_2)]q_1 - 0.28q_1$. Its first-order condition is $d\pi_1/dq_1 = 1 - 0.001(2q_1 + q_2) - 0.28 = 0$. If we rearrange the terms, the first firm's best-response function is $q_1 = 360 - \frac{1}{2}q_2$. Similarly, the second firm's best-response function is $q_2 = 360 - \frac{1}{2}q_1$. By substituting one of these best-response functions into the other, we learn that the Cournot-Nash equilibrium occurs at $q_1 = q_2 = 240$, so the equilibrium price is 52¢.

26. Using Equations 6A.13 and 6A.14, we find that the equilibrium quantities are $q_1 = (a - 2m_1 + m_2)/3b = (90 + 30)/6 = 20$ and $q_2 = (90 - 60)/6 = 5$. As a result, the equilibrium price is $p = 90 - 20 - 5 = 65$.

29. Firm 1 wants to maximize its profit:

$$\pi_1 = (p_1 - 10)q_1 = (p_1 - 10)(100 - 2p_1 + p_2).$$

Its first-order condition is $d\pi_1/dp_1 = 100 - 4p_1 + p_2 + 20 = 0$, so its best-response function is $p_1 = 30 + \frac{1}{4}p_2$. Similarly, Firm 2's best-response function is $p_2 = 30 + \frac{1}{4}p_1$. Solving, the Bertrand-Nash equilibrium prices are $p_1 = p_2 = 40$. Each firm produces 60 units.

32. One approach is to show that the effect a rise in marginal cost or a fall in the number of firms tends to cause the price to rise. Solved Problem 6.2 shows the effect of a decrease in marginal cost (the opposite effect). The section titled "The Cournot Equilibrium and the Number of Firms" shows that as the number of firms falls, market power increases and the markup of price over marginal cost increases. The two effects reinforce each other. Suppose the market demand curve has a constant elasticity of ε. We can rewrite Equation 6.8 as $p = m/[1 + 1/(n\varepsilon)] = m\mu$, where $\mu = 1/[1 + 1/(n\varepsilon)]$ is the markup factor. Suppose that marginal cost increases to $(1 + \alpha)m$ and the drop in the number of firms causes the markup factor to rise to $(1 + \beta)\mu$; then the change in price is $[(1 + \alpha)m \times (1 + \beta)\mu] - m\mu = (\alpha + \beta + \alpha\beta)m\mu = m/[1 + 1/(n\varepsilon)]p$. That is, price increases by the fractional increase in the marginal cost, α, plus the fractional increase in the markup factor, β, plus the interaction of the two, $\alpha\beta$.

39. Appendix 6A shows the general formulas for the linear demand, constant marginal cost Cournot model.

   a. For the duopoly, $q_1 = (15 - 2 + 2)/3 = 5$, $q_2 = (15 - 4 + 1)/3 = 4$, $p_d = 6$, $\pi_1 = (6 - 1)5 = 25$, $\pi_2 = (6 - 2)4 = 16$. Total output is $Q_d = 5 + 4 = 9$. Total profit is $\pi_d = 25 + 16 = 41$. Consumer surplus is $CS_d = \frac{1}{2}(15 - 6)9 = 81/2 = 40.5$. At the efficient price (equal to marginal cost of 1), the output is 14. The deadweight loss is $DWL_d = \frac{1}{2}(6 - 1)(14 - 9) = 25/2 = 12.5$.

   b. A monopoly equates its marginal revenue and marginal cost: $MR = 15 - 2Q_m = 1 = MC$. Thus, $Q_m = 7$, $p_m = 8$, $\pi_m = (8 - 1)7 = 49$. Consumer surplus is $CS_m = \frac{1}{2}(15 - 8)7 = 49/2 = 24.5$. The deadweight loss is $DWL_m = \frac{1}{2}(8 - 1)(14 - 7) = 49/2 = 24.5$.

   c. The average cost of production for the duopoly is $[(5 \times 1) + (4 \times 2)]/(5 + 4) = 1.44$, whereas the average cost of production for the monopoly is 1. The increase in market power effect swamps the efficiency gain so that consumer surplus falls while deadweight loss nearly doubles.

Answers to Questions for Cross-Chapter Analysis

Frequent Flier Programs

1. For the given values, the equilibrium price would be $p = \$150/[1 + 1/(2 \times -1.75)] = \$210$ if only the elasticity had changed. If only the marginal cost changed, the equilibrium price would be $p = \$160/[1 + 1/(2 \times -2)] \approx \$213.3$. Thus the change in both the marginal cost and the elasticity contributes to the increase in the equilibrium price.

2. In this example, profit increases substantially. Given that the marginal cost equals the average cost, the profit is $\pi = (p - MC)Q = (p - MC)50{,}000{,}000p^{\varepsilon}$. Prior to the FFP, the firm's profit is $(\$200 - \$150)1{,}250 = \$62{,}500$. After the FFP, the profit is approximately $(\$224 - \$160)3{,}855 = \$246{,}727$.

Definitions

I hate definitions. —Benjamin Disraeli

bandwagon effect: The situation in which a person places greater value on a good as more and more other people possess it.* (4)

Bertrand equilibrium: a *Nash equilibrium* in prices; a set of prices such that no firm can obtain a higher profit by choosing a different price if the other firms continue to charge these prices. (6)

best response: the strategy that maximizes a firm's profit, given its beliefs about its rivals' strategies. (6)

bundling (*package tie-in sale*): a type of tie-in sale in which two goods are combined so that customers cannot buy either good separately. (5)

cartel: a group of firms that explicitly agree to coordinate their activities. (6)

Cournot equilibrium: a *Nash equilibrium* in quantities; a set of quantities sold by firms such that, holding the quantities of all other firms constant, no firm can obtain a higher profit by choosing a different quantity. (6)

cross-price elasticity of demand: the percentage change in the *quantity demanded* in response to a given percentage change in the price of another good. (3)

demand curve: the *quantity demanded* at each possible price, holding constant the other factors that influence purchases. (2)

dominant strategy: a strategy that strictly dominates (gives higher profits than) all other strategies, regardless of the actions chosen by rival firms. (6)

duopoly: an oligopoly with two firms. (6)

elasticity: the percentage change in a variable in response to a given percentage change in another variable. (3)

equilibrium: a situation in which no one wants to change his or her behavior. (2)

excess demand: the amount by which the *quantity demanded* exceeds the *quantity supplied* at a specified price. (2)

excess supply: the amount by which the *quantity supplied* is greater than the *quantity demanded* at a specified price. (2)

game: any competition between players (firms) in which strategic behavior plays a major role. (6)

game theory: a set of tools that economists, political scientists, military analysts, and others use to analyze decisionmaking by players that use strategies. (6)

incidence of a tax on consumers: the share of the tax that falls on consumers. (3)

income elasticity of demand (or *income elasticity*): the percentage change in the *quantity demanded* in response to a given percentage change in income. (3)

Law of Demand: consumers demand more of a good the lower its price, holding constant tastes, the prices of other goods, and other factors that influence consumption. (2)

Lerner Index: the ratio of the difference between price and marginal cost to the price: $(p - MC)/p$. (4)

market: an exchange mechanism that allows buyers to trade with sellers. (1)

market power: the ability of a firm to charge a price above marginal cost and earn a positive profit. (4)

microeconomics: the study of how individuals and firms make themselves as well off as possible in a world of scarcity and the consequences of those individual decisions for markets and the entire economy. (1)

minimum efficient scale (*full capacity*): the smallest quantity at which the average cost curve reaches its minimum. (6)

model: a description of the relationship between two or more economic variables. (1)

monopolistic competition: a market structure in which firms have market power but no additional firm can enter and earn positive profits. (6)

monopoly: the only supplier of a good for which there is no close substitute. (4)

multimarket price discrimination (*third-degree price discrimination*): a situation in which a firm charges different groups of customers different prices but charges a given customer the same price for every unit of output sold. (5)

---

*Numbers refer to the chapter where the term is defined.

Nash equilibrium: a set of strategies such that, holding the strategies of all other firms constant, no firm can obtain a higher profit by choosing a different strategy. (6)

natural monopoly: situation in which one firm can produce the total output of the market at lower cost than several firms could. (4)

network externality: the situation where one person's demand for a good depends on the consumption of the good by others. (4)

nonuniform pricing: charging consumers different prices for the same product or charging a single customer a price that depends on the number of units the customer buys. (5)

normative statement: a conclusion as to whether something is good or bad. (1)

oligopoly: a small group of firms in a market with substantial barriers to entry. (6)

patent: an exclusive right granted to the inventor to sell a new and useful product, process, substance, or design for a fixed period of time. (4)

perfect price discrimination (*first-degree price discrimination*): situation in which a firm sells each unit at the maximum amount any customer is willing to pay for it, so prices differ across customers and a given customer may pay more for some units than for others. (5)

positive statement: a testable hypothesis about cause and effect. (1)

price discrimination: practice in which a firm charges consumers different prices for the same good. (5)

price elasticity of demand (or *elasticity of demand*, ε): the percentage change in the *quantity demanded* in response to a given percentage change in the price. (3)

price elasticity of supply (or *elasticity of supply*, η): the percentage change in the *quantity supplied* in response to a given percentage change in the price. (3)

prisoners' dilemma: a game in which all players have dominant strategies that result in profits (or other payoffs) that are inferior to what they could achieve if they used cooperative strategies. (6)

quantity demanded: the amount of a good that consumers are willing to buy at a given price, holding constant the other factors that influence purchases. (2)

quantity discrimination (*second-degree price discrimination*): situation in which a firm charges a different price for large quantities than for small quantities but all customers who buy a given quantity pay the same price. (5)

quantity supplied: the amount of a good that firms *want* to sell at a given price, holding constant other factors that influence firms' supply decisions, such as costs and government actions. (2)

quota: the limit that a government sets on the quantity of a foreign-produced good that may be imported. (2)

requirement tie-in sale: a tie-in sale in which customers who buy one product from a firm are required to make all their purchases of another product from that firm. (5)

reservation price: the maximum amount a person would be willing to pay for a unit of output. (6)

residual demand curve: the market demand that is not met by other sellers at any given price. (6)

shortage: a persistent excess demand. (2)

snob effect: the situation in which a person places greater value on a good as fewer and fewer other people possess it. (4)

strategy: a battle plan of the actions a firm plans to take to compete with other firms. (6)

supergame: a game that is played repeatedly, allowing players to devise strategies for one period that depend on rivals' actions in previous periods. (6)

supply curve: the *quantity supplied* at each possible price, holding constant the other factors that influence firms' supply decisions. (2)

tie-in sale: a type of nonlinear pricing in which customers can buy one product only if they agree to buy another product as well. (5)

transaction costs: the expenses of finding a trading partner and making a trade for a good or service beyond the price paid for that good or service. (2)

two-part tariff: a pricing system in which the firm charges a consumer a lump-sum fee (the first tariff or price) for the right to buy as many units of the good as the consumer wants at a specified price (the second tariff). (5)

References

Adelaja, Adesoji O., "Price Changes, Supply Elasticities, Industry Organization, and Dairy Output Distribution," *American Journal of Agricultural Economics*, 73(1), February 1991: 89–102.

Agcaoili-Sombilla, Mercedita C., *The World Rice Market: A Model of Imperfect Substitutes*, Ph.D. University of Minnesota, 1991.

Aigner, Dennis J., and Glen G. Cain, "Statistical Theories of Discrimination in Labor Markets," *Industrial and Labor Relations Review*, 30(2), January 1977:175–187.

Akerlof, George A., "The Market for 'Lemons': Quality Uncertainty and the Market Mechanism," *Quarterly Journal of Economics*, 84(3), August 1970:488–500.

Akerlof, George A., "Labor Contacts as Partial Gift Exchanges," *Quarterly Journal of Economics*, 97(4), November 1982: 543–569.

Alexander, Donald L., "Major League Baseball," *Journal of Sports Economics*, 2(4), November 2001:341–355.

Allingham, M. G., "Progression and Leisure," *American Economic Review*, 62(3), June 1972:447–450.

Anderson, Keith B., and Michael R. Metzger, *Petroleum Tariffs as a Source of Government Revenues*. Washington, D.C.: Bureau of Economics, Federal Trade Commission, 1991.

Arrow, Kenneth, *Social Choice and Individual Values*. New York: Wiley, 1951.

Ayres, Ian, and Joel Waldfogel, "A Market Test for Race Discrimination in Bail Setting," *Stanford Law Review*, 46(5), May 1994:987–1047.

Baldwin, John R., and Paul K. Gorecki, *The Role of Scale in Canada/U.S. Productivity Differences in the Manufacturing Sector, 1970–1979*. Toronto: University of Toronto Press, 1986.

Baldwin, Robert E., and Paul R. Krugman, "Industrial Policy and International Competition in Wide Bodied Jet Aircraft," in Robert E. Baldwin, ed., *Trade Policy Issues and Empirical Analysis*. Chicago: University of Chicago Press, 1988.

Bar-Ilan, Avner, and Bruce Sacerdote, "The Response to Fines and Probability of Detection in a Series of Experiments," NBER Working Paper 8638, December 2001.

Battalio, Raymond, John H. Kagel, and Carl Kogut, "Experimental Confirmation of the Existence of a Giffen Good," *American Economic Review*, 81(3), September 1991: 961–970.

Becker, Gary S., *The Economics of Discrimination*, 2nd ed. Chicago: University of Chicago Press, 1971.

Benjamin, Daniel K., William R. Dougan, and David Buschena, *Journal of Risk and Uncertainty*, 22(1), January 2001: 35–57.

Berck, Peter, and Michael Roberts, "Natural Resource Prices: Will They Ever Turn Up?" *Journal of Environmental Economics and Management*, 31(1), July 1996:65–78.

Berry, Steven, James Levinsohn, and Ariel Pakes, "Voluntary Export Restraints on Automobiles: Evaluating a Trade Policy," *American Economic Review*, 89(3), June 1999: 400–430.

Besley, Timothy J., and Harvey S. Rosen, "Sales Taxes and Prices: An Empirical Analysis," *National Tax Journal*, 52(2), June 1999:157–178.

Besley, Timothy J., and Harvey S. Rosen, "Vertical Externalities in Tax Setting: Evidence from Gasoline and Cigarettes," *Journal of Public Economics*, 70(3), December 1998: 383–398.

Bhuyan, Sanjib, and Rigoberto A. Lopez, "What Determines Welfare Losses from Oligopoly Power in the Food and Tobacco Industries?" *Agricultural and Resource Economics Review*, 27(2), October 1998:258–265.

Bhuyan, Sanjib, "Corporate Political Activities and Oligopoly Welfare Loss," *Review of Industrial Organization*, 17(4), December 2000:411–426.

Billikopf, Gregory Encina, "High Piece-Rate Wages Do Not Reduce Hours Worked," *California Agriculture*, 49(1), January–February 1995:17–18.

Bishai, David M., and Hui-Chu Lang, "The Willingness to Pay for Wait Reduction: The Disutility of Queues for Cataract Surgery in Canada, Denmark, and Spain," *Journal of Health Economics*, 19(2), March 2000:219–230.

Black, Dan A., Seth Sanders, and Lowell Taylor, "The Economic Rewards to Studying Economics," *Economic Inquiry*, 41(3), July 2003:365–377.

Blanchflower, David G., and Alex Bryson, "Union Relative Wage Effects in the United States and the United Kingdom," Industrial Relations Research Association Proceedings, 2004.

Blanciforti, Laura Ann, "The Almost Ideal Demand System Incorporating Habits: An Analysis of Expenditures on Food and Aggregate Commodity Groups." Doctoral thesis, University of California, Davis, 1982.

Bordley, Robert F., and James B. McDonald, "Estimating Aggregate Automotive Income Elasticities from the Population Income-Share Elasticity," *Journal of Business and Economic Statistics*, 11(2), April 1993:209–214.

Borenstein, Severin, James Bushnell, and Matthew Lewis, "Market Power in California's Gasoline Market," University of California Energy Institute, CSEM WP 132, May 2004, **www.ucei.berkeley.edu/PDF/csemwp132.pdf**.

Borenstein, Severin, and Nancy L. Rose, "Competition and Price Dispersion in the U.S. Airline Industry," *Journal of Political Economy*, 102(4), August 1994:653–683.

Borjas, George J., "The Labor Demand Curve Is Downward Sloping: Reexamining the Impact of Immigration on the Labor Market," *Quarterly Journal of Economics*, 118(4), November 2003:1335–1374.

Boroski, John W., and Gerard C. S. Mildner, "An Economic Analysis of Taxicab Regulation in Portland, Oregon," Cascade Policy Institute, **www.cascadepolicy.org**, 1998.

Boskin, Michael J., Ellen R. Dulberger, Robert J. Gordon, Zvi Griliches, and Dale W. Jorgenson, "The CPI Commission:

Findings and Recommendations," *American Economic Review*, 87(2), May 1997:78–93.

Boskin, Michael J., and Dale W. Jorgenson, "Implications of Overstating Inflation for Indexing Government Programs and Understanding Economic Progress," *American Economic Review*, 87(2), May 1997:89–93.

Brander, James A., and Anming Zhang, "Market Conduct in the Airline Industry: An Empirical Investigation," *Rand Journal of Economics*, 21(4), Winter 1990:567–583.

Brander, James A., and M. Scott Taylor, "The Simple Economics of Easter Island: A Ricardo-Malthus Model of Renewable Resource Use," *American Economic Review*, 88(1), March 1998:119–138.

Brown, Robert W., "An Estimate of the Rent Generated by a Premium College Football Player," *Economic Inquiry*, 31(4), October 1993:671–684.

Brown, Stephen P. A., and Daniel Wolk, "Natural Resource Scarcity and Technological Change," *Economic and Financial Review* (Federal Reserve Bank of Dallas), First Quarter 2000:2–13.

Brownlee, Oswald, and George Perry, "The Effects of the 1965 Federal Excise Tax Reductions on Prices," *National Tax Journal*, 20(3), September 1967:235–249.

Brozovic, Nicholas, David L. Sunding, and David Zilberman, "Prices and Quantities Reconsidered," University of California, Berkeley, working paper, 2002.

Brunk, Gregory G., "A Test of the Friedman-Savage Gambling Model," *Quarterly Journal of Economics*, 96(2), May 1981:341–348.

Busch, Susan H., Mireia Jofre-Bonet, Tracy Falba, and Jody Sindelar, "Tobacco Spending and its Crowd-out of Other Goods," *Applied Health Economics and Policy*, forthcoming.

Buschena, David E., and Jeffrey M. Perloff, "The Creation of Dominant Firm Market Power in the Coconut Oil Export Market," *American Journal of Agricultural Economics*, 73(4), November 1991:1000–1008.

Card, David, and Alan B. Krueger, *Myth and Measurement: The New Economics of the Minimum Wage*. Princeton, N.J.: Princeton University Press, 1995.

Caputo, Michael R., and Quirino Paris, "An Atemporal Microeconomic Theory and an Empirical Test of Price-Induced Technical Progress," *Journal of Productivity Analysis*, forthcoming.

Carlson, Steven, "An Overview of Food Stamp Cashout Research in the Food and Nutrition Service," in Nancy Fasciano, Darryl Hall, and Harold Beebout, eds., *New Directions in Food Stamp Policy Research*. Alexandria, Va.: U.S. Department of Agriculture, Food and Nutrition Service, 1993.

Carlton, Dennis W., and Jeffrey M. Perloff, *Modern Industrial Organization*, 4th ed. Reading, Mass.: Addison Wesley Longman, 2005.

Carter, Colin A., and Jacqueline Huie, "Market Effects of Searching for Mad Cows," *ARE Update*, 8(1), September/October 2004:5–7.

Caves, Richard E., and David R. Barton, *Technical Efficiency in U.S. Manufacturing Industries*. Cambridge, Mass.: MIT Press, 1990.

Chouinard, Hayley H., David Davis, Jeffrey T. LaFrance, and Jeffrey M. Perloff, "The Effects of a Fat Tax on Dairy Products," University of California, Berkeley Working Paper, 2005.

Chouinard, Hayley, and Jeffrey M. Perloff, "Incidence of Federal and State Gasoline Taxes," *Economic Letters*, 83(1), April 2004:55–60.

Christensen, Laurits R., and William H. Greene, "Economies of Scale in U.S. Electric Power Generation," *Journal of Political Economy*, 84(4, pt. 1), August 1976:655–676.

Chung, Sangho, "The Learning Curve and the Yield Factor: The Case of Korea's Semiconductor Industry," *Applied Economics*, 33(4), March 2001:472–483.

Coase, Ronald H., "The Nature of the Firm," *Economica*, 4(16), November 1937:386–405.

Coase, Ronald H., "The Problem of Social Cost," *Journal of Law and Economics*, 3, October 1960:1–44.

Connolly, Marie, and Alan B. Krueger, "Rockonomics: The Economics of Popular Music," NBER Working Paper 11282, **www.nber.org/papers/w11282**, 2005.

Crawford, David, John Del Roccili, and Richard Voith, "Comments on Proposed Tax Reforms," Econsult Corporation, June 9, 2004.

Deacon, Robert T., and Jon Sonstelie, "The Welfare Costs of Rationing by Waiting," *Economic Inquiry*, 27(2), April 1989:179–196.

Delipalla, Sophia, and Michael Keen, "The Comparison Between Ad Valorem and Specific Taxation Under Imperfect Competition," *Journal of Public Economics*, 49(3), December 1992:351–367.

de Melo, Jaime, and David Tarr, *A General Equilibrium Analysis of U.S. Foreign Trade Policy*. Cambridge, Mass.: MIT Press, 1992.

de Melo, Jaime, and David Tarr, "VERs under Imperfect Competition and Foreign Direct Investment: A Case Study of the US–Japan Auto VER," *Japan and the World Economy*, 8(1), March 1996:11–33.

Dewan, Sanjeev, and Vernon Hsu, "Adverse Selection in Electronic Markets: Evidence from Online Stamp Auctions," *Journal of Industrial Economics*, LII(4), December 2004: 497–516.

Diewert, W. Edwin, and Alice O. Nakamura, eds., *Essays in Index Number Theory*, Vol. 1. New York: North Holland, 1993.

Dixit, Avinash K., and Robert S. Pindyck, *Investment Under Uncertainty*. Princeton, N.J.: Princeton University Press, 1994.

Duffy-Deno, Kevin T., "Business Demand for Broadband Access Capacity," *Journal of Regulatory Economics*, 24(3), 2003: 359–372.

Dunham, Wayne R., *Moral Hazard and the Market for Used Automobiles*. Economic Analysis Group Discussion Paper 96–4. Washington, D.C.: U.S. Department of Justice, Antitrust Division, 1996.

Dunn, L. F., "Quantifying Nonpecuniary Returns," *Journal of Human Resources*, 2(3), Summer 1977:347–359.

Dunn, L. F., "An Empirical Indifference Function for Income and Leisure," *Review of Economics and Statistics*, 60(4), November 1978:533–540.

Dunn, L. F., "Measurement of Internal Income-Leisure Trade-offs," *Quarterly Journal of Economics*, 93(3), August 1979:373–393.

Eastwood, David B., and John A. Craven, "Food Demand and Savings in a Complete, Extended, Linear Expenditure System," *American Journal of Agricultural Economics*, 63(3), August 1981:544–549.

Economides, Nicholas, "The Economics of Networks," *International Journal of Industrial Organization*, 14(6), October 1996:673–699.

Econsult Corporation, *Choosing the Best Mix of Taxes for Philadelphia: An Econometric Analysis of the Impacts of Tax Rates on Tax Bases, Tax Revenue, and the Private Economy*, Report to the Philadelphia Tax Reform Commission, 2003.

Edell, Richard J., and Pravin P. Varaiya, "Providing Internet Access: What We Learn from the INDEX Trial," **www.index.berkeley.edu/reports/99-010W**, April 1999.

Exxon Company, U.S.A., *Competition in the Petroleum Industry*. Submission to the U.S. Senate Judiciary Subcommittee on Antitrust and Monopoly, January 21, 1975.

Farrell, Joseph, and Matthew Rabin, "Cheap Talk," *Journal of Economic Perspectives*, 10(3), Summer 1996:103–118.

Farrell, Lisa, Roger Hartley, Gauthier Lanot, and Ian Walker, "The Demand for Lotto," *Journal of Business & Economic Statistics*, 18(2), April 2000:228–241.

Fasciano, Nancy, Daryl Hall, and Harold Beebout, eds., *New Directions in Food Stamp Policy Research*. Alexandria, Va.: U.S. Department of Agriculture, Food and Nutrition Service, 1993.

Federal Trade Commission, "Federal Trade Commission Advertising Cases Involving Weight Loss Products and Services," 1927, February 2003.

Fisher, Franklin M., "The Social Cost of Monopoly and Regulation: Posner Reconsidered," *Journal of Political Economy*, 93(2), April 1985:410–416.

Foster, Andrew D., and Mark R. Rosenzweig, "A Test for Moral Hazard in the Labor Market: Contractual Arrangements, Effort, and Health," *Review of Economics and Statistics*, 76(2), May 1994:213–227.

Fraker, Thomas M., "The Effects of Food Stamps on Food Consumption: A Review of the Literature," in Nancy Fasciano, Darryl Hall, and Harold Beebout, eds., *Current Perspectives on Food Stamp Program Participation*. Alexandria, Va.: U.S. Department of Agriculture, Food and Nutrition Service, 1990.

Frech, H. E., III, and William C. Lee, "The Welfare Cost of Rationing-by-Queuing Across Markets: Theory and Estimates from the U.S. Gasoline Crisis," *Quarterly Journal of Economics*, 102(1), February 1987:97–108.

French, Ben C., and Gordon A. King, "Demand and Price-Markup Functions for Canned Cling Peaches and Fruit Cocktail," *Western Journal of Agricultural Economics*, 11(1), July 1986:8–18.

Friedlaender, Ann F., Clifford Winston, and Kung Wang, "Costs, Technology, and Productivity in the U.S. Automobile Industry," *Bell Journal of Economics and Management Science*, 14(1), Spring 1983:1–20.

Friedman, Milton, and Leonard J. Savage, "The Utility Analysis of Choices Involving Risk," *Journal of Political Economy*, 56(4), August 1948:279–304.

Fudenberg, Drew, and Jean Tirole, "A 'Signal-Jamming' Theory of Predation," *Rand Journal of Economics*, 17(3), Autumn 1986:366–376.

Fullerton, Don, "On the Possibility of an Inverse Relationship Between Tax Rates and Government Revenues," *Journal of Public Economy*, 19(1), October 1982:3–22.

Fullerton, Don, and Li Gan, "A Simulation-Based Welfare Loss Calculation for Labor Taxes with Piecewise-Linear Budgets," *Journal of Public Economics*, 88(11), September 2004:2339–2359.

Gallini, Nancy T., "Demand for Gasoline in Canada," *Canadian Journal of Economics*, 16(2), May 1983:299–324.

Garratt, Rod, Mark Walker, and John Wooders, "Behavior in Second-Price Auctions by Highly Experienced eBay Buyers and Sellers," University of California at Santa Barbara Economics Working Paper 1181, 2005.

Garrett, Thomas A., "An International Comparison and Analysis of Lotteries and the Distribution of Lottery Expenditures," *International Review of Applied Economics*, 15(20), April 2001:213–227.

Garrett, Thomas A., and Russell S. Sobel, "Gamblers Favor Skewness, Not Risk: Further Evidence from United States' Lottery Games," *Economics Letters*, 63(1), April 1999: 85–90.

Gasmi, Farid, D., Mark Kennet, Jean-Jacques Laffont, and William W. Sharkey, *Cost Proxy Models and Telecommunications Policy*, Cambridge, MA: MIT Press, 2002.

Gasmi, Farid, Jean-Jacques Laffont, and Quang H. Vuong, "Econometric Analysis of Collusive Behavior in a Soft-Drink Market," *Journal of Economics and Management Strategy*, 1(2), Summer 1992, 277–311.

Genesove, David, "Adverse Selection in the Wholesale Used Car Market," *Journal of Political Economy*, 101(4), August 1993:644–665.

Gilbert, Richard J., "Patents, Sleeping Patents, and Entry Deterrence," in Steven C. Salop, ed., *Strategy, Predation, and Antitrust Analysis*. Washington, D.C.: Federal Trade Commission, 1979.

Golec, Joseph, and Maurry Tamarkin, "Do Bettors Prefer Long Shots Because They Are Risk Lovers, or Are They Just Overconfident?" *Journal of Risk and Uncertainty*, 11(1), July 1995:51–64.

Goolsbee, Austan, "What Happens When You Tax the Rich? Evidence from Executive Compensation," *Journal of Political Economy*, 108(2), April 2000:352–378.

Goolsbee, Austan, "In a World Without Borders: The Impact of Taxes on Internet Commerce," *Quarterly Journal of Economics*, 115(2), May 2000:561–576.

Goolsbee, Austan, "Competition in the Computer Industry: Online Versus Retail," *Journal of Industrial Economics*, XLIX(4), December 2001:487–499.

Grabowski, Henry G., and John M. Vernon, "Brand Loyalty, Entry, and Price Competition in Pharmaceuticals After the 1984 Drug Act," *Journal of Law and Economics*, 35(2), October 1992:331–350.

Gray, Wayne B., and Ronald J. Shadbegian, "'Optimal' Pollution Abatement: Whose Benefits Matter, and How Much?," NBER Working Paper 9125, 2002, **www.nber.org/papers/ w9125**.

Green, Richard, Richard Howitt, and Carlo Russo, "Estimation of Supply and Demand Elasticities of California Commodities," manuscript, May 2005.

Grossman, Michael, and Frank Chaloupka, "Demand for Cocaine by Young Adults: A Rational Addiction Approach," *Journal of Health Economics*, 17(4), August 1998:427–474.

Grossman, Philip J., Marco Pirozzi, and Jeff Pope, "An Empirical Test of Free-Rider Behaviour," *Australian Economic Papers*, 32(60), June 1993:152–160.

Gruber, Harald, "The Learning Curve in the Production of Semiconductor Memory Chips," *Applied Economics*, 24(8), August 1992:885–894.

Gruber, Jonathan, Anihdya Sen, and Mark Stabile, "Estimating Price Elasticities When There Is Smuggling: The Sensitivity of Smoking to Price in Canada," NBER Working Paper 8962, May 2002.

Guillickson, William, and Michael J. Harper, "Multifactor Productivity in U.S. Manufacturing, 1949–83," *Monthly Labor Review*, 110(10), October 1987:18–28.

Gundersen, Craig, and Victor Oliveira, "Food Stamp Program and Food Insufficiency," *American Journal of Agriculture Economics*, 83(4), November 2001:875–887.

Hahn, Robert W., Robert E. Litan, and Jesse Gurman, "Paying Less for Real Estate Brokerage: What Can Make It Happen?" AEI-Brookings Joint Center Working Paper 05-11, 2005.

Hall, Robert E., and David M. Lilien, "Efficient Wage Bargains Under Uncertain Supply and Demand," *American Economic Review*, 69(5), December 1979:868–879.

Hamilton, Stephen F., "The Comparative Efficiency of Ad Valorem and Specific Taxes Under Monopoly and Monopsony," *Economics Letters*, 63(2), May 1999:235–238.

Harkness, Joseph, and Sandra Newman, "The Interactive Effects of Housing Assistance and Food Stamps on Food Spending," *Journal of Housing Economics*, 12(3), September 2003:224–249.

Hatton, T. J., G. R. Boyer, and R. E. Bailey, "The Union Wage Effect in Late Nineteenth Century Britain," *Economica*, 61(244), November 1994:435–456.

Haughwout, Andrew F., Robert P. Inman, Steven Craig, and Thomas Luce, "Local Revenue Hills: Evidence from Four U.S. Cities," NBER Working Paper 9686, **www.nber.org/papers/w9686**, 2003.

Hausman, Jerry A., "Efficiency Effects on the U.S. Economy from Wireless Taxation," *National Tax Journal*, 52(3, part 2), September 2000:733–742.

Hausman, Jerry A., and Gregory K. Leonard, "The Competitive Effects of a New Product Introduction: A Case Study," *Journal of Industrial Economics*, 50(3), September 2002: 237–263.

Hausman, Jerry A., and Gregory K. Leonard, "Superstars in the NBA: Economic Value and Policy," *Journal of Labor Economics*, 14(4), October 1997:586–624.

Hay, George A., and Daniel Kelley, "An Empirical Survey of Price-Fixing Conspiracies," *Journal of Law and Economics*, 17(1), April 1974:13–38.

Helland, Eric, and Alexander Tabarrok, "Contingency Fees, Settlement Delay, and Low-Quality Litigation: Empirical Evidence from Two Datasets," *Journal of Law, Economics, and Organization*, 19(2), Special Issue, October 2003:517–542.

Hennart, Jean-François, "Upstream Vertical Integration in the Aluminum and Tin Industries," *Journal of Economic Behavior and Organization*, 9(3), April 1988:281–299.

Herndon, Jill Boylston, "Health Insurer Monopsony Power: The All-or-None Model," *Journal of Health Economics*, 21(2), March 2002:197–206.

Holt, Matthew, "A Multimarket Bounded Price Variation Model Under Rational Expectations: Corn and Soybeans in the United States," *American Journal of Agricultural Economics*, 74(1), February 1992:10–20.

Hosoe, Nobuhiro, "Crop Failure, Price Regulation, and Emergency Imports of Japan's Rice Sector in 1993," *Applied Economics*, 36(10), June 2004:1051–1056.

Hotelling, Harold, "The Economics of Exhaustible Resources," *Journal of Political Economy*, 39(2), April 1931:137–175.

Houthakker, Hendrik S., "An International Comparison of Household Expenditures Patterns, Commemorating the Centenary of Engel's Law," *Econometrica*, 25(3), December 1957:532–551.

Hsieh, Wen-Jen, "Test of Variable Output and Scale Elasticities for 20 U.S. Manufacturing Industries," *Applied Economics Letters*, 2(8), August 1995:284–287.

Hui, Kai-Lung, and Ivan P. L. Png, "Piracy and the Legitimate Demand for Recorded Music." *Contributions to Economic Analysis & Policy*, 2(1), 2003: article 11.

Hummels, David, and Alexandre Skiba, "Shipping the Good Apples Out? An Empirical Confirmation of the Alchian-Allen Conjecture," *Journal of Political Economy*, 112(6), December 2004:1384–1402.

Ida, Takanori, and Tetsuya Kuwahara, "Yardstick Cost Comparison and Economies of Scale and Scope in Japan's Electric Power Industry," *Asian Economic Journal*, 18(4), December 2004:423–438.

Imbens, Guido W., Donald B. Rubin, and Bruce I. Sacerdote, "Estimating the Effect of Unearned Income on Labor Earnings, Savings, and Consumption: Evidence from a Survey of Lottery Players," *American Economic Review*, 91(4), September 2001:778–794.

Irwin, Douglas A., and Peter J. Klenow, "Learning-by-Doing Spillovers in the Semiconductor Industry," *Journal of Political Economy*, 102(6), December 1994:1200–1227.

Irwin, Douglas A., and Nina Pavcnik, "Airbus versus Boeing Revisited: International Competition in the Aircraft Market," *Journal of International Economics*, 64(2), December 2004:223–245.

Ito, Harumi, and Darin Lee, "Assessing the Impact of the September 11 Terrorist Attacks on U.S. Airline Demand," *Journal of Economics and Business*, 57(1), January-February 2005:75–95.

Jacobson, Michael F., and Kelly D. Brownell, "Small Taxes on Soft Drinks and Snack Foods to Promote Health," *American Journal of Public Health*, 90(6), June 2000:854–857.

Jagannathan, Ravi, Ellen R. McGrattan, and Anna Scherbina, "The Declining U.S. Equity Premium," *Quarterly Review* (Federal Reserve Bank of Minneapolis), Fall 2000:3–19.

Jetter, Karen M., James A. Chalfant, and David A. Sumner, "Does 5-a-Day Pay?" *AIC Issues Brief*, No. 27, August 2004.

Jha, Prabhat, and Frank J. Chaloupka, "The Economics of Global Tobacco Control," BMJ, **bmj.com**, 321, August 2000:358–361.

Jha, Raghbendra, M. N. Murty, Satya Paul, and Balbir S. Sahni, "Cost Structure of the Indian Cement Industry," *Journal of Economics Studies*, 8(4), 1991:59–67.

Johnson, Ronald N., and Charles J. Romeo, "The Impact of Self-Service Bans in the Retail Gasoline Market," *Review of Economics and Statistics*, 82(4), November 2000:625–633.

Kakalik, J. S., and N. M. Pace, *Costs and Compensation Paid in Tort Litigation.* Santa Monica, Calif.: RAND Corporation, Institute for Civil Justice, 1986.

Kalirajan, K.P., and M.B. Obwona, "Frontier Production Function: The Stochastic Coefficient Approach," *Oxford Bulletin of Economics and Statistics*, 56(1), 1994:87–96.

Karp, Larry, "Global Warming and Hyperbolic Discounting," *Journal of Public Economics*, 89(2–3), February 2005: 261–282.

Karp, Larry S., and Jeffrey M. Perloff, "The Failure of Strategic Industrial Policies Due to the Manipulation by Firms," *International Review of Economics and Finance*, 4(1), 1995:1–16.

Katz, Michael L., and Carl Shapiro, "Systems Competition and Network Effects," *Journal of Economic Perspectives*, 8(2), 1994:93–115.

Keeler, Theodore E., Teh-Wei Hu, Paul G. Barnett, and Willard G. Manning, "Taxation, Regulation, and Addiction: A Demand Function for Cigarettes Based on Time-Series Evidence," *Journal of Health Economics*, 12(1), April 1993:1–18.

Keeler, Theodore E., Teh-Wei Hu, Michael Ong, and Hai-Yen Sung, "The U.S. National Tobacco Settlement: The Effects of Advertising and Price Changes on Cigarette Consumption," *Applied Economics*, 36(15), August 2004:1623–1629.

Kennickell, Arthur B., "An Examination of the Changes in the Distribution of Wealth from 1989 to 1998: Evidence from the Survey of Consumer Finances," Federal Reserve, 2001.

Kennickell, Arthur B., "A Rolling Tide: Changes in the Distribution of Wealth in the U.S., 1989–2001," Federal Reserve Board, 2003, **www.federalreserve.gov/pubs/oss/ oss2/papers/asa2003.7.pdf.**

Kennickell, Arthur B., and R. Louise Woodburn, "Consistent Weight Design for 1989, 1992, and 1995 SCPs, and the Distribution of Wealth," working paper, Board of Governors of the Federal Reserve System, August 1997.

Kim, E. Han, and Vijay Singal, "Mergers and Market Power: Evidence from the Airline Industry," *American Economic Review*, 83(3), June 1993:549–569.

Kim, H. Youn, "Economies of Scale and Scope in Multiproduct Firms: Evidence from U.S. Railroads," *Applied Economics*, 19(6), June 1987:733–741.

Kim, Hongjin, Gloria E. Helfand, and Richard E. Howitt, "An Economic Analysis of Ozone Control in California's San Joaquin Valley," *Journal of Agricultural and Resource Economics*, 23(1), July 1998:55–70.

Klein, Lawrence R., "The Use of the Input–Output Tables to Estimate the Productivity of IT," *Journal of Policy Modeling*, 25(5), July 2003:471–475.

Klemperer, Paul, *Auctions: Theory and Practice,* Princeton University Press, 2004.

Krattenmaker, Thomas G., and Steven C. Salop, "Anticompetitive Exclusion: Raising Rivals' Costs to Achieve Power over Price," *Yale Law Journal*, 96(2), December 1986:209–293.

Kridel, D. J., P. N. Rappoport, and L. D. Taylor, "An Econometric Model of the Demand for Access to the Internet," in *The Future of the Telecommunications Industry: Forecasting and Demand Analysis,* eds. D. G. Loomis and L. D. Taylor, Boston, MA: Kluwer Academic Publishers, 1999.

Kridel, D. J., P. N. Rappoport, and L. D. Taylor, "An Econometric Model of the Demand for Access to the Internet by Cable Modem," in *Forecasting the Internet: Understanding the Explosive Growth of Data Communications,* eds. D. G. Loomis and L. D. Taylor, Boston, MA: Kluwer Academic Publishers, 2001.

Krupnick, A. J., and Paul R. Portney, "Controlling Urban Air Pollution: A Benefit-Cost Assessment," *Science*, 252, April 1991:522–528.

Lenard, Thomas M., "The Efficiency Costs of the Postal Monopoly: The Case of Third-Class Mail," *Journal of Regulatory Economics*, 6(4), December 1994:421–431.

Leslie, Phillip J., "A Structural Econometric Analysis of Price Discrimination in Broadway Theatre," working paper, University of California, Los Angeles, November 15, 1997.

Levin, Richard C., Alvin K. Klevorick, Richard R. Nelson, and Sidney G. Winter, "Appropriating the Returns from Industrial Research and Development," *Brookings Papers on Economic Activity*, 3(Special Issue on Microeconomics), 1987:783–820.

Levy, Douglas E., and Ellen Meara, "The Effect of the 1998 Master Settlement Agreement on Prenatal Smoking," NBER Working Paper 11176, March 2005, **www.nber.org/ papers/w11176.**

Liebenstein, Harvey, "Bandwagon, Snob, and Veblen Effects in the Theory of Consumers' Demand," *Quarterly Journal of Economics*, 64(2), May 1950:183–207.

Lopez, Rigoberto A., and Emilio Pagoulatos, "Rent Seeking and the Welfare Cost of Trade Barriers," *Public Choice*, 79(1–2), April 1994:149–160.

MacAvoy, Paul W., "Tacit Collusion Under Regulation in the Pricing of Interstate Long-Distance Services," *Journal of Economics and Management Strategy*, 4(2), Summer 1995:147–185.

MacCrimmon, Kenneth R., and M. Toda, "The Experimental Determination of Indifference Curves," *Review of Economic Studies*, 56(3), July 1969:433–451.

Machina, Mark, "Dynamic Consistency and Non-Expected Utility Models of Choice Under Uncertainty," *Journal of Economic Literature*, 27(4), December 1989:1622–1668.

MacKie-Mason, Jeffrey K., and Robert S. Pindyck, "Cartel Theory and Cartel Experience in International Minerals Markets," in R. L. Gordon, H. D. Jacoby, and M. B. Zimmerman, eds., *Energy: Markets and Regulation: Essays in Honor of M. A. Adelman.* Cambridge, Mass.: MIT Press, 1986.

MaCurdy, Thomas, David Green, and Harry Paarsch, "Assessing Empirical Approaches for Analyzing Taxes and Labor Supply," *Journal of Human Resources*, 25(3), Summer 1990:415–490.

Madden, Janice F., *The Economics of Sex Discrimination.* Lexington, Mass.: Heath, 1973.

Maddock, Rodney, Elkin Castano, and Frank Vella, "Estimating Electricity Demand: The Cost of Linearizing the Budget Constraint," *Review of Economics and Statistics*, 74(2), May 1992:350–354.

Marks, Steven V., "A Reassessment of Empirical Evidence on the U.S. Sugar Program," in S. V. Marks and K. Maskus, eds., *The Economics and Politics of World Sugar Policy*, Ann Arbor: University of Michigan Press, 1993.

McAfee, R. Preston, "The Real Lesson of Enron's Implosion: Market Makers Are In the Trust Business," 1(2), 2004: Article 4.

Medoff, Marshall H., "A Pooled Time-Series Analysis of Abortion Demand," *Population Research and Policy Review*, 16(6), December 1997:597–605.

Moffitt, Robert, "Estimating the Value of an In-Kind Transfer: The Case of Food Stamps," *Econometrica*, 57(2), March 1989:385–409.

Moschini, Giancarlo, and Karl D. Meilke, "Production Subsidy and Countervailing Duties in Vertically Related Markets: The Hog-Pork Case Between Canada and the United States," *American Journal of Agricultural Economics*, 74(4), November 1992:951–961.

Nash, John F., "Equilibrium Points in *n*-Person Games," *Proceedings of the National Academy of Sciences*, 36, 1950:48–49.

Nash, John F., "Non-Cooperative Games," *Annals of Mathematics*, 54(2), July 1951:286–295.

Nemoto, Jiro, Yasuo Nakanishi, and Seishi Madono, "Scale Economies and Over-Capitalization in Japanese Electric Utilities," *International Economic Review*, 34(2), May 1993:431–440.

Norman, G., "Economies of Scale in the Cement Industry," *Journal of Industrial Economics*, 27(4), June 1979: 317–337.

O'Donoghue, Ted, and Matthew Rabin, "Doing It Now or Later," *American Economic Review*, 89(1), March 1999:103–124.

Ouchi, Hiromi, Jill J. McCluskey, and Thomas I. Wahl, "Implications of the Consumer Response to Emerging Technologies and Diseases for International Trade: The Case of Japan," *Western Economics Forum*, 3(1), Spring 2004:11–16.

Organization for Economic Cooperation and Development, *Agricultural Policies In OECD Countries: Monitoring And Evaluation 2005*, 2005.

Oxfam, *Dumping Without Borders*, Oxfam Briefing Paper 50, 2003.

Panzar, John C., and Robert D. Willig, "Economies of Scale in Multi-Output Production," *Quarterly Journal of Economics*, 91(3), August 1977:481–493.

Panzar, John C., and Robert D. Willig, "Economies of Scope," *American Economic Review*, 71(2), May 1981:268–272.

Perry, Martin K., "Forward Integration by Alcoa: 1888–1930," *Journal of Industrial Economics*, 29(1), September 1980: 37–53.

Perry, Martin K., "Vertical Integration: Determinants and Effects," in Richard Schmalensee and Robert D. Willig, eds., *Handbook of Industrial Organization*. New York: North Holland, 1989.

Polinsky, A. Mitchell, "Controlling Externalities and Protecting Entitlements: Property Right, Liability Rule, and Tax-Subsidy Approaches," *Journal of Legal Studies*, 8(1), January 1979:1–48.

Pollak, Robert A., *The Theory of the Cost-of-Living Index*. New York: Oxford University Press, 1989.

Posner, Richard A., "The Social Cost of Monopoly and Regulation," *Journal of Political Economy*, 83(4), August 1975:807–827.

Prescott, Edward C., "Why Do Americans Work So Much More Than Europeans?" *Federal Reserve Bank of Minneapolis Quarterly Review*, 28(1), July 2004:2–13.

Rabin, Matthew, "Psychology and Economics," *Journal of Economic Literature*, 36(1), March 1998:11–46.

Ransom, Michael R., "Seniority and Monopsony in the Academic Labor Market," *American Economic Review*, 83(1), March 1993:221–233.

Rappoport, P. N., D. J. Kridel, L. D. Taylor, and K. T. Duffy-Deno, "Residential Demand for Access to the Internet," in *The International Handbook of Telecommunications Economics*, vol. II, ed. Gary Madden, Chelthenham, U.K.: Edward Elgar, 2002.

Rawls, John, *A Theory of Justice*. New York: Oxford University Press, 1971.

Reimer, Jeffrey J., and Thomas W. Hertel, "International Cross Section Estimates of Demand for Use in the GTAP Model," Global Trade Analysis Project Technical Paper No. 23, 2004.

Reinstein, David A., and Christopher M. Snyder, "The Influence of Expert Reviews on Consumer Demand for Experience Goods: A Case Study of Movie Critics," *Journal of Industrial Economics*, 53(1), March 2005:27–51.

Richard, Oliver, "Flight Frequency and Mergers in Airline Markets," *International Journal of Industrial Organization*, 21(6), June 2003:907–922.

Ries, John C., "Windfall Profits and Vertical Relationships: Who Gained in the Japanese Auto Industry from VERs?" *Journal of Industrial Economics*, 41(3), September 1993:259–276.

Rob, Rafael, and Joel Waldfogel, "Piracy on the High C's: Music Downloading, Sales Displacement, and Social Welfare in a Sample of College Students," NBER Working Paper 10874, 2004, **www.nber.org/papers/w10874**.

Roberts, Mark J., and Larry Samuelson, "An Empirical Analysis of Dynamic Nonprice Competition in an Oligopolistic Industry," *Rand Journal of Economics*, 19(2), Summer 1988:200–220.

Robidoux, Benoît, and John Lester, "Econometric Estimates of Scale Economies in Canadian Manufacturing," Working Paper No. 88-4, Canadian Department of Finance, 1988.

Robidoux, Benoît, and John Lester, "Econometric Estimates of Scale Economies in Canadian Manufacturing," *Applied Economics*, 24(1), January 1992:113–122.

Rohlfs, Jeffrey H., *Bandwagon Effects in High-Technology Industries*, Cambridge: MIT Press, 2001.

Rohlfs, Jeffrey H., "A Theory of Interdependent Demand for a Communications Service," *Bell Journal of Economics and Management Science*, 5(1), Spring 1974:16–37.

Roth, Alvin E., and Axel Ockenfels, "Last-Minute Bidding and the Rules for Ending Second-Price Auctions: Evidence from eBay and Amazon Auctions on the Internet," *American Economic Review*, 92(4), September 2002: 1093–1103.

Rosenberg, Howard R., "Many Fewer Steps for Pickers—A Leap for Harvestkind? Emerging Change in Strawberry Harvest Technology," *Choices*, 1st Quarter 2004:5–11.

Rousseas, S. W., and A. G. Hart, "Experimental Verification of a Composite Indifference Map," *Journal of Political Economy*, 59(4), August 1951:288–318.

Ruffin, R. J., "Cournot Oligopoly and Competitive Behavior," *Review of Economic Studies*, 38(116), October 1971: 493–502.

Salop, Joanne, and Steven C. Salop, "Self-Selection and Turnover in the Labor Market," *Quarterly Journal of Economics*, 90(4), November 1976:619–627.

Salop, Steven C., "The Noisy Monopolist: Imperfect Information, Price Dispersion, and Price Discrimination," *Review of Economic Studies*, 44(3), October 1977:393–406.

Salop, Steven C., "Strategic Entry Deterrence," *American Economic Review*, 69(2), May 1979:335–338.

Salop, Steven C., "Practices That (Credibly) Facilitate Oligopoly Coordination," in Joseph E. Stiglitz and G. Frank Mathewson, eds., *New Developments in the Analysis of Market Structure*. Cambridge, Mass.: MIT Press, 1986.

Salop, Steven C., and David T. Sheffman, "Cost-Raising Strategies," *Journal of Industrial Economics*, 36(1), September 1987:19–34.

Schaller Consulting, *The New York City Taxicab Fact Book*, 2004, **www.schallerconsult.com**.

Scherer, F. M., "An Early Application of the Average Total Cost Concept," *Journal of Economic Literature*, 39(3), September 2001:897–901.

Schmalensee, Richard, Paul L. Joskow, A. Denny Ellerman, Juan Pablo Montero, and Elizabeth M. Bailey, "An Interim Evaluation of Sulfur Dioxide Emissions Trading," *Journal of Economic Perspectives*, 12(3) Summer 1998:53–68.

Schoemaker, Paul J. H., "The Expected Utility Model: Its Variants, Purposes, Evidence and Limitation," *Journal of Economic Literature*, 20(2), June 1982:529–563.

Scott, Robert E., "The Effects of Protection on a Domestic Oligopoly: The Case of the U.S. Auto Market," *Journal of Policy Modeling*, 16(3), June 1994:299–325.

Shadbegian, Ronald J., and Wayne B. Gray, "What Determines Environmental Performance at Paper Mills? The Roles of Abatement Spending, Regulation and Efficiency," Center for Economic Studies working paper CES 03–10, 2003.

Shapiro, Carl, and Joseph E. Stiglitz, "Equilibrium Unemployment as a Worker Discipline Device," *American Economic Review*, 74(3), June 1984:434–444.

Shapiro, Carl, and Hal R. Varian, *Information Rules: A Strategic Guide to the Network Economy*, Boston: Harvard Business School Press, 1999.

Shearer, Bruce, "Piece Rates, Fixed Wages and Incentives: Evidence from a Field Experiment," *Review of Economic Studies*, 71(2), April 2004:513–534.

Skeath, Susan E., and Gregory A. Trandel, "A Pareto Comparison of Ad Valorem and Unit Taxes in Noncompetitive Environments," *Journal of Public Economics*, 53(1), January 1994:53–71.

Slade, Margaret E., "Product Rivalry with Multiple Strategic Weapons: An Analysis of Price and Advertising Competition," *Journal of Economics and Management Strategy*," 4(3), Fall 1995:224–276.

Smiley, Robert, "Empirical Evidence on Strategic Entry Deterrence," *International Journal of Industrial Organization*, 6(2), June 1988:167–180.

Sood, Neeraj, Abby Alpert, and Jay Bhattacharya, "Technology, Monopoly, and the Decline of the Viatical Settlements Industry," NBER Working Paper 11164, March 2005, **www.nber.org/papers/w11164**.

Spence, A. Michael, *Market Signaling*. Cambridge, Mass.: Harvard University Press, 1974.

Spence, A. Michael, "The Learning Curve and Competition," *Bell Journal of Economics and Management Science*, 12(1), 1981:49–70.

Spencer, Barbara J., and James A. Brander, "International R&D Rivalry and Industrial Strategy," *Review of Economic Studies*, 50(4), October 1983:707–722.

Stewart, Mark B., "Union Wage Differentials in an Era of Declining Unionization," *Oxford Bulletin of Economics and Statistics*, 57(2), May 1995:143–166.

Stiglitz, Joseph E., "The Theory of 'Screening,' Education, and the Distribution of Income," *American Economic Review*, 65(3), June 1975:283–300.

Stiglitz, Joseph E., "Equilibrium in Product Markets with Imperfect Information," *American Economic Review*, 69(2), May 1979:339–345.

Stiglitz, Joseph E., "The Causes and Consequences of the Dependence of Quality on Price," *Journal of Economic Literature*, 25(1), March 1987:1–48.

Stuart, Charles, "Swedish Tax Rates, Labor Supply, and Tax Revenues," *Journal of Political Economy*, 89(5), October 1981:1020–1038.

Stuart, Charles, "Welfare Costs per Dollar of Additional Tax Revenue in the United States," *American Economic Review*, 74(3), June 1984:352–362.

Sullivan, Ashley F., and Eunyoung Choi, "Hunger and Food Insecurity in the Fifty States: 1998–2000," Center on Hunger and Poverty, Brandeis University, August 2002.

Sullivan, Daniel, "Monopsony Power in the Market for Nurses," *Journal of Law and Economics*, 32(2, pt. 2) October 1989:S135–S178.

Swinton, John R., and Christopher R. Thomas, "Using Empirical Point Elasticities to Teach Tax Incidence," *Journal of Economic Education*, 32(4), Fall 2001:356–368.

Tarr, David G., *A General Equilibrium Analysis of the Welfare and Employment Effects of U.S. Quotas in Textiles, Autos and Steel*. Washington, D.C.: Bureau of Economics Staff Report, Federal Trade Commission, 1989.

Terrell, Katherine, "Technical Change and Factor Bias in Polish Industry (1962–1983)," *Review of Economics and Statistics*, 75(4), November 1993:741–747.

Tideman, T. Nicholaus, and Gordon Tullock, "A New and Superior Process for Making Social Choices," *Journal of Political Economy*, 84(6), December 1976:1145–1159.

Timmer, C. Peter, "Choice of Technique in Rice Milling on Java," in Carl K. Eicher and John M. Staatz, eds., *Agricultural Development in the Third World*. Baltimore: Johns Hopkins University Press, 1984.

Tullock, G., "The Welfare Cost of Tariffs, Monopolies, and Theft," *Western Economic Journal*, 5(3), June 1967:224–232.

Tyler, John H., Richard J. Murnane, and John B. Willett, "Estimating the Labor Market Signaling Value of the GED," *Quarterly Journal of Economics*, 115(2), May 2000:431–468.

Urban, Glen L., Theresa Carter, and Steven Gaskin, "Market Share Rewards to Pioneering Brands: An Empirical Analysis and Strategic Implications," *Management Science*, 32(6), June 1986:645–659.

Vandermeulen, Daniel C., "Upward Sloping Demand Curves Without the Giffen Paradox," *American Economic Review*, 62(3), June 1972:453–458.

Van Ravenstein, Ad, and Hans Vijlbrief, "Welfare Cost of Higher Tax Rates: An Empirical Laffer Curve for the Netherlands," *De Economist*, 136(2), 1988:205–219.

Varian, Hal R., "Measuring the Deadweight Cost of DUP and Rent-Seeking Activities," *Economics and Politics*, 1(1), Spring 1989:81–95.

Varian, Hal R., *Microeconomic Analysis*, 3rd ed. New York: Norton, 1992.

Varian, Hal R., "The Demand for Bandwidth," **www.sims. berkeley.edu/~hal/Papers/brookings.pdf**, February 2002.

Villegas, Daniel J., "The Impact of Usury Ceilings on Consumer Credit," *Southern Economic Journal*, 56(1), July 1989: 126–141.

Viscusi, W. Kip, *Employment Hazards*. Cambridge, Mass.: Harvard University Press, 1979.

Viscusi, W. Kip, *Pricing Environmental Risks*. Policy Study No. 112. St. Louis, Mo.: Center for the Study of American Business, Washington University, 1992.

Von Hippel, F. A., and W. F. Von Hipple, "Sex Drugs and Animal Parts: Will Viagra Save Threatened Species?" *Environmental Conservation*, 29(3), 2002:277–281.

Von Hippel, F. A., and W. F. Von Hipple, "Is Viagra a Viable Conservation Tool? Response to Hoover, 2003," *Environmental Conservation*, 31(1), 2004:4–6.

von Neumann, John, and Oskar Morgenstern, *Theory of Games and Economic Behavior*. Princeton, N.J.: Princeton University Press, 1944.

Waldfogel, Joel, "The Deadweight Loss of Christmas," *American Economic Review*, 83(5), December 1993:1328–1336.

Waldfogel, Joel, "Does Consumer Irrationality Trump Consumer Sovereignty?" working paper, 2004.

Walton, Clarence C., and Frederick W. Cleveland, *Corporations on Trial: The Electric Cases*. Belmont, Calif.: Wadsworth, 1964.

Warner, John T., and Saul Pleeter, "The Personal Discount Rate: Evidence from Military Downsizing Programs," *American Economic Review*, 91(1), March 2001:33–53.

Weiher, Jesse C., Robin C. Sickles, and Jeffrey M. Perloff, "Market Power in the U.S. Airline Industry," D. J. Slottje, ed., *Economic Issues in Measuring Market Power, Contributions to Economic Analysis*, Volume 255, Elsevier 2002 forthcoming.

Weitzman, Martin L., "Prices vs. Quantities," *Review of Economic Studies*, 41(4), October 1974:477–491.

Wellington, Donald C., "The Mark of the Plague," *Rivista Internazionale di Scienze Economiche e Commerciali*, 37(8), August 1990:673–684.

Whinston, Michael D., and Scott C. Collins, "Entry and Competitive Structure in Deregulated Airline Markets: An Event Study Analysis of People Express," *Rand Journal of Economics*, 23(4), Winter 1992:445–462.

White, Michelle J., "The 'Arms Race' on American Roads," *Journal of Law and Economics,* 47(2), October 2004: 333–355.

Whitmore, Diane, "What Are Food Stamps Worth?" Princeton University Working Paper #468, July, 2002, **www.irs. princeton.edu/pubs/pdfs/468.pdf**.

Williamson, Oliver E., *Markets and Hierarchies: Analysis and Antitrust Implications*. New York: Free Press, 1975.

Williamson, Oliver E., "Credible Commitments: Using Hostages to Support Exchange," *American Economic Review*, 73(4), September 1983:519–540.

Willis, Robert J., "A New Approach to the Economic Theory of Fertility Behavior," *Journal of Political Economy*, 81(2, pt. 2), March–April 1973:S14–S64.

Winicki, Joshua, "Low-Income Families Participating in Fewer Assistance Programs," *Food Review*, May–August, 2001: 38–44.

Womer, N. Keith, and J. Wayne Patterson, "Estimation and Testing of Learning Curves," *Journal of Business and Economic Statistics*, 1(4), October 1983:265–272.

Yellen, Janet L., "Efficiency Wage Models of Unemployment," *American Economic Review*, 74(2), May 1984:200–205.

Chapter 1

Flu Vaccine: Prices, Exhortation, or Government Intervention: "State Accuses Lauderdale Firm of Price Gouging for Flu Vaccine," **sun-sentinel.com**, October 13, 2004; Patrick O'Neill, "CDC Hopes to Inoculate against Recurrence of Flu-shot Shortage," *The Oregonian*, September 7, 2005; "Maine Health Officials Don't Foresee Flu Vaccine Shortage," **WMTW.com**, September 8, 2005.

Twinkie Tax: Jacobson and Brownell (2000); Bartlett, Bruce, "The Big Food Tax," *National Review Online*, April 3, 2002; Lemieux, Pierre, "It's the Fat Police," *National Post*, April 6, 2002; Tobler, Helen, "Call for Tax War on Obesity," *Australian IT*, August 16, 2002; "Soda Pop to Be Banned in L.A. Schools," CBSNEWS.com, August 28, 2002; Chouniard, et al. (2005).

Income Threshold Model and China: "Next in Line: Chinese Consumers," *Economist*, 326(7795), January 23, 1993:66–67; Pelline, Jeff, "U.S. Businesses Pour into China," *San Francisco Chronicle*, May 17, 1994:B1–B2; *China Statistical Yearbook* (Beijing: China Statistical Publishing House, 2000); **www.us china.org/statistics/2005foreigninvestment_2.html**.

Putting Saturn in Orbit: Edwards, Martin, "We're Not Dealing: Fixed-Price Sales Find Fans," *Business Journal of North Carolina*, 7(33), November 30, 1992:20; Pelline, Jeff, "No-Dicker Stickers for New Cars," *San Francisco Chronicle*, April 15, 1993:D1; Pelline, Jeff, "GM Sold on New Pricing," *San Francisco Chronicle*, July 2, 1993:D1; "Automakers Urge Dealers to Quit Haggling," *Plain Dealer*, February 20, 1994:43K; Glover, Mark, "There's No Haggling over GM Sales Jump," *Sacramento Bee*, February 4, 1994:D1; Martin, Tim, "'No-Dicker' Sticker Has Mixed Success," *Nashville Tennessean*, April 12, 1994; Levy, Michael, "Auto Sales Undergoing a Revolution: New Pricing, Mega-Dealerships Change Business," *Buffalo News*, April 24, 1994:Business, 15; Kenzie, Jim, "Saturn Homecoming Celebrated First Decade," *Toronto Star*, August 14, 1999; Kaltenheuser, Skip, "At Car Dealers, a No-Haggle Policy Sets Off a Battle," *New York Times*, August 29, 1999:4; Flavelle, Dana, "Tiny, Tough Cynthia Trudell in Driver's Seat," *Toronto Star*, September 11, 1999.

Chapter 2

Sideways: ACNielsen Press Release, "ACNielsen Examines Sales Trends Since Popular Movie's Release," February 21, 2005; Richard Kinssies, "On Wine: 'Sideways' Has Intoxicating Effect on Pinot Noir Sales, Some Say," *Seattle Post-Intelligencer*, February 23, 2005; John Harlow, "Oscar Winner Knocks Sales of Merlot Wine Sideways," *The Sunday Times*, March 6, 2005.

Aggregating the Demand for Broadband Service: Duffy-Deno (2003).

Mad Cow: Jason Henderson, "FAQs about Mad Cow Disease and Its Impacts," *The Main Street Economist*, December 2003; "Japan Deems Beef Standards Lax in Canada and U.S." *San Francisco Chronicle*, January 20, 2004:D3; George Raine, "Beef Sales Up Despite Mad Cow," *San Francisco Chronicle*, January 14, 2004:B1, B2; Jon Ortiz, "More Mad Cows Likely," *Sacramento Bee*, February 8, 2004; Peggy Hernandez, "Ban on U.S. Beef Leaves Japanese with a Craving," *Boston Globe*, February 20, 2004:A10; Carter and Huie (2004); Ouchi, et al. (2004); George Raine, "Staging a Comeback," *San Francisco Chronicle*, January 1, 2005:D1, D4.

American Steel Quotas: Crandall, Robert W., "The Effects of U.S. Trade Protection for Autos and Steel," *Brookings Papers on Economic Activity*, 1, 1987:271–288; Burnham, James B., *American Steel and International Trade: The Challenge of Globalization*, Center for the Study of American Business Contemporary Issues Series 95 (Center for the Study of American Business Contemporary Issues, September 1999); Mitchell, Alison, "By a Wide Margin, the House Votes Steel Import Curb," *New York Times*, March 18, 1999:A1, C23; "EU Retaliates with Its Own Steel Tariffs," *San Francisco Chronicle*, March 26:2002: B3; Andrews, Edmund L., "Panel Rejects Effort to Add a Steel Tariff," *New York Times*, August 28, 2002:A1.

Zimbabwe Price Controls: "Mugabe's Election Victory May Be Short-Lived," *The Daily News*, March 15, 2002; "Smuggling Results in Sugar Shortages in Zimbabwe," *Harare*, April 21, 2002; "Construction Industry Faces Bleak Future," *Zimbabwe Standard*, May 5, 2002; "Zimbabwe Raises Cement Prices to Ease Shortage," *Harare*, May 7, 2002; "Makoni Admits Price Controls to Blame for Thriving Black Market," *The Daily News*, May 10, 2002; "Supermarkets Adjust Price of Chicken," *The Daily News*, May 17, 2002; James, Stanley, "Bakeries Scale Down Operations," *The Independent*, September 6, 2002; "Zimbabwe Faces Food Shortages," **cnn.com**, May 24, 2005; "Zim Slaps Price Control on Food," News24, **finance24.com**, June 4, 2005.

Chapter 3

Willingness to Surf: Edell and Varaiya (1999); Varian (2002); Ahmad, Nadia, "Internet Fees Alter Network Use," *Daily Californian*, May 21, 1999:1, 3; **www.index.berkeley.edu/reports/99-01w**; Kridel et al. (1999, 2001), Rappoport et al. (2002), Varian (2002), Duffy-Deno (2003).

Substitution May Save Endangered Species: Von Hippel and Von Hippel (2002, 2004).

Oil Drilling in the Arctic National Wildlife Refuge: Dwight Lee, "To Drill or Not to Drill: Let the Environmentalists Decide," *The Independent Review*, Fall 2001, pp. 217–226; Energy Information Administration, "The Effects of Alaska Oil and Natural Gas Provisions of H.R. 4 and S. 1776 on U.S. Energy

Markets," February 2002; United States Geological Survey, "Arctic National Wildlife Refuge, 1002 Area, Petroleum Assessment, 1998, Including Economic Analysis." **pubs.usgs.gov/fs/fs-0028-01/fs-0028-01.pdf**; "Oil Companies Could Benefit from Alaska Drilling," VNU Business Media, In., November 22, 2004; Severin Borenstein, "ANWR Oil and the Price of Gasoline," U.C. Energy Institute, *Energy Notes,* 3(2), June 2005.

Taxing to Discourage Smoking and Raise Revenue: Keeler, Hu, Barnett, and Manning (1993); "A Tax We Can Live With," *University of California at Berkeley Wellness Letter,* 9(9), June 1993:7; "Tobacco: Armageddon and Appalachia," *Economist,* 32(7820), July 17, 1993:25; "In Canada, They're Cutting Sin Taxes," *Business Week,* February 21, 1994:44; Farrell, Christopher, "This Sin Tax Is Win-Win," *Business Week,* April 11, 1994:31; Marshall, Jonathan, "Life Is Very Good for Silicon Valley Residents," *San Francisco Chronicle,* January 13, 1997:B3; Grossman, Michael, "Health Economics," *NBER Reporter,* Winter 1998:1–5; **www.ash.org**; Besley and Rosen (1998); **tobaccofreekids.org** (2002); **ash.org/cigtaxfacts.html** (2002); "Government Announces Tobacco Tax Increases to Discourage Smoking," Canada NewsWire, June 17, 2002; "Online Cigarette Sales Under Fire," *San Francisco Chronicle,* August 13, 2002:B4; Gruber, Sen, and Stabile (2002); Jha and Chaloupka (2000); CDC, "Annual Smoking-Attributable Mortality," *MMWR Weekly,* 51(14), April 12, 2002:300–303; Paul Geitner, "EU, Philip Morris Near Deal on Smuggling," *San Francisco Chronicle,* April 6, 2004:C3; Keeler et al. (2004); Levy and Meara (2005); U.S.D.A., "Tobacco Outlook—Summary," ERS-TBS-258, April 2005; **www.cdc.gov/mmwr/preview/ mmwrhtml/mm5114a2.htm**.

Chapter 4

Apple's iPod: "The History of Apple's iPod," osviews.com/modules.php?op=modload&name=News&file=article&sid=4259; Brad Gibson, "First on TMO," www.macobserver.com, November 3, 2004, and May 4, 2005; "A Brief History of the iPod," www.uberreview.com/history.htm, 2004–2005; en.wikipedia.org/wiki/Ipod, July 28, 2005; en.wikipedia.org/wiki/Ipod, July 28, 2005.

Electric Power Utilities: Christensen and Greene (1976).

Creating and Destroying an Auto Monopoly: Chee Yoke Heong, "Malaysia's Proton Struggles On," *Asia Times Online,* www.atimes.com, August 26, 2003; "Malaysian Government Buys Back Stake in Proton," *Mercury News,* January 12, 2005; Reuters, "Auto Sales Expected to Slow in Malaysia," secure.detroitnewspapers.com, January 26, 2005; and Sidek Kamiso, "Dr Mahathir: Proton Has to Raise Output," thestar.com.my, February 12, 2005.

Botox Patent Monopoly: Weiss, Mike, "For S.F. Doctor, Drug Botox Becomes a Real Eye-Opener," *San Francisco Chronicle,* April 14, 2002:A1, A19; Abelson, Reed, "F.D.A. Approves Allergan Drug for Fighting Wrinkles," *New York Times,* April 16:2002; Harriet Tramer, "Docs Detecting How to Boost Botox Profitability," *Crain's Cleveland Business,* March 7, 2005:17; Natasha Singer, "Botox Plus: New Mixes for Plumping and Padding," *New York Times,* July 14, 2005. The graph shows an inverse linear demand curve of the form $p = a - bQ$. Such a

linear demand curve has an elasticity of $\varepsilon = -(1/b)(p/Q)$. Given that the elasticity of demand is $-400/375 = -(1/b)(400/1)$, where Q is measured in millions of vials, then $b = 375$. Solving $p = 400 = a - 375 \times 1$, we find that $a = 775$. The height of triangle $A + B + C$ is \$750 = \$775 − \$25, and its length is 2 million vials, so its area is \$750 million.

Internet and Other Pirates: Protecting Intellectual Property Rights: Joseph Kahn, "The Pinch of Piracy Wakes China Up On Copyright Issue," *New York Times,* November 1, 2002:C1, C5; Benny Evangelista, Nick Wingfield, "Online Swapping of Music Declines in Wake of Suits," *Wall Street Journal,* January 5, 2004:B4; Connolly and Krueger (2005); Jane Wardell, "Software Piracy Rate Is Steady," *San Francisco Chronicle,* May 19, 2005; Carrie Kirby, "Survey Shows Little Progress in Effort to Halt Pirated Software," *San Francisco Chronicle,* May 19, 2005; Deborah Charles, "U.S. Court Rules against Grokster in File-Share Case," Reuters, June 27, 2005; Carolyn Said, "Pay to Play—Or Else," *San Francisco Chronicle,* June 28, 2005.

Chapter 5

Disneyland Pricing: Disneyland.

Amazon Is Watching You: Streitfeld, David, "Amazon Pays a Price for Marketing Test," *Los Angeles Times,* October 2, 2000:C1, www.managingchange.com/dynamic/survey/analysis.html.

Botox Revisited: See Chapter 11, "Botox Patent Monopoly."

Smuggling Prescription Drugs into the United States: Tim Harper, "Canada's Drugs 'Dangerous,'" *Toronto Star,* August 28, 2003:A12; Christopher Rowland, "FDA Sting Targets Medicine Supplier Springfield," *Boston Globe,* August 28, 2003; Tony Pugh, "Canadian Online Pharmacies Struggle to Find Suppliers," *San Diego Union-Tribune,* September 7, 2003:A-3; Gardiner Harris, "U.S. Moves to Halt Import Of Drugs From Canada," *New York Times,* September 10, 2003:C2; Ceci Connolly, "Hopefuls Back Drug Reimports," *Washington Post,* October 8, 2003:A6; Lolita C. Baldor, "FDA Questions Canada Drug Import Safety," Associated Press Online, December 23, 2003; "Survey: U.S. Families Struggle to Pay for Drugs," MSNBC News, February 23, 2004; Robert Pear, "U.S. to Study Importing Canada Drugs," *New York Times,* February 26, 2004:A16; Victoria Colliver, "U.S. Drug Prices 81% Higher than in 7 Western Nations," *San Francisco Chronicle,* October 29, 2004:C1, C6; Heather Timmons, "Court Refuses To Hear Case on European Drug Pricing," *New York Times,* June 1, 2005:C7.

Unions That Have It All: Peter Sleeth and Jim Lynch, "Lockout Disaster Averted," *Sunday Oregonian,* October 13, 2002:F1; George Raine, "Port Talks Turn Positive," *San Francisco Chronicle,* November 2, 2002:A1, A16; David Moberg, "What's Up on the Docks?" *These Times,* November 11, 2002:12; www.ilwu.org; Carl Biers and Marsha Niemeijer, "Members Angry Over Multi-Tier Wage and Benefit System," **www.labornotes.org**, June 2004; *Pacific Coast Longshore Contract Document,* July 1, 2002–July 1, 2008.

Consumers Pay for Lower Prices: Borenstein and Rose (1994); Varian, Hal, "Priceline's Magic Show," *Industry Standard,*

April 17, 2000; "PMA Coupon Council Celebrates September as National Coupon Month," *PR Newswire*, September 3, 2002; www.couponmonth.com/pages/allabout.htm (2005); www.pmalink.org/about/press_releases/release80.asp (2005).

IBM: *IBM v. United States*, 298 U.S. 131 (1936).

Blue Fries, Green Ketchup: "Heinz Unveils New Blue Ketchup," *USA Today,* April 7, 2003; Mathew Emmert, "Stocks Fools Love: H.J. Heinz," fool.com, February 10, 2005.

Welfare Gain from More Toilet Paper: "Going Soft?" *The Economist,* March 4, 2000:59; Hausman and Leonard (2002).

Chapter 6

Catwalk Cartel: William Sherman, "Catwalk Rocked by Legal Catfight," *Daily News*, March 14, 2004; Warren St. John, "Behind the Catwalk, Suspicion and Suits," *New York Times,* April 18, 2004:sec.9, 1, 12; Neil Chandler, "Models in GBP 28m Wage Battle," *Daily Star,* June 6, 2004:8; *Carolyn Fears et al. v. Wilhelmina Model Agency, Inc., et al.,* 02 Civ. 4911 (HB), United States District Court For The Southern District Of New York, 2004 U.S. Dist. Lexis 4502; 2004–1 Trade Cas. (CCH) P74,351, March 23, 2004.

A Government-Created Cartel: Tarr (1989); Ries (1993); Scott (1994); Berry et al. (1999).

Bail Bonds: Ayres and Waldfogel (1994).

Airline Mergers: Market Power versus Flight Frequency: Richards (2003).

Air Ticket Prices and Rivalry: Weiher, Sickles, and Perloff (2002).

Government Aircraft Subsidies: Irwin and Pavcnik (2004); Constant Brand, "EU, Washington Resume Battle Over Boeing," *San Francisco Chronicle,* May 31, 2005.

Deadweight Losses in the Food and Tobacco Industries: Bhuyan and Lopez (1998).

Cross-Chapter Analysis

Frequent Flier Programs: "Qatar Airways the Latest to Reward Frequent Fliers," Customer Loyalty Today, Vol 7, No. 7, July 2000, p. 5; Kyung M. Song, "Frequent-Flier Costs Clip Profit at Alaska Airlines Parent Firm," *Seattle Times*, July 15, 2000; Leah Beth Ward, "Airlines Compete for Business Travelers by Offering High-Tech Promotions," *The Dallas Morning News*, May 25, 2000; Scott Thurston, "Continental Airlines Tops among Frequent Fliers, Survey Shows," *Atlantic Journal and Constitution*, May 10, 2000; Sofia Reeves, "US Airways Cuts Fares, Increases Flier Miles in Wake of Averted Strike," *Pittsburgh Post-Gazette*, March 29, 2000; Bray, Roger, "Fast Lanes for Frequent Flyers," *Financial Times* (London), January 8, 2002:14; Sharkey, Joe, "Reward Miles are Piling Up; Fliers May Face Future Squeeze," *New York Times*, August 17, 2002:B1; Engle, Jane, "As Airlines Change Rules, Passengers Hold the Bag," *Los Angeles Times*, September 15, 2002:L2; http://frequentflier.com; Philip Charlton, "Targeting—The Achilles' Heel of Frequent Flyer Programmes," www.thewise-marketer.com/features/read.asp? id=42, February 2004; "By the Numbers," July 26, 2005, www.montrosetravel.com/print_ver-sion/75/Frequent Flyer Programs-July 26, 2005.html; webflyer.com.

Credits

Index

Symbols Used in This Book

α [alpha] = ad valorem tax (or tariff) rate, or an exponent in a Cobb-Douglas production function

Δ [capital delta] = change in the following variable (for example, the change in p between Periods 1 and 2 is $\Delta p = p_2 - p_1$, where p_2 is the value of p in Period 2 and p_1 is the value in Period 1)

ε [epsilon] = the price elasticity of demand

η [eta] = the price elasticity of supply

$\mathcal{L}$ = lump-sum tax

π [pi] = profit = revenue − total cost = $R - C$

ρ [rho] = profit tax rate

τ [tau] = specific or unit tax (or tariff)

θ [theta] = probability or share

ξ [xi] = the income elasticity of demand

Abbreviations, Variables, and Function Names

AFC = average fixed cost = fixed cost divided by output = F/q

AVC = average variable cost = variable cost divided by output = VC/q

AC = average cost = total cost divided by output = C/q

AP_Z = average product of input Z (for example, AP_L is the average product of labor)

C = total cost = variable cost + fixed cost = $VC + F$

CRS = constant returns to scale

CS = consumer surplus

CV = compensating variation

$D(q)$ = market demand function

$D_r(q)$ = residual demand function

DRS = decreasing returns to scale

DWL = deadweight loss

EV = equivalent variation

F = fixed cost

i = interest rate

I = indifference curve

IRS = increasing returns to scale

K = capital

L = labor

LR = long run

m = constant marginal cost

M = materials

MC = marginal cost = $\Delta C/\Delta q$

MP_Z = marginal (physical) product of input Z (for example, MP_L is the marginal product of labor)

MR = marginal revenue = $\Delta R/\Delta q$

MRS = marginal rate of substitution

MRT = marginal rate of transformation

$MRTS$ = marginal rate of technical substitution

n = number of firms in an industry

p = price

PPF = production possibility frontier

PS = producer surplus = revenues minus variable costs = $R - VC$

Q = market (or monopoly) output

$\bar{Q}$ = output quota

q = firm output

R = revenue = pq

r = price of capital services

s = per-unit subsidy

$S(q)$ = market supply function

$S_o(q)$ = supply of all the other firms in the industry

SC = a measure of economies of scope

SR = short run

T = tax revenues (αpQ, τQ, $\rho\pi$)

U = utility

U_z = marginal utility of good Z

VC = variable cost

w = wage

W = welfare

Y = income or budget

Featured Applications in This Book

Cross-Chapter Analysis